Texas Devils

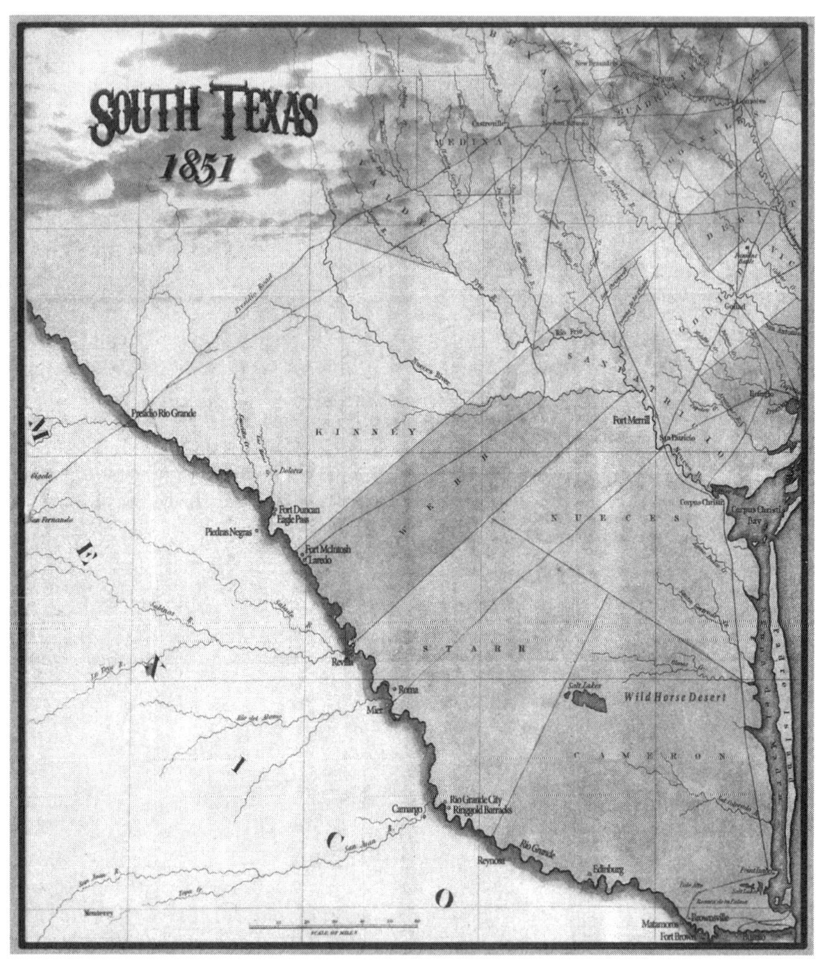

South Texas in 1851 as depicted by the General Land Office of Texas, J. P. Eppinger and F. C. Baker, surveyors. Courtesy of Lauren K. George, Wichita Falls, Texas.

Texas Devils

Rangers and Regulars on the Lower Rio Grande, 1846–1861

Michael L. Collins

University of Oklahoma Press : Norman

Also by Michael L. Collins

That Damned Cowboy: Theodore Roosevelt and the American West, 1883–1898 (New York, 1989)

(ed. with Kenneth E. Hendrickson Jr.) *Profiles in Power: Twentieth-Century Texans in Washington* (Arlington Heights, Ill., 1993)

(ed.) *Tales of Texoma: Episodes in the History of the Red River Border* (Wichita Falls, 2005)

Library of Congress Cataloging-in-Publication Data

Collins, Michael L., 1950–
Texas devils : Rangers and regulars on the lower Rio Grande, 1846–1861 / Michael L. Collins.
p. cm.
Includes bibliographical references and index.
ISBN 978-0-8061-3939-5 (hardcover : alk. paper)
ISBN 978-0-8061-4132-9 (paper)
1. Lower Rio Grande Valley (Tex.)—History—19th century. 2. Lower Rio Grande Valley (Tex.)—Ethnic relations—History—19th century. 3. Texas Rangers—History—19th century. 4. Texas militia—History—19th century. 5. Mexicans—Texas—Lower Rio Grande Valley—History—19th century. 6. Culture conflict—Texas—Lower Rio Grande Valley—History—19th century. 7. Frontier and pioneer life—Texas, South. 8. Frontier and pioneer life—Texas—Lower Rio Grande Valley. 9. Texas, South—Relations—Mexico. 10. Mexico—Relations—Texas, South. I. Title.
F392.R5C65 2008
976.4'4905—dc22

2008001816

The paper in this book meets the guidelines for permanence and durability of the Committee on Production Guidelines for Book Longevity of the Council on Library Resources, Inc. ∞

2 3 4 5 6 7 8 9 10

For Ben and Phoebe,
both genuine Texan originals,
each remarkably gifted

Contents

Illustrations

Figures

Map

Acknowledgments

I owe a tremendous debt of gratitude to a number of individuals who assisted me immeasurably during the course of my research and writing. First, my friends at the Midwestern State University Moffett Library have always provided me with all the support and assistance that any serious scholar could ever expect. My former administrative assistant, Terri McCleskey, deserves my appreciation for all her technical expertise and advice in the preparation of the manuscript. The professional staff of the Center for American History at the University of Texas at Austin never failed to lend me their time and their talents, sharing a treasure trove of knowledge about the manuscript collections that formed much of the body of this work. In particular, my friend Patrick Cox saved me on more than one occasion from trailing off into the blind alleys of my zealous interest in all things Texan. A special note of acknowledgment is also more than appropriate for Donaly Brice and the staff of the Texas State Library and Archives Commission. Without Donaly's wealth of understanding and his many leads, I might still be combing through files in Austin, looking aimlessly for the evidence that proved to be at the very core of my study.

My loving wife, Carol, and my children—Russell and Lauren and her husband, Douglas—never wavered in offering encouragement, if not advice. And my dear friends Ben and Phoebe Procter deserve special mention. They were the first outside the Collins household to view the manuscript and offer invaluable editorial suggestions and enthusiasm for the project. Finally, to the tearful Tejana who in February 1994 inspired me to continue the trail of historian Walter Prescott Webb, I am eternally grateful. After hearing a paper that I delivered to a diverse audience at the Second Palo Alto Conference in Brownsville—the effort being my first foray into "Rangerology"—she approached me and said approvingly, "It is about time one of your people told the truth about this story." I shall never forget her.

Texas Devils

Introduction

The lore and literature of the Lone Star State are as rich, magnificent, and immense as the land itself. A vast region shrouded in the mists of history, Texas continues to loom large in the American imagination. At the very center of Texas history stands the romantic figure of the Ranger, immortalized in film, folklore, dime novels, poetry, and even history texts. The mythic Ranger riding to the rescue of embattled pioneers and defending the good while punishing the evil—such is the stuff of American mythology.

To be sure, the storied frontier institution of the Texas Rangers stands as unique in the annals of military history. From the earliest appearance of Texan mounted volunteers in 1823 to the deployment of ranging companies serving the Republic of Texas to the formation in 1874 of the fabled Frontier Battalion that patrolled the borders of Indian country and policed the sprawling cattle ranges, this legendary fighting force has been justly celebrated in song, cinema, and popular literature. Few images familiar to peoples the world over are more closely identified with the Lone Star State as that of the intrepid Texas Ranger.

On horseback, with six-shooter or repeating rifle in hand, the hard-riding, straight-shooting Ranger remains resolutely heroic in the minds of admirers. Simply put, the mythic Ranger commands his rightful place with the cowboy and the fallen defender of the Alamo in the holy trinity of Texas tradition. No matter that he is as much a product of popular fiction as of historical fact, that he lives on in the imagination as much as in the history of the American Southwest, the Ranger persists as an enduring symbol of unflinching courage and unyielding determination in the face of insurmountable odds.

With the publication in 1935 of *The Texas Rangers: A Century of Frontier Defense*, historian Walter Prescott Webb completed the apotheosis of the storied horsemen in the service of the Lone Star State. Webb's classic study soon took its place among the classics of Texas historical literature and for four generations of Texans has stood as historical canon, to be read but not questioned. Professor Webb's narrative, telling the epic story of the state's frontier origins and tradition, has become central to the Anglo-Texan creation myth. Yet, while it confirmed that the Ranger tradition rested at the very core of the state's colorful yet barbaric heritage, the book failed to establish fully that the Ranger experience should also lead Texans to reexamine the burdens of their tribal past, burdens that continue to manifest themselves today, especially along the U.S.-Mexican border where races and cultures converge and sometimes collide. Shortly before his death in an automobile accident in 1963, Professor Webb admitted that succeeding generations of scholars should rewrite the story of the Rangers. Although the present study does not revise the entire history of the Texas Rangers as an institution, it does seek to provide a corrective lens for viewing the story of the state partisan forces that operated in South Texas and on both sides of the Rio Grande beginning in 1846.[1]

According to Webb and the next two generations of Texas historians, the Ranger was a product of his harsh and unforgiving environment. Hewn by the primitive conditions of the frontier, he was largely defined by his interaction with the raw forces and unpredictable elements of nature. According to the traditional story, border wars with Mexico shaped his basic character. Webb summarized the evolution of the Rangers and their tempering by the stern lessons of revolution and nation building. "The affair of the Alamo had taught them to expect no mercy; the massacre of Fannin's men . . . [at Goliad] had taught them distrust of Mexican honor; the fate of the Mier prisoners in Perote prison had taught them never to surrender; and the victory of San Jacinto had taught them contempt for Mexican valor."[2]

But Webb failed to take stock of a discomforting truth: the Ranger experience, particularly along the Rio Grande border, understandably instilled a deep-seated contempt for Anglo-Texan audacity and avarice in the peoples of Mexico and Texans of Mexican heritage. That legacy also taught Tejanos not to trust the Texan system of laws and justice. Just as significant, in extolling the virtues of volunteers known variously as state partisans, minute companies, and Mounted Rangers, Webb neglected or ignored critically important evidence revealing volunteer Ranger forces as sometimes ineffective, oftentimes brutal, and almost always more concerned with the rule of force than the rule of law.

In sum, the documentary record of early Ranger service in the Rio Grande Valley and the Nueces Strip between the Rio Grande and the Nueces River belies the pristine Hollywood image of "good guys in white hats" who "always get their man." A honest examination of the border strife from 1846 to 1861 reveals that during that time the real Texas Ranger, rather than standing for the triumph of individual freedom and social justice, was far more likely to represent racism, prejudice, and even hatred toward Mexicans and Indians, traits that then characterized the Anglo populace of the Lone Star State. Instead of quelling violence on the South Texas frontier and bringing peace and order to the region, as the tradition has it, volunteer Rangers frequently contributed to the cycle of violence that swept the region. No matter how objectionable to some Anglo-Texans, the grim reality is that the Rangers were oftentimes brutal in committing injustices against the Spanish-speaking population of the border.

Yet while Rangers were not always heroic and selfless in their service to their state, they were not always villainous either. Nor were all Tejanos and Mexicanos innocent victims of indiscriminate Anglo-Texan terror as meted out by *los Rinches* (the Rangers). In the final analysis, the objective historian must conclude that devils existed on both sides of the border, and many people of Mexican heritage fell victim to outrages committed by their own people. In sum, the barbaric code of conduct that prevailed along the Rio Grande frontier in the nineteenth century knew no boundaries, racial or otherwise.

Thus under the careful scrutiny of objective historical investigation, the Ranger Myth cultivated for generations simply does not hold up. Professor Webb's largely sanitized history of the Rangers falls short of acknowledging many of the past wrongs committed by the state volunteers toward the Spanish-speaking people of the border. Even recent scholars, who have devoted too little attention to the Mounted Rangers along the lower Rio Grande, either ignore or simply apologize for the misdeeds and atrocities committed by Texas volunteer militia along the Rio Grande during the mid-nineteenth century. As one historian explained away that bitter legacy: "Despite the hatred and prejudices of the past, and the occasional rogue Ranger, each Ranger performed his duty as he saw it. Each was molded by the time and place in which he lived." Or as the biographers of Ranger immortal Leander McNelly recently wrote, their subject could be "terribly brutal and cruel," and on occasions he even encouraged his men to "shoot first and ask questions later," yet he was "nevertheless effective in the time and place in which . . . [he] worked." Thus in the biographers' opinion, the Ranger should not be held to the same moral standards that apply today.[3]

A disquieting reality is amplified in the historical evidence relating to the Mexican border, particularly that documenting the actions of Texas minute companies serving along the lower Rio Grande. Texas Mounted Rangers—long before they evolved into law enforcement units—served as instruments of Anglo-American conquest. In 1846, when they first rode into Mexico as agents of Anglo-American "manifest destiny," and during the decade that followed, Ranger forces time and again exacted a terrible retribution upon peoples of Mexican heritage. More than a shield to defend the border from the ravages of Mexican banditti and Indian marauders, they served as a spear for the expansionist designs of ambitious leaders who remained dissatisfied with the conquest confirmed by the Treaty of Guadalupe Hidalgo in 1848. Even after the war with Mexico, many of the young recruits mustered into the ranging service and their officers surely were little more than mercenaries, soldiers of fortune, and filibusters determined to extend the boundaries of Texas and the United States south of the Rio Grande. In the end, the Texas state partisans' ambitions included lands not only for themselves but also for the southern slaveholding gentry who inspired and led them.

These petulant and undisciplined state partisans dispatched to the Rio Grande between 1846 and 1861 stood as a constant source of agitation and even trouble for federal forces stationed along that volatile river frontier. In other words, more often than not, the Rangers serving in South Texas proved as much a hindrance as a help in ongoing federal efforts to provide for an effective border defense. In the end, Ranger campaigns in the Rio Grande Valley—including those of the so-called Cortina War of 1859–1860—produced strained relations between the United States and Mexico as well as friction between Washington and Austin. And this mistrust and ill will only served as a further wedge between leaders of the Lone Star State and those of the Union during the eventful years leading up to the secession crisis of 1861.

The record of Confederate and Union military operations on the lower Rio Grande between 1861 and 1865 yields yet another significant fact. The experience of the Mounted Rangers did not abruptly halt with the coming of the American Civil War, as Webb's neglect of this critical period might suggest. Although the outbreak of the struggle for southern independence preempted Texan designs of conquest in Mexico, Ranger traditions—the best and worst of those traditions—continued uninterrupted during the war years. The Confederate home guard in the Rio Grande District, specifically the Second Texas Mounted Rifles, utilized many of the same unconventional tactics as the Ranger companies of the Mexican War and the state militia raised to fight the elusive Comanches. Even the Confederate commanders in South Texas, among them the already legendary John S. "Rip" Ford, were the very same officers who led the "spy companies" (as companies of scouts and couriers were known) deployed at the vanguard of U.S. regulars during their march into Mexico and the minute companies later raised to pursue Plains Indian warriors into their haunts and hunting grounds.

Following the trail of Walter Prescott Webb is no easy task. Any historian, professional or otherwise, who willingly takes on the formidable challenge of retracing the tracks of such a venerable scholar or questioning some of his conclusions about the iconic Texas Rangers should expect a measure of criticism, especially from Anglo-Texans who exhibit an understandable pride in their heritage. The following volume will perhaps provoke a debate among laypersons and academics alike as to the rightful place of the early Texas Rangers in border history. At least that is the hope.

There is an old expression that "legends die hard." It is true. And sometimes, at least in the minds of many people, the legends never die at all. For it is only from the shadows of popular myth that the true story emerges, the tale that Webb and his disciples never told—that of the riders from hell who were justly reviled and feared by peoples of Mexican heritage as symbols of racial repression and cultural conquest. This story is not about the Rangers of legend who bravely defended the border from lawlessness and savagery but about the Rangers of historical record who tortured and even lynched prisoners, who joined in filibustering expeditions to the Rio Grande and beyond, and who wrought a terrible vengeance upon their enemies.

They ride still somewhere on the unsettled borders between Texan myth and Mexican lore. To the Spanish-speaking peoples living along the lower Rio Grande they are remembered as *los diablos Tejanos*—"the Texas devils." This is their story.

1
The Rangers

"Of this far famed corps—so much feared and hated by the Mexicans—I can add nothing to what has already been written," Captain Luther Giddings of the First Ohio Volunteers recollected of the most memorable fighting men he encountered on the fields of the U.S.-Mexican War. "The character of the Texas Ranger is now well known by both friend and foe. As a mounted soldier he has no counterpart in any age or country. Neither Cavalier nor Cossack . . . are like him; and yet, in some respects he resembles them. . . . Chivalrous, bold and impetuous in action, he is yet wary and calculating, always impatient of restraint, and sometimes unscrupulous and unmerciful. He is ununiformed and undrilled, and performs his active duties thoroughly, but with little regard to order or system. He is an excellent rider and a dead shot. His arms are a rifle, Colt's revolving pistol and a [bowie] knife."[1]

Given the character of these Texans, it is little wonder that in May 1846, when the electrifying news of war with Mexico flashed across Texas like a lightning bolt, more than five thousand of them rushed to volunteer for service in the field. From the banks of the Guadalupe and the rocky hills above the Colorado, from countless farms that dotted the prairies and from the timberlands stretching along the lower Brazos, from the streets of San Antonio and a hundred other villages, volunteers came, eager for a fight. Each was a veritable arsenal on horseback, eager to be greeted with another opportunity to avenge the martyrs of the Alamo and Goliad and to exact punishment for other Mexican atrocities, both real and imagined.

That spring, Texans found themselves on the front lines of another conflict with Mexico. Nothing could have pleased them more, and Texas Mounted Rangers mustered into service at the beginning of the U.S.-Mexican War were the first volunteers to join General Zachary Taylor's regulars along the Rio Grande. During the opening engagements of the campaign, at the Palo Alto prairie on May 8, and the following day at Resaca de la Palma upriver from Fort Brown, they served alongside the U.S. regulars. Ranger captains Samuel Walker and Ben McCulloch and their Texan spy companies became the eyes and ears of General Taylor's dragoons. Riding in advance of American forces during the subsequent march to Monterrey that fateful summer, at times ranging far ahead of regular units, they spurred their mounts deep into the deserts and mountainous regions of northern Mexico. Whether reconnoitering enemy troop movements and possible routes into the interior theaters of war, carrying vital intelligence to American commanders, or interdicting Mexican supply lines and "procuring" horses and mules for regular units, the Rangers proved indispensable to Taylor's success.

An Outlaw Appearance

In appearance, the Rangers were unique, easily distinguishable from the regular dragoons and infantrymen who served under General Taylor, the grizzled and sometimes profane officer immortalized by his troops as "Old Rough and Ready." Samuel C. Reid, a native of New York who joined Ben McCulloch's company while it was encamped on the Rio Grande below Fort Brown, described his fellow Rangers as looking more like a mob than a military unit. "Here was a scene worthy of pencil," he recalled. "Men in group with long beards and mustaches, dressed in every day variety of garment, with one exception, the slouched hat, the unmistakable uniform of a Texas Ranger, and a belt of pistols around their waists. . . . A rougher looking set we never saw." With no evidence of rank, no unit standards or insignias, no regular uniform, and their "rough exterior, it was hard to tell who or what they were," Reid confessed. "Notwithstanding their ferocious and outlaw look, there were among them doctors and lawyers, and many a college graduate." Another of McCulloch's men, Jonathan Duff Brown, added that, while there were physicians, surveyors, teachers, and journalists among them, he did "not recall any ministers of the Gospel in our party." Like Reid, Brown served at the post known as "Camp Maggot," situated in the marshes along the murky, mosquito-infested waters of the Rio Grande opposite Matamoros, Mexico. He admired the Texans' stealth and valor in battle and soon realized that their appearance belied their prowess and value as soldiers. Reid admitted that "one would have thought from the savage looking mien of the men, with their long matted hair and beards, and their singular costumes, that we were a band of brigands."[2]

Private Samuel Chamberlain of the U.S. Army found the Texas volunteers to be surly in appearance and sullen in mood. The New Hampshire–born artist and adventurer had only recently enlisted in the regulars, and nothing he had experienced while growing up near the seaports of New England and later on the prairies of Illinois had prepared him for the shock of meeting the irregulars from Texas. "A motley crowd of desperate characters" was his first impression of Captain McCulloch's Rangers. "A more reckless, devil-may care set it would be impossible to find this side of the infernal regions," he observed. "They presented a strange and terrific appearance, faces and clothes all covered with a mixture of mud, mortar, powder and blood, eyes blood-shot, with a hungry savage look which was truly fearful. Their costumes and arms added to the *Banditti* like effect of the command." Some of them wore buckskin shirts black with grease and stained with tobacco and blood, while others sported red or blue shirts, with trousers tucked into high boots. Still others donned jackets of Mexican leather, while a number were draped in serapes that hung loosely over deerskin leggings and moccasins. All were armed with a brace of Colt revolvers and huge bowie knives, otherwise known as "Texas tooth picks" to the volunteers. "Take them altogether," Chamberlain noted, "with their uncouth costumes, bearded faces, lean and brawny forms, fierce wild eyes, and swaggering manners, they were fit representatives of the outlaws which made up the Lone Star State." Lieutenant Napoleon Dana agreed. His impression of the Texas volunteers when he first set eyes upon them: "the best of them looked as if they could steal sheep."[3]

Correspondent George Kendall of the New Orleans *Picayune* echoed the sentiment: "these Mounted Riflemen are a rather rough-looking set of customers . . . they will be hard to deal with." S. Compton Smith, an army surgeon assigned to General Taylor's advancing force, concurred in his assessment of the hellions from Texas. "The so-called Texas Rangers . . . were mostly made up of adventurers and vagabonds whose whole object was plunder," he observed. "Like Falstaff's ragamuffins, they were . . . never soldiers, but discarded, unjust serving men . . . revolted tapsters, and hostlers trade-fallen . . . ten times more dishonorable and ragged than an old-faced ancient!"[4]

Lieutenant Albert Gallatin Brackett of the Fourth Regiment of Indiana Volunteers, serving in General Joseph Lane's command, concurred in his assessment of the mounted guerrillas from Texas. "They were certainly an odd-looking set of fellows," he noted of Colonel John Coffee "Jack" Hays's regiment of Rangers. "It seems to be their aim to dress as outlandishly as possible. Bob-tailed coats and 'long-tailed blues,' low and high-crowned hats, some slouched hats and others Panama, with a sprinkling of black leather caps, constituting their uniforms." He confirmed that these unwashed, unkempt hellions from Texas, "with a thorough coating of dust all over . . . covering their huge beards," were "savage in appearance." He further observed that their horses, which "ranged from little mustangs to large American full-bloods, and . . . [of] every shade and color," were the best-groomed members of the Texas volunteer units.[5]

In fact, regular officers and enlisted men envied the magnificent mounts the Texans rode and credited the Rangers with incomparable knowledge of horseflesh as well as careful selection and meticulous care of these animals. Furthermore, despite the fact that many formally trained regulars viewed the undisciplined Texans with disdain, they acknowledged that the Rangers proved their worth as scouts and shock troops to be feared by any enemy. Of these irregulars, Brackett observed in awe: armed with "a pair of Colt's revolvers . . . a hundred of them could discharge a thousand shots in two minutes . . . and with precision" and deadly accuracy.[6]

An Outrageous Character

Ranger Nelson Lee refused to apologize for the unorthodox, sometimes outrageous character of the Texas volunteers who fought with him in Mexico and their penchant for the unconventional. "The qualifications necessary in a genuine Ranger were not . . . such as are required in a regular soldier," he said. "Discipline, in the common acceptance of the term, was not regarded as absolutely essential. A fleet horse, an eye that could detect the trail, a power of endurance that defied fatigue, and the faculty of 'looking through the double sights of his rifle with a steady aim'—these distinguished the Ranger, rather than any special knowledge of tactics."[7]

The rough-hewn frontier types who enlisted in the Texas volunteer units had been shaped by many teachers. From the vaquero of South Texas they had learned that a good horse was essential to survival on the plains. From the Comanche they had learned the fearless mounted charge and ferocity in pursuit of the enemy. From the Lipan Apache they had learned to read horse tracks like handwriting and to understand that deception was the first rule of warfare. From their own officers they had learned skirmish tactics, precision movements on horseback, and the full shock effect of the .44-caliber Walker Colt, which enabled them to powder burn their foe in close-quarter fighting. And from their fathers they had acquired skills in marksmanship, horsemanship, and other arts of war. Perhaps Ranger adjutant John S. "Rip" Ford best summarized the recruits who galloped alongside him into the storms of the U.S.-Mexican War: "They ride like Mexicans; trail like Indians; shoot like Tennesseans; and fight like the devil."[8]

Understandably, the Rangers' reputation preceded them into battle. As Lieutenant Rankin Dilworth aptly commented, "[T]he Mexicans dread the Texians more than they do the devil, and they have good reason for it." From Matamoros to Monterrey to Mexico City, their fame—or their infamy—spread like news of the plague. Simple villagers and humble peons in the countryside shuddered in terror upon hearing word of the advance of *los sangrientos Tejanos*, "the bloody Texans." Even the most seasoned Mexican lancers learned how frightening was the specter of screaming Rangers charging hell for leather into their lines with bullets flying from both fists. As one contemporary observed of the tattered volunteers from Texas: "they ask for no quarter and will show none."[9]

Although Rip Ford insisted that his fellow Rangers were, for the most part, "men of good character," he also admitted that motives of revenge more than a sense of patriotism guided many in Colonel Hays's regiment. "The command had men in it who had suffered the loss of relatives by Mexicans massacring prisoners of war," Ford acknowledged. "There were men who had been Santa Fe prisoners, Mier prisoners, and prisoners made at San Antonio by Vasquez and Woll." (The latter refers to the Mexican incursions into South Texas in 1842.) "Was it a wonder that it was difficult to restrain these men . . . who were standing face to face with the people whose troops had committed . . . such bloody deeds?" he asked.[10]

References to wanton acts of violence committed by Rangers against the civilian populace of northern Mexico filled contemporary accounts. At the same time, however, during the campaigns of 1846 and 1847, roaming gangs of Mexican banditti raided ranchos, ransacked villages, and pillaged the properties of peasants and landlords alike; their misdeeds were sometimes wrongfully assigned to *los malvados Tejanos*, "the evil Texans." As Samuel Chamberlain recalled, "[B]etween the Rangers and [Mexican] guerillars [*sic*] the unfortunate inhabitants of the states of Nuevo Leon and Tamaulipas had a hard time of it . . . plundered by both sides, their lives often taken, and their wives and daughters outraged and carried off. The names of 'Old Reid,' Captain Bayley [*sic*], Harry Love, Ben McCullough [*sic*] and more terrible than all, [Mabry] 'Mustang' Gray, will always remain fresh in the memory of Mexicans, as the atrocities committed by them now form part of the . . . [dark] legends of the country."[11]

Even the Texas Mounted Rangers' most determined apologists could not deny that the Rangers used harsh methods in obtaining information about the disposition of Mexican troops, their location, and their strength in arms. The Texans, like their enemies, sometimes pistol-whipped or even choked prisoners to extract vital information. In the event of the capture of a civilian "guerrilla," they might even loop a rope over the prisoner's neck and hoist him off the ground to improve his memory or drag him through the cactus until he agreed to talk. On occasion, the victims were innocent noncombatants. Samuel C. Reid admitted, "[O]ur orders were most strict not to molest any unarmed Mexican, but if some of the most notorious of these villains were found shot, or hung up in the chaparral . . . [the U.S. Army] was charity bound to suppose that during some fit of remorse and desperation, tortured by conscience for the many evil deeds they had committed, they had recklessly laid violent hands upon their own lives! *Quien sabe*?"[12]

Seldom did the Rangers return from a scout without at least one empty saddle. And rarely did they take prisoners. After all, in the field they had no practical way of guarding and providing for captives. But Private Alexander Lander, a member of the Texas volunteer unit known informally as the Galveston Rifles, confessed that as he and other young men of his company were forced to live off the land, they often came into violent conflict with civilian noncombatants. "We had several skirmishes with rancheros where we stopped," he recalled. "We were *Texans* and would help ourselves . . . to the beef, poultry, and other eatables. . . . They sometimes tried to prevent us from taking what we wanted, or tried to compel us to pay more than it was worth," he recounted. "We killed about fifteen of the rancheros" during the campaign in northern Mexico, he casually recorded.[13]

Such incidents may not have been isolated, especially given the barbarity of the war, the extreme privations of life in the field, and the general character and temper of the Texas partisans. One of the most infamous of the Rangers, at least according to General Taylor and his staff, was a protégé of Mustang Gray's named John Glanton, a half-savage Indian fighter with a penchant for scalping the enemy. Originally from South Carolina, Glanton was a mercenary who had accompanied the Rangers into Mexico. Described by Sam Chamberlain as a short, stocky, swarthy ruffian with bronzed, weather-beaten skin and "deep sunk" bloodshot eyes that gave him the appearance of a "wild beast," Glanton was a loathsome desperado of the worst description. Said to sport a violent temper along with his cache of weapons, he was known to be inspired to bloodshed after imbibing strong drink. Typically dressed in the serape, leather garb, and broad-brimmed hat of a Mexican herdsman, he seemed to enjoy pistol play and knife fights as much as games of chance. Chamberlain saw Glanton slash the throat of a handsome young Ranger after a brief exchange of insults in a San Antonio cantina. In his memoirs, Rip Ford remembered how Glanton, after a "drink or two," once threatened an entire company of disgruntled, homesick Rangers with a firing squad and a "quick, short journey" to hell if they so much as complained about the rancid food and lack of comforts in camp. In his memoirs of the war, General Walter P. Lane recalled how Glanton, one day after the American victory at the Battle of Monterrey (September 21–23, 1846) had chased down a fleeing Mexican soldier, shot him in the back at close range, then appropriated the slain man's mount. It was even widely reported that Glanton had once committed the unforgivable sin of murdering a priest. Unfortunately, when General Taylor ordered officers to arrest the tomahawk-wielding rogue and bring him in irons to headquarters so he could be charged with murder, Lane refused. Lane, who defended Glanton's actions, persuaded the scalp hunter to escape to Texas rather than face a court martial and possible execution as a war criminal.[14]

Although Glanton represented the worst elements to infest the ranks of the irregulars known as the Texas Mounted Rangers, he by no means stood alone. According to Samuel Chamberlain, sometime early in 1847 a company of Rangers roared into Hacienda del Patos, located in the foothills near a strategic mountain pass north of Buena Vista. As was their custom, the Texans—apparently low on their whiskey "rations"—were bent upon having a good time, even at the expense of the local villagers. No doubt seeking the comforts of pretty senoritas and the encouragement of tequila, they tumbled into a cantina and imbibed ample quantities of liquid spirits. Upon departing hours later, however, they unwittingly left behind a lone comrade who had enjoyed too much mescal.[15]

The unfortunate and unnamed Ranger made a fatal error that winter afternoon, not merely by remaining behind in the village but also by committing a foolish and unforgivable act of sacrilege. In preparing to rejoin his company, the drunken Texan mounted up and began screaming insults, at the same time firing his pistol wildly into the air before spurring his fleet horse across an open courtyard toward the town chapel. Then he brashly galloped into the sanctuary with rope in hand. After tossing the riata over a large wooden crucifix, he dragged the religious relic into the plaza. A gray-haired priest ran in front of the frenzied rider, holding his arms up as if to plead with the Texan to untie the precious statue. He was knocked to the ground and trampled beneath the horse's hoofs. Within moments, a crowd had gathered around the bloodied body of the priest. One enraged Mexican cried, "*Que mueren los Tejano diablo?*" The question of how the villagers would kill the Texas devil would soon be answered. Before the young Ranger could wheel his horse around and race to safety, several angry villagers pulled him from the saddle and began kicking and beating him.[16]

What happened next could only be described as horrifying. As reported by Samuel Chamberlain, the enraged mob stripped and tied the Texan to a post, then literally skinned him alive with rawhide whips before hanging his limp frame on a huge cross that rose above the town plaza. Before the sun set that day, a company of Texas volunteers returned for their lost companion. What they found in the center of the village filled them with a terrible resolve. "They saw their miserable comrade . . . [on] the cross, his skin hanging in strips, surrounded by a crowd of Mexicans," Chamberlain wrote. "With yells of horror, the rangers charged on the mass with Bowie knife and revolver, sparing neither age nor sex in their . . . fury." After the Texans had carried out their retribution, the bodies of slain men and women littered the courtyard. Only when the bloody deed was done did the Rangers discover that the subject of their revenge was still alive but in "awful agony." As the blood-splattered Rangers cut him down, the young man was said to have begged his friends to end his suffering. "Finding him beyond hope," Chamberlain recorded, "the Ranger Captain put a bullet through the brain of the wretch."[17]

As the shocking slaughter at Hacienda del Patos proved, the Rangers could match and exceed the brutality of even the worst of their enemies. Captain Mabry Gray, commander of a company of volunteers raised in Corpus Christi, stood as a case in point. Texan John Linn remembered the native South Carolinian as an "assassin" from the days of the republic. According to Linn, between 1840 and 1842 Gray led a "company of organized bandits and cut-throats" known as the "Cowboys," who committed numerous acts of violence in the Nueces Strip and along the border. During General Taylor's advance into northern Mexico, Gray and his men, described by one officer as a "gang of miscreants," reportedly murdered "in cold blood . . . the entire male population of the Rancho Guadalupe, where not a single weapon . . . could be found."[18]

Three Heroes for Texas

The horrors of war are never truly offset by the heroism of battle. And yet history is filled with accounts of uncommon courage and selfless sacrifice, reminding us that while warfare brings out the worst in some men, it summons forth the best in others. The U.S.-Mexican War is no exception; the annals of the Texas Rangers include true accounts of daring and bravery that almost defy belief. Yet unlikely as some of these tales may seem, many have been documented as fact. Not even the most imaginative Hollywood scriptwriter could have created a more unlikely pageant of personalities than those who rode into this real historical drama.

Few of these true-to-life warriors were more revered and respected than an intrepid young officer who emerged as perhaps the first genuine hero of the war: Captain Samuel H. Walker of the First Regiment of Texas Mounted Riflemen. At first glance, the Maryland-born Walker looked like anything but a fighter. Chamberlain described Walker as a "small, wiry mild-looking man"; another contemporary wrote that he was "about medium size, with light hair and a mild expression of countenance." One observer thought Walker's "intellect was mediocre and not much cultivated," while another remembered the captain as "an ordinary man" who was by his unassuming nature "silent, retiring, mild . . . and rather melancholy."[19]

Samuel Walker's contemporaries assigned one word more than any other to the fair-skinned, sandy-haired Ranger: "gallant." Although not large or physically imposing, Walker towered in the saddle as he led scouting parties in advance of armies commanded by the disheveled-looking General Zachary Taylor and his successor in the later campaigns, the stubborn, stodgy General Winfield Scott, "Old Fuss and Feathers." Whether as a courier bearing dispatches through Mexican lines to the besieged and bombarded post of Fort Brown, as commander of a spy company daring to take on the most dangerous reconnaissance missions, or a Ranger captain leading a headlong charge into columns of Mexican lancers at Monterrey, Walker inspired his men to be as fearless as he.[20]

"In our continued and varied experience in the army it has never been our fortune to meet a grander and nobler soldier than Captain Walker," recalled J. Jacob Oswandel of the U.S. regulars. "Walker I am told is not so much of a drilled officer . . . but for leading a charge, or for following a retreating enemy, there is no braver or daring officer in the United States Army." Oswandel wrote admiringly that "war was his element . . . and the battlefield his playground. . . . [H]e could fight and chase guerrillas all day, and dance the highland fling all night; he was a splendid horseman and unsurpassed for firm riding and endurance." General Joseph Lane remembered Walker as "one of the most chivalric, noble-hearted men that ever graced the profession of arms." Shaped by the hardships and privations of frontier life, Walker had also been hardened by the sting of battle and the cruelty of imprisonment in Perote Castle following the failed Mier expedition of 1842.[21]

Thus when American units occupied Perote (which lay between the seaport of Veracruz and Mexico City) in the spring of 1847, that event held a special significance for Walker. Surely, the sight of the imposing stone walls and towering turrets of the medieval structure reminded him of the many months of misery his fellow Texans had endured there. Even the familiar stench of the prison caused him to recall the dank dungeons where his comrades had languished so long in darkness. In helping to hoist the Lone Star flag and the Stars and Stripes above the gray walls of the prison, he fulfilled a vow made to fallen comrades five years earlier that he would return one day.

Yet Walker continued to be haunted by the memory of the "cold-blooded murder" of his fellow prisoners. Most vividly he recalled the death march from Mier and the infamous "black bean" incident at Salado on March 25, 1842, in which 176 Texan prisoners were forced to draw lots to determine which 17 among them would die before a firing squad. Walker remained tormented by the recollections of Mexican musket fire that dreadful night as well as by the mournful cries and moans of the dying Texans, who had so bravely stood before their executioners. As he had scribbled in his journal during his imprisonment, he could never forget the embrace of his condemned comrades who "desired their murder to be remembered and revenged by their countrymen." And he remembered their last warnings to tearful Mexican officers who were repulsed by the orders of execution that many other Texans would return someday to avenge them and that "their deaths may yet cause them the blood of thousands." For Walker, memories of their executions would be "more lasting than the massacre of Fannin."[22]

Following his release from Perote prison, Walker wrote home to his family in Maryland that he had "suffered greatly" at the hands of his Mexican captors. Defiant in spirit, resolute in his determination, he vowed "I shall remain in the service [of Texas] until the final settlement of all our difficulties with Mexico." Understandably, then, the U.S.-Mexican War was intensely personal for Walker. No matter that he had already gained fame on the battlefields of this war; his work was not finished. This "distinguished partisan chief, the thunderbolt of the Texan rangers," as Oswandel labeled him, was justly respected by officers and enlisted men alike, regular as well as militia. Perhaps more important, Mexican guerrilleros, who knew of his standing practice of treating ununiformed combatants as *robadores* and bandidos, feared him. "Captain Samuel Walker takes no prisoners," Oswandel said succinctly. "Should Captain Walker come across the guerrillas God help them; the Captain and most all of his men are very prejudiced and embittered against every guerrilla in the country." Walker's "bold and daring feats," Oswandel concluded, "struck terror in the hearts of these highway robbers."[23]

Word of Walker's raids and of his policy of no quarter to Mexican guerrilleros spread far and wide. While at Perote on June 6, 1847, Walker wrote of his exploits in Mexico to his brother, Jonathan, admitting that he had recently taken "summary measures" with several Mexican captives who were, in his judgment, "guilty of many acts of barbarity." As he wrote his brother, "I doubt not that you have heard many exaggerated stories about the affair." Then he predicted that, by the Fourth of July, General Scott would be entering Mexico City. "I hope I shall be with him."[24]

But it was not to be. The next that the Walkers of Baltimore would hear of their beloved Samuel would be the stunning news of his heroism and death at the town of Huamantla on October 9, 1847. Lieutenant William D. Wilkins of the Fifteenth U.S. Infantry recalled the spectacle of two thousand of Santa Anna's brightly clad lancers galloping from the picturesque city of eight thousand inhabitants. The sun gleamed from the lances of the Mexican cavalry as they "drew up in line" and charged General Lane's columns. "We all held our breath with excitement," Wilkins wrote home to his family. "Suddenly a small body of horse[men] broke from our ranks, headed by a tall cavalier, and dashed like a thunderbolt into the midst of the glittering

Mexicans. They wavered a moment, then broke, and fled in confusion into the town. . . . It was Walker with his Rangers who performed the gallant feat, and with 80 men dispersed 2,000 lancers."[25]

Captain Walker led his Texans through narrow streets and into the main plaza, his men riding four abreast. Then sniper fire rang out. Walker tumbled from the saddle, mortally wounded, one bullet having pierced his lung, another having shattered his skull. Legend has it that, even in death, he still clutched a Colt revolver. At the age of thirty, he had become a martyr. According to at least one account, the Rangers wept like children at the sight of their commander's body. The grim scene recalled the sacrifice of the Texas Revolution and rekindled the racial hatreds that fueled an ongoing sanguinary war.[26]

Whether or not Walker died at the hands of a "cowardly assassin," as some Texans reported, made little difference to the result. Convinced that he had been, Walker's "men resolved from this day out that they would take no prisoners, and death to all Mexicans found with firearms in their possession," Oswandel wrote in his memoir. "[T]he death of Captain Walker has and will cause the [loss of] life of many a poor innocent Mexican. Our men look upon Captain Walker's death as murder." Reprisal came immediately, as Captain Samuel Peter Heintzelman reported. Explaining that he witnessed the Texans sweeping the town, killing "every Mexican they saw," he described the Rangers' sack of Huamantla and the scene of "dead Mexicans about in every direction." Labeling the irregulars from Texas a "drunken lot [such as] I never saw," he concluded in frustration, "I could do nothing with them."[27]

Lieutenant Wilkins also described the horrible carnage that followed the victory at Huamantla. Claiming that General Lane had urged the Texans to avenge the death of Captain Walker, Wilkins observed an orgy of violence in which many volunteers looted liquor from cantinas, then proceeded to break into shops and "took all we could lay hands on." Worse yet, "old women and girls were stripped of their clothing—and many suffered still greater outrages. Men were shot by dozens while . . . churches, stores, and dwelling houses [were] ransacked." Wilkins continued, "Shouts, screams, the reports of firearms and the crash of timber and glass" filled the streets as crazed vandals strewed articles of clothing and furniture and stuffed their bags with jewelry, money, and other valuables. "Dead horses and men lay about pretty thick, while drunken soldiers, yelling and screeching, were breaking open houses or chasing some poor Mexicans who . . . fled for their life. Such a scene I never hope to see again. It gave me a lamentable view of human nature [and] . . . made me for the first time ashamed of my country."[28]

Mexican journalist Ramón Alcaraz confirmed that the Texans, who already had "sown death and fear along the roads from Vera Cruz," now plundered public buildings and the houses of civilians, "murdering those unfortunate ones who resisted immediate surrender of their belongings." No wonder that the infamy of such atrocities preceded the Rangers during their march to Mexico City. As for the fallen Captain Walker, his body was carried into a nearby convent yard and, according to Oswandel, "buried without a coffin in a secluded spot." Soon, Walker's fame as a fallen hero of the war with Mexico would spread across the United States. After the war, his name would live on in another respect. The .44-caliber revolver that Texans carried into battle would justly be called the Walker Colt. Several years earlier, Walker had traveled east by steamer, all the way to Paterson, New Jersey, to meet with a struggling inventor and arms manufacturer named Samuel Colt and help him design a better revolver. The Walker Colt eliminated the flaws of its predecessor, the Paterson model, making it a more practical weapon for men on horseback. The heavier, sturdier, more reliable revolver was better adapted to plains warfare and thus more suited to the needs of the Texas Mounted Rangers. Complete with a trigger guard to help prevent accidental discharges, a rotating cylinder and rammer for rapid reloading, and a grip and long barrel perfectly balanced for improved accuracy, the eight-pound pistol even proved serviceable as a club when empty.[29]

After Huamantla, Walker's men remained fiercely loyal to their late leader and his growing legend. Two of the most faithful were Green and Wiley Marshall, twin brothers reared on the Texas borderlands and raised in the martial traditions of the Lone Star State. Described by one comrade as "recklessly brave and . . . perfect in the use of arms and expert in horsemanship," they learned almost every trick and tactic of guerrilla warfare from the captain they so admired. Fearless, inseparable as friends and brothers in arms, with an unwavering confidence in their own skills and in those of their fellow Texans, they were equal to any fighting man. In the words of Ranger Horace Bell, they rode into battle as the "the beau ideal of the . . . frontier Ranger." Like others of the regiment, they kept alive the spirit of their fallen commander, never forgetting his heroism.[30]

Of the scouts who served General Taylor during the first year of the war, none proved more resourceful or cunning than Ben McCulloch, a native of Tennessee. Like Walker, McCulloch bore an appearance that concealed his stealth, courage, and toughness. Samuel C. Reid remembered McCulloch as "a man of rather delicate frame, of about five feet ten inches in height, with light hair and complexion" and "quick, bright blue eyes." McCulloch's receding hairline and cleft chin further accentuated soft facial features that were shaded beneath a broad-brimmed, floppy hat, which was typically turned up in front. His sun-parched skin gave him a "weather-beaten cast," according to Reid. McCulloch exuded a quiet confidence and a reserved self-assurance that inspired others. Thin, angular, almost frail in stature, he looked more like a preacher than a partisan Ranger. Surely, no one could have guessed that the tight-lipped "Captain Ben" had been, during his youth in Tennessee, a personal friend and protégé of David Crockett.[31]

Ben McCulloch may not have looked like a "ring-tailed roarer," but no one could have doubted his bravery in battle or his knowledge of plains craft, particularly Indian-style methods of unconventional warfare. A veteran of the Battle of San Jacinto who had settled at Gonzales after the Texas Revolution of 1836, McCulloch distinguished himself during the summer of the Comanche moon. In August 1840, several hundred Comanche warriors went on a rampage through South Texas. They attacked the towns of Victoria and Linnville and rode off with the spoils. Like dozens of other young Texans, Ben McCulloch saddled up and set off in pursuit. Riding alongside such men as the grizzled Edward Burleson of San Marcos, the much-heralded Matthew Caldwell (affectionately known as "Old Paint"), and young John Coffee Hays from San Antonio de Bejar, McCulloch helped to trail the largest Comanche raiding party ever known to sweep across Texas, tracking them for more than two days before intercepting them near present-day Lockhart.

On August 11, 1840, along the waters of Plum Creek, some eighty-eight mounted Rangers, many of them armed for the first time with Colt service revolvers as well as rifles, ambushed the raiders and scattered them across the plains in a running battle that saw the Indian horsemen doing most of the running. At day's end, the bodies of more than sixty Comanches littered the prairie west of Plum Creek. The terrible lessons learned and the losses inflicted would live long thereafter in the memories of whites and Indians alike.[32]

McCulloch's education in the finer arts of frontier warfare continued during the next two years when he served with Captain Hays during the campaigns to frustrate and defeat the invasions of South Texas by the Mexican forces of General Raphael Vasquez and General Adrian Woll. Serving under "Captain Jack," McCulloch learned guerrilla-style hit-and-run tactics, the method of surprising a superior enemy by taking advantage of the terrain, the effectiveness of night raids on supply trains and pony herds, and the importance of doggedly pursuing a demoralized, hungry foe in retreat, even if it meant chasing him all the way to hell. The word "defeat" was not in McCulloch's vocabulary; neither was "patience."

But McCulloch's reputation and, indeed his legend, would forever rest upon his daring exploits as commander of a Texan spy company riding at the vanguard of General Taylor's march into Mexico. In February 1847, General Taylor instructed McCulloch and sixteen handpicked Rangers to cross some thirty-five miles of open desert to scout the location and strength of General Antonio Lopez de Santa Anna's army at the mountain passes near the village of Encarnacíon. On February 14, during the first of two missions, McCulloch engaged and routed a company of Mexican cavalry; during the second, on the night of February 20, he penetrated the perimeter of Santa Anna's defensive lines near Encarnacíon to determine the strength of the enemy force.[33]

The following morning, McCulloch and his men—disguised as Mexican herdsmen—slipped through enemy pickets, avoided detection by Santa Anna's sentries, and made their way back to General Taylor at Agua Nueva. McCulloch reported to Taylor that an estimated 20,000 enemy troops, well positioned and heavily fortified, lay in wait for the Americans. It was a critical moment in the war and in the history of both nations. Captain Luther Giddings recalled, "General Taylor was induced by the information brought him by that trusty and accomplished scout, Captain McCulloch, to change his ground from Agua Nueva to the gorge of Buena Vista." Taylor confirmed that the intelligence yielded by McCulloch's reconnaissance was of the "highest importance" in convincing him not to attack a superior force but to withdraw to a defensive position and await General Santa Anna, the "Napoleon of the West." Another contemporary termed McCulloch's service "invaluable." Ranger historian Walter Prescott Webb agreed, going so far as to credit McCulloch with sparing Taylor the humiliation of an almost certain defeat. "Success here would have enabled Santa Anna to meet Scott at Vera Cruz with a victorious army supported by a united nation. That Ben McCulloch contributed much to the [ensuing] American victory [at Buena

Vista] no one can doubt," Webb concluded. "If Taylor had made mistakes, the Texas Rangers had helped him to escape their consequences."[34]

Speculation aside, the fact remains that Taylor's forces dealt Santa Anna a devastating blow at the Battle of Buena Vista on February 22–23, 1847, and his victory, together with the fame it brought him, was enough to catapult him into the presidency of the United States two years later. Although Old Rough and Ready acknowledged that the Rangers' contributions to the U.S. war effort were vital, he also understood that he had to be willing to accept the vices of the Texas volunteers along with their virtues. Or else he had to bring himself to dismiss them from service and send them home. According to one official report, during a celebration following the triumph at Buena Vista, scores of the raucous Texans became deliriously drunk and picked a fight with Taylor's regulars. No fewer than two companies of dragoons rushed to the scene to quell the riot. Afterward, Taylor penned in disgust, "[T]he mounted men from Texas have scarcely made one expedition without unwarrantably killing a Mexican."

Taylor reluctantly concluded that he could either fight the Mexican army or control the volunteer Rangers from Texas; he could not do both. Following the engagement at Monterrey the previous September, Taylor had discharged two Texas volunteer regiments from service, believing the corps of irregulars to be undisciplined, insubordinate, and insolent in behavior. Now, as before, he complained to officials of the U.S. Department of War that he "found it entirely impossible to enforce . . . repeated orders . . . against [the Texans'] marauding and other irregularities." In a subsequent communication of June 16, 1847, Taylor confessed that the Rangers had carried out "extensive depredations and outrages upon . . . peaceable inhabitants" of Mexico and that "there is scarcely a form of crime that has not been reported to me as committed by them." Lieutenant George Gordon Meade confirmed Taylor's claims, acknowledging that he, too, was "disgusted" by the "poor discipline" shown by the volunteers from Texas. Meade even charged that the Texans appeared "always drunk . . . and killed for their own amusement." Understandably, therefore, following the battle at Buena Vista General Taylor recommended that the Texan spy companies be mustered out of service and that no more be sent to replace them.[35]

As it turned out, Taylor was the one replaced. After Buena Vista, General Winfield Scott took command of all U.S. forces in the theater of war. On March 9, 1847, General Scott landed an army of 12,000 regulars at Veracruz.

After this successful amphibious operation, the first of its kind in U.S. military history, Scott lay siege to the town, which surrendered twenty days later. Then he began his march to Mexico City, following roughly the same invasion route used by Hernán Cortéz nearly 330 years earlier. Scott soon received five companies of recruits that appeared every bit as imposing as any legion of Spanish conquistadores. To clear the road through the mountain passes, which pointed the way toward the interior valleys of Mexico, this detachment of Texas scouts and couriers arrived, all frontiersmen fresh from fighting Indians.

In command of these units stood a conqueror whose reputation seemed to approach that of the dreaded Cortéz himself. Only thirty years of age, this seasoned Ranger leader, recently commissioned as a colonel in the U.S. Army, had already come to be known by the Mexican populace as the scourge of the South Texas borderlands—so much so that he had earned in battle the sobriquet *El Diablo*, "the Devil."[36]

His name was John Coffee "Jack" Hays. A native of Tennessee who had migrated to Texas in 1837, he had first established himself there as a surveyor and engineer of considerable skill. A prominent contemporary once recommended the handsome young Hays to Mirabeau B. Lamar, president of what was then the Republic of Texas, as "a gentleman of the purest character and of much energy and ability" who was "fully competent to any work in his line." Although he rode with Burleson, McCulloch, Caldwell, and others at the Battle of Plum Creek in 1840, Hays did not distinguished himself during this decisive engagement. Over the next two years, however, the quiet, unpretentious Hays emerged as one of the most feared and respected men on the border. Commanding Ranger insurgents from their enclaves in the wilderness in attacks on Mexican supply trains and reconnaissance forces during the bloody year of 1842, he helped his fellow Texians (as citizens of the Lone Star Republic then styled themselves) recapture San Antonio—and reclaim Texan honor—from the likes of Generals Vasquez and Woll.

As an Indian fighter, he knew no equal. In 1841, the Comanches learned firsthand of his fearless spirit and badgerlike tenacity at Enchanted Rock, nestled in the hills near the head of the Pedernales River. According to legend, and to contemporary reports, from his perch atop the rock formation Hays, alone, reportedly held off an estimated one hundred Comanche warriors for nearly an hour, killing as many as ten before a detachment of Rangers arrived to disperse the rest. So fearful were the Comanches of the "silent, white devil," as they came to call Hays, that they spread the word from the Texas hill country to the high plains of the Llano Estacado that Captain Jack was a ghost, not a mortal; surely this demon on horseback had been dispatched by evil spirits from the netherworld.[37]

Scholars disagree on whether the fight at Enchanted Rock happened as reported. True or not, Texans *believed* that it happened, and Hays's reputation rose accordingly. Hays neither corroborated nor denied such stories—he did not need to.[38]

Others created the legend of Jack Hays. During this period Hays's Lipan Apache scout, Flacco, recalled how "Devil Jack" would willingly ride straight up to death, showing no fear. Little wonder that during the U.S.-Mexican War Jack Hays was a name already known by friend and foe alike. "We had heard so much of Colonel Hays," Samuel C. Reid wrote, remembering his eager anticipation of meeting the commander of his regiment. "A delicate looking young man, of about five feet eight inches in stature," Reid recalled, "he was dressed very plainly, and wore a thin jacket, with the usual Texan hat, broad brimmed with a round top . . . with a black handkerchief tied negligently around his neck. He has dark brown hair, and large and brilliant hazel eyes . . . with very prominent and arched eyebrows." Reid went on, "His broad, deep forehead is well developed; he has a Roman nose. . . . He is naturally of a fair complexion, but from his long exposure on the frontier has become dark and weather-beaten. He has rather a thoughtful and care-worn expression . . . and his long acquaintance with dangers . . . [has] given him a habitual frown." Reid added, "[H]e wears no whiskers, which gives him a still more youthful appearance." Lieutenant Napoleon Dana wrote that Jack Hays was "a very remarkable man, and one of the most daring of the day," observing further that he was also the "best looking" officer in the Texas ranks. Yet another veteran of the war compared the soft-spoken Hays to the Homeric warrior Hector, recalling that "his services stand preeminent for daring and endurance, for privation, suffering, and hard fighting." The very "terror of his name," this contemporary remembered, was enough to strike fear into even the bravest of foes.[39]

Lieutenant Albert Brackett remembered his astonishment upon first seeing the legendary Hays. "I could scarcely realize that this wiry-looking fellow was the world-renowned Texas Ranger," he began. "Jack was very modest. . . . He was plainly dressed, and wore a blue roundabout, black leather cap, and black pants, and had nothing about him to denote that he belonged to the army or held rank in it." Brackett also recalled that "his face was sun-browned; his cheeks gaunt; and his dark hair and dark eyes gave a shade of melancholy to his features; he wore no beard or mustache; and his small size—he being only five feet eight—made him appear more like a boy than a man. Hays was no great talker . . . [and he] avoided speaking as much as possible; still he was very kind, and did not seem to put on any unnecessary airs." Another contemporary wrote, "[S]o many were the stories that went the rounds in camp of his perilous expeditions . . . , daring adventures, and his cool and determined bravery, that when we saw the man who held such sway over his fellow beings, we were first inclined to believe that we had been deceived." Colonel Hays's adjutant, Rip Ford, remembered his amusement upon seeing new arrivals attempting to search out the famed Ranger commander: "Colonel Hays was a rather small man and wore no uniform. Some large, good looking Ranger would [often] be taken for him." Apparently, everyone enjoyed the standing camp joke. Of course, no one had the nerve to tell the wiry little commander of such cases of mistaken identity.[40]

Although Jack Hays was no conversationalist and did not appear the least bit intimidating at first glance, he proved through his deeds and his daring that he deserved the highest respect from all who served under him. As historian Walter Prescott Webb would have put it, Hays did not merely command troops in the field; he *led* them. Rip Ford remembered, "[N]o officer ever possessed more completely the esteem, the confidence, and the love of his men." Ranger Robert Hall wrote admiringly of the charismatic, though humble, Hays. "He was all that has been said of him, and more. . . . So much faith did all of us have in . . . this extraordinary man that any half dozen veterans would have followed him in a charge against the whole Mexican army." Samuel C. Reid observed, "His word is law among his men . . . [and] there is something about the man which prevents one from taking the slightest liberty with him." Without question, all who knew Jack Hays agreed that he was the quintessential leader.[41]

That he proved at the Battle of Monterrey. On September 21, 1846, the guns of El Diablo led the way. From the cornfields north of the city, Colonel Hays commanded a bold charge against Mexican cavalry, a furious attack that helped General William Worth's forces secure the strategic Saltillo road that led to the fortified city. According to an admiring Lieutenant Dana, although the regular infantry raised a "tremendous shot" at the opening of the charge, it was Hays and his Texans who rushed "ahead like devils," hurling themselves headlong into the enemy and slamming into the lines of Mexican lancers. As

Dana recalled, with the blood-curdling battle cries of the Rangers, "terror soon found [its] way to the hearts of the foe."

According to another contemporary account, when a legion of Mexican lancers advanced toward American forces that day, Hays and his mounted Texans rode ahead with wild abandon to meet them. As the columns of combatants collided, the Rangers "poured into them a shower of rifle and pistol balls." Following the charge into the wall of Mexican cavalry, "both columns reeled before the terrible shock," the observer wrote, as "horse and rider were crushed to the earth . . . [amid the] hurry of wild confusion." After the initial surge of the pistol-wielding Texans, the battlefield dissolved into ferocious hand-to-hand combat as Mexican horsemen, armed with lance and sword, "sunk beneath the fierce rangers [*sic*] aim." During this chaotic clash, the daring Captain McCulloch reportedly advanced so rapidly that he became separated from his unit; soon surrounded by the enemy, he was forced to fight his way through the phalanx of Mexican cavalrymen, in the process expending every round from his two revolvers while spurring his mount back to the Texas ranks.[42]

After two rain-soaked days of fighting, the drenched American columns entered the city and advanced along the Calle de Monterrey. Through slippery side streets, Hays directed McCulloch's and Walker's companies as they fought with the desperation of wounded wildcats, swarming house to house and scrambling along tile rooftops, their rifles and revolvers taking a heavy toll on the enemy. Then over the walls surrounding the Bishop's Palace, Hays and company scaled to the heights of the city's most prominent landmark. As Texas volunteer James Holland remembered, the boys from the Lone Star State frightened soldier and civilian alike with "such shouting and huzzaing [*sic*] . . . to let the enemy know that Texas had come to town."[43]

Among the casualties in this epic battle lay the much-respected Ranger Captain Robert Gillespie, who, according to legend, inspired his fellow Texans to fight on. "Monterrey is ours," the mortally wounded Texan reportedly uttered confidently as he drew his last breath. "Boys, place me behind that ledge and rock and give me my revolver. I will do some execution on them yet before I die."[44]

Reid remembered well the ferocity of the battle that rainy day of September 23. "The street-fight became appalling," he recalled, "the artillery of both sides raked the streets, the balls striking the houses with a terrible crash, while amid the roar . . . were heard the battering instruments used by the Texans.

Doors were forced open, walls were battered down—entrances made through the longitudinal walls, and the enemy driven from room to room, and from house to house." Reid could not forget the "shrieks of women, and the sharp crack of the Texan rifles. Cheer after cheer was heard in proud and exulting defiance, as the Texans or regulars gained the housetops by means of ladders, while they poured a rain of bullets from the enemy on the opposite houses." He concluded, "[I]t was a strange and novel scene of warfare."[45]

Ranger Nelson Lee, too, never forgot the horrific picture of death and destruction. He remained haunted by the sickening image of "ghastly corpses" that filled the streets of Monterrey. Years later he still claimed to hear vividly the "groans and shrieks and agonizing cries for water and for mercy" that came from dying men and women throughout the defeated city. Another chronicler underscored the fierceness and vicious nature of the house-to-house fighting when he noted that the Rangers "unsated [*sic*] with slaughter . . . waited to avenge singally [*sic*] the . . . wrongs suffered during their long war of independence. The capitulation of the 24th, of course, disappointed all their sweet and long cherished hopes of vengeance." Ramón Alcaraz recalled that Monterrey looked like a "great cemetery" filled with "unburied corpses and . . . dead animals," the bodies in the streets creating a "terrifying scene."[46]

Despite the fact that the Texans were driven by their desire to collect on past "debts" and often entered battle still inspired by the liquor they termed "snake bite medicine," General Worth seemed little concerned about the reports of crimes against Mexican civilians. He even acknowledged his admiration for Colonel Hays and his Mounted Rangers. "Hereafter, they and we are brothers," he wrote proudly, "and we can desire no better guarantee of success than by their association."[47]

But General Taylor's dismissal of the Texas volunteers made clear his disapproval of their brutal methods and mercenary motives. "With their departure we may look to a restoration of quiet and order in Monterrey," Taylor informed the adjutant general of the army on October 6, "for I regret to report that some shameful atrocities have been perpetrated by them since the capitulation of the town." Equally disturbed by the Rangers' "lawless and vindictive spirit," Captain Luther Giddings gladly observed the departure of the Texans with "the hope that all honest Mexicans were at safe distance from their path."[48]

Hays's Texans could best be termed a military organization in name only. Colonel Ebenezer Dumont of the Fourth Regiment of Indiana Volunteers observed Hays leading Rangers into Puebla. He remembered that most of the Texans rode astride their horses, but some stood erect in the saddle, others slouched while clutching their pommel horn, and still others rode sideways with a leg slung over the saddle. Although most were mounted atop beautiful, well-proportioned American thoroughbreds, others rode small, shaggy-maned mustangs, a few rode mules, and at least one rode a jackass. "Here they came, rag-tag and bobtail, pell-mell, helter-skelter. The head of one covered with a slouched hat, that of another with a towering round top, another bear headed whilst twenty others had caps made of the skins of every variety of wild and tame beasts." Yet "a nobler set of fellows than these same Texian tatterdemalions never unsheathed a sword in their country's cause or offered up their lives on their country's altar. Young and vigorous, kind, generous, and brave, they have purposely dressed themselves in such a garb, as to prove to the world at a glance that they are neither regulars nor volunteers common, but Texas Rangers—as free and unrestrained as the air they breathe." Of the same scene, Lieutenant Albert Brackett added: "I watched them closely as they went silently by me, and could distinguish no difference between the officers and men."[49]

Neither could the Mexicans in battle, and it was on that field that Hays and his Rangers proved their worth once again. Late in November 1847, during an expedition against the city of Izúcar de Matamoros, Hays and a company of 135 mounted Rangers advanced more than sixty miles in less than twenty-four hours, ahead of General Lane's columns through the cold and rain to lead an American assault upon a fortified Mexican garrison. During a spectacular attack upon enemy defenses on the outskirts of town, Hays drove his column into Mexican pickets with stunning success, killing more than sixty, among them Colonel José de las Piedras. Afterward Hays' men freed twenty-one American prisoners, seized an arsenal of weapons, including three pieces of artillery and twelve tons of shot, then rounded up a herd of horses before riding out to rejoin the main force at Puebla. At the narrow mountain pass of Galaxara, American columns composed of regular and Ranger units collided with a force of some five hundred lancers and guerrillas. Of Hays's bravery in riding to the front to engage the enemy and thus allow U.S. dragoons to withdraw, General Lane wrote: "Never did any officer act with more gallantry than did Colonel Hays in this affair of the 24th. When we found it necessary to retire for the purpose of reloading . . . he halted in their rear, and, as the enemy advanced, deliberately shot two of them dead [with revolvers at close range], and covered his retreat until the arrival of reinforcements." Owing to Hays's swift and decisive reaction to the ambush, only two American soldiers died upon the field, while Mexican casualties were estimated at seventy.[50]

Los Diablos Tejanos

On December 6, 1847, Hays's motley collection of Mounted Rangers rode into an already occupied Mexico City. The appearance of the Texans aroused no small measure of interest. "Our entrance into the City of Mexico . . . produced a sensation among the inhabitants," Rip Ford recalled. "They thronged the streets along which we passed. The greatest curiosity prevailed to get a sight of *los diablos Tejanos*—'the Texas devils.'" Colonel Dumont echoed the report that as the Ranger companies passed through the city and approached the ruins of the temples and palaces of Montezuma, they were the "subject of much curiosity. The . . . streets were lined with spectators of every hue and grade, from a major general of the North American Army to a Mexican beggar. Quietly they moved along. Not a word was spoken. They seemed unconscious that they were the observed of all the observers." Another eyewitness recorded that the arrival of the Texans "excited as much lively interest as if President Polk and the American Congress had suddenly set themselves down in front of the [National] Palace." The unnamed observer went on to describe that "crowds of men flocked to see them . . . and women, affrighted, rushed from the balconies into the houses."[51]

Ranger Nelson Lee also recollected that the dramatic Texan entrance into the city of Montezuma resembled both a peculiar parade and a freakish carnival that attracted thousands of the gawking and curious. "We were some nine hundred strong," he began, "and perhaps no body of men ever presented a rougher or more ridiculous appearance." Recalling that the "accumulated dust" of a thousand miles "lay thick" upon the Texans, he acknowledged that the men who rode alongside him were "ragged and unwashed," more unkempt than their mounts. As for their horses, he admitted that the varied assortment of animals ranged from spirited, well-bred geldings and mares to pack mules and "long-haired jacks." With throngs lining the streets, he continued, "all the batteries of their wit were discharged upon us, even the little boys hooting and the women laughing in derision. At length they carried their jokes to the extent of pelting us with dirt and pebble stones."[52]

The crowds would soon learn that the arrival of the Texas devils was no laughing matter. On that December day, an eerie silence spread through Mexico City, a silence punctuated only by the sounds of horse hoofs clattering against cobblestone streets. A correspondent for the New Orleans *Picayune* also offered a colorful description of the strange and slow procession. "As the Gallant Rangers filed through the streets, covered with mud and dust accumulated on their long journey, it would have done you good to see the Mexicans stare, particularly when they were informed that these were the much dreaded . . . *Tejanos.* Dressed as Rangers always are in anything that comes to hand . . . but well mounted and well armed, they presented a sight never before seen in the streets of Mexico," the reporter wrote. "The usually noisy *leperos* [outcasts] were as still as death while they were passing." Colonel Hays "appeared to be the object of peculiar interest," he continued, "and the better informed class of Mexicans were particularly anxious to have pointed out to them the man whose name has been the terror of their nation."[53]

On the same day, December 6, General Ethan Allen Hitchcock noted his first reaction to the mounted volunteers from Texas. "Hays' rangers have come—their appearance never to be forgotten," he wrote in his diary. "Not in any sort of uniform, but well mounted and doubly well armed: each man has one or two Colt's revolvers besides ordinary pistols, a sword, and every man his rifle. All sorts of coats, blankets, and head-gear, but they are strong athletic fellows. The Mexicans are terribly afraid of them."[54]

As the horsemen passed through the city, one unidentified Ranger's pistol fell from his belt and struck the pavement, causing the weapon to discharge, accidentally striking an unarmed Mexican in the leg. This unfortunate incident—for which U.S. military officials later tried to charge the young Ranger with attempted murder—turned out to be a portent of things to come. When Hays rode triumphantly into the Grand Plaza and halted his columns in front of the National Cathedral, a crowd of more than one thousand pressed forward to get a closer look at the grim-faced Texans, who remained on horseback rather than dismounting in the midst of such a large throng. According to Ford, a Mexican street vendor passed by the

Rangers with a basket of assorted candies on his head. When one young Texan called him over and reached into the basket to retrieve first one fist full of candy, then another without offering to pay for the treats, the Mexican became incensed. Thinking the Ranger a thief, the merchant grabbed the Texan's hat, then bent over, picked up a small stone, and hurled it at the horseman "with great force." As an observer wrote, "It was the last stone he ever threw, for quicker than thought, a flash was seen, a report was heard, and the offender fell dead. A flash from the Eternal Throne could not have more speedily called him to account. The Ranger quietly replaced the pistol in his belt, reclaimed his cap and rode on." A single gunshot was all that was needed to cause a stampede as men and women trampled one another in a desperate attempt to escape.[55]

As if tensions were not high enough, later that same evening while several Rangers stood quietly preparing to enter a theater, a mischievous young Mexican, hardly more than a boy, dashed by them and grabbed a bandana from around the neck of one of the Texans. Before the street urchin could run to safety, however, the offended Ranger leveled his pistol and blew the youngster off his feet, killing him instantly. No sooner had the gun smoke cleared the air than the Texan walked over, retrieved his bandana, and according to Rip Ford, "went on his way as if nothing had happened."[56]

In the ensuing days, hardly a sunrise passed without at least one *Norte Americano* being found dead in the streets and alleys of the sprawling city, either shot or, more often, stabbed during the previous night's violence. One December night, a young Ranger of Captain Jacob Roberts's company foolishly ventured alone into a sordid district of the city known appropriately as "Cutthroat," the squalid area inhabited by what Ford termed men and women of "the lower orders." Almost predictably, several knife-wielding assassins attacked the young man, stabbing him repeatedly and leaving him for dead. Ford noted that the Texan's chest wounds were so ghastly (one gash supposedly deep enough to reveal his pulsating heart) that even the most battle-hardened soldiers were sickened by the sight of the suffering man, who apparently lived just long enough to ask his fellow Rangers to avenge his death.

Such incidents were "not reported" to U.S. officials, Ford later admitted. But neither were they forgotten—nor forgiven—by the Rangers, who waited less than twenty-four hours to settle this particular debt. An "ominous silence reigned among the Rangers" for the rest of the day, Ford recalled. "Not one of them appeared to speak of their murdered comrade." And yet Ford knew that a "scheme to wreak a bloody vengeance" was afoot. Hays's men were hell-bent on vengeance, and nothing would stop them.

Later that evening, a tense Colonel Hays sat in his headquarters at 26 Doncella Street, talking with Captain P. W. Humphreys of the U.S. Army and Adjutant Ford. Suddenly the conversation was interrupted by the crack of gunfire, unmistakably the reports of six-shooters. When Humphreys queried Hays about the origin of the shots, the colonel dismissed the firing as the work of U.S. Marines engaged in target practice. "They are always making noise," Hays explained the issue. Just then, the firing increased and became more general, the pattern of the shots indicating that a skirmish was moving through a nearby neighborhood in a somewhat orderly manner.

Around midnight, the gunfire ceased, and a deadly calm fell over the city. In the strange silence, Ford heard the unmistakable sound of a single pair of boots clomping against the stone street. Humphreys walked to the window and casually commented that General Scott's personal orderly was fast approaching. "For once Colonel Hays seemed intimidated," Ford recollected. Pushing back from the table, Hays stood and excused himself. "Ford, if he comes in tell him I am not in," the colonel ordered. Old Rip remembered that Humphreys had not actually seen the general's aide but was merely testing Hays as to his knowledge of the source of the gunshots. "We all knew they were Texians," Ford confessed.[57]

Around ten o'clock the following morning, Captain Humphreys reported to Ford that during the night a unit of regular military police had been dispatched to investigate the disturbances and that they too had apparently "joined in" the indiscriminate shooting. The result, he informed Ford, was that the bodies of fifty-three Mexican civilians had already been placed in carts by the city police. By sundown, Humphreys updated the estimate to eighty corpses that had been transported in death wagons to a nearby morgue, where they were laid out like cordwood. "It was a fearful outburst of revenge," Ford confessed.[58]

Several days later, General Scott summoned Colonel Hays to confront him with the report that six more Mexican civilians had been gunned down by Rangers in broad daylight. Hays stood ready for a reply. He admitted that his men had fired on a group of Mexicans because they had stacked rocks on rooftops and were stoning the Rangers as they rode through the streets below. His men had acted in "self defense," he insisted. Scott asked no further questions, and the matter died there.[59]

As the winter of American military occupation settled over the ancient city of the Aztecs, the signs of seasonal change appeared everywhere. The days grew shorter, and the afternoon shadows longer. Every day, darkness fell sooner over the Mexican nation. Even the winter skies seemed to turn more sullen and grayer. Then as Christmas drew closer, a chilling gale swept down from the north.

The United States now appeared poised to secure through negotiations what had been already won on the fields of battle. As the year 1847 hastened to a close, so did the war, if not the conflict that had led to it. With Scott's army occupying the capital, an obscure former clerk of the U.S. Department of State, Nicholas P. Trist of Virginia, pressed forth in asserting President James K. Polk's war aims. Already Trist was demanding a treaty that would provide for the U.S. acquisition of the sprawling Pacific coastal province called California as well as the New Mexico territories, thus effectively reducing the Republic of Mexico by nearly half while also ensuring the United States' position as the supreme continental empire stretching from one great ocean to another. More concerned about the defense of their own state borders, Texans would soon have cause to rejoice upon hearing of the settlement of the Rio Grande boundary dispute. Mexican claims to the Nueces River as a northern border had long been lost. No matter that history and geography favored Mexico on this question, the fortunes of war and diplomacy did not.

In December 1847, Christians throughout the capital and countryside were observing the traditional Advent and preparing for the holy celebration of the coming of the Christ child. Great cathedrals and little chapels alike were displaying scenes of *la Navidad*, images of the Madonna and Child, and the words of hope: *paz en la tierra, buena voluntad a los hombres*—"peace on earth, good will toward men."

Before long the war would be over, as much as any war can ever truly be over. Not since the conquest of Cortéz had Mexico known such defeat. Not since the "Great Dying" that followed in the path of the famed conquistador in 1519 had the peoples of the Valley of the Aztecs experienced such sorrows and shed so many tears. And just as the natives of Mexico would long remember the dark legend of Cortéz, even three centuries after the fall of Montezuma's empire, so, too, would they remember the specter of the dreaded demons on horseback who brought death and destruction to their country. For the Texas Rangers had ridden across their land and into their lore, like the horsemen of the apocalypse, never to be forgotten, feared for their ferocity and brutality in battle. So it was that another legend was born in the collective memories of the Mexican people, that of the terror from the north that would be forever feared and known as los diablos Tejanos.

2
The River

Somewhere between heaven and hell there is a place called the Nueces Strip. In time, as in space, it stretches along the borders of Texas myth and physical reality. Rising slowly from the sea, sweeping inland, seemingly to the horizon and beyond, this harsh and desolate country extends south from the Nueces River to the Rio Grande and westward from the Gulf of Mexico to the Devils River. Sprawling over 15,000 square miles of low-lying plains, the South Texas savannahs cover an area almost twice the size of Massachusetts. Throughout the region, dense thickets of gnarled mesquite and tangled chaparral choke the prairies. So do scattered clusters of cactus and clumps of creosote. Nearer the waters of the Gulf, salt marshes, brackish lagoons, and undulating sand dunes characterize an otherwise monotonous landscape. It is a forbidding land that reaches as far as the human imagination can travel. Hot, dry, dusty in summer, the country is even more barren and windswept in winter. While each spring the cool ocean breezes bring showers of life-giving rain, leaving the earth carpeted with lush grasses and cascades of wild flowers, in summer the land inevitably surrenders again to the sun.

Predictably, the searing heat and unrelenting drought of July return these rattlesnake-infested plains to their featureless form. Little wonder that Anglo-Texans and Tejanos of the nineteenth century, as well as the Spaniards and American Indians before them, saw this barbaric though magnificent country as a land of contrasts, one with an almost spiritual quality, a mystique that transcended racial, cultural, and geographic boundaries. So it is that, for generations of Texans, this unforgiving country existed as much in the mind as on any map.[1]

The Nueces Strip is a wild, even savage, land that has inspired the growth of legends. Across the lore as well as the landscape of southernmost Texas runs a crooked river that meanders for a thousand miles and more, separating two nations, two cultures, and two peoples. The Rio Grande winds lazily across sun-spangled plains, descending gently toward the blue-green waters of the Gulf of Mexico. Past sleepy adobe villages and beneath spreading palms that shade the river's banks, the muddy current moves slowly, seeking a path to the sea. Over the years, the course of the channel has changed, leaving dry beds that serve as mute reminders of the unpredictability of both nature and history. Narrow and shallow by the standards of great rivers, the Rio Grande finds its way through a serene land inhabited by a gentle people. It is a peaceful river.[2]

Yet even today the corridos and *rancheras*, or border ballads, sung along both banks of the river tell of a time when death was common in the brush country and of a day when "the Valley" (as it has been misnamed) was transformed into a blood-stained battleground. Songs still speak of the time when men were all too willing to kill for any cause, noble or otherwise. And, as the lyrics proclaim, through the center of it all runs the river.

The Rio Grande, or Rio Bravo del Norte (fierce river of the north) as Spaniards also called it, has always been a source of conflict, always more of a political than a geographic barrier. Since the U.S.-Mexican War and the signing in 1848 of the Treaty of Guadalupe Hidalgo, which formally established the Rio Grande as an international boundary, the serpentine river has become a symbol of the racial and cultural divide between peoples of two republics. And it represents more—much more. To the people who live and work along the waters of the lower Rio Grande today, the river still serves as a daily reminder that a confluence of commerce and cultures has shaped the character of the region, making it a meeting place of past and present. Today, as in earlier generations, the Rio de las Palmas (river of palms) is a juncture of diverse peoples of different destinies yet common dreams, of divided loyalties though shared hopes and fears. The river also reveals to residents on both banks that the ties of blood, beliefs, and language bind people together more than any artificial boundaries divide them. The waters suggest other universal truths—truths that cross all borders and are as timeless as the land itself—namely that in the uncertain course of human affairs not much separates the fortunes of those who have so much from the fate of those who have so little. In the final analysis, despite their apparent differences, people on both sides of the border must share the same space and the same future.[3]

Ford Begins the Pursuit

To be sure, the wild cattle, millions of them that once roamed freely over the ranges of the Nueces Strip, knew no boundaries. From the day of the earliest Spanish entradas, to the romantic era of the Texas cowboy and the long drive, the hardy though obstreperous beasts known as longhorns wandered across the grasslands of this border country in need of practically no attention or care. Lean, angular, with shoulders and ribs protruding like sharp blades, the unpredictable animals predictably did what they do best—they grazed, bred, multiplied, and migrated across the open range without regard to river or legal claims. They were an independent lot, just like the frontiersmen who coveted them.[4]

Following the U.S.-Mexican War, the advancing Anglo-Texans considered these vast herds—all of them—to be "Texas cattle," there for the taking. But to the Tejanos who farmed and raised livestock north of the Rio Bravo, and to the Mexican peons and vaqueros living south of the river, the animals were nana's (grandmother's) cattle. And no treaty nor court of the gringos could ever change that.[5]

Following the war, yet another reality remained—the seemingly insatiable demand for cattle in the hide and tallow markets of Matamoros, Reynosa, Camargo, and other border towns upriver. No matter whose brand the animals bore on their bony hips, they could always be rounded up and easily sold in the slaughterhouses on either side of the river. During the war, ranchos on both sides of the Bravo had been destroyed or abandoned, and wild cattle roamed on the open prairies. So it was that eager buyers along the river engaged in the lucrative trade for leather as well as that for the animals' horns and hoofs, which could be melted into soap and candles, then shipped to markets in Mexico, the Caribbean islands, and the United States.[6]

Anglos and Mexicans were not the only ones competing to round up the countless wild cattle wandering throughout this border country. What nature and the agents of both nations did not claim, the American Indians did. During these years, the Comanches ranged southward—as they had for centuries—from their settlements on the Llano Estacado to raid as far south as the Rio Grande and beyond. In the process, their forays often found them on both sides of the international border, not just rustling cattle but also stealing entire herds of wild horses that thundered over the plains of South Texas and northern Mexico. Naturally, Texas and U.S. officials blamed an unstable and corrupt government in Mexico City for harboring the "thieving" Indians, while Mexican authorities pointed the finger at malevolent and grasping gringos and their "protectors" north of the Rio Grande, whom they charged could not control the marauders.[7]

The two sides agreed, however, that the Comanches were their common enemy and that something had to be done. Not surprisingly, officers of the state of Texas acted first. In the summer of 1849, Texas governor George T. Wood ordered state adjutant general John D. Pitts to authorize the formation of three companies of Mounted Rangers to patrol the borderlands of the Colorado, Nueces, and Rio Grande. These volunteers were not only to act in support of regular army units stationed on that defensive perimeter but also to range far to protect the frontier and punish the plains tribesmen for their recent rapine and plunder. Little was reported of these ranging companies, other than the fact that a John Grumbles served briefly as captain of one of them and that for a time his unit was stationed on the Nueces, some seventy-five miles above Corpus Christi. The celebrated Henry Eustace McCulloch, veteran of many border campaigns and the younger brother of Ben McCulloch, commanded the second company, which was posted on the prairies between Goliad and Corpus Christi. As for the third company, Pitts assigned it the most difficult task—that of defending the cattle ranges and settlements in the Nueces Strip and along the lower Rio Grande. To organize and lead this detachment of Mounted Rangers, Pitts appointed the seasoned and savvy John S. "Rip" Ford.[8]

Pitts could not have made a better choice. A native South Carolinian reared in the best of southern martial traditions, Ford first arrived in Texas in June 1836, too late to participate in the rebellion against Mexico. Like so many others, he came to seek a new beginning and possibly to escape a failed marriage, leaving behind his wife, Mary, and never looking back. During the next decade, he established himself as a "practicing" physician in the East Texas town of San Augustine, earning barely enough money to pay bills, living modestly. Then in 1845, he moved to Austin to become editor of the *Texas Democrat* and to hang out a second shingle, this one for a legal practice.

In September, he married a widow named Louisa Lewis, but their apparent happiness ended all too soon. The following June, Louisa fell ill, and despite Ford's best efforts to nurse her back to health, she died. Grief stricken, Ford lapsed into a deep melancholy and may have even temporarily lost his will to live.[9]

Later in 1846, however, with the outbreak of war with Mexico, Ford emerged from his bereavement and joined the First Regiment, Texas Mounted Volunteers, under the command of Colonel Jack Hays. He soon rose in rank to adjutant of the Texas unit. Schooled not only in the letters but also in the ways of the wilderness, he was as knowledgeable about the merits of unconventional warfare as about traditional, linear skirmish tactics on horseback. Although a student of all subjects from military history to modern medicine, he was at his best motivating men. At the same time, while riding alongside the likes of Hays and Ben McCulloch, he learned that a well-armed, well-mounted, and disciplined fighting force posed a most formidable foe for even the fiercest of enemies. Like those captains who rode before him, he learned that the commander of Texas volunteers must, in battle, trust not only his training but also his best instincts. The fact that he was already familiar with the terrain and topography of South Texas also made Ford more valuable to the ranging service than almost any other soldier of his day.[10]

In 1849, therefore, Ford stood alone among his contemporaries. With Jack Hays now gone to the goldfields of California, and with Ben McCulloch soon to follow the forty-niners in search of fortune, Ford was the last Ranger legend to survive both the war with Mexico and the subsequent delirium of the gold fever. Now it was Ford's turn to make his imprint on the Ranger traditions.

A merging of classical Renaissance man and plainsman of the Texas frontier, the tall, muscular Rip Ford, with his expressive eyes, fair complexion, and chiseled facial features, represented the best of both archetypes. Whether clad in a gentleman's suit and top hat or in a fringed buckskin tunic, deer hide leggings, and a broad-brimmed sombrero, he appeared comfortable and in his element. Equally at home with the most polished, literate, and well-mannered of Austin society as with the most savage and desperate characters infesting the borders of the Lone Star State, he arguably stood closer than any person then living to being the Texan everyman.

Yet anyone who knew John Ford knew he was anything but common. "Old Rip," the Texan troops had affectionately named him during the late war with Mexico, referring to the many letters of condolences he had written, each ending with the traditional postscript R.I.P. (rest in peace). In two respects, however, Ford belied the nickname bestowed upon him. First, he could not have been considered "old" by any stretch of the imagination, being only thirty-two years of age when he returned from Mexico City in 1848. More ironic still, he hardly knew the meaning of the words "rest" and "peace."

This his Ranger recruits in 1849 soon learned. On August 23, the indefatigable Captain Ford—known to the Comanches as "Bad Finger" because of a digit that had been partially shot away in battle—mustered more than twenty men into service and marched them in a matter of days from San Antonio to Corpus Christi. While on the move and at almost every camp en route, he drilled them in the manual of arms, in target practice, and in wheeling movements, changing fronts, and other maneuvers while mounted and at a full gallop. Each morning he awakened his Rangers, allowed them a little time for breakfast, then pushed them and their horses for thirty miles and more, until darkness fell and it was time again to pitch camp and stretch out under the stars.[11]

Ford's command was typical of those volunteer units known variously as state partisans, minute companies, and Mounted Rangers. Most of the recruits were young and unmarried; they were also lacking in military experience, although not in courage or in a sense of duty. They were well mounted and heavily armed, although in most cases with mere muzzle-loaders and single-shot pistols. As was the custom, they provided their own horses, a simple necessity to ensure that even the least seasoned of them rode a reliable and fleet mount. Only a few carried service revolvers manufactured by Mr. Colt. Several of them, like their captain, also wielded bowie knives and, on occasion, shotguns for close-quarter fighting. Their commanding officer made certain that each of them had both the will and the skill to use every weapon in their personal arsenal. Although Ford later claimed that the men received $23 a month, no official quartermaster records have apparently survived for this company. Given the circumstances of the times, though, their pay was doubtlessly low and usually slow in coming. Sometimes it probably never came at all.

When he first saw his men, Ford lamented that "a dozen determined Indians could have defeated the whole command with heavy loss." Yet, while admitting his Rangers' natural aversion to discipline, he still recognized "a company of sober and brave men" capable of being trained to fight together. During their march down the valley of the Nueces, the captain and his men learned that in late summer even the most courageous could be deterred by the elements. In the last days of August 1849, the skies opened up as tropical storms rolled in from the Gulf of Mexico, transforming the parched prairies into a veritable quagmire. "The rain fell in torrents," Ford remembered, "dry creeks were converted into rivers; their waters were deep, their currents impetuous. We waded and swam, and splashed through mud and bogs. . . . For many days no one had dry clothes." More troublesome still, in these conditions their horses grew agitated and "lost flesh daily." After camping for a few days near the swollen Nueces, first at a site eight miles upriver from Corpus Christi, then fifteen miles to the south at the future site of Captain Richard King's Santa Gertrudis Ranch, Ford led his men through sheets of rain on a sweeping reconnaissance of the region. Up the Nueces and westward to the road from San Antonio to Laredo, he rode over the drenched plains that were overrun by droves of mustangs and drifting herds of wild cattle. After stopping at Fort McIntosh on the Rio Grande, he moved down river more than forty miles to Rancho Davis and the settlement of Rio Grande City.[12]

But the Comanches were nowhere to be found. Owing to the heavy seasonal rains washing away all signs, not a trail nor a trace could be located. The boredom and inactivity added to the daily drudgery and lack of amenities, which made camp life on such a scout anything but romantic. For a bed, each man settled at night for a blanket and the hard, or sometimes muddy, ground. For a pillow, his saddle sufficed. Only when at a permanent outpost, where they camped for a week or more, did the Rangers pitch tents for shelter. For food, they lived off the land, shooting any wild game that wandered their way, whether turkey, quail (or prairie hens), peccary (wild hogs), and rattlesnakes. Sometimes they enjoyed what dried beef they could procure before going into the field. Beans and soggy cornmeal were usually reserved for those occasions when the men had time to cook as was the delicacy of fresh beef, always available on the savannahs of South Texas, where wild cattle ranged freely across the region. Such were the conditions that awaited the young Texans who rode in the ranging service.[13]

Ford's detachment disbanded in the fall, and the men returned home for the winter. No muster rolls have survived to document their dismissal, but Old Rip reconstructed from memory the roll of officers and staff of the company reorganized the following February. Twenty-eight year-old Lieutenant Andrew Jackson Walker, an experienced scout from Corpus Christi, was promoted to second in command, and twenty-two-year-old Malcijah Benjamin Highsmith of Bastrop County was appointed quartermaster and commissary, with young David Level now acting as orderly sergeant, and the twenty-six year-old Philip N. Luckett of Corpus Christi continuing as surgeon. All were veterans of the recent conflict with Mexico. A Mexican guide and interpreter, Rocque Maugricio, also signed on; described as a half-blood Comanche who spoke three languages, he was familiar with every square mile of the Nueces Strip. Ford also respected Rocque as a skilled tracker and recognized his uncanny sense of smell.[14]

Ford and his men had not even seen, much less come close enough to smell, a Comanche the previous fall. In the spring of 1850, however, their scouting expeditions would prove to be as productive as their previous ones had been unsuccessful. In early April, Ford and his company of more than forty Rangers arrived on the border without incident. They established camp at a sandy site they called San Antonio Viejo—Old San Antonio—near the Rio Grande, some forty-five miles upriver from Ringgold Barracks. From there Ford could command a strategic crossing of the Rio Bravo while remaining no more than four days' hard ride from San Antonio, Corpus Christi, or Brownsville.

Sometime after the first of May, after Ford's company had returned to Fort McIntosh, they left the post on a scout of the upper Nueces. Near the headwaters of that river, Rocque picked up the trail of a Comanche raiding party. The captain was confident that his guide would quickly locate the marauders and set out on their trail. On the morning of May 12, within hours of breaking camp at a river ford known as Comanche Crossing, Ford and his men encountered the Indian warriors. The Rangers swiftly engaged them in a four- or five-mile running fight. During the chase, Ford's Rangers broke from formation to ride up behind their enemy. Each rider positioned himself closely behind the right rear flanks of an Indian war pony, where the Indian horseman could not turn and fire upon his pursuer. Thus the Rangers could "draw down" with pistols on the fleeing raiders at close range or at the least shoot their horses from under them. The Texans killed four Comanches and wounded several others who escaped; they also captured a dozen horses. One Ranger received a minor wound, according to Ford, who lost his own mount that morning.[15]

The next day, after discovering that two of his company's horses had been stolen in the night, Ford resumed the trail, riding several miles downstream, then doubling back that afternoon to a point near his original camp at Comanche Crossing. Frustrated that the tracks of the Indian ponies seemed only to lead in circles, Ford ordered his men to bed down beneath a full moon that illumined heavens and prairies alike. Not even in the brightness of what Texans termed a "Comanche moon" could the Rangers continue the pursuit. The elusive plains tribesmen seemed to have escaped again.

The following morning, Ford and company moved down the Nueces. They scoured the river valley for any sign of the Comanches and constantly scanned the horizon for movement. Eventually, they reached Fort Merrill, the army post located on the river's north bank where the San Antonio Road crossed en route to the coastal town of Corpus Christi. After purchasing rations for his men and horses, Ford established camp nearby, then continued alone to Corpus Christi, where he attempted to procure a suitable horse to replace his favorite mount, which had been killed in the previous fight. Unsuccessful in this endeavor, as well as in his effort to requisition new Colt revolvers, he returned to camp on May 25 and prepared to lead another scout.

This time the result would be different. In the predawn darkness of May 26, the loud popping sounds of rifle fire awakened the company. As Rangers scrambled to their feet and grabbed their weapons, the moans of an unidentified man were heard in the brush. A young Comanche brave had been mortally wounded and, in Ford's words, was "in the agonizing throes of death." Apparently, Ford's sentries had foiled an attempt to stampede the Rangers' horses.[16]

At daybreak, the Texans were in the saddle. Leaving a squad to defend the camp, Ford and his men rode the perimeter for several miles. But once again, the Comanche party had slipped away. Later that day, Ford scribbled a message to Captain J. B. Plummer, commander at Fort Merrill, detailing recent events. According to Ranger courier Edward Burleson, Jr., of San Marcos, Plummer responded with skepticism and little concern about the reports of rifle fire and Comanche raiders so near post. By Burleson's account, Plummer even seemed to blame the trigger-happy Texans for disturbing his troopers' sleep. More bizarre still, later that day one of Plummer's regulars, described by Ford as "loony," passed through the Texans' camp, holding up the severed head of the young Comanche as his personal trophy. By nightfall, no one could blame Ford for being frustrated and restive.[17]

On the morning of May 29, 1850, Ford and his Rangers began their long ride back to the Mexican border and to their camp at San Antonio Viejo. They did not get far before locating and engaging the Comanche, near the Rancho Amargosa (the Spanish word for "bitter"), about eight miles northwest of present-day Alice. Around midmorning Rocque picked up fresh Indian pony tracks, certain evidence that a war party was nearby. Ford ordered his men to form skirmish lines, then dispersed them at proper intervals. Four miles ahead, near Agua Dulce Creek (aptly named for its sweet water), the Rangers came in sight of a Comanche camp nestled in a tangle of mesquite. At a gallop, the column of Rangers advanced toward the unsuspecting enemy. Faster still they rode as the Indians jumped on their ponies and dashed away, with the pistol-wielding Texans in close pursuit. In the desperate struggle that followed, Ford's Rangers engaged the Comanches, shooting them and their horses at near point blank range. By Ford's count, they killed four raiders and wounded at least seven others.

For their actions, however, the Rangers paid a heavy price. During the exchange, young William Gillespie was bringing up the rear. Judged by Ford to be a "good soldier and a splendid shot," Gillespie watched a Comanche tumble from his horse with one shot through the neck and another through his back. Gillespie rode by the fallen warrior's body, assuming him to be dead. Out of the corner of his eye, however, he saw the young man move. Gillespie wheeled his horse around and took aim with his pistol, but as he pulled the trigger, his horse lurched, causing the weapon to discharge into the ground. While the Texan struggled to reload, the wounded Comanche rolled over and sent an arrow deep into his side; the shaft pierced his lung, leaving him slumped in the saddle, mortally wounded.[18]

Once Ford realized that he had lost at least one man, he apparently suspended the chase and ordered several Rangers to cover his flanks and directed another squad to retrieve their dying comrade and carry him to a place of safety. Then the captain reformed his lines. For several tense moments, the Comanches held their ground, believing the demoralized Texans to be in retreat. They were wrong. The Rangers charged headlong into their enemy, scattering what remained of the raiding party over the prairie. Abandoning their wounded, the Indian horsemen fled toward a timberline about a mile away, but not before Ranger David Steele placed a shot behind the ear of the presumed leader, knocking him from his horse. The rest of the Comanche raiders outran the Rangers; escaping into the brush, they taunted the Texans with shrill, blood-curdling cries and defiant gestures.[19]

In the aftermath of this battle, the Rangers discovered that several of their horses had been injured. They also found, hiding in the mesquite thickets, a wounded Comanche. A mere adolescent, the boy was sitting upright, not even flinching from the pain of two gunshot wounds. Speaking to the young brave in his native tongue, Shoshonean, Rocque assured him that he would not be harmed any further. Looking surprised, the prisoner rose up and saluted Ford. Then the captive explained to the interpreter that his people had bestowed upon him the dubious name Carne Muerta (as translated into Spanish), or "Dead Meat." He also claimed to be the son of a Comanche war chief. Were it not for the death of young Gillespie in camp that evening, the incident might have been looked upon with some amusement.[20]

There was no humor in what followed, however. That night Ford's solemn command marched to a camp occupied by a detachment of Captain Grumbles's company. The following morning, the Rangers tied Gillespie's body to a mule and walked to a nearby hill overlooking the Agua Dulce, where the men of both units attended a brief burial ceremony described by Ford as "sad though simple." They wrapped the corpse in a blanket while Ford read a few appropriate words from the scriptures. Then several Rangers gently lowered the body—boots, hat, and all—into a shallow grave and shoveled dirt upon the remains. Like his uncle, Robert Gillespie, who had fallen at the Battle of Monterrey just three years earlier, the youthful William had died far from home and in the service of Texas.

Throughout the funeral, the young Comanche captive sat and stared at the open grave, as if it were meant for him. Perhaps he wondered whether the Texans might seek their revenge by killing him next, that his name might be prophetic. After all, he must have known of the Rangers' reputation for executing captives. Ford ordered his men not to kill Carne Muerta, however, to carry him with them, perhaps as a bargaining chip in negotiations or as live bait to lure the Comanches into another fight.[21]

The Raids Grow Worse

That spring, as the grasses grew lush to provide excellent forage for their horses, the Comanches conducted a series of bold raids into Webb County and southward along the lower Rio Grande. Riding down from the high plains like the hordes of Genghis Khan, they swept across the sunbaked plains of the Nueces Strip, each time galloping away with horses and cattle and in the process sending herdsmen and farmers scurrying for the safety of large border settlements such as Laredo.

So widespread were these depredations and so great was the fear along the Rio Bravo that General George M. Brooke, commander of the Eighth Military Department of Texas, wrote to General Winfield Scott on May 28, 1850, and implored him to station still more garrisons of U.S. regulars on the border. "The predatory war now going on will be continued for ever, unless we exercise the strength we possess to put it down at once," Brooke informed the commanding general of the army. "The number of posts must be increased on the Rio Grande," he insisted. Not only were the Comanche devastating the South Texas frontier, he reported, but they were also crossing the river into Chihuahua and Coahuila, "laying the whole country [to] waste." In the final analysis, he recommended that U.S. government officials consider paying annuities to the Comanches in exchange for peace along the entire line of settlements that extended from Eagle Pass to the upper Trinity River.[22]

Yet General Brooke did not want to call upon the governor of Texas to provide state Rangers for protection of the frontier. As he stated succinctly, "[T]heir feeling, and you may say, general natural hostility to Indians would be very apt to bring about what we wish to avoid—a general war." The people of South Texas, however, did not agree with Brooke's assessment. In an undated petition, forty-four landowners of the lower Rio Grande—most of them with Spanish surnames—insisted that Governor Peter H. Bell reinforce the Ranger units operating in South Texas. Claiming that their homes had been for more than a year "the favourite lurkeing [*sic*] place" of Comanche marauders, they reported in distress: "our flocks have been destroyed . . . [and] scarcely a month has passed that some one or more of our citizens have not either been murdered or dragged into captivity."[23]

For the moment, however, Ford and his Mounted Rangers were all that stood between these stockmen and the roving bands of Comanches. During the second week in June, Captain Ford led a detachment of twelve volunteers on another reconnaissance of the vast expanses stretching from the upper Nueces to the Rio Grande. They did not have to look long or far for their foe. Picking up a trail across the sandy bed of the Nueces, they followed it all the way to the Rio Grande. As they rode to Don Basilio Benavides's rancho, located twenty miles below Laredo, they came upon a band of Comanche rounding up wild horses near a large bend of the Rio Bravo. Ordering his men to dismount and watch the Comanches from the brush, Ford waited patiently and quietly for them to approach with their stolen herd. Noticing that the marauders were mounted on horses "of inferior quality and in bad condition," the captain allowed them to ride within pistol range.

A furious fight erupted with an initial exchange of gunfire. Completely surprised by the Rangers' ambush, the Comanches galloped away, with the Texans in fast pursuit. No more than a mile and half into the chase, the Rangers closed in on the Indian horsemen, whose ponies were slowed by fatigue and lack of nourishment.

A brief but bloody struggle unfolded, with the Rangers hurling themselves into the Comanches with a vengeance. As Ed Stevens and Jose Morales of Bexar County rode up to two warriors, one of the Indians launched an arrow that struck Stevens in the back of his scalp, then glanced off the rear of his skull, stopping only when it "bulged the skin at the top of his head," Ford remembered. Angered, but not gravely injured, Stevens leveled his rifle, rode forward, and placed the muzzle at the temple of the bowman. When he fired, Ford recalled, the concussion of the blast "scattered the Indian's brains into the face and one eye of Morales's horse." When the other Indian, now on foot, tried to bring down Stevens, Morales swiftly spurred his horse forward and trampled the warrior, then shot him. In all, the Texans killed seven Comanches during this fight. Remarkably, Stevens was the only Ranger wounded that day.[24]

Following the savage struggle, while the Rangers were recovering Benavides's stolen horses, they discovered a young Comanche who appeared to be dying from both his wounds and a broken hip, presumably suffered during a fall from his horse. Although the Rangers carried the injured prisoner back to Benavides's ranch house, Ford and his surgeon, Philip Luckett, soon pronounced the warrior's condition hopeless. Ford ordered an "act of mercy," insisting that one of his men put the Comanche out of his misery. When no Ranger volunteered to carry out the execution, a Mexican muleskinner stepped forward to finish the onerous task. An eerie stillness fell over the camp; the silence was suddenly pierced by a single gunshot. Then all fell quiet again.

For the remainder of the sweltering summer of 1850, Ford's company fanned out across the exposed frontier between the upper Nueces and the Rio Grande. To cover the vast ranges of the region and to maximize the effectiveness of his force, Ford split his company into three detachments. Lieutenant Walker's squad of twenty men patrolled the ranches below Laredo, while Lieutenant Highsmith's command of twenty-six Rangers was stationed at San Antonio Viejo, where they were strategically positioned to respond to any contingency. Ford even left his personal field glasses with Highsmith so he could keep an eye out for Comanche raiding parties. Meanwhile, with a smaller escort Ford rode upriver to Fort McIntosh, where he turned Carne Muerta over to Captain Sidney Burbank, the likeable post commander, described by Ford as "mild yet firm in his methods," a professional who "merited the esteem and confidence of the officers and men."[25]

Burbank agreed to take custody of the Comanche captive, much to Ford's relief. The captain feared that the young Indian had become more of a liability than a reliable source of information or a pawn in negotiations. Now Burbank and his interpreter could interrogate him, feed him, and listen to his seemingly endless boasts and empty threats.

Ford soon learned of a more tangible danger. Hearing from a courier that Comanche raiders had struck his own camp during his absence, he led his squad more than seventy miles across the rugged prairies to San Antonio Viejo. Upon Ford's arrival, Highsmith assured his commanding officer that, while besieged for two days and nights by a large party of Comanches, he had neither suffered nor inflicted any casualties. Highsmith reported that only a handful of animals had been stolen, including Ford's obstreperous old horse Higgins; little of importance had been lost. The only fatality during the siege had been a fat mule the raiders slaughtered for meat within sight of camp. Despite the theft of a few more horses and mules in the following days, not much happened during the next two months. The summer droned on, and the searing Texas heat continued to take its toll upon the land and all living things there.

In late August, Captain Ford moved his camp to Los Ojuelos, situated some forty miles east of Laredo on the main road to Corpus Christi. If he and his men actually believed that they had the Comanches on the run, they would soon think otherwise. Just weeks after establishing camp near the small stream, Ford learned that three of his young Rangers had been overtaken and two of them slain by Comanches somewhere on the sandy mesquite-covered plains southwest of where Richard King's Santa Gertrudis Ranch would be located three years later.[26]

Ford was distressed though not surprised, when he learned of the loss. Following the fight near Amargosa on May 29, 1850, Ford had reluctantly allowed John Wilbarger, Doc Sullivan, and Alpheus Neal to return to their homes near Bastrop to attend to personal matters. Before they parted, however, Ford had warned them of the perils of traveling alone or in small parties across the desolate Nueces Strip.

Judging by what transpired as the three men attempted to return to Ford's company nearly three months later, Old Rip had understated the dangers. On August 20, as the three Rangers rode over the prairies south of the Nueces and stopped at midday to rest beneath the shade of clustered mesquite, they were discovered by a roving band of Comanches. They mounted up, and rather than trying to escape, they chose to stand and fight.[27]

That turned out to be a fatal mistake. Before the three Rangers could even ready themselves, a rifle shot struck Sullivan in the chest, curling him over in the saddle. While the twenty-year-old Wilbarger returned fire, Neal pulled Sullivan from his horse, tied the animal to a tree, and offered comfort to his companion. Mortally wounded and gasping for breath, young Sullivan urged Neal to save himself. Seeing his companion's situation as hopeless, Neal tried to mount his pony to ride away; however, the terrified animal raced under the rope tied to Sullivan's horse, knocking the Ranger down before he could even swing into the saddle. Desperately Neal tried to hold on to the pommel horn while being dragged away. By the time the Comanche warriors caught up with him, Neal had lost his grip and spilled to the earth. As he scrambled to his feet and started to run a burning sensation penetrated deeply into his back. Struck by one arrow, then another, and yet another, he reeled from the shock, then staggered and fell. He had as many as eight arrows lodged in his legs, arms, and torso. Stunned and bleeding, he lay motionless while the Comanches stripped him of his boots and clothing.[28]

Meanwhile, Wilbarger also made a break for the open prairie, but the swift-riding Comanches closed in on him after a frantic two-mile chase. By all indications, the young Ranger fought fiercely before being brutally killed. When his body was found several days later, pools of dried blood covered the site of his killing, as if several wild animals had been butchered there. Not much was left to bury as Wilbarger's remains were "terribly mangled," according to Ford.[29]

What happened to the boyish Alpheus Neal was nothing less than remarkable. Left for dead by the Comanches, Neal recovered consciousness. Despite the loss of blood, he managed to pull several arrows from his body and broke off at least two more. Disoriented and in agonizing pain, he somehow walked more than sixty-five miles to San Patricio. The story has it that he stumbled into town naked, sunburned, and blistered beyond recognition, his lips cracked open, his tongue swollen from his mouth, and his wounds festering. Looking more like a ghoul than a man, he had nevertheless lived to tell of his terrifying experience. Neal's story must rank among the most amazing survival tales in the annals of Texas.[30]

Fortunately for Ford's Rangers, the remainder of 1850 passed without further event of note. Other than Old Rip's falling ill that autumn and seeking medicines in Laredo, only routine reconnaissance missions occurred. With the coming of winter, the scouts ceased, at least until after Christmas. Like the grasses that provided forage for their ponies, the Comanches typically remained dormant during the winter months.[31]

All that changed with the coming of the New Year. During the first week of January 1851, Ford received an order from Captain Burbank to escort Carne Muerta to San Antonio, whereupon the prisoner would be returned to his people. Ford detailed Lieutenant Burleson and a detachment of twenty men to carry out the task. It was only a four-day ride from Camp Los Ojuelos to the Alamo City.

In the meantime, Ford dispatched Andy Walker to scout the prairies along the Arroyo Gato (Cat Creek), some fifty miles northeast of Laredo. On January 19, Walker and eighteen other Rangers came upon a remuda of horses and mules that had been hobbled, their legs tied together to allow them to graze but not to drift far or run away. Walker and his men understood full well the meaning of their discovery. A party of Comanches had recently crossed into Mexico and had left fresh mounts for their return trip. Surely, they would come back soon. When they did, the Rangers would be there to meet them.[32]

Walker posted sentries, staked out the high ground below the stream, and waited. For five bitter days and chilling nights, his vigil continued. Late in the afternoon of the sixth day his patience paid off. Rangers John Wilson and Andrew Wheeler signaled to their lieutenant that a Comanche party of at least twenty was fast approaching, returning from their raid into Mexico with as many as two hundred horses and mules. Walker allowed the lead horsemen to pass his position, holding his fire until the main body came to within close range. At that point, he gave the command for attack. Out of the brush the Rangers rode full speed into the face of the enemy, their charge being so swift and sudden as to leave the startled Indians stunned and confused. Walker's men slammed into the war party with such fury that the field became a swirling maelstrom of dust and gunpowder. In Ford's words, the "combatants formed a struggling mass of men and horses."[33]

Above the din of battle, the Indian leader sounded a shrill whistle to alert his warriors. But it was too late. The Comanche ranks failed to hold as most of the horsemen quickly scattered into the chaparral. But the Comanche headman had collapsed, mortally wounded by the Texans' deadly fire. Then Lieutenant Walker and Rangers Wallace McNeill, Alfred Wheeler, John Wilson, and David Level engaged what remained of the enemy at close quarters, firing on their foes at point blank range. Walker and his men even fought Comanche style, dropping to the sides of their horses and shooting over their saddles, a tactic that no doubt resulted in at least two of the Rangers' mounts being shot from under them. During such a maneuver, an arrow pinned Sergeant Level's hand to his saddle bow and another pierced his horse's neck, sending the animal to the ground with a fatal wound. With one hand trapped under his horse, Level only escaped the lance of a charging warrior when John Wilson placed a ball through the Indian's side, doubling him over and sending him stumbling into the thickets.[34]

Within a matter of minutes, the fight along the Arroyo Gato was decided. Walker and company had killed several Comanches, recaptured the entire herd of horses and mules, and sent the surviving raiders into flight northward with word of their defeat at the hands of the Texas devils. Understandably, Ford could not have been more pleased when he learned of Walker's success.

Ford could hardly have expected more from Lieutenant Burleson's squad, which had been dispatched to San Antonio to deliver Carne Muerta. On a cold blustery January 27, 1851, as Burleson headed back to Camp Los Ojuelos, he crossed the Nueces and struck the main road to Laredo, where his detachment unexpectedly rode upon three Comanches. What ensued was termed by chronicler John Wesley Wilbarger "one of the most desperate Indian fights" in the history of Texas border warfare. As soon as the Comanches saw the Texans, they wheeled their ponies and made a dash across the open prairie. Seeing the flight of the horsemen, Burleson led seven of his men in pursuit, after commanding the remainder of the detachment to continue along the trail to Laredo. For three miles, Burleson chased the Indians until he looked ahead and was surprised to see at least a dozen more warriors on foot.

They were waiting for him. At that point, the Rangers galloped to within one hundred meters of the enemy so that Burleson could size up the situation. Mistakenly, and apparently against Burleson's better judgment, several of the Texans then dismounted and drew their weapons. Seeing this maneuver, the Comanches charged and engaged the Rangers in a savage fight that descended into hand-to-hand combat. With Burleson remaining on horseback, frantically directing his men in this life-and-death struggle, the scene quickly became a terrifying tangle of men and weapons. Revolvers and rifles discharged in close quarters, arrows flew with deadly accuracy, lances were thrust, Texan knives clanged against Indian hatchets and cold steel tore into human flesh.[35]

Four of the Comanches died, and at least eight others were wounded in this clash; the Rangers also suffered heavy casualties. Every Texan on the field that afternoon received at least one wound, and two died in the battle. Baker Barton fell dead and William Lackey lay dying of multiple wounds, any one of which may well have been mortal. Jim Carr reportedly received four serious injuries, although none proved fatal. The same was true of Jack Spencer, Alf Tom, Jim Wilkerson, and a Ranger identified only as Leech. Young Warren Lyons, an interpreter who had been raised a Comanche, was also bleeding from multiple injuries. As for the citizen farmer turned soldier, the fearless Lieutenant Burleson, he received an arrow through the scalp, which penetrated his hat, pinning it to his head just beneath his ear.[36]

After what was probably no more than three minutes, the Comanches retreated, so hastily that they did not even stop to collect their dead. Although bloodied, their faces blackened from powder, Burleson and six of his Rangers were still standing on a field covered with arrows. According to Comanche accounts, the Texans then brutally scalped the slain warriors and dismembered their corpses in reprisal or perhaps merely for sport. The following day, Burleson dispatched courier Sam Duncan to Fort McIntosh to request that Captain Burbank send army ambulances to carry those wounded who were able to travel.

As for the Comanche raiders, they headed northward to their winter camps on the high plains. Yet as they planned to return in the spring to capture mustangs, mules, and cattle, they surely knew that, when they did, the Rangers would be there to meet them again. Indeed, on March 23, 1851, Ford's company of mounted volunteers formed in Laredo and mustered for another six months of duty.[37]

Fortune Seekers Infest the Borderlands

As the Rangers continued their reconnaissance for Indian raiders, the region of the Nueces Strip was fast becoming a breeding ground for some of the worst elements ever to infest the Texas borderlands. All types of fortune seekers—both good and bad, but mostly bad—rushed into this untamed region after 1848. It was almost as if the lowest of American society drained into Texas and down into the valley of the lower Rio Grande. Undeterred by the ever present threat of marauding Indians, they came by the thousands: mercenaries, muleskinners, army deserters, prostitutes, scalp hunters, prairie bandits and brigands of every description, bounty hunters in search of runaway slaves, mustangers seeking to round up vast herds of wild horses running freely over the plains, and Anglo filibusters looking for an opportunity to extend the United States into northern Mexico. A motley collection of malcontents and miscreants, they mingled with the more established population of soldiers, steamboat operators, merchants, missionaries, lawyers, farmers, and herdsmen.[38]

What a combustible mixture! John Russell Bartlett, a member of the team of surveyors that traversed the region in the autumn of 1850, observed that a "bad population" reigned virtually unchallenged along the Rio Bravo. "Murders were common . . . and it had been too often the case that the guilty escaped justice," he commented. Protestant missionary Melinda Rankin, a native of New England who opened a school in Brownsville in 1852, wrote that during her first months on the border she "suffered much anxiety, and kept almost constant watch through the . . . night" because of the "number of lawless . . . [types] prowling about for the purposes of theft." She further noted that "there were plenty who would take my life for the dress I took off that night." Major William Emory of the U.S.-Mexican Boundary Commission, which surveyed the lower Rio Grande in 1853, likewise reported on what he termed the "reckless character of the persons . . . infesting that frontier." He commented that the newly established international boundary was little more than an "imaginary" line that bandits could cross freely and "any offence [*sic*] can be committed on either side with impunity." Frederick Law Olmsted, a young easterner who traveled across the region in 1856, agreed that the population on the lower Rio Grande was "composed of runaway vagabonds and outlaws of all nations."

A French Catholic priest, P. F. Parisot, in Brownsville, later concurred, "[G]reat crimes committed in open day remained unpunished and men depended for protection more upon their own witty brains and stout arms rather than upon the shelter of the laws." Distressed to discover that his parish was made up largely of refugees from repression and revolution south of the river and ruffians and rogues from north of the border, the missionary confessed ministering to men and women who were "as willing to promote earthly fortunes by foul means, as by those that were fair and honorable." In short, he noted that a "moral blight" existed throughout the region and that the residents on both sides of the river were "not as a rule the wisest and best of their respective populations." But perhaps the wife of an officer stationed at Fort Brown summarized it best. "[T]here never was a country more unfitted by nature to be the home of civilized man," wrote Teresa Viele. "It seems only to be intended as a home for desperate men, escaped refugees from the law . . . [and] men who live in the saddle."[39]

Newspaper editor Ovid Johnson of Brownsville described the situation aptly in 1849; in his opinion, the lower Rio Grande Valley was a veritable breeding ground for violent and wicked men who lived by their own set of rules. "It is not to be regarded as extraordinary that after the close of the late war with Mexico, and the disbanding of our forces on that frontier, a large number of persons were found dispersed along that line who felt little inclination to observe the law, or to respect the rights of the neighboring citizens of Mexico," he explained. "All wars and commotions leave behind them a refuse population," he submitted, and "on both sides of the Rio Grande, these persons have stationed themselves." Surely, as Johnson observed, bandits and bad men of all types seemed to lurk in the brushes near every bend of the river and beyond into the maze of thorny mesquite that offered instant concealment for armed horsemen of uncertain motives.[40]

Captain Abner Doubleday, a veteran of the late war with Mexico, returned to the region in 1854, stopping off in the coastal village of Corpus Christi before continuing across the brush country below the Nueces. As he traveled to his new assignment at the isolated post of Fort Duncan, situated on the Rio Grande near Eagle Pass, he learned firsthand that this harsh country was no place for the meek. He later recalled sarcastically that the Nueces Strip seemed to be a "charming place for people who dislike the restraints of civilization." Moreover, he noted, "there was no law there but that of the Bowie knife and pistol." He surmised that most of the characters he encountered along that frontier had fled to South Texas "on account of the crimes they have committed" and that the border country had become a "refuge for a great many criminals." Horse thieves, cattle rustlers, and highway robbers—"felons of the worse kind"—infested this lonely land, he lamented, noting that not even martial law could tame these desperate characters. Doubleday remembered that one of his fellow officers from the East aptly commented, "Isn't it strange that every gentleman to whom I have been introduced here has murdered somebody?" Even the bustling, festive city of San Antonio, he discovered, "was not regulated by law to any great extent." And beyond the outskirts of the Alamo City, roaming bands of marauding Comanches still claimed the wilderness as their own. To this well-educated young officer from New York, the country of the lower Rio Grande seemed truly Godforsaken.[41]

A southern gentleman serving on the South Texas border two years later would agree. Traveling across the desolate, parched plains of the Nueces Strip in the fall of 1856, Colonel Robert E. Lee of the Second U.S. Cavalry would wonder why everything that grew from the ground stuck him and why everything that slithered and crawled across the earth tried to sting or bite him. After suffering an infected finger from the prick of cactus needles from a Spanish bayonet, he wrote home from his quarters at Ringgold Barracks that "every branch and leaf in this country are armed with a point, and some poison the flesh. What a blessed thing the children are not here," the homesick colonel informed his wife, Mary. "They would be ruined." To Lee, accustomed to the breathtaking beauty of his beloved Virginia, with its spectacular forests and lush green meadows, the stark region of the lower Rio Grande spread before him like a "desert of dullness," a denuded, drought-stricken land of swirling dust storms. Not even his experiences in the war with Mexico had prepared him for such a forbidding frontier as that which awaited him on the Rio Bravo.[42]

Violence and Vigilantism Rule the Border

The war between the United States and Mexico may have formally concluded in 1848, but for many—living both north and south of the border—that conflict would never end. The succeeding years brought only continuous social, political, and economic upheaval within Mexico, and with only token garrisons of U.S. troops stationed at remote army posts scattered along the lower Rio Grande, the populace living along the river resorted to the unwritten laws of the frontier. In the absence of moral and legal authority, and with no extradition agreement between the two nations, public violence and vigilantism ruled this border region, and private killings—as a result of individual acts of revenge—were all too common. Each man professed to be a law unto himself. And in those cases where disputes were not settled immediately with six-shooters, twenty feet of rope was never far away. A jury of twelve or one hundred could always convene on short notice, sit in hurried judgment of the unfortunate "accused," and swiftly carry out the seemingly preordained verdict. In other words, those presumed guilty of horse theft, cattle rustling, or lesser crimes (such as murder) were promptly given a "fair trial." Then they were hanged.[43]

"It is the stern and primary law of self-preservation—this border custom of bringing criminals before the whole body of citizens for judgment," observed Jane Cazneau (the wife of trader William Cazneau) of Eagle Pass, who wrote under the pseudonym Cora Montgomery. Simply stated, the first law enforced on this frontier was the Old Testament injunction "an eye for an eye." It was a code older than the scriptures and one more easily understood than the U.S. Constitution. Not surprisingly, therefore, one of the first casualties in the ongoing conflict of cultures and classes along the Rio Grande was the Bill of Rights.[44]

No one understood the reality of life in the region better than the Tejanos who were left by the fortunes of war within the borders of Texas. They comprehended little of the laws of the Lone Star State—laws that all too often left their lands and their legal rights at the mercy of Anglos and their attorneys in the courts of Texas. If in the Nueces Strip and along the Mexican border possession was nine points of the law, then the tenth was the exercise of armed force. Without question the exacting of gunpowder justice was complemented by the more subtle exercise of political influence over those who interpreted and enforced the law. Still, for the poor and powerless, the result was the same: no matter the promise of protection under the U.S. Constitution and the laws of their adopted state, what mattered most in settling land claims in the courtrooms of South Texas was that the victors received the spoils.

No sooner had most U.S. regulars been removed from the border than the region along the Rio Grande was beset by hundreds of disputes over land tenure and title. A welter of conflicting claims and resulting legal challenges threatened to clog the court dockets and to disrupt the peace (such as it was) along the border. Early in January 1850, aware of the explosive potential of these disputes, Governor Bell requested that the Texas State Legislature authorize a commission to investigate the legitimacy of land titles and to adjudicate the outcome of the contested deeds in the counties of the trans-Nueces region. Particularly vexing and especially volatile were overlapping land surveys—some grants having been issued as early as the eighteenth century under the authority of Spain, other titles after 1821 by the Republic of Mexico, and still others more recently by the Republic of Texas or its sovereign successor, the Lone Star State.[45]

Even the rumor of such a commission touched off a firestorm of controversy in the lower Rio Grande Valley. On the evening of February 2, 1850, a "mass meeting" of angry and apprehensive citizens gathered in Brownsville at the schoolhouse of R. N. Stansbury. The announced purpose of the assembly was to consider the creation of a Territory of the Rio Grande and a provisional government that would answer not to Austin but to Washington City. Scores of outspoken separatists and secessionists—many of them Anglos, but some Tejanos—raised the specter of an armed insurrection should a state commission even consider stripping them of their lands, most of which had been acquired since 1836. Following a tumultuous exchange of harsh words, epithets directed mostly at Governor Bell and other state officials, those in attendance adopted a series of stinging resolutions renouncing the authority of the Lone Star State and calling on the U.S. Congress to create a territorial government with jurisdiction over the region south of the Nueces River. These "territorialists" even went so far as to announce a convention on March 16 in Brownsville to consider the formation of such a sovereign entity, separate from the state of Texas. "The time has at length arrived when the people of this Valley must act," one resolution proclaimed. "We have too long confided in the justice of the people of Texas—too long tamely submitted to her unauthorized political jurisdiction. Our confidence has been misplaced," the document declared. "Let us knock on the door of Congress for that protection which Texas denies us." Accusing state authorities of threatening to "annul the titles in real estate between the Nueces and the Rio Grande," the statement further predicted that any commission formed to litigate disputed land claims would create even more uncertainty and thus undermine the confidence of land merchants as well as the labors of "men of the soil." The pronouncement demanded: "If you desire the prosperity of this Valley—a rapid development of its agricultural resources, and the quiet enjoyment of your property, which you have acquired by years of industrious toil, you must look to the United States for a disinterested government and an independent judiciary."[46]

Yet another important moral undercurrent lay just beneath the surface of the rhetoric. Although the town meeting focused largely upon the pressing issues of property rights and border security, the broadsides that circulated in Brownsville announcing the gathering were apparently distributed only to those citizens who were known opponents of slavery. A faction of Cameron County residents, who termed themselves Friends of Free Soil and Territory, evidently saw the growing unrest as an opportunity to voice their views on that most volatile of issues. Their attempts to interject the slave question into border politics was but a portent of things to come.[47]

The remonstrance did not end there. Within two weeks, the territorialists submitted to the U.S. Congress two petitions demanding the immediate formation of a Territory of the Rio Grande. Almost all of the signatories to the first petition were of Mexican origin, notable among them Juan Nepomuceno Cortina, a disgruntled ranchero who mistrusted the Texans and their government and who suspected that his family's estates in Cameron County would not be recognized by any tribunal appointed by Governor Bell. The second petition of protest listed such prominent Anglos as steamboat owner and rancher Richard King and merchant Stephen Powers who, like Cortina, were both destined for decades to play a central role in the history of the Rio Grande Valley.[48]

Apparently, not all residents of the Nueces Strip shared the fears being fomented by these separatists. On the night of February 5, 1850, what was termed a "large assemblage" gathered in Brownsville at Stansbury's schoolhouse to voice support for Governor Bell and his tribunal "to investigate and quiet land titles" in the counties of the Rio Grande Valley. This gathering of citizens headed by resident Israel Bigelow—and apparently composed entirely of Anglo-Americans—proclaimed their undivided loyalty to the state of Texas. They further charged that an alliance of land speculators, lawless brigands, and abolitionists had banded together to promote the dismemberment of Texas and the secession of the Trans-Nueces in order to serve their own individual designs and self-interests.[49]

In an effort to quell the discord spawned by the separatist movement in South Texas, Governor Bell responded with a letter to the people of Cameron and surrounding counties. On February 22, the governor wrote from Austin that his purpose in forming an investigative commission was "to quiet, not to disturb or invalidate," land holdings along the border. Attempting to reassure his readers, he announced his determination to protect the property of rightful landowners from the fraudulent or forged claims of those who held no lawful title, only "squatter's rights." He then tried to allay what he believed to be unwarranted fears about the investigations of the commission, which he asserted would be "composed of men free from prejudice, and with no hostile feelings toward the claimants or their causes." Finally, he implored the residents along the Rio Grande to "await, with patriotic forbearance, the action of the tribunal which you seem so much to dread. That tribunal," he pledged, "is intended to augment . . . [the] validity to your land titles, and to place you in . . . undisturbed possession."[50]

By the time the governor's words reached South Texas, the legislature had already authorized the creation of a two-man commission to investigate and adjudicate land claims in the counties between the Nueces and the Rio Grande. Specifically, legislators instructed the commissioners to recognize and validate "all claims to lands . . . provided such claim had its origin in good faith prior to the second day of March, in the year eighteen hundred and thirty-six." In so doing, the framers of the enabling legislation all but assured a morass of future legal entanglements by excluding those grants made by the Republic of Texas and those subsequently made by the state of Texas.[51]

As anticipated, Bell wasted no time in appointing two commissioners whose task was to tour the counties of the Nueces Strip to ascertain the legality of land titles embroiled in pending litigation. Although both men enjoyed a reputation for honesty and fairness, neither was fluent in Spanish nor knew anything about the rapidly changing and highly volatile state of affairs along the border. A native of Kentucky and a physician by training, James B. Miller had settled near San Felipe to practice medicine. Early in 1836, after establishing himself as a confidant of Stephen F. Austin, he stood alongside the likes of William Barret Travis as a leader of the so-called war faction. After the revolution, he operated a plantation in Fort Bend County before serving in the senate of the Republic of Texas, then as secretary of the treasury under President Sam Houston.

The other commissioner, William H. Bourland, also originally from Kentucky, immigrated to Lamar County in 1840. By 1843, he had been elected to the congress of the republic. Then, after the outbreak of war with Mexico in 1846, he left his seat in the state legislature to enlist in the army, where he rapidly rose to the rank of major in the Texas volunteers assigned to General Zachary Taylor's regulars. So neither appointee was a stranger to responsibility, or to the specter of Anglo-Mexican conflict.[52]

Understandably, as word spread about the appointment of the two commissioners, suspicion and mistrust preceded them on their tour of the border, especially among the Hispanic population of South Texas. Despite the fact that Governor Bell had vowed that the tribunal would be impartial and judicious during its deliberations, Tejanos looked upon the board, perhaps unfairly, as merely representative of a land-hungry Anglo-Texan elite. From the moment Bourland, Miller, and their interpreter, a respected attorney and judge named Robert J. Rivers, arrived in Laredo in June 1850, they were neither wanted nor welcomed. "When we first entered upon the discharge of our official duties," the commissioners later reported, "we had to encounter much opposition and embarrassment, growing out of an impression which seemed to prevail in the valley of the Rio Grande that . . . the board was devised to destroy, rather than protect their rights . . . to their lands. We were not prepared for that opposition." The commissioners later concluded that, were it not for the intercession of Hamilton Bee, clerk of Webb County, they would have been unable to overcome that resistance and complete their work. As the summer droned on, the commissioners traveled to Rio Grande City, then to Brownsville, in each town holding public hearings, subpoenaing witnesses, testimony, and evidence, accepting depositions and documents.[53]

After concluding the hearings, Bourland, Miller, and Rivers parted company and headed north by different routes. Deciding to return to Austin by water, Miller boarded the steamer *Anson* in Brownsville late in November. Two days out to sea, however, a storm swept over the South Texas coast, and the little steamboat capsized and sank a few miles off Matagorda Island. Although Dr. Miller escaped drowning, the commission suffered a terrible setback. Miller lost his luggage, which included a trunk containing the complete records and documents assembled by the commission—among them all the original land titles presented by claimants to the board. Thus the commissioners and Governor Bell faced the daunting prospect of starting over again the next year.[54]

The following summer, therefore, Bourland and Miller again toured the South Texas counties in order to obtain, where possible, duplicates of the lost land titles and to reconstruct as best they could the testimony and documentation obtained earlier. At last on November 11, 1851, some twenty-one months after the formation of the Bourland-Miller Commission, the two members issued their final report to Governor Bell and the General Land Office of Texas. In all, the commissioners recommended 76 percent of all petitions for confirmation, while they rejected the remaining 24 percent on various grounds ranging from "abandonment" to earlier forfeiture for failure to pay taxes to the absence of proper documents proving ownership prior to March 2, 1836.[55]

The commissioners appeared somewhat biased in their decisions. Of the forty-nine petitions denied by the commission, forty had been filed by men of Mexican or Spanish origin, while only nine of those rejected had been entered by claimants of Anglo or Celtic ancestry. Not surprisingly, regardless of the findings of the Bourland-Miller Commission, disputes concerning overlapping titles would underlay racial strife and cultural conflict along the border for many years to come. Even those Tejano titleholders whose lands were "confirmed" by the board were left to the mercy of an Anglo-American legal system and elected leaders unsympathetic to their plight. No wonder that many of them remained unconvinced that justice had been served.

Anglo-Texans—inspired by a simple belief in their own superiority—insisted that a "higher law" prevailed over the poorly documented claims of Hispanic peons and rancheros. Moreover, they believed it was their right, indeed their responsibility, to press forward with the "blessings of liberty." In the process of extending the dominions of democracy, they saw themselves as carrying out a divine commission to "civilize" the "heathen," subjugate and convert the "infidel" of the Roman Church, and subdue and develop an untamed wilderness—regardless of the cost. It was their manifest destiny, they claimed.[56]

Even if God was *not* on their side—and they insisted that He was—surely the judicial system of the state of Texas favored them. Jane Cazneau candidly acknowledged that issues of race and nationality strongly influenced the administration of justice along the border. Writing in 1852 from the squalid outpost of Fort Duncan, she admitted, "[T]here is a disposition [among the Texans] to judge the Mexicans with severity and to deal with them beyond the law." Referring to the peasants who tilled the fields and tended to the herds along the Rio Grande, she contended, "[T]he soil has been torn from them by the great landowners who monopolize what should support a thousand . . . families." Frederick Law Olmsted, who traveled through the region several years later, likewise noted the "unhappy condition" of Tejanos who had been dispossessed by the recent arrival of the Norte Americanos. More specifically, he concluded that "they were too poor and too ignorant to . . . insist upon their rights." Olmsted further offered, "[T]here is . . . between our Southern American and the Mexican, an unconquerable antagonism of character, which will prevent any condition of order where the two come together."[57]

Olmsted also observed that the Hispanic population on both sides of the border harbored "fear and hate for the ascendent race." Rip Ford agreed that the Spanish-speaking population of the border "hated Texians horribly, yet feared them" for they held a "lively remembrance" of the brutality of the "bloody Texans" during Mexico's war with the United States. As for the Texans, they still remembered the Alamo and Goliad as well as the more recent atrocities committed during their ongoing sanguinary war with Mexico. To them, their continuing conflict with the Mexican nation was defined in simple terms. Too many Texan martyrs had died in the struggle against tyranny for their sons and daughters to be denied their "rightful inheritance"—and that included the grasslands of the Nueces Strip. Texan John Linn recollected that during those times his countrymen were "remorseless" in seizing all that had been allegedly left "abandoned" along the border. "The restless spirit of the adventurers by which Texas was flooded induced them to enter into competition . . . in appropriating livestock left grazing on the prairies. Anything that belonged to a Mexican," he admitted, "was legitimate game." He also confessed that Texans claimed as the spoils of victory "immense numbers" of horses that were rounded up on both sides of the river.[58]

An Economic War Is Waged

Disputes over ownership of lands and livestock loomed large in the Nueces Strip, disputes that kept alive memories of the U.S.-Mexican War. All the while, a war of a different sort raged along the Rio Grande, an economic one waged with tariffs, trade restrictions, and the transport of smuggled goods. As with most wars, much was at stake. Soon after the signing of the Treaty of Guadalupe Hidalgo, the congress of the Republic of Mexico imposed prohibitive import duties and restrictive trade policies intended to stifle the flow of commerce across the border. But such measures, intended mostly to deny Americans access to the markets as well as the raw materials of Mexico, only incensed merchants, manufacturers, and people of commerce north of the border. At the same time, such regulations and constraints threatened to strangle the economic livelihood of the border states of Tamaulipas,

Coahuila, Nuevo Lefin, and Chihuahua, thus inciting the peoples of these northern provinces to insurrection or at the very least forcing them to display a blatant disrespect for any distant law and authority. Not surprisingly, smuggling became a way of life along the river. So did the trafficking of fugitive slaves who had fled to the freedom afforded by Mexican soil.[59]

The situation was rife for rebellion. Severe financial losses to traders along the Bravo, and more important the fear of even greater economic hardships, combined with political instability within Mexico and the natural antipathy of Texans toward Mexicans to produce a tinderbox of trouble. So as filibusters gathered in San Antonio and elsewhere throughout the Lone Star State and plotted to invade Mexico for the purpose of seizing lands as far south as the Sierra Madre Mountains, bands of armed insurrectos and secessionists collected near the southern bank of the Rio Grande and hatched schemes to overthrow local Mexican authorities and declare an independent Republic of the Sierra Madre.[60]

Only a spark was needed to ignite the resulting border disturbances known as the "Merchant's War." A disgruntled Mexican renegade leader, the Texas-born and Virginia-educated general José María de Jesús Carvajal, provided that spark. In September 1851, Carvajal recruited Texas merchants and mercenaries to aid him in capturing border towns and recovering confiscated goods from Mexican customs officials. On September 19, with as many as three hundred fellow *filibusteros*—described by one contemporary as "desperate looking men" recruited from both sides of the river—he captured, albeit for only a brief time, the town of Camargo. According to Colonel Persifor F. Smith of the U.S. Army, this motley mob included dozens of Anglos, former Texas Rangers described as "men of unsettled habits . . . left without occupation or means of subsistence" after the war and who were consequently "ready for anything that offered to supply their necessities." Four weeks after occupying Camargo, Carvajal's rabble of insurrectionists, known as the "Liberating Army of Northern Mexico," marched triumphantly to the outskirts of Matamoros, only to be confronted there by a superior force of Mexican regulars under the command of General Francisco Avalos. For several days, beginning on October 21, fierce street-to-street and house-to-house fighting raged within that city, and a spectacular pitched battle and artillery duel transformed the town plaza into a war zone. Helen Chapman, wife of Major William Chapman, reported from her quarters at Fort Brown that she heard "the rattle of musketry and the roar of cannon" through the night. Black clouds of smoke drifted across to the river from Matamoros while dozens of "wild, strange looking beings," as Helen Chapman described them, gathered in Brownsville to cross and participate in the fighting. All the while, the streets of Brownsville spilled over with families of peons ferried across the river who were fleeing northward, their carts and wagons filled with all their earthly belongings.

At last, outgunned and without proper logistical support to sustain his campaign, Carvajal had little choice but to retreat, abandoning Matamoros to the Centralist forces, which included both Mexican regulars and their Seminole Indian scouts. Before they withdrew, however, Carvajal's insurrectos suffered numerous dead and scores of wounded.[61]

One of the injured, who suffered only a scalp wound, was Rip Ford, who had raised a company of thirty "free Rangers," or mercenaries, to join in Carvajal's little revolution. The ranks of these rebels also included Andy Walker, who had served with Ford in the recent campaign against the Comanches. Ford later recalled the ferocity of the struggle in Matamoros, specifically the frustration of defeat at the hands of an old adversary, General Avalos. Still, he remembered how he and his defiant fellow Rangers fought bravely against overwhelming odds and how they had inflicted heavy casualties on the hated *federales* and Seminoles, dispatching many to the "happy hunting grounds." What he failed to mention in his memoir was that his filibusteros put the torch to the town, then reportedly fired upon unarmed Mexicans who attempted to stop the spread of the flames from the village plaza to adobe dwellings nearby.[62]

Ford later recollected that, although two young Texans had been taken prisoner during the battle and were purportedly condemned to be executed, they were instead freed. "A suggestion was made to shoot them," Ford recounted. But General Avalos ordered their release, replying, "Shoot these two Texians and a thousand more will come to their funeral." Like his fellow countrymen, Avalos had learned well in the late war the terrible resolve of los diablos Tejanos.[63]

Other American soldiers of fortune taken prisoner by Avalos during the three-day battle were not so lucky. As reported by Father Emanuel Domenech, a French priest recently arrived in Brownsville, a group of some eight "American adventurers" had been imprisoned in a squalid jail in Matamoros for weeks before word came from Mexico City that President Mariano Arista had ordered their execution. On a rainy day in October

1851, the condemned men, along with a dozen other unfortunate prisoners detained on charges of insurrection, were marched under armed guard to an untilled field more than a mile from Matamoros, where they were tied to posts, blindfolded, and shot by a firing squad. "The bodies were placed on a dung cart," Father Domenech sadly recalled, "and conveyed to the cemetery" two miles away. "Slow and on foot, under the pelting rain, I walked behind the cart, from which the blood trickled down, recommending the victims to the mercy of God." They were buried, without ceremony, tossed together into a long shallow ditch that served as a makeshift grave. Such was often the fate of filibusters who failed in pursuit of grandiose dreams of conquest.[64]

Carvajal's border insurrection soon collapsed, and his mercenary force, composed primarily of Anglos, quickly disbanded. The next year, General Carvajal, described by one contemporary as a "brave and enterprising" revolutionary who was "more a distinguished soldier . . . than a good leader," attempted to foment two more rebellions along the Rio Bravo. Both movements were predicated upon a pronunciamento calling for constitutional reform and a sweeping redistribution of land. Yet behind this so-called Plan of La Loba, and the *grito,* or cry, for land and liberty in a newly established, independent buffer state in northern Mexico, there may have been another design, a more sinister motive known only to a few. "During those days slaves held in Texas, induced to run away from their masters by Mexicans, found refuge beyond the Rio Grande," Ford wrote. "It was calculated that there were, at that date, three thousand colored men north of the Sierra Madre who were owned by men living in Texas," he estimated. "General Carvajal acceded to a proposition to have them surrendered to their masters." Furthermore, Ford purported that Carvajal had pledged to impose a stringent fugitive slave law if his border revolution succeeded.[65]

Carvajal, although never realizing his ambitious schemes, succeeded in further inciting the embittered population of the border. Moreover, his failure left his patrons in Texas, including upstart steamboat operators Richard King and Mifflin Kenedy as well as several other prominent merchants in Brownsville, with dreams and designs yet unrealized. His aborted rebellion likewise left in its wake many enemies in northern Mexico who were understandably suspicious of Carvajal's motives as well as the intentions of his Anglo supporters in Texas. But mostly, his movement—called a "pale-faced revolution" by cynical Mexicans and Tejanos—engendered along the lower Rio Grande a growing climate of lawlessness and a general disrespect for established authority.[66]

Carvajal's border rebellions did not go unnoticed in Washington, D.C. Concerned about the fragile weave binding the Compromise of 1850, particularly with enforcement of the controversial fugitive slave law that provided for harsh penalties for anyone abetting runaways, President Millard Fillmore bristled in anger when he learned that Texas filibusters had joined Carvajal and his movement to establish a buffer republic in northern Mexico. On October 22, 1851, Fillmore admonished any American citizens who fomented violence and revolution in Mexico, and he issued a stern warning that the U.S. government would not lift a hand to spare any captured Americans caught on the wrong side of the river from a certainty of a Mexican noose. The president also issued an executive order that day commanding Colonel Persifor Smith of the Eighth Military Department of Texas to interdict and suppress any illegal invasions of sovereign Mexican soil by any members of the U.S. land or naval forces or any state militia units that violated the territorial integrity of the Republic of Mexico and thus destabilized the Rio Grande border.[67]

From his headquarters in San Antonio, on October 21, Colonel Smith had already taken preemptive measures to halt any further efforts of Texans to support Carvajal's rabble. Smith ordered Colonel William S. Harney to hasten to the border with several companies of the Second U.S. Dragoons. As instructed, Harney deployed horse-mounted regulars to patrol the river frontier, establish pickets at fords and ferry crossings, and intercept any Mexican rebels or Texas filibusters attempting to reenter Mexico.

The following month, Mexican federal officials received reinforcement of a different type. In a series of formal communiqués, U.S. secretary of state Daniel Webster reassured Mexico's minister Luis de la Rosa that the Fillmore administration would use any and all means at its disposal to apprehend or destroy any bands of insurrectionists staging on Texas soil. Webster seemed satisfied enough with de la Rosa's polite response. Still the secretary of state must have wondered whether these border troubles were but a hint of things to come.[68]

Just three years after the signing of the settlement at Guadalupe Hidalgo, therefore, many mercenaries and soldiers of fortune along the unsettled border with Mexico remained dissatisfied with the terms of the treaty, in particular the Rio Grande boundary. No matter that the U.S. conquest of the Nueces Strip—and much more—had already been confirmed by force of arms and by diplomatic agreement. For Texas adventurers and land seekers, and the Mounted Rangers who served as instruments of their ambitions, the war with Mexico continued, as if transcending the boundaries of time and place. Like the waters of the river that divided the two nations, the sources of that conflict continued to run deep. And the currents never seemed to end.

3
The Renegades

On September 23, 1851, Rip Ford's company of Mounted Rangers gathered one last time in the Laredo town plaza to be mustered out of service. As was the custom, the captain called roll, then read a prepared statement, thanking each of his men for his devotion to duty and service under the most difficult of circumstances. Ford recalled that a general "feeling of sadness" prevailed and that most of his volunteers choked back their emotions. "We knew that many of us would be separated, never to meet again in this world," he recollected. It was only natural at such a time that soldiers would wonder if they would ever experience such camaraderie again. And perhaps haunted by memories of missing friends, their thoughts wandered back to Gillespie, Wilbarger, Sullivan, Barton, and Lackey—fallen comrades who now lay buried beneath the land they had loved and coveted for their own. "We had lived more like a band of brothers than as a military company," Old Rip wrote in his memoirs, remembering the scene with a romantic, even Shakespearean, sense of the dramatic. It was almost as if this parting of company was far more difficult than any hardship or pain Ford and his men had endured while riding together.[1]

For the next five years, the Texas Mounted Rangers all but disappeared from the forlorn landscape of the Nueces Strip. During this formative period, a financially strapped state of Texas failed to find the funds for frontier defense or for almost anything else. Yet even if officials in Austin seemed to quickly forget the state partisan forces, citizens in South Texas did not. "Now that the company is disbanded," the San Antonio *Ledger* editorialized in early October 1851, "the Indians, who have so much dreaded its presence as to abandon their visits altogether . . . can again carry devastation and death, with little dread of molestation, from the Nueces to the Rio Grande. Again they can resume their cattle stealing and scalping forays along the whole line of settlements from the farms and ranches above Laredo, to Davis's ranch [Rio Grande City], and thence across the country to Corpus Christi." Reflecting the views of many South Texas residents, the editorialist argued that Ford's Rangers had performed "good service" and that the recent encounters had taught the Comanches "that Rangers could ride, shoot, and manoeuvre rather differently from mounted infantry." The newspaper implored Governor Peter H. Bell to "recall them immediately to protect the frontier, or it will again be devastated and destroyed."[2]

A Cry for Help

In the coming months, however, neither Bell nor the state legislature would respond to such calls to protect the frontier, particularly along the line from San Antonio to Eagle Pass and down the Rio Grande to Point Isabel. The following year, on June 15, Sheriff Peter Nickels of Cameron County informed the governor that "the Indians are at it again in their old neighborhood." An unidentified raiding party had recently stolen two flatboats filled with cargoes valued at $2,000, in the process killing one young man and seriously wounding another.[3]

By all indications, this act of river piracy was merely one in a series of bloody incidents that had made the spring of 1852 one of the most violent in the annals of South Texas. That same week, Thaddeus M. Rhodes of Brownsville reported to Governor Bell that raiders committed daily depredations along the Rio Grande, stealing cattle and horses with alarming regularity. The sources of these raids, he claimed, were "armed bands of Mexicans and Indians" who routinely crossed north of the Rio Grande to rob ranchos before slipping back into their sanctuaries on the south bank. The reported leader of these raiders, Rhodes said, was a renegade chieftain named Pedro Villereal, a nefarious figure and known cattle thief who allegedly made a fortune selling stolen livestock to the Mexican army. Claiming that terrified Americans were abandoning their homes and farms in droves and fleeing to the safety of border settlements, Rhodes also alleged that travel throughout the lower Rio Grande was at best unsafe, at worst suicide, and all commerce had been paralyzed. He concluded, "I know of no remedy for our troubles short of one or two companies of rangers."[4]

On June 30, merchant E. J. McLane of Brownsville echoed Rhodes's sense of urgency. Writing Governor Bell to allege that Mexican officials in Matamoros and elsewhere were not only harboring but also encouraging the raiders, he reported that there was a growing public outrage in the wake of continued depredations. In response to the emergency, he informed the governor that he and fellow citizen W. W. Dunlap had already organized two companies of volunteers to patrol the river frontier. He requested that the state furnish his men with rifles and revolvers. "We can equip ourselves if the state has no arms but muskets," he continued. "Only give us the proper authority and commission."[5]

Such calls did not go unheeded. Although he insisted that he had no authority to call out volunteer units without supporting action from the legislature and believed that frontier defense was a federal responsibility first, he began to forward reports and complaints of border raids to General Persifor F. Smith, recently promoted to commander of the Eighth Military Department of Texas, headquartered at San Antonio. When that tactic failed, he went one step further. On August 20, 1852, the governor dispatched a letter to President Millard Fillmore, informing him that the "desperate situation and insecurity of life and property" in the entire Rio Grande Valley was a result of ongoing raids from roaming bands of renegades. Bell described to Fillmore an entire region of the state that was "rapidly depopulating and on the verge of ruin." Unless the federal government took "prompt and energetic measures" to end the depredations, Bell predicted the "total disorganization and destruction of the whole line of the Rio Grande."[6]

Believing that a state of emergency now existed along the border with Mexico, Bell authorized Texas adjutant general James S. Gillett to organize three companies of Rangers to take the field. One, under the command of Owen Shaw, mustered into service in San Antonio on August 18. Not until September 14 did G. K. Lewis manage to find enough recruits to form the second company in Corpus Christi. One week later, Henry Clay Davis, one of the most respected ranchers and landowners in Starr County, mustered in the third unit at Rio Grande City. By executive order, these state partisans were to serve in support of regular army units then scattered along the vast border with Mexico.[7]

Bell may or may not have expected the U.S. government to pay for these Ranger units. What he never expected was the message he received that autumn from U.S. secretary of war Charles M. Conrad. In response to growing Texan claims that marauding Mexicans, Indians, and half-bloods were crossing regularly from Mexico to plunder the estates of the Rio Grande Valley, a skeptical Conrad wrote, "[T]here is reason to suspect that these statements are somewhat exaggerated." Besides the natural tendency of fearful persons "under the influence of fear" to "magnify the danger . . . some of the signers of these papers have strong motive to do so." The secretary even contended that General Smith had privately pronounced some of the claims "entirely unfounded." Thus Conrad reported to Bell that no further federal reinforcements along the lower Rio Grande were necessary and Texas Ranger companies would not be "received into the service of the United States." Even if most Texan claims proved to be true, he admitted, outlawry conducted across the international boundary should be dealt with by the civilian authorities of Texas and Mexico, not by the U.S. military. If Bell placed Rangers in the field, the government of Texas would be solely responsible for paying for them.[8]

Implicit in the correspondence was the threat that Bell would be held personally responsible for the Rangers' actions along the border with Mexico. Conrad further suggested that the people of Texas were at least partially at fault for the border disturbances. The Texans' support for Carvajal's failed revolution had provoked leaders in Mexico City, he argued, and the governor of Texas should have expected reprisal. Officials of the U.S. government were already bringing appropriate diplomatic pressures to bear in an attempt to suppress raids launched from the Mexican side of the Rio Bravo, he assured Bell. Besides, he reminded the governor, General Persifor Smith had recently stationed five regular rifle companies at posts along the northern banks of the Rio Grande. No matter that these horse- and mule-mounted infantry were of little use in warfare against the Plains Indians. No matter that they possessed neither the mounts nor the weapons to effectively engage the Comanches. Bell could not count on more federal support, the secretary stated bluntly.[9] Stunned and angered by Conrad's attitude, which revealed a dangerous ignorance of the situation along the border, Bell was determined to take action himself. So were the young Rangers already forming in the field.

Reacting to reports that Indian marauders had crossed into Texas and sacked several ranches as far south as Roma, Captain Owen Shaw and his company swept the exposed area along the San Antonio road leading northward from Laredo. Other than an encounter with Comanches that September in which nine raiders were killed and twenty-three horses recovered, little else was worthy of official report. Captain Clay Davis's far-ranging patrols along the border that autumn likewise failed to produce much of note. By the close of 1852, the sprawling plains of South Texas appeared quiet again, with only the incessant winds from the north murmuring winter's presence.[10]

During the next two years, the Comanches were not the only threat to the horse- and cattle-rich region of the Nueces Strip. Renegade bands of displaced Lipan Apaches, Kickapoos, and Seminoles continued to grow in numbers on the south bank of the Rio Bravo. Operating from their safe harbors on Mexican soil, they regularly crossed into Texas to help themselves to the livestock left wandering in the South Texas brush country. Like the Comanches, who continued their bold forays into Mexico, these raiders recognized neither national border nor legal boundary as barriers. To them, the Rio Grande remained no more of an obstacle than the thin line of garrisons manned by slow-moving infantrymen of the U.S. Army.

In the summer of 1855, Lipan Apaches, reportedly aided by Seminoles, conducted some of their most daring raids yet. They crossed into Texas and struck settlements as far north as the Blanco and Guadalupe rivers, taking horses, cattle, and scalps along the way. News of these depredations stirred the governor of Texas, Elisha M. Pease, to action. Aware that Texas frontiersmen were frustrated with the inadequate defense afforded by the few federal garrisons scattered along the border, Pease authorized the formation of a company of Rangers to protect the frontier and punish the marauders. Pease apparently feared that, should he fail to respond decisively to the situation, Texas minutemen might take matters into their own hands and march off to Mexico.[11]

Ironically, Pease turned to one such impulsive Texas leader, James Hughes Callahan. A native of Georgia, Callahan had come to Texas during the revolution of 1836, a twenty-four year-old volunteer in the Georgia Battalion of the Texian army assigned to Colonel James Fannin's command. Following the battle at Coleto Creek, he had been spared execution by his Mexican captors, probably because they considered him useful as a skilled mechanic. As a prisoner, he was assigned to a labor detail in Victoria. Although fortunate to survive, he never forgot that Palm Sunday in 1836 when many of his fellow prisoners were brutally massacred at Goliad. Although he had not stood with Houston on the plain of San Jacinto one month later, he had no doubt gloried at the news of Santa Anna's defeat and capture. In the ensuing months, the republic rewarded Callahan for his service with a commendation and a tract of land near Sequin in Caldwell County. A farmer and store owner there, he served with distinction as a citizen-soldier during the campaigns between 1840 and 1842, when volunteer companies of Rangers doggedly pursued both Comanche raiders and Mexican cavalry from the frontier line then extending along the San Antonio River. During this critical time, he learned the art of unconventional warfare from such notable Ranger captains as Ben McCulloch and El Diablo, Captain Jack

Hays. Then in the autumn of 1842, he participated in General Alexander Somervell's expedition to the Mexican border. Although no evidence exists that he fought at Mier with Captain William S. Fisher and his recalcitrant volunteers, many of the men mustered into service with him were killed there. Others were later executed by Mexicans at Salado, while many more were marched off to central Mexico and imprisoned for two years in the dank dungeons of Perote Castle. Surely, like other Texans of the times, Callahan brooded over this humiliating defeat and for years seethed in anger about the barbaric treatment of the survivors of the ill-fated Mier expedition.[12]

Unsurprisingly, Callahan quickly stepped forward in response to Governor Pease's call to protect the frontier and punish the marauders. In addition to the stridently anti-Mexican feelings he held as a veteran of the border wars, he had lost several cattle to raiders during a recent foray along the Blanco, an assault he considered to be a personal affront demanding revenge. A seasoned soldier and veteran of border wars and well respected by the frontiersmen of the region, Callahan was a logical choice to lead a company of Indian fighters.[13]

On July 5, 1855, Governor Pease ordered Callahan to muster into service a company of mounted riflemen for a punitive expedition. Specifically, he instructed Callahan to recruit able-bodied men who could supply their own horses, weapons, and ammunition and who would enlist for three months. The governor informed Callahan that, with no appropriated funds to support such a venture, all volunteers must agree to "rely upon the justice of the Legislature to reimburse them later." Pease thus commissioned Callahan to track down and engage the Indian raiders, or in his words, "to follow them up and chastise them wherever they may be found." Although the governor made no mention of the Rio Grande border, his directive was clear.[14]

The forty-year-old Callahan needed no further instructions; he understood his mission. During the ensuing weeks, he had little trouble enlisting volunteers. Texans needed no encouragement or inducement to take up arms in defense of their families and friends, not against the Lipan, Kickapoo, and Seminole Indians or anyone else. Moreover, if reports out of Austin and San Antonio could be believed, any volunteers who rallied to Callahan's side were almost certain to track the Indian marauders onto Mexican soil. Most Texans welcomed the opportunity to cross into Mexico again and possibly engage enemy forces in battle. Besides, the aging president of the Republic of Mexico was said to be on the brink of being toppled from power in a Liberal revolution that summer. Many Texans realized that this was perhaps one last chance to strike a blow against the much hated "butcher of the Alamo," Antonio Lopez de Santa Anna. Nothing could have been more motivating.[15]

At San Antonio on July 20, 1855, Captain Callahan mustered into service a company of eighty-eight Rangers. Most were seasoned Indian fighters, some of them veterans of the late war with Mexico still intent upon avenging the past, others inexperienced farm boys eager for a fight with the enemies of their fathers, a few of them soldiers of fortune and filibusters fiercely determined to make a name for themselves. In certain ways, the expeditionary force resembled a mob more than a military unit. According to later allegations of the Mexican government, some of these adventurers may have been driven by the most mercenary of motives—bounties offered for the recovery of runaway slaves who had found refuge south of the Rio Grande.[16]

No one knows for sure, but evidence does strongly suggest that one of the primary goals of Callahan's expedition was the retrieval of fugitive slaves. As General Persifor Smith wrote later that year, "[A] report was current that a party was organizing to go into Mexico and take negroes that had run away from Texas, and horses that had been stolen, and I presume that the party of Capt. Callahan was the one alluded to." Smith concluded, "[I]f so, their design was covered by the persuit [*sic*] of a trail of Lipans escaping with their booty."[17]

In an August 15 letter to Lieutenant Edward Burleson, Jr., of San Marcos, Callahan explained his plans to reward volunteers with more than just the hope of recompense from a parsimonious state legislature. "I want every man to understand that if he goes with me to the Devil's River or any place I wish to go and if anything is taken . . . it belongs to those that go and will be divided accordingly," he affirmed. Further clarifying his intentions, he vowed, "I wish you to inform the men under your command that if any property is taken from the Indians by any of the scout it belongs to the men that take it." He concluded that if "those in camp receive no share in such . . . this will induce the boys to go on scouts." Again, on August 31, from his camp at Enchanted Rock near Fredericksburg, he hinted that more was on his mind than simply punishing Indian marauders. "Some of the boys have found out the arrangements . . . but . . . I think it the best move to keep the matter as secret as possible for I am bound to go to the Rio Grande if nothing happens."[18]

Is it possible that the "arrangements" to which Callahan alluded might simply have been a reference to his distribution of the spoils of the expedition to his recruits? Did he merely wish to keep from others his intention to cross into Mexico? Or could the correspondence suggest a veiled reference to the bounties slave owners paid for fugitive slaves? The matter of Callahan's primary mission remains a mystery.

Regardless of the motives of the men who made up this expedition, one thing seems certain. The so-called Indian problem on the southwestern borders of Texas had become inexorably linked to the ongoing boundary troubles along the Rio Grande, troubles that had continued to kindle the burning embers of mistrust between the United States and Mexico. By 1852, scattered bands of renegade Seminoles and Lipan Apaches, in league with Mescalero Apaches, Kickapoos, and others, had established safe harbor on the Mexican side of the river, south of Eagle Pass near the spurs of the Sierra Madre Mountains. And from these enclaves, the displaced natives had conducted raids with impunity as far north as the Colorado River, each year retiring with their booty to the safety of their sanctuaries south of the Rio Bravo. Moreover, these marauders had reportedly received not merely encouragement but also bounties from Mexican scalp buyers, horse traders, cattle rustlers, and even Mexican officials who had tacitly sanctioned the forays to plunder Texan settlements along the frontier. All the while, Mexican magistrates had privately insisted that such Indian villages below the Bravo had served the peoples of northern Mexico as an effective buffer against depredations conducted by Comanches living in Texas. Indians on both sides of the border, therefore, had emerged as surrogate warriors in the continuing struggles between the United States and Mexico.[19]

The Wild Cat

No figure along that frontier was as widely hated by whites as the renegade Seminole chieftain Coacoochee, better known as "Wild Cat." A disciple of legendary Florida warrior Osceola, Wild Cat had earned his reputation as a fierce and formidable foe, even before he first set foot on Texas soil. During the Second Seminole War in Florida between 1835 and 1838, he had bedeviled the U.S. Army with his evasive tactics, which included attacking U.S. dragoons before vanishing into the malarial swamps of the

Everglades. His acumen during the war and his refusal to be humbled by treaty makers raised Wild Cat's stature as a defiant warrior worthy of respect. Only grudgingly did he leave the wetlands of Florida to resettle in the recently established Seminole reserve near Fort Gibson, Indian Territory, in 1841. After squabbling with Cherokee leaders over conflicting land claims in that region, he accompanied Indian agent Pierce M. Butler on a trek across Texas in 1845, hoping to negotiate a peace pact with the Comanches. Following the trek, the proud Seminole chieftain returned to the borders of Arkansas convinced of two things: the swift-riding Comanches who ruled the plains of West Texas could not be trusted, and neither they nor Anglo-Texans would ever welcome the Seminoles into the sprawling empire of bison and grass that lay beyond the line of settlements west of Austin and San Antonio.[20]

After the U.S.-Mexican War, Wild Cat actively encouraged the Kickapoo, Lipan, and others to join him in establishing a safe haven south of the Rio Grande. In an alarming letter to Governor Bell on October 20, 1850, U.S. Indian agent Marcus Duval warned that the renegade chieftain was inspiring hundreds of slaves to escape bondage and unite with the Seminoles in Coahuila, below Piedras Negras, near the town of San Fernando, where they would enjoy the protection of the Mexican government. Duval cautioned Governor Bell that Wild Cat was determined to "keep up a constant excitement on your border" and that he was "not likely to be kept still except by force or fear." Then he urged that "speedy action is necessary for the interest of the Government of Texas." Indian agent John H. Rollins concurred in a letter to Governor Bell ten days later. Condemning Wild Cat as a dangerous master of deceit and duplicity, he charged that the Seminole chieftain had lied to his own people and to fugitive slaves, persuading them that Texas leaders had first promised them a homeland, then betrayed them by withdrawing the offer of sanctuary. "Indeed it is the intrigue of the times," Rollins insisted, "when a single chief boldly enters upon the execution of a plan that unless speedily frustrated must end in a general war with possibly all of the Indian tribes."[21]

Swift action, however, was not forthcoming. Federal agents remained reticent to engage Wild Cat, federal garrisons of troops along the Rio Grande border being too few in number and located too far apart. Moreover, Governor Bell's successors, James W. Henderson and Elisha M. Pease, failed to address the threat that lay less than sixty miles beyond the waters of the Bravo. In those days, therefore, the only thing lower than the morale of Texas frontiersmen was the state appropriation to defend their borders from marauding Indian raiders and Mexican robadors. Professor Webb stated it best when he wrote that during these years the state partisan Rangers became "little more than a historical expression."[22]

The result should have been predictable. Buoyed by a success measured in the swelling numbers of renegades and runaway slaves who came to his side, an emboldened Wild Cat—soon commissioned a colonel in the Mexican army—built alliances with the Kickapoo, Lipan, and Mescalero. Consequently, he grew more confident in his conduct of raids against Comanches and Anglo-Texans, whom he hated with equal intensity. Captain Abner Doubleday remembered that, during his time at Fort Duncan, situated on the north bank of the Bravo near Eagle Pass, Wild Cat acted brazenly, going so far as to threaten any American bluecoat who challenged him and his renegades. "They sent us word that [if we pursued them across the river] they would hang up the right arm of every one of us in the square of the neighboring town of San Fernando in Mexico."[23]

Jane Cazneau, who met Wild Cat on several occasions, wrote that he looked more noble than savage, although she also insisted that the native chieftain was unusually vain. Frontiersman William Banta agreed, offering a colorful portrait of the charismatic Seminole leader, whom he met on many occasions. Towering over six feet tall, Wild Cat wore his raven black hair in braids that hung down his back, with several silver decorative plates dangling loosely from the tresses. At the bottom of the plait descended a handful of silver bells that jingled when he walked. Below a thick silver headband adorned with assorted bird feathers rose a furrowed forehead, accented by heavy black eyebrows and eyes peering "like an eagle." With buckskin leggings and a blue beaded tunic draped over his broad shoulders, he covered his long frame with a brightly colored Mexican blanket. A silver cross swayed from his neck, although he professed a greater love for jewelry than any faith in the "Jesus road." From his hip hung a long silver-plated tomahawk that could also be used as a smoking pipe. With two wives normally at his side, he carried himself with a regal bearing. "He was very communicative, polite, and firm in conversation," Banta recalled of the renegade leader, a fierce, determined, and fearless warrior.[24]

The Callahan Expedition

By 1855, Texas frontiersmen were well acquainted with Wild Cat and his threats against Anglo settlers. On September 18, when Callahan's company left Bandera Pass some thirty miles northwest of San Antonio, few if any of the Texans had reservations about their mission. In fact, some of the Rangers were filibusters who had recently fomented insurrection south of the Rio Grande, including William Robertson "Big" Henry, a native Virginian purported to be Callahan's second-in-command. A physical giant as determined as the menacing Seminole chieftain, Henry was an adventurer in every sense of the word. A colorful, boisterous combustible with an ego to match his large frame, Henry had first come to Texas during the Mexican War as a sergeant in the U.S. Army. Following that conflict, he settled down in San Antonio and became a respectable and popular, though somewhat controversial, figure among his fellow citizens. Soon after the war, he married Consolation Arocha, who later bore him three children. In 1854, he successfully campaigned for the post of city marshal. One historian has described Henry as "supremely confident and even fearless," while admitting that "his boldness often bordered on folly." A well-known contemporary, Ranger William A. "Big Foot" Wallace—himself a seasoned veteran of border wars with Mexico—commented that Henry "had rather exalted notions, and was difficult to control. He was brave and possessed merit, but had the . . . [reputation] of interferring [*sic*] with his superior officers."

To be sure, no one who knew Big Henry should have been surprised when they learned that the moody, impulsive, and sometimes insubordinate dreamer had raised a party of some twenty soldiers of fortune for his own personal invasion of Mexico in the spring and summer of 1855. Or that he reportedly offered his services to the Mexican insurgent, General Carvajal, leader of the secessionist movement in northern Mexico. Or that he published a proclamation in various newspapers urging Texans to "take matters into their own hands and correct the evils on the frontier" and to wage a "war to the death against Santa Anna and his government."

Henry assured Governor Pease just weeks before crossing the border with Captain Callahan that he was "engaged . . . in an honorable cause . . . assisting a down trodden people to cast off the Yoke of Tyranny" and to "overturn the despotic sway" of Santa Anna. To Henry, who seemed part patriot and part privateer, both mercenary and agent of "manifest destiny," surely a man given to grandiose schemes and designs, this expedition was more than a cause. It was a crusade. But who would have expected anything less from such an incendiary who was the great-grandson of Revolutionary War leader Patrick Henry?[25]

On September 25, 1855, Callahan's Rangers reached Encina on the Leona River, less than thirty miles from the border settlement of Eagle Pass. Before their arrival on the border, the expedition had been beset by delays as well as by dissension and disobedience within the ranks. Heavy rains had turned the plains into a quagmire, slowing the company's progress to no more than six or seven miles a day. To make matters worse, flooding conditions had pushed both the Frio and Nueces rivers beyond their banks, making it difficult for Callahan to safely ford the swollen streams. Then, after sloshing across the South Texas prairies for a week, tempers flared as a dispute erupted among the officers over the issue of command. Fear of desertions combined with disagreements over even the most petty of issues eventually led the force to divide into three columns—one commanded by the charismatic Callahan, a second by the headstrong Henry, and a third by the less experienced Nat Benton of Seguin, (nephew of U.S. senator Thomas Hart "Old Bullion" Benton), whose force of some thirty volunteers had caught up with Callahan only days earlier.[26]

All three parties advanced toward the Rio Grande. On September 29, the Texans reached the flooded river, which stretched out before them some three hundred yards in width. Upon surveying the scene, they could see that the currents were too swift for a crossing. Because of recent rains, the river rushed by with tremendous force, the currents discouraging even the boldest among the Texans. The parties had little choice but to encamp on the bluffs overlooking the Bravo some four miles above Eagle Pass, opposite Piedras Negras. The expeditionary force waited for four days before the waters finally subsided enough to cross. The Texans transported their horses and provisions across the river by boats reportedly seized at gunpoint by the impatient Captain Henry. Only a handful of men remained on the Texas side to guard the pack train. By October 3, a hundred well-armed, confident, and restless Mounted Rangers had arrived on the south banks of the river, prepared for any contingency or conflict in arms. Or so they thought.[27]

Divided in their loyalties and in their choice of leaders, they nevertheless stood united by their determination to fight Indian raiders, Mexican regulars, or anyone else. The Mounted Rangers moved beyond the sand hills that hugged the river banks. For more than twenty miles, they rode westward, through mesquite and chaparral thickets that strangled the trail to San Fernando. Callahan had been informed that ahead lay a party of Lipan Apaches and Seminoles, reportedly under the leadership of Wild Cat, who was also said to command a band of "Seminole Negroes" (men of mixed African and Native descent). As the Rangers approached Escondido Creek later that afternoon, a fusillade of gunfire erupted from a distant timberline. A force of Mexican troops and Indian scouts had been concealed there. Then some seven hundred of the enemy swarmed out of the thickets. Callahan halted his troops and ordered them to form a skirmish line; the captain rode to the front of his command shouting encouragement over the din of confusion. Incredibly, he ordered them to charge. As the Texans hurled themselves forward, their foes greeted them with a thunderous volley.[28]

Texas frontiersman and chronicler A.J. Sowell recorded that a "desperate fight" ensued. "Pistols, rifles, and shotguns rang out on every side, mingled with the yell of the Texans, the war whoop of the Indians, and the loud imprecations of the Mexicans," he reported. During the furious charge and exchange of gunfire, at least one Mexican officer and several of his men fell on the field, while four Texans tumbled from their saddles mortally wounded, among them young Willis Jones, the son of William Jones, the judge of Val Verde County. According to Sowell, six Rangers, including Captain Nat Benton and his son Eustis, suffered serious wounds.

By the time Callahan's Mounted Rangers had galloped through enemy lines, another column of Mexican infantry, numbering perhaps two hundred, appeared from a nearby tree line. Recognizing the danger, the captain ordered his men to retreat swiftly to a ravine some three hundred yards away, where they dismounted and made a stand. Several of the riflemen who had their horses shot from under them scrambled for the cover of an irrigation canal.[29]

The Rangers then witnessed perhaps the most heroic single act of the battle. Wesley Harris of Seguin and several of his comrades noticed that young Eustis Benton had fallen from his horse and lay exposed on the prairie. Without hesitation, they rode back onto the field of fire to retrieve his seemingly lifeless body. When they reached him, they discovered that although the ball had pierced the young Ranger's skull and remained lodged somewhere behind his eye, he was still breathing.[30]

Harris and his fellow horsemen also recovered the body of Willis Jones. But the other dead were by necessity left on the field. While the thick smoke and smell of gunpowder still hung in the air, both sides disengaged from the fight. Then night fell. Callahan and one of his subordinates later claimed that the Rangers had killed at least sixty *rurales* (rural mounted police) and Indians during the chaotic exchange that day. General Emilio Langberg, the military commander of the state of Coahuila, refuted that claim, reporting the loss of only four dead and three wounded. He also insisted that no Indians had participated in the skirmish, although according to Texan William Kyle, an eyewitness to the event, the four-hour battle was "one of the hardest Indian fights ever fought." No one knows for sure, but it is probable that Wild Cat was among the Texans' enemy that day, wearing the blue and red jacket of the Mexican cavalry. Regardless, as Callahan's company retreated hastily toward Piedras Negras, the Mexican troops withdrew and regrouped near San Fernando.[31]

That night, the Texans were still on Mexican soil, establishing a defensive perimeter and preparing for the possibility of another attack. But no second ambush awaited them so the next morning they cautiously fell back to Piedras Negras, then a settlement of approximately 1,500 inhabitants. Sometime before sunset on October 4, Callahan and his Rangers occupied the outskirts of the town, a collection mostly of modest adobe dwellings and mud-chinked jacales (primitive wooden structures with thatched roofs). According to J. S. McDowell, a member of the expedition, shortly after dawn the next day Callahan "demanded to the Alcalde to surrender the town. . . . In case of refusal he proposed sacking it forthwith." As McDowell recollected, "[A] deputation of Piedras Negras citizens came down. They accepted the terms of an unconditional surrender. We then marched in regular order . . . and halted in front of the Alcalde's house, attached to which was a rude stone fort, which we made our headquarters." At that point, the local magistrate, "a short fleshy man, waddled out, nervously waving a hastily improvised flag on a short stick. With many smiles and gracious bows he gave up his keys and authority to our leader. He also promised to have all the arms and munitions delivered immediately at the guard house." McDowell recalled that this arsenal "constituted quite a military museum." Callahan could now boast that he had occupied the town and that he had done so without facing even token opposition.[32]

One critically important fragment of evidence suggests that, after taking the border town, Callahan and others may have been planning an even larger campaign into the interior of Mexico. After apparently returning from Piedras Negras to San Antonio on October 7, William Kyle noted that "we have Piedras Negras in possession" and "have plenty of artillery" to wage an offensive campaign south of the border. (This may have been the same William Jefferson Kyle who was a prominent Fort Bend County sugar plantation owner and slaveholder.) Moreover, he estimated that as many as five or six hundred more men could be raised for an invasion force. "Old Rip is here and will go without fail," he announced in reference to the presence of the grizzled John Ford. The famed Ranger captain and newspaper publisher was known to favor the annexation of Mexico or at the very least the establishment of a buffer Republic of the Sierra Madre. "I will be back in Mexico in less than fifteen days," Kyle boldly predicted.[33]

Meanwhile, in Piedras Negras, with a small garrison of U.S. regulars across the river looking on from Fort Duncan, and with many of the town's residents fleeing with their belongings in carts and wagons down the road to San Fernando, Captain Callahan had every reason to reassure his men that their position was secure. But that soon changed. Within hours of seizing the town armory, Callahan got word that a large force of Mexican cavalry, perhaps numbering more than one thousand, was rapidly advancing on Piedras Negras. Some accounts contended that, upon hearing this news, a handful of Texans deserted and fled across the Rio Bravo, fearful that they would face certain death if they remained. With fewer than one hundred volunteers, the knowledge that U.S. troopers at Fort Duncan under the command of Captain Sidney Burbank remained under strict orders *not* to cross the river, and a swollen Rio Grande at his back, Callahan concluded that only extreme measures might spare the remainder of his men from annihilation or, at best, from capture. Determined that his command would not suffer a fate similar to that of Travis at the Alamo or Fannin at Goliad, he ordered his Rangers to set fire to the prairie and the jacales scattered along the western edge of town. If nothing else, he hoped, putting the torch to fields and thatched hovels between himself and the enemy would provide precious time needed to evacuate his command by ferry across the river.[34]

That decision would have devastating consequences. No sooner had the Texans torched the perimeter of the town than the wind-whipped flames quickly spread, leaping from one hut to another until a raging inferno had engulfed dozens of dwellings. Entire families fled in terror, scurrying through the chaos to some point of safety. As Callahan had planned, the Mexican federales and their Indian allies, who were closing in on the town, had no choice but to fall back from the blaze that separated them from the Texans. "Dense volumes of smoke were seen issuing from every house," wrote a correspondent for the New Orleans *Picayune*, who described the scene from the Texas side of the river. "In the twinkling of an eye the entire village was in flames, except a few houses around the plaza where the Texans intended to make a stand. They were now surrounded by a wall of flame, and the Mexican commander, [Colonel] Manschaca . . . withdrew his eight hundred men without firing a shot." The reporter recounted that "as night drew on . . . the flames of the village, built almost entirely of wood and straw, mounted into the heavens, illuminated the river and surrounding country with the brightness of day—the explosions of powder in the burning buildings, the . . .[gun]fire from the Texans upon spies and scouts from the enemy's camp, the shouting of the 'filibusteros' as they darted about, as it seemed from this side, amidst the very flames" made for "a mixture of sights and sounds never to be forgotten."[35]

Across the river at Fort Duncan, an exasperated Captain Burbank—who had not even been aware of Callahan's crossing days earlier—observed the horrible scene. "The Texans commenced firing the town and in a few minutes nearly every house in the place was in flames," he later reported to U.S. adjutant general Samuel Cooper. Burbank also stated that, although Callahan sent a courier across the Bravo with a message requesting protection and assistance for his Rangers, Burbank flatly refused to render aid. Even two additional dispatches apparently failed to persuade Burbank to commit his forces in support of Callahan's men.[36]

Still, as Callahan ordered a retreat back across the river, Burbank hastened a battery of small artillery pieces to the riverbank to help cover the Rangers' movement. As it turned out, the cannon were not needed. Through the billowing, black smoke, which covered their escape, the Texans crossed the river in skiffs. According to one eyewitness, they left approximately thirty of their horses on the Mexican side of the river—horses Callahan later reported as "captured." To a man the company retired safely to the north bank with their wounded, including young Eustis Benton, who would miraculously recover from his head wound. But they did not depart until they had sacked the town and reduced it to cinders and ashes.[37]

J. S. McDowell denied that widespread pillaging and looting occurred that "night of sorrows." He insisted, "If any property was plundered and appropriated for private use by our men, except for forage and to appease hunger, such was an exception and not the rule." Yet another eyewitness, Jesse Sumpter of Eagle Pass, told a different story. "Callahan's party commenced hauling their plunder off the bank of the river which consisted of a large quantity of corn, beans, flour, and produce." He admitted that "there were a good many men riding about the town of Eagle Pass [later that night] and every one that I saw had . . . jewelry displayed about his neck and breast, such as gold necklaces, chains, ear-rings, finger-rings, watches and other articles . . . which they seemed to take delight in displaying." Sumpter also noted that "one of Callahan's men rode up to my house. He seemed to have more of the jewelry than any of the others. . . . He was riding on a silver-mounted Mexican saddle, and the owner, Prado, happened to be in my house. When he saw his saddle, he knew it and pointed it out to me as being his. He told me he valued it at $100. While he was talking to me," Sumpter recalled, "he cried like a child, for he had lost everything he had except what he had on." If the Texans had not succeeded in holding Piedras Negras, they had apparently managed to take much of it with them.[38]

What Callahan's Rangers did not carry away, they destroyed. General Langberg summarized the carnage soon thereafter. "Piedras Negras offers now a scene of devastation," he reported. "A multitude of innocent families are without shelter—homeless and ruined." General Persifor Smith admitted to Governor Pease the following week that many of the residents of Piedras Negras were left in "utter destitution" and reduced to "seeking food on this side of the river to save themselves from starving." Captain Burbank concurred, writing to the adjutant general that the Mexicans who had fled their town before it was set ablaze were "in a state of great destitution." He even recommended that, given the emergency of the situation, the U.S. government "hastily" dispatch provisions to the scene to alleviate the suffering. Otherwise, he feared reprisal from the people of the border in response to the entire affair, which he termed "embarrassing." The razing of an entire border town—and in the presence of the U.S. garrison at Fort Duncan—had an incendiary effect upon U.S.-Mexican relations, just as

Burbank predicted. Already smoldering in suspicion, intrigue, and even open animosity, the border situation would only grow worse. As Langberg summarized the entire affair, "[T]he shame of this barbarous and unjustifiable act shall be as lasting as the remembrance of the occurance [*sic*]."[39]

The Fallout

The incident was over, but not forgotten—or forgiven. By almost any measure, all that Callahan's reckless incursion had accomplished was to stir up old embers of hatred, fear, and mistrust along the border. The Callahan expedition rekindled and ignited anew the fires of discord and anger on both sides of the river. Predictably, Texans and their spokesmen in Austin as well as allies in Washington rallied to the defense of Callahan. Just one week after the sacking of Piedras Negras, Governor Pease wrote General Smith that the captain "was justified in pursueing [*sic*] the Indians across the Rio Grande . . . when they had been committing depredations upon our citizens." Moreover, he stated, "if this leads to a border warfare between the Citizens of this State and the Mexicans and Indians no one will regret it more than myself, but the fault lies with the United States Government, whose neglect to furnish protection to our settlements . . . rendered it necessary." Pease further exonerated Callahan in an address to the Texas State Legislature on November 5. Again he defended the captain's decision to burn the village in view of the recent raids against Texan settlements conducted by Indians allegedly based below the Bravo. After all, he charged, Mexican officials in Coahuila had "made common cause" with the Indian raiders and had even harbored them.

A public meeting of citizens in San Antonio also applauded Callahan's actions, the rowdy assemblage going so far as to pass a resolution commending the Ranger for his courageous determination to punish those who plundered the frontier. Likewise, newspapers such as the *Texas State Gazette*, *The Texas State Times*, and the San Antonio *Herald* strongly supported military action, agreeing with Pease that Texans had the right to defend their property and their persons from the onslaught of *los bárbaros Indios* (the barbaric Indians) who enjoyed sanctuary south of the border.[40]

U.S. secretary of state William L. Marcy, in a series of dispatches to Mexico's minister to the United States, Juan N. Almonte, also supported Callahan's actions. He agreed that the Texans' expedition would never have occurred had local authorities in Coahuila suppressed the Lipan raiders living within their boundaries. More specifically, he reminded Almonte that the Mexican government had not fulfilled its treaty obligations to maintain order and peace along the border and that such negligence was also a clear violation of article 33 of an 1831 accord between the two nations. He further insisted that, according to accounts that had crossed his desk, "the Rangers were invited across the Rio Bravo . . . by a Mexican officer, who, it is presumed they believed to be competent for the purpose." Even if no such formal invitation had been issued to Callahan, he reasoned, the border crossing was still "justifiable by the law of nations." He then accused unnamed Mexicans living in and near Piedras Negras of "treacherously" leading the Texans into an ambush near Escondido Creek. As for the burning of the town and the conduct of both the Texans and Captain Burbank's regulars who assisted in their retreat, Marcy dismissed the events of that October night as "laudable" acts of self-defense. Moreover, he concluded that both the Rangers and troopers from Fort Duncan deserved "praise and not reproach."[41]

U.S. minister to Mexico James Gadsden offered similar arguments. Writing to the minister of foreign affairs of Mexico, Miguel M. Arrioja, on November 29, 1855, the American diplomat who had recently negotiated the purchase of the Gila River region for the United States, went so far as to define the Ranger company as a "regular organized military Corps in the service, and acting under the orders of the Executive of Texas." He claimed that Callahan's company had only been dispatched to the border "for the purpose of protecting the lives of its citizens from the scalping-knife and the tomahawk" and their property "from the plundering instincts of Savages instigated and known to be in the service of Mexico." He even stated that the "humane expedition" of Texans acted under the "higher law of self-preservation," which transcended the terms of any treaty or international convention.[42]

Not surprisingly, Mexican authorities disputed such claims. Learning at his station in Washington of a violation of his country's sovereignty by a company of Texas Rangers, Juan Almonte vehemently protested the border intrusion. Writing to Secretary Marcy on January 14, 1856, Almonte expressed outrage at what he repeatedly termed an "invasion" of Mexico by Callahan's company. He accused both Governor Pease and Captain Burbank of "connivance" in planning and implementing the expedition. Denying that any Mexican official had authorized the Texans to cross the border and insisting that there had been "atrocities committed by the aggressors," he demanded a formal investigation into the behavior and acts of "the fillibuster [*sic*] company of Captain Callahan." He likewise called for a military inquiry into the actions—or inaction—of the federal troops at Fort Duncan. More specifically, he singled out "the fillibuster [*sic*] Captain Henry," questioning his role in the incursion and thus reinforcing his complaints to Marcy earlier in the year that the unpredictable Henry had raised mercenaries and engaged in mischief within the borders of Mexico. Lastly, on behalf of his government, Almonte requested that the "wicked men" who had participated in the expedition as well as the sponsoring governments of Texas and the United States be held responsible for the resulting damages and that the inhabitants of Piedras Negras be "properly indemnified."[43]

Perhaps Mexican officials did not realistically expect that any reparations would be paid to the residents of Piedras Negras. Indeed, none was forthcoming. Nor did these officials expect that leaders in Austin or Washington would ever admit that there might have been more to the military expedition than simply the punishment of Indian raiders. But for many years, rumors and reports persisted that at least some of the Texans had enlisted in what they understood to be a mission to recover runaway slaves from south of the border. And that these volunteers fully expected to be paid handsome bounties for any returned fugitives. The truth shall probably remain buried with Callahan and Henry.[44]

To Anglo-Texans, Callahan and his men were freedom fighters, brave defenders of the borders, indeed patriots. To people of Mexican heritage—on both sides of the river—the Texas devils were nothing more than filibusters, soldiers of fortune, and privateers, not heroic Rangers but riders from hell.

4
The Rubicon

"Do not picture the Ranger as you read of him in newspapers, the personification of the brave and reckless—wild perhaps, but with a redeeming trait of lofty chivalry," Lieutenant Albert J. Myer of the U.S. Army Medical Corps wrote. "Rangers are rowdies, rowdies in dress, manner and feeling. Take one of the lowest Canal drivers, dress him in ragged clothes . . . put a rifle in his hand, a revolver and big Bowie knife at his belt—utterly eradicate any little traces of civilization or refinement that may have by chance been acquired, then turn him loose, a lazy, ruffianly scoundrel in a country where little is known of, less cared for, the laws of God or man, and you have the material for the Texas Mounted Ranger." The New York–born Myer thus characterized the archetypical Ranger of the day as "an animal—perhaps I should say a brute—of whose class some hundreds are at present mustered into the service to fight Indians. There are exceptions," he conceded. "My invective is not meant for all." Few contemporaries painted a more unflattering and less romantic portrait of the Ranger than this army physician who traveled along the Rio Grande frontier en route to his post at Fort Davis early in 1855.[1]

Myer was not the only one who held a jaded view of the Texas partisans. Not three years earlier, Indian agent John Rollins had echoed the sentiment when he reported to Indian commissioner C. S. Todd, then stationed in San Antonio, that the Texas Mounted Rangers were anything but a source of pride for the people of the Lone Star State. Rollins admitted that most of the army regulars serving on the South Texas frontier appeared as though they had been enlisted in the "drinking houses" of the northern cities and generally seemed to be "creation's outcasts." But the state volunteers, Rollins continued, were in character "worse than the regulars." Moreover, while the bluecoats "occupied themselves very fully and satisfactorily in doing no good," the rabble from the borders of Texas continually "managed to refresh themselves with an alarming amount of mischief."[2]

An Irish-born traveler and adventurer, Michael Baldridge, agreed. When the Rangers captured a suspected marauder, whether "red" or white, "they always went upon the presumption that he had committed enough crimes to hang him, or if he had not, the probabilities were very strong that he . . . [could have or] would." Baldridge further observed of the Texas irregulars that "they never gave the prisoner the benefit of a doubt or a trial by jury."

"These Rangers were a peculiar people, and led a wild life," Baldridge continued. "It would seem as if pistols and Bowie knives had been their toys and playthings in childhood, and they knew how to use them. . . . They are free commoners, and are well received wherever they go, on account of the protection they give. They very seldom attend church," he noted, "were never known to decline when asked to drink, live upon excitement, and find their principle source of amusement in playing. . . . draw poker."[3]

By the end of the 1850s, Randolph Marcy's adventures in Texas would make this U.S. army officer a leading authority not only on the state's terrain, its natural history, and its native inhabitants but also on its frontier culture. Marcy often described with awe and wonder the geography and the animal populations of Texas and on occasion complimented the various Indian peoples that resided within the state's borders. His general impression of the land's Euro-American inhabitants, however, was less laudatory. He expressed general praise for the members of the Texas Ranger units but also reservations about them, describing those volunteers as "frontier settlers, whose sinews of iron and frames of oaken firmness had undergone such a system of training that they were . . . capable of enduring almost any amount of exposure and fatigue." Yet Marcy also wrote that, even though "many worthy citizens" emigrated from the United States to Texas when Mexico first opened the land to Anglo settlers, these "worthy citizens . . . were commingled with adventurous spirits, who sought excitement and danger; also individuals of desperate fortunes, who had nothing to lose; as well as refugees from justice, who deemed this [Texas] the safest asylum to escape the penalties due their crimes." Marcy judged the resulting Texas society to be "eminently impulsive, unsettled, and lawless."[4]

Little wonder that the Tejano people of the lower Rio Grande lived in constant fear that Los Diablos Tejanos were never far away. Nor were soldiers of fortune and filibusteros, mercenaries operating independently of government or cause, men who were quick to seize any opportunity to advance their own self-interests at the expense of any person, nation, or ideal standing in their paths. Gathering in this seemingly forsaken no-man's-land of the Nueces Strip, they constituted a curious collection of romantics, revolutionaries, rogues, and border ruffians, adventurers imbued with a sense of their self-proclaimed racial and religious superiority. "The Americans of the Texas frontiers are, for the most part, the very scum of society, bankrupts, criminals, old volunteers, who, after the Treaty of Guadalupe Hidalgo, came into a country protected by nothing that could be called a judicial authority, to seek adventure and illicit gains," observed Father Emanuel Domenech, who served during these years at a mission in Brownsville. A longtime resident of the lower Rio Bravo, William Neale, agreed that "when the land bordering on the north side of the Rio Grande became Texas property, thousands of immigrants came pouring in from the states as well as people returning from California dazed with the gold craze. All began to settle and partition the lands amongst themselves," he remembered, "all claiming squatter's rights on what they called vacant lands. Naturally the heir of the land resented the encroachment of the Americans and bad blood began to boil between the squatters and the rightful owners of the land."[5]

South Texas indeed provided a fertile ground for those frontiersmen and fortune seekers who professed to advance the ideals of Protestantism and patriotism. But behind the lofty pronouncements stood a more proprietary and pecuniary motive—the desire for land and the wealth it represented. To be sure, those who rushed in to populate the lower Rio Grande Valley prior to the American Civil War were typical of the border types that seemed to people every frontier. They lived a restless and sometimes reckless existence. They distrusted any distant authority, even defied the law, and were surely ambitious for themselves and for their American nation. They embraced a simple faith in the presumed superiority of their institutions and ideals. Jealous and protective of their freedoms, certain of their invincibility, they would willingly fight anyone who dared to challenge them. Always proud, sometimes pious, often profane, they practiced a simple code of survival: "do unto thy enemies before they do unto you." Their frontier society sanctioned, even encouraged, the exercise of retributive violence as a means of settling disputes. As a class, they extolled physical strength and courage as the greatest of virtues. Armed with every conceivable instrument of death, from Colt revolvers to Springfield rifle muskets, they were walking arsenals. And no one dared question their will or their skill to use any weapon in their possession or their "divine right" to do so in "self-defense." It has been said of such men that they were fiercely determined to keep the Sabbath and everything else they could get their hands on.[6]

Filibustering along the Border and Beyond

Such frontier types—certain they were advanced agents of civilization—provided perfect fodder for filibustering activities along the Mexican border and beyond. Moreover, the proximity to a chronically unstable Republic of Mexico, the twin impulses of manifest destiny and the martial spirit so strong in Texas, and the compelling allure of land all combined to provide a breeding ground for adventurism and aggression. In the autumn of 1855, while sentiments over Callahan's expedition still ran an emotional crest, Rip Ford returned to Austin and wasted little time in organizing a secret society dedicated to the "liberation" of the "oppressed island" of Cuba, even if it meant war with Spain. The mystical organization, known as the "Lone Star of the West," also appeared in San Antonio that winter, although it seemed to gather little popular support and no statewide momentum. Its elaborate rituals, secret passwords and handshakes, and other clandestine trappings may even have been the object of much ridicule.[7]

Undeterred by this failure, Rip Ford turned his attention back to the forceful acquisition of Mexico. On February 15, 1856, he expressed the feelings of many fellow Texans when he proposed to Edward Burleson, Jr., that a people's army be raised for the purpose of a military invasion of Mexico. "If you, or [Henry] McCulloch, or Callahan would go upon the Brazos you could get money," Ford encouraged his friend.

> I look upon the movement as a political necessity—a duty we owe to Texas and the South. It has occupied my thoughts for years. I do not wish to take a prominant [*sic*] part in getting up the thing, because I have said and written so much on the subject, I begin to think people do not believe me. Why may not others of less note secure a slice [of Mexico] . . . and place it under American control? There is no government in Mexico. Everything is in confusion. The people are oppressed, ground down by despotism, debased by ignorance and paralyzed by the influence of priests. She is a dangerous and harmful neighbor. Her people aid in the taking of our property, in fact they rob us. They allow hostile expeditions to be fitted out against us upon their territory. We have the right by the laws of nations, by the right of self-preservation and self-defense which we acquired from God himself to demand "indemnity for the past and security for the future."

> These can only be obtained by placing the country between the Rio Grande and the Sierra Madre under the control of Americans and by giving protection to slave property in Texas and the South. I conscientiously believe that . . . Heaven would bless the enterprise with success.[8]

The plans of the Almighty aside, wealthy planters and slaveholders no doubt would have blessed such an effort with monetary and moral support. Although some Texans such as Old Rip were talking and writing about territorial expansion, with an eye toward perpetuating and extending that "Peculiar Institution" of slavery beyond the border and even throughout the Caribbean Basin, others were already preparing to take up arms in the cause. They needed only to look to the tropics of Nicaragua for a crusade worthy of their energies and ambitions. During the spring and summer of 1856, hundreds of Texas volunteers rushed to enlist in the army of freebooters commanded by the most famous filibuster of them all, that "gray-eyed man of destiny" from Nashville, General William Walker, who had recently invaded the coast of Nicaragua and proclaimed an independent republic with himself as president. No doubt enticed by the promise of adventure, glory, land, and money—although not necessarily in that order—scores of frontiersmen joined the movement to "liberate" Nicaragua from "despotism" and the threat of British colonial rule.[9]

These soldiers of fortune no doubt held designs of their own. During the months of June and July, at weekly meetings in Galveston and Houston cash was collected and volunteers were recruited for the enterprise. The Houston *Telegraph* reported on August 25 that Colonel Samuel A. Lockridge, one of Walker's principal officers, was living in Seguin and that he planned on traveling overland to Galveston with as many as 250 armed volunteers, all eager to make their way by steamboat to the malarial-ridden Mosquito Coast. There they would join Walker's "Immortals" in their struggle to create an independent nation, the "Republic of Nicaragua" (as Walker would term it), a tropical paradise where slavery would surely be legal. In September, the *Telegraph* confirmed that more than 200 Texan adventurers crowded aboard a steamer in New Orleans bound for the coast of Central America. Two months later, the New Orleans *Picayune* revealed that Lockridge himself left port with a company of 283 Texas volunteer Rangers. By the end of the year, one of Walker's advanced agents had even contracted with William L. Cazneau of Eagle Pass to provide another thousand recruits for Walker's army. In January 1857, the Galveston *News* reported that E. J. C. Kewen, appointed by Walker as the "Commissioner General for the Republic of Nicaragua," had named Major W. C. Capers to serve as "Official Commissioner of the Republic of Nicaragua for the State of Texas." Capers had clearly received instructions to raise both money and recruits for the cause, and according to the *News*, he succeeded in enlisting a company of some 60 volunteers to accompany him to the sweltering jungles of Nicaragua.[10]

During the ensuing months, leaders in the Lone Star State intensified their efforts to support and even subsidize Walker's filibustering war. On January 22, 1857, the Galveston *News* published a letter from twenty-nine "Texas Rangers" in Nicaragua who were serving under Colonel John Waters and Colonel Lockridge, their call for aid announcing that Colonel G. W. Crawford would soon be recruiting yet more volunteers in Galveston. On February 16, the Houston *Telegraph* reported that Major Capers would be raising another company of Rangers to depart Galveston for Nicaragua. Two days later, Crawford and his recruits attended a dinner at the Methodist Church, followed by a lavish ball at the Tremont House. It was hosted by such notables as Hardin R. Runnels, the wealthy Trinity River cotton planter who would be elected governor of Texas the following December, and Francis R. Lubbock of Houston, the soon-to-be lieutenant governor and a future Confederate governor of Texas. At the social gathering on the evening of February 18, Colonel Crawford proudly announced to the assembled crowd that each of his men would be outfitted with a "Texas saddle" and a Colt revolver, courtesy of their generous patrons.[11]

The following morning, the steamship *Louisiana* docked in Galveston with a force of 104 more volunteers from San Antonio under the command of Captain Marcellus French and Captain Sam Jackson. Fittingly, these young mercenaries and adventurers had insisted on being styled the "Alamo Rangers," and their unit flag bore a Lone Star and the motto, "Remember You Are Texans." According to one contemporary, these swaggering and intrepid border fighters composed "a splendid body of men." At the rendezvous in Galveston was another company of Rangers from Corpus Christi under Captain Henry A. Maltby, who had recently resigned as the town's mayor in order to fight alongside General Walker. So the steady stream of volunteers continued to pour into the seaport.[12]

Thus loosely organized, but well-armed, well-financed, and highly motivated, hundreds of idealistic and impulsive Texans struck off for the steaming rain forests of Central America to live out their dreams of conquest and to assist Walker in carrying out his design of establishing in Nicaragua a base for the African slave trade.

By the spring of 1857, however, the initial enthusiasm for the Nicaragua venture had begun to wane—and for good reason. Word came of the defeat of Colonel Lockridge's Rangers at the hands of native rebels, as well as dissension within the ranks of Walker's brigade. Lists of known dead soon appeared in Galveston newspapers as did published accounts of purported acts of insubordination and even desertions by those disgruntled and disillusioned with their leaders. One report held that General Walker himself dismissed Colonel George B. Hall and Captain J. E. Farnham of the Texas Regiment for what was termed "intemperance." Still more stories circulated of young men dying from tropical fevers. On May 16 the Galveston *News* carried what may have been the first report of Texas boys returning home from the isthmus, many of them in a "destitute condition." They had apparently had enough of filibustering.[13]

Despite deserting Walker's command, the contentious and obstinate Colonel Lockridge—a genuine incendiary from Mississippi—remained committed to the cause of an independent Nicaraguan nation, where southern slaveholders might enjoy an expanding base for their plantation economy as well as the imported labor from Africa. While on yet another recruiting trip along the Texas Gulf Coast in June, Lockridge stopped off again at Galveston en route to New Orleans. As he explained to editor Willard Richardson of the Galveston *News*, his supporters would surely provide additional resources to assist him in raising another regiment of five hundred Rangers, perhaps more. Despite remaining disaffected with Walker and disassociating himself from the controversial leader, Lockridge continued to encourage the establishment of a southern-style republic in Central America.[14]

Even in Lockridge's absence, and despite the news of a series of disastrous defeats suffered by Walker's forces, recruiting efforts for the adventure continued and even intensified in Texas. By all appearances, the central figure in these efforts was none other than the brawling, brooding figure of William R. Henry of San Antonio. On September 5, 1857, the Galveston *News* published a letter from the notorious Captain Henry, who implored his "old frontier comrades to join me forthwith in the city of Galveston." During the next three weeks, Richardson editorialized on behalf of Henry's call for recruits, going so far as to compare General Walker to Moses Austin (the empresario who first opened Texas to Anglo settlement) and the Marquis de Lafayette! "We believe that slavery may be seriously affected by events in Central America," Richardson prophesied.[15]

The following month, Hamilton Stuart of the Galveston *Civilian* commented that "considerable Nicaraguan excitement" had gripped the city again and that more "immigrants" were preparing to leave for the shores of Central America. "We of the South are in favor of the extension of slavery," he proclaimed. "We need more territory over which we can extend or maintain it." More men, money, and material support must be brought into service, he claimed, if such an endeavor was to prevail.[16]

The "Nicaraguan fever" continued to spread across Texas. On November 26, the Galveston *News* reported again that Captain Hardin Runnels—the Democratic nominee for governor—had assembled more than a hundred enlistees in Houston, while Captain Henry had gathered seventy-five more volunteers in San Antonio. Similar companies were springing into existence in Brazoria and Austin. From the fertile plains of the lower Brazos to the rocky, rugged hill country above the Colorado, young Texans were lured into armed service by the promise of large land grants in the lush valleys of Nicaragua and by the adventure of a lifetime. All of them were no doubt fighting to extend their own personal wealth. Most surely believed that by joining the cause, they prepared the way for an even greater future for the American South, especially for a Texas, which was so dependent upon cheap slave labor to sustain the cotton and sugar plantations of the rich bottom lands of the Brazos, Colorado, and Red rivers. Some, in their religious-like zeal, sought their own destinies, which they believed to be linked to the Central American nation. None doubted the righteousness of their cause or the certainty of their inevitable triumph.[17]

Failure in Nicaragua

One Texan seemed to embody the dream of a southern empire of cotton and slavery sweeping across the Caribbean Basin and the mainland of Central America: former president of the Republic of Texas Mirabeau Buonaparte Lamar. Lamar longed to extend the territories of the United

States into the tropics of Honduras, Costa Rica, and Nicaragua, as he had once proposed to cast the Lone Star flag across northern Mexico, all the way to the Pacific coast of California. The elder statesman, who had stood as Sam Houston's chief rival for more than two decades, insisted that the moral authority of the United States must be imposed over Central America and the Caribbean. In 1854, following the failure of the so-called Ostend Manifesto (President Pierce's effort to acquire Cuba from Spain), Lamar had openly advocated an American invasion of that island, the overthrow of Spanish colonial authority, and the imposition of U.S. hegemony over the "pearl of the Antilles."

Having failed in that scheme, he was determined to be in a position to effect his goals on the mainland. On December 23, 1857, he accepted President James Buchanan's commission as U.S. minister to Nicaragua. The following month, he assumed the title of minister to Costa Rica as well. For the next eighteen months, he served in these posts, all the while remaining vigilant as Buchanan's eyes and ears in the region. During his tenure as minister, Lamar defended his countrymen in their mission to fulfill what he termed a "divine mandate" to bring "civilization"—and slavery—to the equatorial forests of Nicaragua and neighboring nations.[18] Lamar, while apparently never openly inciting revolution in Nicaragua, seemed always ready to rationalize Walker's adventurism on behalf of "liberty."

Lamar also stood poised to uphold the right of U.S. shipping companies and their steamboats to carry commerce to and from the Mosquito Coast. On March 20, 1858, in perhaps his most strident defense yet of the filibuster's mischievous means and methods, he wrote Don Gregorio Juárez, minister of foreign relations for the Republic of Nicaragua, warning him that "mighty changes" would soon transform his nation and open the region's natural resources and riches to the "talents, energy, and industry" of the Norte Americanos. "Man is not made to abide eternally in indolence and ignorance," he proclaimed. "That is not his natural condition." Then the old poet and prophet of U.S. expansionism lectured the Nicaraguan diplomat: "You say this is filibusterism. Well, Sir, there are two great filibusters in this age whose career it is impossible to check. They are now stalking through the world with colossal strides and giant power. . . . These filibusters are *Knowledge* and *Virtue*." He then concluded, "[T]hey are the great executioners of the will of Providence. God has sent them forth with the two-fisted swords of Truth and Justice."[19]

Walker also had no doubts that the Almighty stood with him. Still, his earthly enterprise turned out to be doomed. Three more years of schemes, machinations, and guerrilla warfare in Nicaragua ended in final defeat for the filibusteros and in the capture and execution of the ambitious General Walker. As for those soldiers of misfortune from Texas who had joined in his struggle, some paid the ultimate price for their ambitions—their lives; others simply disappeared into the misty tropics of Central America. Still others eventually staggered back home in tatters. Some of these were ready to turn their guns on Mexico.[20]

General Walker may have never set foot in Texas, but many of his most ardent supporters had. Some of them saw the lower Gulf Coast and the Rio Grande border as a staging ground for filibustering activities throughout the Caribbean and Central America. None was more determined than Colonel Samuel Lockridge, now living in Brownsville and actively raising money, men, and arms for a planned invasion of Spanish Cuba. On March 29, 1858, the longtime Walker protégé wrote to Governor Santiago Vidaurri in Monterrey, asking for the Mexican leader's aid in launching a military expedition from the port of Veracruz. Boasting that he would be able to put fifteen hundred soldiers of fortune in the field, Lockridge also claimed to have the financial backing of prominent U.S. citizens from as far away as New Orleans. He even urged Vidaurri to call upon the "brave children" of Mexico to join in his noble cause to "liberate" Cuba. First, however, Lockridge reiterated his longtime support for the creation of a border Republic of the Sierra Madre, where an army of Cuban liberation could be raised. In closing, the brazen adventurer requested that Vidaurri secretly direct his written response in care of Charles Stillman of Brownsville, the trusted cotton merchant and steamboat operator who apparently shared Lockridge's lofty designs.

Nine days later, Colonel Lockridge further informed Governor Vidaurri that one of William Walker's patrons and supporters had arrived in Corpus Christi and traveled to the border towns of Camargo and Laredo on a recruiting tour. Among those he wished to solicit was the longtime filibustero General Carvajal. "If you accept his proposals, which I included in my letter of March 29," Lockridge assured Vidurrai, "I will lend you all the aid you desire, including weapons and men, as you need. . . . General Hennings speaks your language and will probably visit Monterrey," Lockridge closed. ("General Hennings" is most likely a reference to British philanthropist and adventurer Charles F. Henningsen.)[21]

A War against Mexican Texans

While such men as Lockridge and William Henry were hatching plans of conquest elsewhere, another kind of war was being waged in South Texas during the summer of 1857. This conflict was a racial and ethnic war against Mexican Texans who earned a modest living freighting supplies from the port of Indianola to San Antonio and southward to settlements along the Rio Grande. Simply put, Texas teamsters and the merchants who backed them enjoyed the profitable business of transporting commerce across the wilderness of South Texas, and they especially resented the competition of Mexican carters who hauled supplies for less money than their Anglo counterparts did. That July, isolated attacks against caravans of Mexican oxcart brigades raised tensions in the trans-Nueces region. Bigotry and violence erupted when brush men and border ruffians fell upon Tejano teamsters, murdering them and stealing their carts loaded with valuable merchandise. What Texan John Linn termed the "disgraceful business" of assassination and thievery failed to move most local authorities, however; according to Linn, they regarded "the whole thing with supine indifference, as they made no efforts whatever either to suppress the crimes or to bring the criminals to justice."[22]

In response to the reports of lawlessness, General David E. Twiggs, commander of the Eighth Military Department of Texas, dispatched military escorts to protect Mexican freighters, but only those under government contract carrying military stores. Only after authorities in Mexico issued formal protests to U.S. secretary of state Lewis Cass did federal officials pressure Texas governor Elisha M. Pease to end the campaign of robbery and death. As Pease announced to the state legislature on November 30, 1857, "[I]t is now very evident that there is no security for the lives of citizens of Mexican origin engaged in the business of transportation, along the road from San Antonio to the Gulf." The lawmakers responded by approving the expenditure of state funds for armed guardsmen to protect Tejano carters. By the end of the year, the so-called Cart War had subsided.[23]

The racial prejudice underpinning the conflict, however, could not be eliminated by enacting legislation, appropriating money, or dispatching military escorts. Even those Texans who sympathized with the offended cart drivers refused to acknowledge the Tejanos as their equals, the Anglos seeing the Tejanos as people of an inferior order. On December 19, 1857, the *Nueces Valley Weekly* affirmed that "there is evidently a large amount of prejudice existing among our people against the greaser population, which often breaks out in acts of violence and lawlessness, altogether indefensible." Yet the editorial continued, "[T]he fact of their being low in the scale of intelligence is no excuse for our making them the scape goats for all the outrages that have been committed during the progress of this unfortunate war. Let us rather, by better examples and kind treatment, endeavor to elevate their moral and social condition, thereby making them respectable members of our community."[24]

Under the circumstances of prevailing racial attitudes, Mexican Texans no doubt needed federal military protection more than their Anglo counterparts did. During the decade of the 1850s, the U.S. War Department maintained a thin line of army outposts along the lower Rio Grande, the isolated forts existing not only to defend the border from marauding Indians and Mexican banditti but also to protect that exposed frontier from heavily armed gangs of mercenaries and freebooters—*los malvados gringos*—who would rob, raid, and plunder with impunity. From Fort Duncan, a squalid post situated on a bluff overlooking the Rio Grande near Eagle Pass, descending downriver past the Falls of Presidio to Fort McIntosh, a cluster of stone structures located one mile above Laredo, to Ringgold Barracks, a few frame buildings rising near a sweeping bend of the Bravo a half mile below Rio Grande City, southward to Fort Brown—the string of isolated posts stationed on the north bank of the river stretched along a frontier that spanned almost five hundred miles paralleling the meandering stream. A few outposts garrisoned by several companies of horse-and mule-mounted infantrymen, or dragoons, the forts were separated by many miles, each garrison manned by a handful of troopers poorly prepared and ill equipped to handle the swift-moving Comanches, elusive Lipan Apaches, and evasive bandits on both sides of the river. It was a far-flung perimeter of defense, one as imaginary as the border that the army proposed to protect.[25]

Like many Texans of the day, Jane Cazneau had little faith that these remote posts could provide any effective defense for the lower Rio Grande. "The utter absence of connected, judicious lines of communication along this whole frontier is absolutely incredible," she lamented in 1852. "It is rather to the neglect of Congress and the inertia of three or four of the highest officers in the army than to the Cabinet that this glaring default is to be imputed," she opined. "Three or four skeleton companies—and very thin skeletons they are—are all the government can allow for four or five hundred miles of this river frontier," she wrote in disgust. "There is no use sending them after Indians," she observed of the slow-moving, mounted infantrymen. "Posts are scattered in aimless confusion" and are "generally strongest where there is nothing to defend, and always weakest where there is the most peril." No leader in Washington, therefore, should have been surprised when the people of this frontier resorted to extra-legal methods to defend themselves by "any means at their disposal." Then she warned, "[I]f the government forgets to take care of us, we will take care of ourselves."[26]

Proposal for a Protectorate

Few individuals in the Lone Star State better understood the fierce independence exhibited by Texans than U.S. senator Sam Houston. And few expressed less confidence in the ability of the federal government to safeguard the Rio Grande border. Houston had never held much faith in large standing armies, not even as president of the late Republic of Texas. More recently, as the senior senator from Texas, he had consistently opposed any attempts to expand the regular army in the West, certainly not on the Texas frontier, specifically along the Rio Grande border. Such units had already proved ineffective in the face of marauding Indians and bandits. Houston's opposition in early 1858 to Mississippi senator Jefferson Davis's so-called New Regiment's Bill, which proposed to increase War Department appropriations to provide for additional forces on the frontier, was thus consistent with his past positions on military policy and expenditures.[27]

One disgruntled Texan agreed, bitterly complaining that the federal outposts "might as well be in Philadelphia or . . . Washington" for all the good they served in frontier defense. Another observer scoffed at the regular dragoons and scorned those officials who defended their effectiveness against Indian marauders, concluding that such stationary posts were "as much out of place as a sawmill upon the ocean."[28]

Throughout his public career, Houston had always preferred to rely upon state volunteer Rangers for frontier defense—understandably so. Experienced in Indian warfare, knowledgeable in plains craft and the ways of the wilderness, the Rangers had demonstrated time and again that they were more than a match for the fleet Comanches and fierce Apaches. From the days of the Texas Revolution, to the border campaigns during the decade of the republic, and throughout the recent war with Mexico, Rangers had consistently proved to be a most formidable foe. Seemingly fearless, even ferocious in battle, they had learned well how to track and pursue their enemies, to deceive and surprise them, and to overtake them on the open prairies. In a hundred engagements, the Rangers had employed skirmish tactics and a relentless charge, which made them feared and respected, even hated. Their unequaled skill on horseback, their knowledge of horseflesh, their stealth as spies, their legendary endurance in trailing marauders, and their use of the Colt six-shooter in close-quarter fighting had combined to create in the field a shock effect virtually unparalleled in the annals of modern warfare. In short, a single company of Rangers could constitute a mobile, mounted arsenal unlike any other military force in the world. On horseback, armed with rapid-fire revolvers and rifles, they were dogged and persistent, even tenacious, surely as terrifying an enemy as any man might imagine.

And Houston knew that. On March 1, 1858, one day before Sam Houston was to celebrate the twenty-second anniversary of Texas independence as well as his own sixty-fifth birthday, he rose in the Senate chamber to introduce a bill proposing the organization of a regiment of Texas mounted volunteers for protection of the southwestern frontier. He requested authorization for the president of the United States, in time of national emergency, to activate into the federal service up to four more regiments of state volunteers. Of course, he also recommended to his skeptical colleagues that federal funds be allocated to pay for these military units, which would be, by the terms of his measure, commanded by officers appointed by the governor of Texas. Almost predictably, Houston's bill to muster into regular service state Ranger units failed to marshal any measurable support outside the Lone Star State.[29]

Just two weeks earlier, Houston had aroused the suspicions and even the indignation of many of his fellow senators by introducing a controversial resolution calling for the United States to establish a "protectorate" over Mexico, Costa Rica, Guatemala, Honduras, and Nicaragua. Arguing that it was the responsibility of the United States to "maintain order and good government" over Mexico and the orphan states of Central America, he insisted that such a paternalistic act was "necessary to secure for the people of said states the blessings of stable Republican government." A mere two days after introducing this proposal, Houston called for the Committee on Foreign Relations to take up the issue. Several anti-slavery senators from the North, including the future secretary of state William H. Seward, of

New York, challenged Houston's motives for such action. Houston stood defiantly to defend his ambitious proposal. His blue eyes flashed in anger as he denied that he was trying to promote "the filibustering spirit that is abroad in the land." He insisted that "the very opposite is my belief and intention. I have always denounced filibusterism." The tall Texan, typically dressed in a Mexican serape, panther skin waistcoat, and deerskin leggings and moccasins, proclaimed eloquently (if not persuasively) that his resolution was "not offered with a view of extending our dominion, but with the view of improving our . . . [hemisphere]. These people are contiguous to us; our commerce has connection with them; and our political relations have necessarily been extended to them. Their defenseless situation," he reasoned, "is well calculated to invite aggression from other nations, or from individuals who, either from vicious or enterprising considerations, see proper to invade them." Then he exclaimed, "[T]hey are not in condition to defend themselves." Finally, he implied that, if the United States did not accept the responsibility to restore and maintain stability and order in Mexico and Central America, the Old World powers surely would.[30]

On April 20, Houston again rose to address his fellow senators, this time to offer a substitute resolution, one that recommended establishing a protectorate over Mexico only. Focusing his attention upon "our poor, distracted, adjoining neighbor" to the south, he cautioned that anarchy and revolution in Mexico provided a breeding ground for lawlessness, violence, and bloodshed along the sprawling border with the United States. Such chaos would be an open invitation to the most dangerous and destructive of elements, he declared. The only viable option for leaders in Washington, therefore, was military intervention—for the good of Mexico as well as for the good of the United States. The consequences of inaction, he warned, and the risks of U.S. neglect would be grim and even dreadful, for the people on both sides of the border. "To suffer her [Mexico] to be parceled out by filibusters—each perhaps a despot—would be," he claimed, "to fraternize with every desperate adventurer in our own land, and to invite to our continent all the wild, vicious spirits of the other hemisphere."[31]

"The protectorate must be self-protecting," Houston conceded. As much as $12 million could be raised from Mexico's customs receipts over the next decade, and that revenue could defray the costs of general administration as well as the expense of maintaining the five thousand troops necessary to establish and preserve order and stability within Mexico. Only then would free institutions, financial health, and economic growth be possible south of the Rio Bravo. "What a salutary change this would be, not only for both countries, but for the world at large," he boldly predicted. In his harshest words yet, he charged that the enfeebled nation of Mexico was "but little better than a national outlaw. She is powerful in the commission of wrongs, but powerless for their redress."[32]

He reminded his colleagues that citizens from the Lone Star State, particularly those from the border region of South Texas, had filed countless grievances and held millions of dollars in unsettled claims against the Republic of Mexico. The U.S. Department of State, he charged, seemed a mere "repository" for such depositions, at best impotent and at worse indifferent in its futile pursuit of indemnities for alleged crimes and outrages committed north of the Rio Grande by citizens of Mexico who found sanctuary across the river. Although admitting that "those grievances are doubtless magnified in a pecuniary point of view," he still insisted that such claims should be addressed "when ascertained to be valid."[33]

Next he spoke in an ominous tone about the imminent threat of the British Empire. With the theatrical skill of a thespian, he dramatized the ever present dangers of Old World imperialism. He reminded his peers that Mexico's $55 million national debt was "chiefly owned in England and on the Continent," thus intimating that there was a growing possibility of European intervention in the affairs of America's nearest neighbor to the South. He wondered aloud if the United States would someday be forced to "extricate the hand of our unfortunate neighbor from the [British] lion's mouth."

Houston then spoke about the days of his youth when he served the people of Tennessee in the House of Representatives. As he gazed around the great chamber of the Senate, he declared: "Mr. President, I have looked, but in vain, in both wings of this Capitol, for a fellow member who was . . . with me when the celebrated Monroe Doctrine was announced. Of the two hundred and sixty-one Senators and Representatives who constituted the Congress which commenced its session on the first Monday of December, 1823, I stand here alone . . . as one who regards himself as among the last." Tears filled his eyes and his normally strong voice seemed choked with emotion as he remembered his colleagues of that earlier time when both he and the nation were young and still untested. "All those worthy spirits, alas! have one by one, quit earth with the exception of President Buchanan, ex-President Van Buren," and a handful of elder statesmen who had long since retired from the public arena. He recalled the "full meridian of strong intellect" in that "great Congress" and how to a man—Jackson, Clay, Calhoun, Webster, and all the others—were now gone. Digressing from the topic at hand, he spoke eloquently about patriotic duty and personal honor as the principles that had guided his every decision in public life. He pleaded with his colleagues to remember the spirit and intent of President James Monroe's momentous policy statement delivered on that December day thirty-five years earlier. His hand trembled ever so slightly as he lifted from his desk a copy of Monroe's address. After reminding his fellow senators that he was the only surviving member of that Congress "to whom it was addressed," he began reading from the historic message known as the Monroe Doctrine.[34]

A silence fell over the chamber as the familiar figure with the distinct cleft chin and receding hairline recited from the lengthy text crafted more than a quarter of a century earlier by Monroe's secretary of state, John Quincy Adams. Perhaps it was ironic that the Texan, whom Adams once termed sardonically "that magnificent barbarian," spoke with eloquence, invoking the memory and message of Mr. Monroe and his brilliant chief diplomat. For the old protégé of the late Andy Jackson, in decrying the demons of anarchy that endangered Mexico and her border with the United States, was calling upon the very guiding principle formulated by Adams and Monroe, that fundamental doctrine which had come to provide the mooring of U.S. foreign policy. "We owe it, therefore, to candor, and to the amicable relations existing between the United States and those Powers [of Europe], to declare that we should consider any attempt on their part to extend their system to any portion of this hemisphere as dangerous to our peace and safety." He punctuated his address with particular emphasis upon the next passage: "With the existing colonies or dependencies of any European power we have not interfered, and shall not interfere. But with the Governments who have declared their independence, and maintained it, and whose independence we have on great consideration, and on just principles, acknowledged," he explained," we could not view any interposition for the purposes of oppressing them, or controlling in any other manner their destiny by any European Power in any other light than as the manifestation of unfriendly disposition towards the United States."[35]

Houston contended that Monroe had foreseen that, someday, circumstances might dictate, even demand, that the United States "exercise a controlling influence over one or another of those young Republics" of

Latin America. And he claimed that, rather than allow these weak states to be subjugated by the great imperial powers of Europe, the United States might be forced to intervene, even militarily, in order to "nourish . . . and protect such as could not take care of themselves." He further predicted that "the unlocking of the rich, varied, natural stores of Mexico, would redound not only to an enlarged welfare of that country, but to the good of every country interested in commerce and in enlightened civilization. . . . We must make her respectable and respected," he declared. Nearly a half century before President Theodore Roosevelt formulated his historic corollary to the Monroe Doctrine, therefore, the elder sage from Texas interpreted Monroe's words to mean that in order to ensure peace and stability in the Western Hemisphere, the United States must be ever prepared to police and protect it from enemies abroad, as well as from adversaries and anarchists lurking within these neighboring states. The aging hero of San Jacinto then folded his speech and took his seat.[36]

Sam Houston towered as a man whose vision transcended that of most of his contemporaries. More than an elder sage of the Senate, he remained as the last giant of his age, summoning his fellow citizens to answer America's call to national greatness. The following summer he continued to promote his grandiose plans for Mexico. Speaking to a public gathering on August 17, 1858, at Hempstead on the lower Brazos, he expressed regret over the defeat of his resolution proposing the protectorate, and he even suggested that, were he younger, his conscience would compel him to lead an expedition south of the Rio Grande. He intimated that, like Julius Caesar, he stood poised to cross the Rubicon of his day and extend a Pax Americana south of the border. And he had no doubt that thousands of his fellow Texans—most with experience as Rangers—would be at his side to complete the war that had been left unfinished.[37]

Although in reality the greatest hero Texas would ever know had neither the youthful energy nor the fiery passion to accomplish such a feat, younger and brasher Texans were ready to seize the opportunity and carry the Lone Star banner and the Stars and Stripes across the river that bordered both republics. And that is precisely what Houston feared—those hell-roaring ruffians who rode with the devil's abandon, soldiers of fortune and misfortune who could conquer but not govern, at least not without his leadership. Perhaps he had such fanatics and their designs on Mexico in mind when he lamented to his wife, Margaret, on April 22, 1858, a mere two days after delivering in the Senate chamber his rambling speech favoring a protectorate over Mexico, "I cannot control the destiny of this Country. [But] were I its *ruler*, I could rule it well."[38]

5
The Red Robber

On February 5, 1859, sixty-eight-year-old general David E. Twiggs, commander of the Military Department of Texas, issued a general order from his headquarters in San Antonio instructing Company L of the First U.S. Artillery to abandon Fort Brown. At the same time, he ordered the transfer of these troops to Fort Duncan at Eagle Pass. During the ensuing weeks, he also directed the closure of Ringgold Barracks at Rio Grande City and Fort McIntosh at Laredo, dispatching units from those posts northward to Camp Hudson on the Devils River, where they would be better positioned to defend the road from San Antonio to El Paso. Such improvident decisions might have been expected from "Old Davey" Twiggs. Cautious and aging, crippled with arthritis and debilitated by other ailments (some real, others imagined), he seemed too consumed by his many maladies to tour the Rio Grande and inspect these posts. So he failed to determine for himself the condition of the border and thus the need for troops stationed along that frontier. Affable and kind, the general preferred not to travel to the Rio Bravo del Norte but to remain within the comfort of his headquarters near the Military Plaza in San Antonio.

According to Captain Anderson, Twiggs suffered from dyspepsia, constantly complained of bowel obstructions, and expressed a continuing fear that his inflamed gall bladder might burst. "He was assuredly unfit for any important business and ought to have been retired for life," Anderson concluded. Future events would prove that it was Twiggs's judgment, rather than his body, that had failed. For his orders to evacuate the posts along the lower Rio Grande left the entire border unprotected and exposed to lawlessness, banditry, and insurrection.[1]

Not surprisingly, more than ninety merchants in Brownsville, as well as men of commerce from as far away as Corpus Christi, quickly reacted to the orders of evacuation. On March 9, 1859, Francis W. Latham, collector of customs at Brownsville and the coastal port of Brazos Santiago, and scores of other concerned citizens protested to U.S. secretary of war John B. Floyd, predicting that Mexican banditti, highwaymen, and marauding Indians would interpret the withdrawal of federal troops from the Rio

Grande as an open invitation to raid, pillage, and kill. But their warnings went unheeded. To Floyd's admonitions, Twiggs responded that such fears were without merit, that there was not "any danger of the Mexicans . . . crossing the river to plunder or disturb the inhabitants" of South Texas. "[T]he outcry" for federal protection, the general claimed, was "solely to have an expenditure of the public money."[2]

Twiggs could not have been more wrong. In less than six months, a squall of violence would sweep across the lower Rio Grande, and the border from Laredo to the Laguna Madre would be transformed into a bloodstained battleground. By the summer of 1859, tensions had mounted higher than ever along the Rio Bravo as racial relations, already beset by simmering resentment and fear, became further inflamed by reports of continuing Anglo mistreatment of Mexicans and Tejanos. A war of reprisal seemed imminent. All that was needed was a spark to ignite it.

A War Is Ignited

The spark occurred on the morning of July 13, 1859, when a lone horseman rode into Brownsville, ostensibly for coffee and conversation. The ruddy-faced rider, a pistol strapped to his hip, dismounted and hitched his horse to a post in front of Gabriel Castel's cantina on the east side of market plaza. Inside the cantina, the ranchero sat at a table talking with other patrons. No one could say for sure what business had brought him to Brownsville that day; perhaps he spoke of his recent indictment for cattle rustling, issued by a Cameron County grand jury. His appearance in the dusty town streets, and the quiet confidence he exuded, however, seemed to belie the fact that he was a wanted man. But then Juan Nepomuceno Cortina was a man of many mysteries and contradictions.[3]

The details of what happened in Brownsville that summer day are subject to dispute. But according to local tradition, as Cortina peered out the window of Castel's, he saw a disturbing scene, one that would change his life and that of the land he loved. City marshal Robert Shears, a coarse and rough-hewn lawman said by some to have a penchant for violence, had arrested an old vaquero named Tomás Cabrera and dragged him from the Cometa grocery and dry goods store. Of Shears, Brownsville resident William A. Neale recalled, "[H]e was considered by his comrades one of the most fearless of men. . . . His only faults were that he used chewing tobacco to the excess, leaving a pool of . . . juice wherever he stood or sat, and . . . would on the spur of the moment issue a flow of curses and words that would require a rosary to keep track."[4]

Whether Shears seized Cabrera for public intoxication, horse theft, or resisting arrest—or perhaps all of them—matters little. What mattered was that Cabrera was a longtime friend and employee of Cortina and that Shears had brutally pistol-whipped the aging Tejano, bludgeoning him into submission. Cortina considered this act humiliating not only to the victim but also to Cortina himself as well as an offense against all people of Mexican heritage. So while the tobacco-stained marshal manhandled the prisoner toward the old courthouse near Tenth and Levee, Cortina left the cantina and mounted his horse. Riding up to Shears, the ranchero demanded Cabrera's release. During the brief exchange of angry words that followed, Cortina's horse bumped into the lawman. In an instant, Shears had pulled his pistol and fired, striking the pommel of Cortina's saddle. Before Shears could get off another shot, Cortina wheeled his horse around and fired twice. The first shot missed the marshal, but the second hit him in the left shoulder, knocking him to the ground. As a few stunned spectators watched, Cortina swept down, swung Cabrera up on his horse, and galloped away. In the space of a few minutes, life in the lower Rio Grande Valley had been forever altered.[5]

Nothing would ever be the same. The shots fired in the town plaza that July morning proved to be only the first in a border war that would soon engulf the entire Rio Grande Valley. That bloody conflict, known to history as the Cortina War, led to the birth of a genuine Texas legend, one that still lives along the muddy waters of the Rio Bravo—that of the Red Robber of the Rio Grande.

Years later, Cortina recalled this defining moment when he wounded the "squinting sheriff," as he called his adversary. "Indignantly, I asked him, 'Why do you ill treat this man?' He answered me insolently, and then I punished his insolence and avenged my countryman by shooting him with a pistol and stretching him at my feet. Immediately, I mounted my horse, with my protégé behind me, and withdrew amidst the stupor of the Yankees and the enthusiastic hurrahs of the Mexicans." Proudly he said, "[F]rom that moment the Texas Mexicans proclaimed and recognized me as their chief . . . and patriot."[6]

Juan "Cheno" Cortina was not a modest man. Nor did he come from modest beginnings. Born on May 16, 1824, in Camargo, Tamaulipas, the son of Trinidad and Maria Estéfana Cortina, Juan grew to understand that his family's heritage and legacy were both bound up in the sprawling Spanish land grant his mother had inherited from her father and his father before him. In 1772, José Salvador de la Garza, Juan's great-grandfather, had received a sweeping 270,000-acre grant, the Espiritu Santo, from the Spanish crown. By 1836, Dona Maria Estéfana Goseacochea de Cortina had come to hold as much as one-third of that old estate, her Rancho del Carmen lying north of the Rio Bravo in what is today Cameron County, Texas. Following the death of Juan's father, who was a practicing attorney, then the conclusion of the U.S.-Mexican War, Maria Estéfana Cavazos (remarried and widowed again) found herself besieged by a procession of Anglo immigrants, all eager to become part of the new gentry now occupying the lower Rio Grande. Within a few years, she had lost much of what remained of her family fortune, not to land-grabbing gringos but, ironically, to guileful attorneys who defended her lawful land claims in the courts of Cameron County. In 1852, the proud heiress had no choice but to settle legal fees by signing away her rights to a large tract of land that included the township of Brownsville.[7] Thus largely dispossessed, an embittered Maria Estéfana—and more important her son Juan—held little faith in the system of justice dispensed by the Anglo lawyers and judges who represented the conquering Texans.

Juan Cortina was probably the least educated but most intelligent of Maria Estéfana's children. Yet he appeared anything but a likely hero for the desperately poor and disenfranchised peasants (peons) living and laboring on the lands of the lower Rio Grande Valley. Barely five feet six inches in height, he was, according to Lieutenant Benjamin F. McIntyre, "medium in size . . . [of] rather pleasant countenance . . . a genial companion of few words." Rip Ford remembered that Cortina was "rather fairer than most men of his nationality." Although a veteran of the U.S.-Mexican War who had served as a corporal in General Mariano Arista's irregular cavalry during the Palo Alto and Resaca de la Palma battles, Cortina spent much of the time escorting teamsters who freighted supplies to Mexican regulars in the field. By any measure, then, his record as a soldier was not particularly distinguished.[8]

A decade later, little more could have been said about the obscure and unassuming Cortina, except for the fact that a Cameron County jury had issued an indictment against him for cattle rustling. Whether a common cattle thief, according to his detractors, or as his defenders claimed a respectable ranchero who merely rounded up and sold nanita's livestock, no matter what brand they carried, one thing was certain. Before the shooting of Shears hardly anyone outside of Cameron County had ever heard of Juan Cortina.

That soon changed. Following the gunfight with the marshal of Brownsville, Cortina disappeared across the river and spent most of the summer of 1859 in Matamoros, where he walked the streets freely. Most likely, on more than one occasion he recrossed into Texas to visit his mother. During such times, while evading a posse formed by Brownsville sheriff James G. Browne and thus frustrating local officials with his elusiveness, he easily found the aid and assistance of a network of admirers who already looked upon him as a symbol of Mexican resistance to Anglo occupation and repression.[9]

No one in Texas could have predicted what would happen next, not knowing that Cortina was intent upon reprisal against those he believed had wronged him. The principal objects of his revenge included not only Shears but also several of Brownsville's most influential citizens, including Adolphus Glaevecke. A Polish immigrant and veteran of the U.S.-Mexican War who farmed and raised livestock on the Palo Alto prairie some three miles north of Brownsville, Glaevecke exhibited a peculiar talent for finding "lost" cattle and horses. In fact, the same grand jury that had brought charges of cattle theft against Cortina had indicted Glaevecke for rustling. Despite the fact that the brusque Glaevecke had married one of Cortina's relatives, Cheno held a strong disdain for him. During the summer of 1859, he vowed to kill Glaevecke and several other members of what he considered to be a corrupt and repressive clique of cattlemen and county officials. Surely this feud, more than the confrontation in the streets with Shears, underlay Cortina's anger and thus the ensuing border war that bore his name.[10]

A Town Is Taken

At first, nothing seemed particularly unusual about the evening of September 27, 1859. A festive atmosphere prevailed as the barrooms and hotels in both Brownsville and Matamoros echoed with mariachi music and Mexican folk dancing. Tejano and Texan stood side by side, drinking tequila, the Hispanics in a continuing observance of Mexican Independence, the Anglos needing no such excuse as a holiday to engage in their regular revelry. Amid the celebration, Adolphus Glaevecke sat in Jeremiah Galvan's store near the Brownsville market square, commenting to several friends that he had seen Cortina in the street that day. "I remarked . . . that some action ought to be taken to have him arrested, as I did not believe that he was up to any good. . . . At quite a late hour, the party broke up." Glaevecke and the others would have their chance to catch Cortina sooner than they might have thought.[11]

Shortly after four o'clock the following morning, September 28, Cortina rode into the sleeping town at the head of some seventy heavily armed horsemen. Strategically placing sentries along Elizabeth Street to ensure his command of the entire area, he proceeded to the Miller Hotel, where he produced a list of enemies who were to be shot on sight. Four columns of horsemen then fanned out to carry out the executions and to kill anyone else who so much as offered resistance. One squad stormed the town jail, surprising the jailer, Robert Johnston, who the men hated for his harsh treatment of Tejanos. They shot him several times as he fled to a neighboring house owned by a storekeeper named Viviano Garcia. When Garcia rushed out to protect the wounded man, then refused to deliver him to the mob, he, too, was killed. According to one account, Cortina's gunmen then dragged Johnston from the house and "shot him like a dog, but not before he got off a single shot, killing one of his assailants." The raiders emptied the jail of at least ten prisoners before continuing on their violent spree.[12]

Another jailer equally hated for his treatment of Tejanos, George Morris, who in Cortina's words had "perpetrated many Mexican murders," also awakened to the sound of gunfire. Grabbing a pistol, Morris attempted to hide from the approaching Cortinistas (as Cortina's followers came to be known) by scrambling under his house. As soon as he believed his pursuers had detected him, he opened fire, killing at least one of the raiders before they killed him in a hail of lead. According to William A. Neale, the armed and angry crowd then pulled "poor Morris" into the street and brutally bludgeoned his corpse. With knives, they "hacked his body into . . . pieces" to the horror of his wife, Dona Luciana.[13]

With equal determination, another squad of mounted gunmen moved down an alley between Washington and Adams streets until they came to the home of William Peter Neale (the son of the aforementioned William A. Neale), who allegedly had been responsible for the recent killings of two Mexicans. Before young Neale could grab his revolver and defend himself, a pistol-wielding assassin fired through a window of the house, mortally wounding him. Perhaps to protect his wife and young son, Neale then staggered from the house and collapsed beside a woodpile, where he died.

A fifth victim, Clemente Reyes, was also shot dead in the predawn darkness as the streets of Brownsville filled with the shouts of "*viva Cortina*," "*viva la república Mexicana*," and "*mueran los Americanos*."[14]

Alerted by gunshots in the streets that morning, Sheriff Browne managed to evade the Cortinistas, as did Robert Shears, who purportedly took refuge by hiding in a stove. Glaevecke also escaped the bullets surely intended for him. Years later, he recalled that, like nearly two thousand other residents of Brownsville, he was aroused from his slumber by the sounds of gunfire. "I first thought it was some young bloods returning from the ball in Matamoros," he recalled, "but I heard the name of Cortina cried out, and I knew in a minute what had happened." Running down Eleventh Street to Levee Street, then dashing through the darkness to Twelfth Street, he observed the raiders breaking into a store, stealing firearms and ammunition and anything else that they could carry. "Only by some quick movements did I succeed in getting into Galvan's place and barring the door. There I found several citizens preparing the place for a siege. . . . It was almost daylight by that time," Glaevecke recalled, "and I saw Cortina come to a grated window high up from the sidewalk, and look in." Clutching a double-barreled shotgun loaded with "a good big charge of powder and a handful of buck-shot," Glaevecke took aim at his hated enemy, only to pull the weapon down when he realized that, by shooting Cortina, he would bring certain death to himself and those hiding with him.[15]

Even after sunrise, the Mexican avengers, dozens of them, continued to scour the town for those enemies targeted for death. With guns drawn, they moved quietly but methodically from street to street, house to house. Cortina, meanwhile, had established his headquarters in the abandoned cantonment of Fort Brown, where he began issuing commands in the name of justice and the Republic of Mexico. As a sign of his conquest, Cortina wanted to raise the Mexican flag over the fort and nearby market plaza, but his followers were unable to locate enough tackle. Yet flag or no flag, his raiders held undisputed possession of the entire town of more than two thousand inhabitants. As the sun rose over South Texas, an eerie silence gripped the normally bustling border community, now governed by fear. No one dared step outside or speak to the grim-faced gunmen patrolling the streets on horseback.[16]

Sometime after eight o'clock that morning, Cortina received three visitors who had come to persuade him to withdraw his forces to the other side of the river. Ironically, they were Mexican, not Texan. Moreover, they were familiar faces, men Cortina could trust. General José María de Jesús Carvajal , still influential along both sides of the border and a relative of Cortina's, joined Colonel Miguel Tijerina, Cortina's cousin, and young Manuel Trevino, the Mexican consul at Matamoros, in their discussion with Cortina. Confident that his objections had been largely accomplished, Cortina rode out of town, headed north along the road to his mother's Rancho del Carmen, some eight miles upriver. But no one, certainly not the people of Brownsville, believed that they had heard the last of Juan Cortina.[17]

Later that day, collector of customs Frank Latham wrote to General Twiggs that, just hours after the raid on Brownsville, a well-armed and angry mob threatened the federal arsenal at the port authority thirty miles downriver on Brazos Santiago Island. Describing the lower Rio Grande border as being in "perfect turmoil," Latham informed Twiggs that entire families were abandoning their homes and farms to flee across the river to Matamoros. While claiming that he had ordered the powder magazine and musket stores at Brazos Santiago to be guarded by the local garrison of twenty regulars, he expressed a sense of panic that banditti were now loose upon the land and that the village at the mouth of the Rio Grande stood exposed to plunder and destruction. "As all the buildings are built of wood," he scribbled hastily, "once fired all would be lost." Finally, he lamented that the residents of Brazos Santiago and Brownsville were "sadly in need of the protection of the government." He admitted, "[W]e feel somewhat humiliated at the necessity of calling on Mexican authorities for protection."[18]

Following the raid on Brownsville, Cortina's reputation continued to grow, his fame spreading across the land like a wind-whipped prairie fire. Tejanos north of the river and the Mexican populace of Tamaulipas on the other side viewed him as something of a Robin Hood of the border, while Anglo-Texans along the lower Rio Grande forted up in fear of the man they cursed as a cold-blooded killer. As the news raced throughout the region, Hispanics hailed his deed as heroic. In the words of Rip Ford, "[T]o the poor who heard of him, Cortina was a sign of hope in a land where hope had no meaning." Yet to the Anglo-Texans, he stood as a murderous bandit worthy of only the gallows. Thus revered by one people and hated by the other, Juan Cortina had already assured his reputation in the history of the Rio Grande Valley. And his war had only begun.[19]

Terror Rides in Texas

Two days after withdrawing from Brownsville, Cortina issued a pronunciamiento from Rancho del Carmen. Dated September 30, 1859, and addressed to "the inhabitants of the State of Texas, and especially to those of the city of Brownsville," the letter defended Cortina's recent actions, explaining his motives for leading the raid. "There is no need of fear," he assured the people of the border. "Orderly people and honest citizens are inviolable to us in their persons and their interests. Our object . . . has been to chastise the villainy of our enemies. . . . These have connived . . . and formed . . . a perfidious inquisitional lodge to persecute and rob us, without any cause, and for no crime . . . other than that of being of Mexican origin." He then insisted that his attack had been justified as "making use of the sacred right of self-preservation." Referring to Johnston, Morris, and Neale as "criminal, wicked men, notorious . . . for their misdeeds," he also characterized the three as "wretched" and "vile." Together, Cortina said, they "form, with a multitude of lawyers, a secret conclave . . . for the sole purpose of despoiling the Mexicans of their lands and usurp[ing] them afterwards." He further accused Glaevecke of spreading "terror among the unwary, making them believe that he will hang the Mexicans and burn their ranchos" in hopes that all would abandon their fields and livestock to the Norte Americanos. In some of his strongest language, Cortina referred to Shears as "infamous and traitorous," and he charged that, like Johnston, Neale, and Morris, the marshal had carried out legal maneuvers, tactics of intimidation, and even assassinations in his bid to strip Tejanos of their lands and their liberties. "Our personal enemies shall not possess our lands," he warned. "All truce between them and us is at an end. . . . The hour has arrived. Our oppressors number but six or eight."[20]

Whether Cortina actually authored the document, dictated its defiant tone and general content to a more educated man, or requested that another craft it for him entirely remains unclear. What seems more certain is that his grito sounded across the frontier of the lower Rio Grande. Hundreds of Tejanos and Mexicans throughout the region heard it and responded by taking up arms and joining the cause.

Predictably, within days the citizens of Cameron County issued their own appeal. Only this cry would be heard as far away as the capitals of Texas and the United States. Fearing further depredations from partisan guerrillas and demanding protection from the Cortinistas, leaders of Brownsville and Cameron County hastily formed a Committee of Public Safety, which included some of the most influential men of the border, among them Mayor Stephen Powers, collector of customs Frank Latham, and steamboat owner and merchant Mifflin Kenedy. On October 2, members of the committee dispatched an urgent plea to Texas governor Hardin R. Runnels and sent a copy of the letter to President James Buchanan. Describing the "brutal and ruthless" manner in which Cortina's party murdered five residents of the border town, they depicted the whole region as utterly defenseless against marauding and murderous brigands. "Every able-bodied man has been under duty day and night," the plea continued, stating further that each volunteer was "nearly worn down with fatigue."[21]

Given General Twiggs's recent evacuation of the border outposts and the fact that the nearest federal garrison stood more than 220 miles away in San Antonio, the Committee of Public Safety had every reason to fear that another attack might be imminent. Fewer than eighty armed volunteers in Brownsville stood ready to defend that city; these defenders were not only unrested but also untested. Moreover, according to Mayor Powers, they were equipped with Mississippi rifles and outdated muskets borrowed from the armory in Matamoros, which were "in a sad state of efficiency, not more than half in any way serviceable."[22]

U.S. senator John Hemphill understood the extreme urgency of the situation. Writing from his office in Austin, on October 6, and again two days later, he implored President Buchanan to dispatch a regiment of federal regulars to suppress the insurrection and violence along the Mexican border. "I trust that troops will be speedily ordered to the abandoned posts of the Rio Grande," he concluded. A few days later, Mayor Powers likewise asked President Buchanan to "give us that aid our situation demands, and vindicate the majesty of the laws of our country by demanding the extradition of the criminal [Cortina], and thus teach the rabble and human dregs of two frontiers that these things cannot nor shall not be" tolerated.[23]

Frightened that another raid might come before reinforcements could arrive, citizens of Brownsville built barricades with brick and chain across town streets. Around the clock, sentinels patrolled the perimeter of the town. Men slept with their firearms. Few dared to enter or to leave Brownsville, except by way of steamboat traffic on the river. And rumors ran rampant that the Red Robber and his horde might cross the Rio Grande again at any moment. For days, news from the outside world halted with the interruption of the mail. Brownsville became a fortress besieged by fear.

With the exception of Brownsville, the lower Rio Grande had been depopulated by mid-October. North of the river, farms and homesteads had been abandoned, ranchos deserted, entire herds of cattle and flocks of sheep left unattended to roam the mesquite-covered prairies. Roads were devoid of wagons and carts. Hardly a horseman ventured forth. Only an eerie silence moved alongside anyone bold enough to travel across the countryside of Cameron County.[24]

In the early morning mists of October 12, Sheriff Browne headed a posse along the winding trail that led to Rancho del Carmen. His purpose soon became apparent. Before Cortina knew of their movement, the men of the posse had captured his protégé Tomás Cabrera, who worked cattle at the nearby Rancho San Jose. Formally arresting the same prisoner who had escaped the clutches of Marshal Shears less than three months earlier, Browne headed back to Brownsville, apparently without incident. The following week, Mayor Powers informed Governor Runnels of Cabrera's apprehension, observing that, "this is an old man, [who] always lived on the Texas side of the river, and hitherto has been of good character." Perhaps this action was intended to bait Cortina and provoke him into coming out of hiding and crossing the river from Matamoros.[25]

If so, the tactic worked. Before sunset, an angry Cortina demanded Cabrera's release. Otherwise, he threatened, his *bravos* would burn Brownsville to the ground. When city officials refused to comply with his demand, Cortina gathered a mounted force of fifty gunmen and splashed across the Rio Bravo and encamped at Rancho del Carmen. Over the next several nights, Cortinistas crept to the outskirts of Brownsville and fired shots into the city in an attempt to terrorize its inhabitants. By doing so, they ensured that the slumbering border town remained stirred to a state of frenzy and panic.[26]

The events of that autumn awakened state officials to the need for immediate action. On October 13, Governor Runnels authorized William G. Tobin of San Antonio to muster into service a company of one hundred Rangers to assist in quieting the "blood disturbances" that had recently beset the lower Rio Grande. Although Runnels instructed Captain Tobin to "repel any invasion or quell any insurrectionists" in the region, he also cautioned him: "you will be prudent and restrain from disturbing unoffending Mexican or American citizens, or encroaching upon Mexican soil." He then reminded Tobin that the "sole object of your mission . . . [is to] arrest offenders and prevent further violence." The governor thus issued orders that no reasonable person could have misunderstood.[27]

Meanwhile, with still no assurance that state Rangers or federal regulars would arrive anytime soon, the Cameron County Committee of Public Safety issued the call for a company of local militia to defend the town. Only twenty men, led by an inexperienced William B. Thompson, responded. They called themselves the Brownsville Tigers; a name that dignified what was otherwise an undisciplined and untrained rabble. The ranks of the Texan volunteers included merchants, mechanics, herdsmen, and farmers, but not one professional soldier. They were too few in number—even when reinforced by more than forty Matamoros guardsmen—and poorly equipped. Some carried rifles, but most wielded cumbersome and arcane smooth-bore muskets more suited to conventional linear tactics in the open field. For defense of the city, they also appropriated the only artillery piece locally available to them, a brass four-pounder borrowed from one of Mifflin Kenedy's steamboats. Over the river at Matamoros, they found another cannon, an old weapon from a barge. No wonder they inspired little confidence in the Anglo residents of the border and invoked even less respect from their foe.[28]

The natural elements, as well as the ineptitude of the Texans, favored Cortina. On October 23, 1859, Mayor Powers informed Governor Runnels, "[T]his country is now being almost deluged by constant rains and the roads on this account are almost impassible." Even so, he reported, the Brownsville militia (tactfully described as "a crowd of some sixty persons") would "go out to attempt to dislodge the enemy," which he characterized as "a large number of disaffected persons and desperadoes from all the ranches between this place and Camargo, and from both sides of the river."[29]

In fact, several days earlier the militia had gone out to pursue the enemy. "Captain" Thompson and a ranchero named Antonio Portillo had ridden at the front of their force, through the rain and along the river road recently transformed into a quagmire. William Neale later recalled, "I believe that they meant mischief, for my old friend, Henry . . . made his will just before he marched." Trudging past Glaevecke's ranch, they inched along, pulling two small cannon behind them as they plodded through the mud. On the morning of October 24, they engaged Cortina's pickets near Santa Rita, less than two miles below Rancho del Carmen. It had taken them a week to get there. "There, sure enough, they found the enemy," Neale wrote, "or perhaps . . . the enemy found them." After an initial exchange of fire, Thompson ordered his men to halt and "make a stand." The Cortinistas, probably numbering no more than twenty, withdrew and scattered into the tangle of chaparral and mesquite. According to Neale, "[M]uch difference of opinion prevailed among the officers" at that point. For, he added "nearly all of them [acted like] colonels, captains, or majors." Confident that they had routed the enemy, who they were convinced might attempt to flee across the Rio Grande, Thompson and Portillo apparently agreed to hasten the Tejano volunteers to the riverbanks to seize several small boats to prevent an escape. At the same time, Thompson commanded the remainder of his men to dismount and continue into the chaparral on foot.[30]

That decision turned out to be one Thompson would regret. Unseen snipers continued to fire on his men from the surrounding thickets. One of Thompson's volunteers fell dead on the rain-soaked field. Then Portillo's antiquated artillery piece, the one procured in Matamoros, became hopelessly stuck in the mud; when the militiamen attempted to dislodge the gun by firing it, the barrel flew off the carriage and landed in the bog. Abandoning the six-pounder, Thompson commanded his men to bring up Kenedy's smaller piece. When it failed to discharge in the rain, they dragged it to the nearby riverbanks and rolled it into the water. Many of their old rifle-muskets likewise proved useless in the morning mists, as the volunteers had no means of keeping their powder dry. Worse yet, most of the cartridges distributed to Thompson's volunteers turned out to be the wrong caliber.[31]

After huddling in the rain for most of the day while anticipating an attack, and with nightfall nearing, Thompson ordered his men to gather their mounts and withdraw back down the road to Brownsville. "Our retreat was in the utmost confusion," Thompson later confessed. Or as Neale aptly put it, "The Tigers made a desperate charge—for home—leaving their cannon in possession of the enemy, and though it had taken a week to get to Santa Rita, they made much better time in getting back. I was personally acquainted with one of the officers of that famous expedition," Neale recollected, "who, though a cripple, has since frequently declared to me that he got home on that occasion in less than forty minutes." One eyewitness described the pitiful scene in the streets of Brownsville that evening. "Our men commenced arriving in town, some on foot, others on horses, mules, and asses, mostly double, and many of them without arms." By any measure, the expedition had proved at best a humiliation, at worst a debacle.[32]

As for the citizens of Brownsville, or more accurately the 150 or so Anglos in town, the only thing that kept their spirits from total despair was the hope that the Rangers would be coming soon. On October 26, Captain William G. Tobin assured Governor Runnels, "I am now *en route* for the frontier with a company of fifty men" and "am willing to proceed immediately to Brownsville." Meanwhile, Cortina seemed to be gaining the advantage. Emboldened by his successes, he sent word that the people of Brownsville must not only free Cabrera but also surrender Glaevecke, Shears, Browne, Powers, and other offenders of Mexican Texans. Otherwise, he warned, he would sack the town, raze all public buildings, and administer his own brand of justice at the end of a gun barrel. As Frank Latham wrote to Tobin on October 26, "[I]t is desirable that you arrive here with your company at the earliest possible moment as each day the enemy become stronger in numbers." Most local officials, along both sides of the border, feared that Cortina's ranks had already risen faster than the waters of the Rio Grande. Estimates varied from between two hundred and seven hundred men in arms. Regardless of how many guerrillas Cortina actually commanded by the end of October, most observers agreed with Mayor Powers that the Cortinistas were "known, so far as their character is concerned, to be equal to the emergency." But events had proved thus far that the Brownsville Tigers and Matamoros guardsmen were not.[33]

As officials of Cameron County failed in their efforts to quell the insurrection and bring Cortina to justice, the Red Robber enjoyed his victory at Santa Rita. He benefited from the almost daily arrival of recruits, who now posed a formidable threat to peace and security along the border. From villages along the south bank of the Rio Grande and from ranchos and farms north of the river, they came, armed and determined to drive the gringos to the Nueces River. A prison break in Ciudad Victoria, the capital of Tamaulipas, reportedly contributed approximately sixty criminals to the cause, as this collection of rouges, rustlers, and ruffians flocked to Cortina's side, hoping to share in the plunder. One such desperado was Santos Cadena, a bandit from Starr County who reportedly rode to Cortina with forty sordid characters from Agualeguas. A small band of destitute Tampacaus Indians also walked into one of Cortina's camps near the town of Reynosa, apparently believing that by joining the border rebellion they were also defending their homes from the hated Comanche raiders who still frequented Mexico.[34]

For weeks, the elusive Cortina seemed to appear and disappear mysteriously, like Lewis Carroll's Cheshire Cat. Rumors and reports had him in several places at the same time. In many respects, the storied "bandit chieftain" became more a myth than a man of human frailties, as much a product of the Texan imagination as a true threat to the people of the Lone Star State. Newspapers from San Antonio to Corpus Christi to Galveston and beyond carried fabricated accounts, such as claims that Cortina and his marauders had executed every last defender at Brownsville, that they had torched the border town, and then marched northward with the intention of driving all Anglos beyond the Brazos and Colorado rivers. The wildest of these claims speculated that no citizen of Texas was safe, that even the capital of Austin would soon fall, and that state leaders would be put to the sword unless Texans swiftly crushed Cortina's legion of cutthroats.[35]

The most outrageous of these specious reports sprang from one man's fertile imagination. W. J. Miller, a resident of Brownsville who feared that Cortina might make good on his threat to raze the entire city, fled the border town one night late in October. Swimming his horse across the river to Matamoros under cover of darkness, he rode downstream to Brazos Santiago; there he boarded a ferry to South Padre Island and traveled northward to the coastal fishing village of Corpus Christi. Once there, he contributed to the growing panic by claiming that more than four hundred Cortinistas had overrun Brownsville, shouting "death to all Americans." He swore that after a fierce, five-hour battle, marked by savage hand-to-hand combat, the bloodthirsty banditti had massacred hundreds of innocent Texans. He even claimed that he had escaped to safety across the Rio Grande by the "blazing light" of the fire that consumed Brownsville.[36]

Of course, none of that had ever happened. Just as disturbing, the San Antonio *Herald* reported the unsubstantiated story that an army of "greaser pelados" had laid waste to Rio Grande City and that they were now camped on the Arroyo Colorado and would soon march northward to the Nueces. In the words of historian Jerry Thompson, "[T]hroughout Texas, many citizens came to envision little brown-skinned, serape-clad, sombrero-crowned Mexicans riding north from the border, wielding machetes to seize a land that had once been theirs." Terror thus rode far in advance of the Red Robber, but truth did not.[37]

A Heightening of Fear

The hysteria that swept the Lone Star State that autumn was only heightened by the chilling news of John Brown's raid on Harpers Ferry, Virginia, on October 16, 1859. It mattered little that the fanatical abolitionist leader had failed to seize the federal arsenal, that citizen volunteers of the sleepy village overlooking the confluence of the Potomac and Shenandoah rivers had thwarted his scheme to incite a general slave uprising, which he hoped would spread throughout the South. Of no greater consequence was the fact that "Old Osawatomie" Brown and his band of insurrectionists had been captured by a single company of U.S. Marines commanded by Colonel Robert E. Lee. Or even that Brown would soon be tried and convicted of treason and murder, then hanged for his crimes against the state of Virginia. What mattered was the fact that the raid had reawakened a latent fear of slave rebellion in the South. For the ghost of John Brown aroused the worst passions of southerners, who were convinced that other such monsters lurked in every thicket and hollow, poised to foment a slave rebellion. Southerners had terrifying images of fugitive slaves poisoning their masters, of runaways violating southern womanhood, and of knife- and axe-wielding blacks hacking their way across the land, slitting the throats of innocent whites. These visions only led to the further radicalization of opinions from Virginia to Texas. The thunderbolt that struck at Harpers Ferry reverberated around the entire nation, and the rumblings were heard not only along the banks of the Potomac but also as far away as the lower Rio Grande.[38]

To the people of Brownsville and the border, it appeared as if John Brown's timing could hardly have been worse. In reality, however, it could not have been better, at least for those demanding the protection of federal regulars and state partisan Rangers. Amid rumors of imaginary slave rebellions and unfounded reports of the sacking of Brownsville and Rio Grande City, the Texas State Legislature convened early that November to consider the present crises. Rip Ford recalled the scene one day as he walked down Congress Avenue. "A rumor reached Austin that Cortina had taken and burned Corpus Christi," he remembered. Passing in front of the Raymond House, not far from the white limestone capitol, he happened upon state senator Forbes Britton of Corpus Christi, a respected former army officer still referred to as General Britton. As Ford tried to reassure the old soldier that his home and family were safe, none other than Governor Runnels approached and listened intently to Britton's ravings that a mob of "barbarous marauders" had surely destroyed the coastal town and slaughtered many of its inhabitants. "The general's eyes danced wildly in their sockets," Ford recalled, "his chin trembled, and his voice quivered with emotion." Ford even claimed that Britton's performance for the governor was one befitting a "first-class actor." Obviously "deeply moved" by the shocking story, Runnels turned to Old Rip and pleaded, "Ford, you must go; you must start tonight, and move swiftly."[39]

Runnels commissioned Ford a major of state volunteers and formally authorized him to raise a company of Rangers for the purpose of quelling the insurrection on the border. In a letter of November 17, he spelled out three specific orders to be followed. First, the volunteers would elect their officers, as was the early custom with state partisan Rangers. Second, the recruits had to be "able bodied, well mounted, and well armed," the volunteers presumably furnishing their own horses and weapons, as was also the Ranger tradition. Third, Runnels instructed Ford to cooperate fully with any forces of the U.S. Army engaged against Cortina. No mention was made of the Rio Grande and whether Ford's Rangers could pursue the insurrectos into Mexico. Nor did the governor feel compelled to direct Ford to refrain from committing offenses against civilians living on both sides of the Rio Bravo, as he had one month earlier in his orders to Captain Tobin.[40]

Maybe Runnels had more confidence in Ford as an experienced leader of men than he had in Tobin. Perhaps he also knew of Tobin's reputation as a "regulator" who might allow acts of reprisal against people of Mexican origin, including innocent peasants who merely wished to live in peace and farm the alluvial plains along the lower Rio Grande. It is even likely that the governor had become convinced that the situation in South Texas was more serious than he had previously been led to believe. If such was the case, events during the coming weeks would prove Runnels correct on all accounts.

Meanwhile, Tobin's Rangers, numbering nearly a hundred, reached the outskirts of Brownsville after nightfall on November 15. After a long and arduous twenty days and some 240 miles on the trail, they were saddle scalded and slumped over their pommel horns in exhaustion. Little wonder, for in less than a week they had paralleled the Nueces and covered the harsh wilderness between San Antonio and Richard King's Santa Gertrudis Ranch near the coast, where they took on fresh mounts and provisions and rested for a couple of days. Then southward across the forbidding Wild Horse

Desert, they traversed another desolate stretch of country where few streams provided water for men and animals. Ten more days of plodding through sand dunes and thorny thickets found them entering the border town, which had been in a state of siege for more than seven weeks.[41]

As Captain Tobin ordered a bugler to herald the Rangers' arrival, startled residents grabbed their rifles and rushed out to defend the town. A fusillade of musket fire pierced the darkness, but fortunately the volley of grapeshot failed to find its mark, and no one was injured. According to one newspaper account, however, Adolphus Glaevecke, who weeks earlier had ridden northward to the Nueces to guide Tobin's company to the border, received two pieces of shrapnel that ripped through the loose flap of his jacket.[42]

What a fitting welcome for Tobin and his men. A motley assemblage of adventurers and ruffians, they hardly looked like the answer to anyone's prayers. Covered with more than a week's worth of dirt and grime, they were unshaven and unshorn. More important, the weather-beaten riders were surly in mood. Even Ranger historian Walter Prescott Webb admitted that these disreputable and disorderly volunteers represented "a sorry lot." Webb quoted one observer who confessed, "Tobin had one good man, but unfortunately, he fell off a carriage and broke his neck soon after reaching the city." Historian Carl Coke Rister concurred, alleging that "these state troopers were certainly not up to the standard of average rangers and respected law and order but little better than the Mexican outlaws."[43]

On the evening of November 16, every cantina in Brownsville overflowed with liquid spirits and brooding Rangers, who had come to the border hell bent on avenging the much chronicled atrocities of Cortina's banditti. Late that night, what one report described as a "lawless mob" dragged Tomás Cabrera from the town jail and, without even the semblance of a trial or so much as a ceremony, lynched him. As was the ghoulish frontier custom in those days, the crowd left the old man's body hanging from a tree in the market plaza, dangling, twisting, and swinging in the autumn winds as a warning to all who passed. Clearly, this act of retribution was intended to send the unmistakable message that *los diablos Tejanos* had arrived.[44]

But federal regulars had not. Although on November 12 General Twiggs had ordered Major Samuel Peter Heintzelman of the First U.S. Infantry to organize an expeditionary force and march "with all speed to the Rio Grande," he now had second thoughts. Despite his expressed fear that the sizable military stores at Brazos Santiago, which included two complete field batteries of twenty-four-pounders, might have already been seized by Cortina, Twiggs somehow concluded within a few days that those fears were unfounded and that the danger had probably passed. On November 17, from the comforts of his headquarters in San Antonio, he cabled the U.S. secretary of war that the "Cortina affair is greatly exaggerated." Four days later, he dispatched another telegraph expressing his confidence that the reports of border disturbances were "mostly false." Just two days later, he wrote to officials in Washington that "the Cortinas [*sic*] affair is over." Only nine months after Twiggs had ordered the evacuation of the border outposts, it was thus apparent that the situation along the Rio Grande had changed dramatically, but the bilious and incompetent commander of the Military Department of Texas had not. He was as indecisive, inconsistent, and confused as ever. Worst of all, he remained uncertain, uninformed, and even content in his ignorance, something that no good soldier should ever be.[45]

6
The Regulars

Everywhere, it seemed, the scent of burning wood carried in the wind. As a freezing November norther blew across the South Texas plains, men and livestock alike headed for the warmth of the nearest shelter. The season's first frost warned of winter's early arrival, and the wildlife busily prepared their lairs. Migratory birds were already passing through, gathering in southward flight in anticipation of winter's impending siege. Blustery sea breezes carried an unfamiliar bone-chilling cold to the people of the lower Rio Grande. With each passing day, the afternoon shadows grew longer and the hour of dusk shorter. Winter was coming, and a long bitter one it would be, especially for the commander of the U.S. expeditionary force, Major Samuel Peter Heintzelman, dispatched to the border to suppress the Cortina insurrection.

The fifty-five-year-old native of Lancaster County, Pennsylvania, who bore the unmistakable imprint of his German heritage, seemed out of place on the Texas frontier. Stoic, cultured, even refined in his habits and manners, he appeared every bit the West Point graduate and career officer that he set out to be all those many years ago in the Amish enclave of Manheim. Small in stature, slight of frame, he was soft spoken and gentle in his ways. He enjoyed classical music and passed much of his leisure time reading literature or playing chess. He loved fine cuisine, especially when served in a fashionable restaurant or a quaint tavern. Although this veteran of the U.S.-Mexican War could cope with the hardships of the field and the privations of camp life, he had come to expect certain amenities during his assignments back East—among them, comfortable quarters, good food, a firm mattress, and a reliable house servant. Judging by the journal he kept in the summer of 1859 while stationed at Camp Verde, situated in the spectacular Texas hill country, he had difficulty adjusting to the heat of the American Southwest. The harsh climate of Texas seemed to underscore the fact that he was a man who suffered from poor health, as did his wife, Margaret, who demanded the almost constant care of a physician.[1]

Regulars Join the Fight

On November 13, 1859, Major Heintzelman received marching orders from General Twiggs to proceed "with all speed to the Rio Grande." That evening, the major mounted up and moved out of Camp Verde, making his way to San Antonio with Company E of the Second U.S. Cavalry as an escort. After marching all night by moonlight, despite the greeting of a bitter chill, Major Heintzelman and company arrived in the Alamo City the following morning. During the next three days, the major met with General Twiggs on at least two occasions. The general informed Heintzelman that he was to lead troops across the Rio Grande into Mexico only if in "hot pursuit" of Cortina and his marauders. Departing San Antonio on November 17, the major first crossed the Medina River, then Rocky Creek en route to old Fort Merrill, located where the road to Corpus Christi struck the muddy Nueces. On the morning of November 22, he rode through a heavy fog and light rain as he approached the ford of the swollen river, approximately a half mile below Fort Merrill. On the slippery banks of the Nueces, he observed through the mists several vaqueros and the familiar stumpy figure of Captain Richard King, former steamboat pilot and now proprietor of the Santa Gertrudis Ranch, who was riding the open range checking on his herds. The cattleman was known to many as El Cojo (the lame one) because of his slight limp. King, easily recognized by his square jaw, prominent brow, and pointed goatee waved the troopers across the waters and invited them to camp to take cover with him until the skies cleared. According to Heintzelman, King received the troopers "very hospitably" and offered to guide them to Brownsville. Later that afternoon, two light batteries of the First Artillery joined them. After dark, a company of the Eighth U.S. Infantry under Captain Arthur Tracy Lee rode into camp. Understandably, with a five-day, hundred-mile hard ride behind them, Heintzelman and company were more than ready to pitch tents and get a good night's rest.[2]

Exhausted from the forced march, the major decided to stay for three days at Fort Merrill. On Thanksgiving, November 24, 1859, the soldiers celebrated, although Heintzelman admitted that "we did not have much of a feast." More important than their meal of corn, beans, and dried beef was the much anticipated arrival of a company of the Second U.S. Cavalry, commanded by the able Captain George Stoneman, and a second company of the Eighth U.S. Infantry under Captain Charles Jordan. After taking on provisions and allowing horses and mules to forage, Heintzelman continued downriver on November 26. Past the village of San Patricio the following day and southward across the prairies, they rode to King's Santa Gertrudis Ranch, arriving there on November 29. Thus twelve days out of San Antonio, they were still more than a hundred miles from Brownsville. The brush country of South Texas must have seemed even vaster and more daunting than the major's raw recruits could have imagined.[3]

Meanwhile, several other companies of state partisans had responded to this crisis along the border. Karnes County sheriff John Littleton, commanding one company of volunteers, rode into Brownsville shortly after Tobin's Rangers, while another company from Live Oak County, mustered into service under John Donaldson, also headed for the Rio Grande. Typical of the confusion and lack of communication and coordination between such volunteer units, on November 20 Captain Tobin had dispatched Lieutenant Littleton's command of thirty mounted men to ride out to meet Donaldson's company and lead them to Brownsville. But as Tobin later informed Governor Runnels, "[B]y accident each party marched on different roads and . . . [did] not meet." Later that same day, Donaldson's party safely arrived in Brownsville anyway, but Littleton, unaware of their presence, camped on the prairie north of town and waited for them.[4]

The following morning, Littleton's column rode northward, still in anticipation of meeting up with the Live Oak County Rangers. Instead, near the Palo Alto House, not far from the site of the epic artillery duel that announced the beginning of the U.S.-Mexican War thirteen years earlier, Littleton and his men engaged a band of Cortinistas. The Rangers pursued them on foot into the chaparral and mesquite, even though the raiders wielded an artillery piece (probably one of the captured weapons from the Santa Rita affair). Once again, as had been the case with the Brownsville Tigers four weeks earlier, Rangers left afoot to thread their way through a maze of thorny thickets proved ineffective. A furious gun battle raged for more than half an hour before Littleton retired from the field—but not before losing four Rangers, the dead men being identified as William McKay, Thomas Grier, Nicholas Milet, and John Fox. Three other Rangers were wounded, among them Lieutenant Littleton, who received a bullet in the right arm.[5]

Two days after the fight near the Palo Alto House, Captain Tobin rode out to reconnoiter the site and recover the bodies of the dead, as they had been left on the field in the haste of Littleton's retreat. What Tobin and his men found horrified even the most battle-hardened Rangers. The bodies of the four dead Texans had been stripped of their boots and clothing, and their corpses had been badly mutilated. As for young Fox, evidence suggested that he had been taken alive, tortured, and executed, then savagely dismembered. After burying what was left of the dead, Tobin moved westward toward the river, riding to the Rancho Santa Rita, where Cortina was reportedly camped. Finding only a few abandoned jacales, Tobin's men set fire to the huts and moved on. Although rumor spread that the elusive Red Robber had heavily fortified himself in the dense chaparral along the river, Tobin could find no evidence of Cortina's presence.[6]

On November 22, Tobin received most welcome reinforcements. Captain Peter Tumlinson and thirty-nine mounted Rangers arrived from Atascosa County, and another forty volunteers from Brownsville joined them the next evening. The latter group included Mifflin Kenedy, Captain King's longtime partner in the steamboat business. But even with approximately two hundred volunteers now at his command, Tobin implored Governor Runnels to send more. "There must be an increase in forces here before the Banditti Chief Cortina can be beaten and captured."[7]

By the confident tone of his second pronunciamiento, issued from Rancho del Carmen on November 23, Cortina obviously agreed that the forces thus far sent against him posed no threat to his personal safety or to his cause. As in his first grito, issued nearly two months earlier, Cortina called his fellow Mexican Texans to arms. In so doing, he invoked the intervention of the Almighty in an address that sounded as though it was written by a priest rather than a bandit. Referring to his hated enemies in the Cameron County power elite as "vampires in the guise of men," he charged them with "vile avarice," robbery, murder, and the indiscriminate burning of Tejano houses and farms. He further accused the Anglo "monsters" who persecuted people of Mexican origin with not only repression but also racism. "Mexicans! My part is taken," he proclaimed. "The voice of revelation whispers to me that to me is entrusted the work of breaking the chains of your slavery, and that the Lord will enable me with powerful arms to fight against our enemies, in compliance with the requirements of that Sovereign Majesty, who from this day forward, will hold us under his protection." Cortina even declared that he stood prepared to "suffer the death of martyrs" to achieve his goal of exterminating the "tyrants" who ruled over Tejanos.[8]

He then ended the declaration on a note of optimism. He urged his fellow Texans of Mexican origin to rely now on the "good sentiments" of the newly elected governor of Texas, Sam Houston. "Trust that upon his elevation to power he will begin with care to give us legal protection."[9]

Ford Rides Again

If Cortina was truly prepared to "suffer the death of martyrs," several companies of Texas Mounted Rangers were rushing to the border to accommodate him. One such unit was led by the most experienced Ranger commander of them all, a man whose very name had become synonymous with the Texas frontier and with the best of Ranger traditions. Even before the outbreak of the Cortina War, John Salmon "Rip" Ford had established his reputation as a leader who inspired confidence. Already the tall Bible-toting Texan stood as a genuine legend. The venerable Rip Ford, who had served ably under Colonel Jack Hays during the U.S.-Mexican War and had further distinguished himself as a seasoned commander of Rangers that patrolled the Nueces Strip and Rio Grande border, had been elected to the Texas State Senate in 1852. That same year, he reentered the newspaper business and, in partnership with Captain Joe Walker, published the Austin *State Times*, which ran until 1857. The following year, Governor Runnels had commissioned Ford as senior captain of state partisan Rangers and ordered him to raise a company of volunteers to engage marauding bands of Comanches. Ford's 1858 campaign along the Canadian River in Indian Territory brought stunning success, as he and 102 Rangers tracked several hundred Comanche raiders all the way to the Wichita Mountains, routing them in a running fight that lasted seven hours, reportedly killing 76 of the warriors while losing only 2 men. So when Major Ford arrived again on the Rio Grande in mid-November 1859, carrying his commission from Governor Runnels, he appeared poised now to hunt down and capture or kill the caudillo named Cortina.[10]

Surely, the people of Texas could not have hoped for a greater champion. Governor Runnels had every reason to believe that, if Rip Ford could not subdue the menacing swarm of Mexican bandits, no one could. After all, the irrepressible Ford had not failed yet. And he was cut from the same mold as the Ranger legends of the late war with Mexico—McCulloch, Walker, and Hays. Only Ford would have had the audacity to ride into South Texas with just eight armed men and a commission from the governor to suppress the Cortina rebellion. Only Ford had the charisma and presence to raise an entire company of volunteers en route to the border without so much as a dollar of public money or the promise of any payment forthcoming. Author Tom Lea said it best when he wrote admiringly of this courageous leader, known for his wry wit and rocklike determination. "He was no mere fighting man. . . . A good mind and a just sensibility gave an uncommon quality to the mettle in him . . . and made of Rip Ford the . . . loyal friend, the hard foe, a most uncommon fighting man."[11]

No doubt that when Rip Ford and his Rangers rode into Rio Grande City during the second week in November 1859 and camped in the abandoned cantonment of Ringgold Barracks, word quickly spread along the border that los diablos Tejanos had returned. On November 17, Ford informed Governor Runnels that, just days earlier, dozens of Cortina's mounted bravos galloped up to Rancho Davis south of Rio Grande City and filled the compound with gunfire and shouts of anger. As it so happened, when the shooting commenced Ford was standing in front of Clay Davis's establishment appropriately named "The Devil's Door," conversing with a Tejano named Serapio Garcia. Before Ford realized it, the armed horsemen raced by and began firing, wounding Garcia in the arm and just missing Ford's head. "The balls flew about me very thick," Ford reported. Quick to react, Ford and several of his Rangers drew their revolvers and returned fire, wounding two of the attacking party as they rode away. It was not the first time that Old Rip had narrowly escaped death. Nor would it be the last.[12]

Ford soon realized that the situation on the border was even worse than he had previously believed. "We do not know at what moment we may be attacked by some lawless band of Mexicans, " he informed Runnels, "perhaps [by] the same Mexicans who live amongst us." Five days later, Ford warned the governor that Cortina could likely muster six hundred to seven hundred men and that their avowed "object is to make prisoners, rob and kill all passing Americans. The whole Mexican population on both sides of the river are in favor of him." Blaming the unrest on Twiggs's recent decision to withdraw federal troops from the border, Ford warned that the Cortinistas "express determination not to allow any American to live upon the Rio Grande or even go there except by their permission. The contest is in fact for supremacy," he asserted. "If Cortinas [*sic*] is not arrested and punished the Americans will be expelled from the Rio Grande." Contending that Cortina had "spies all over," Ford also informed the governor that the bandit chieftain was now demanding $100,000 from Texas and the United States. If he didn't receive the money, he would continue his war of death and destruction along the border. Then Ford confirmed that, because the Red Robber enjoyed the protection and even support of the wealthy and influential citizens of Matamoros and other Mexican river towns, the Rangers' task would prove much more daunting.[13]

Meanwhile, other Ranger companies were being raised in response to the crisis. By all indications, many of the volunteers who eagerly joined in the fray were patriotic young men from the farms and villages along the Guadalupe, San Antonio, Frio, and Nueces rivers. But alongside these sons of Texas rode a strange cast of characters who could only be described as mercenaries, adventurers, and opportunists, soldiers of fortune who had no official appointment or sanction from the governor or anyone else. Their ranks included Colonel Samuel A. Lockridge and Captain William Robertson "Big" Henry, both recently returned to Texas from their failed filibustering activities in Nicaragua. Now they had come to try their hand along the Rio Grande border and in northern Mexcio.[14]

Major Heintzelman, after learning that Captain Henry had visited his camp at King's ranch on November 29, recorded in his journal, "I feel much disgusted, as I fear I will not get home as soon as I expected." Already, the major understood that filibusters who fight private wars and pursue personal agendas could make his mission much more difficult. Both the forbidding terrain of South Texas and the ominous weather loomed dauntingly enough as Heintzelman led his expedition southward, through the Wild Horse Desert. For several days, Heintzelman and his bluecoats braved blustery north winds and freezing rains. They trudged through deep sands, then threaded through miles of mesquite thickets. Along the way, they found only abandoned ranches and livestock left to roam in the chaparral. Occasionally, they passed a few Mexican herdsmen heading north, away from the troubled border. On Sunday morning, December 4, they crossed the Arroyo Colorado by rope-drawn ferry. Pushing on, Heintzelman insisted upon covering the final thirty miles in less than twenty-four hours, despite the fact that the muddy road across the Palo Alto posed difficult enough passage for mounted men, much less the train of supply wagons laboring behind the lead columns. At last, in the early morning darkness of December 5, Heintzelman's mud-splattered and chilled command rode into Brownsville.

Sunrise found them establishing bivouac and building fires on the abandoned grounds of Fort Brown.[15]

Awakening after a few hours of sleep, Heintzelman surveyed what he termed "a good sized town" where all seemed normal. Stores opened for business, as usual. So did the handful of hotels and restaurants, much to the major's pleasure. Brownsville appeared to be a bustling border city, undeterred by events of recent months. The whistle of the steamboat docked on the river nearby indicated to residents and troopers alike that life had apparently already returned to the ordinary routines of daily commerce and trade. Of the people of this prosperous river town Heintzelman wrote: "how they could fear the outlaws is more than I can see."[16]

Soon he found out. On December 7, Major Heintzelman finally secured a reliable map of the South Texas borderlands. He also met with Captain Tobin, whom he described as a "clever man," and Judge Edmund J. Davis of the Twelfth District of Texas, a Florida native whose jurisdiction covered the six southernmost counties in the state. He also met Brownsville mayor and chief justice of Cameron County Stephen Powers, one of the few slave owners in the region. The three men apprised Heintzelman of the present dangers along the Rio Grande. They convinced him that the reports of depredations along the river, although exaggerated, were nonetheless real. He must take the threat seriously.[17]

Regulars and Rangers in Pursuit

As the December skies darkened and the winter winds swept across the Gulf like a blade of cold steel, a chilling reality also settled over South Texas. Major Heintzelman understood full well that the campaign along the border promised to be anything but easy. His best intelligence reports speculated that Cortina might command as many as seven hundred armed rebels. According to the major's scouts, the chaparral appeared to be crawling with Cortinistas, who seemed ready to ambush anyone sent to engage them. Worse yet, he knew that General Twiggs had refused to allow him to conduct preemptive strikes against Cortina's strongholds on the Mexican side of the river and that the Red Robber was growing in popularity on both sides of the border.[18]

Heintzelman's daily journal entries revealed a reluctance to rely upon the state volunteers, a reticence to trust them. On December 12, as he prepared to scour the border with a combined force of regulars and Rangers, he noted that a near mutiny occurred in Tobin's camp and that the captain did "not appear to have much influence with them." No doubt remembering the Texans' reputation for insubordination during the late war with Mexico, Heintzelman hesitated to allow the Rangers to operate freely, without the restraint or regimen of military protocol. "I cannot get the Rangers to do anything effective in the way of scouting," he penned in disgust. He even claimed after his first scouting expedition in the field that "we would have undoubtedly done better without the Rangers." Seemingly impressed only by the Rangers' undisciplined and disorderly demeanor, he considered the state volunteers more a hindrance than anything else.[19]

As for the Rangers' commanders, Heintzelman obviously respected and admired the likable Major Ford for his unflinching courage and unequaled charisma. But he held less regard for Tobin. "Major Ford and Captain Tobin do not get along well together," he wrote succinctly, noting that Tobin was challenging Ford to hold an election for the commanding office of major. Heintzelman recorded simply, "Tobin thinks he can win . . . and Ford wont [*sic*] order the election." Then he summarized his feelings for both men: "I hope [by] all means that Ford is elected the Major. He is by all odds the better man. He controls his men & Tobin is controlled by his. I would rather have Ford with 50 than Tobin with all his men."[20]

Events of the coming weeks would surely justify Heintzelman's vote of confidence in Old Rip and his doubts about Captain Tobin and his recruits. On the morning of December 12, 1859, the people of Brownsville awakened to the sounds of artillery fire, apparently from across the river. But the roar of cannon at dawn turned out to be nothing more than the sounds of celebration as officials of Matamoros fired a salute to Our Lady of Guadalupe, honoring her day of sainthood. Heintzelman's men had good reason to be nervous and apprehensive, as word spread that morning that a trooper named Featherstone had been found stabbed to death after the supply wagon he was driving broke down on the Arroyo Colorado about fifteen miles north of town.[21]

In the capital that same day, Governor Runnels issued an executive order placing a $500 reward for the arrest or capture of the "desperado," Juan Cortina, if he did not surrender within ten days of the issuance of the proclamation. The decree was distributed across the state in both English and Spanish. Legend has it that, when informed of the reward, Cortina was first amused, then offended. Surely the price on his head did not reflect his importance or value.[22]

At 2:00 A.M. on December 14, Major Heintzelman moved out of Fort Brown at the head of a column of bluecoats, followed by several supply wagons and a battery of horse-drawn artillery and caisson. He met Captain Tobin's Rangers encamped one mile north of Brownsville. From there he moved four miles upriver toward Rancho del Carmen in hopes of surprising and overtaking Cortina's pickets. After failing to persuade Tobin and his volunteers to scout ahead, the major dispatched Judge Edmund Davis to lead a reconnaissance of mounted regulars to locate Cortina's camp. Davis returned before dawn and reported that he found only an abandoned breastwork of mud and logs near the road that snaked its way along the river. Apparently, the only resistance Davis encountered at these deserted fortifications was a barking dog. With a party of axe men clearing the trail, Heintzelman advanced and arrived on the scene, noting that "the remains of fires showed that . . . [the camp] had been occupied for days by a considerable party of men." The campfires, however, were as cold as Cortina's trail.[23]

Sunrise found Heintzelman some two miles north of the abandoned camp, not far from the Rio Grande in a maze of thickets known as El Ebonal because of the ebony-like chaparral that covered the plain. It would be a day that Heintzelman and his men would soon wish to forget. The major recorded in his journal that as he approached Vicente Guerra's rancho, he "tried to keep out the Rangers in advance & on the flanks with little success." Ordering Tobin's Rangers to dismount and move alongside his right flank, Heintzelman moved cautiously through the dense brushes, although he noticed that the Texan volunteers were "not quite confident & held back until I rode ahead." Of the Rangers' reluctance to advance, he wrote: "they were so thoroughly stampeded by their previous expedition that it was only after much difficulty and delay that I could get any of them to go." Moving out in front of Tobin's men, the major and his troopers continued up the road until they caught sight of a lone Mexican in the distance waving a flag. Before the major could react, a cannon shot sounded forth, and a four-pound ball whistled down the trail, sailing harmlessly overhead and landing to the rear. Heintzelman immediately ordered his own pieces "unlimbered" and returned fire. A brief but fierce artillery duel ensued. Remarkably, the only casualties during this pitched battle were one mule and a munitions wagon, which caught fire when a single ball passed completely through the mule, then pierced the wagon laden with powder and friction tubes. Only after putting out the flames were the inexperienced young artillerymen able to sustain cannonade against the enemy position. Heintzelman noted that the Cortinistas must have fired deadly grape and canister directly up the road at his position, as trees were shredded by several bursts, and the pommel on Judge Davis's saddle was actually blown away by one errant piece of shot. "We soon routed them . . . and pursued them up the road," the major recounted. Four miles to the north, near Jesus Leon's ranch, Cortina's men made another stand at a cluster of cabins. After an exchange of rifle fire, Heintzelman reported, "[T]he enemy fled and scurried across the river."[24]

Several miles to the east, Major Ford heard the distant rumble of artillery fire. Unable to rush to the scene by direct route, owing to the dense chaparral and the lack of a reliable guide, Ford left his pack animals in the charge of a "small guard" and hastened southward to Brownsville. Once there, he turned upriver on the same meandering road that Heintzelman had taken in the predawn hours. Ford and his company of fifty Rangers arrived on the scene in the early afternoon, having marched thirty-two miles in four hours. By then the enemy had retreated, many having already crossed the river into Mexico, and Heintzelman had established sentries around his perimeter. Still angry that during the fight Tobin's company had come to within forty yards of the enemy emplacement but then had hesitated to charge the position, Heintzelman welcomed Ford and urged him to assume command of all state partisans. For Heintzelman, it had been a day of frustration.[25]

After allowing his horses to rest for more than an hour, Major Ford resumed the pursuit upriver, scouting ahead and leading the regulars along the road that roughly paralleled the Rio Grande. But his efforts proved to be in vain. He advanced no more than two miles before rain began to fall and a norther blew in, sending the temperature plunging by more than twenty degrees. As the sun fell below the western horizon, Heintzelman ordered a halt and established camp on a muddy prairie about fifteen miles north of Brownsville. That night, the haunting sounds of Mexican bugles were heard in the distance, although several of Heintzelman's scouts sent into the chaparral failed to engage the enemy. "We attempted to lure . . . [Cortina] into attacking us," Ford remembered, "but he refused."[26]

The following morning, Heintzelman and Ford broke camp and returned to Brownsville by way of the only road south along the river, although the trail had become nearly impassible as a result of the previous day's rains. Seeing no sign of Cortina and his banditti, the column of regulars and Rangers undertook other onerous tasks. They stopped to bury young David Herman of Tobin's company, who had been mortally wounded in the fight at Leon's ranch. Along the route to Brownsville, the Rangers also put the torch to several abandoned houses. "I saved some," Heintzelman recorded in his journal, "but most were burned. On Cortinas' [*sic*] rancho [del Carmen] there was a heavy fence [that] made an excellent cover for the enemy. I had that burned down but strictly forbade burning anything without my express order. This is setting a very bad example to Cortinas [*sic*] . . . the Rangers were burning all, friends and foes." Little wonder that the major decided upon his return to Brownsville that, if the Ranger companies were to be better controlled, they should be separated in any future field operation. As far as Heintzelman was concerned, the Texans appeared more intent upon feuding among themselves than with fighting Cortina.[27]

On December 17, from his headquarters at Fort Brown, Major Heintzelman tried to alleviate the tense situation. He ordered Captain Stoneman and a company of the Second U.S. Cavalry to patrol the strategic crossroads at Las Norias, while he instructed Ford to ride with sixty Rangers to Los Fresnos to intercept any bandits attempting to cross into Texas or to flee across the river into Mexico. Tobin and one hundred volunteers were to move downriver to Point Isabel to "attack and disperse" any hostiles lurking near the port of entry below Padre Island and the ordinance depot four miles to the south on Brazos Santiago. As F. F. Fenn, collector of customs at Point Isabel, wrote to Governor-elect Houston, "[T]here is some alarm here, as we do not know at what moment we may be attacked. We are worse situated than ever. . . . Every ranch between this place and Brownsville is deserted—every man whom they can capture is impressed." Lamenting the fact that his mail was being intercepted, ransacked, and read by the Cortinistas, Fenn concluded, "[T]he people . . . have no idea how entirely defenseless we are . . . in fact it is an act of mercy that Cortinas [*sic*] spares us."[28]

The scouting parties failed to locate the enemy and yielded little pertinent information. Captain Stoneman reported finding the body of a "well dressed Mexican" hanging from a tree, his toes almost touching the ground. "As he was not robbed," Heintzelman wrote on December 19, "it is difficult to say who did it." The major contended that the dead man had been last seen looking for cattle, whether his or someone else's was unclear. The following day, however, Captain Tobin returned from the field and admitted to the major that "some of his men . . . hung that poor man." Claiming that "he knew nothing about it & that it was done without his orders or knowledge," Tobin refused to accept responsibility. Heintzelman blamed Tobin, once again, for failing to control his men. "It will have a very bad effect," the major feared.[29] If Tejanos such as Juan Cortina and his supporters from the border states of Tamaulipas, Nuevo Leon, and Coahuila actually believed that newly elected governor of Texas, Sam Houston, could stop such acts of violence against people of Mexican origin, they would be sorely disappointed. And if they thought that the new governor might express sympathy for the cause of the Cortinistas, they would be even more disillusioned. In his inaugural address delivered to the state legislature on December 21, Houston first indicted the government of Mexico for having an "utter disregard of all law and order" within its own boundaries. Referring to the lower Rio Grande as being "in an exposed and excited condition," he blamed Mexico for the troubles on the Texas side of the border. Internal violence and instability within the teetering Republic of Mexico were surely responsible for the outbreak of hostilities in Texas, he claimed, as surely as if Mexican federales had crossed the river. He reminded state legislators and Texans everywhere that two years earlier he, alone, as a U.S. senator had proposed a protectorate over Mexico and that the situation within the neighboring nation was even more "hopeless" now than it had been then. "The Mexican people [are] utterly incapable of framing a government and maintaining a nationality," he announced. "Their history has been a catalog of revolutions, of usurpations and oppression." He conceded that "the Mexicans are a mild, pastoral and gentle people," but they were too often victimized by "demagogues and lawless chieftains, who with armed bands have robbed and plundered the people." The peace and security of the Rio Grande border, and the lives and property of the people along the river, thus rested with the government of Mexico—and also with a Texas state government determined to defend the rights and freedoms of its citizens.[30]

Houston then concluded with a stern warning for leaders south of the border. "Should no change take place in Mexico, restraining their disorders, and should they extend to this side of the Rio Grande, it will demand of the

Chief Executive of the State the exercise of its fullest powers . . . to protect our citizens, and vindicate the honor of the state." Without mentioning Cortina by name, or referring specifically to the besieged Mexican president Benito Juárez, or even the French imperialists who seemed poised to intervene in the fractious nation, Houston thus reinforced the views that he had consistently expressed throughout his career. The aging hero of San Jacinto again stood ready to defend Texas. And perhaps even to carry out a greater design to conquer the enfeebled nation south of the Rio Grande.[31]

If so, Houston was not alone. Other Texans appeared ready to use the Cortina insurrection as a pretext for expansion south of the border. Houston's old friend Ben McCulloch, the brave and blustering Ranger captain of Mexican War fame, had spent the summer and autumn of 1859 in Sonora on unexplained "business." Writing to his mother in Texas that the enterprise would "require my personal attention this fall and winter," McCulloch predicted that "I will either be rich or flat broke in one or two years." In the same letter, he wrote scornfully of the people of Mexico: "a more indolent stupid & worthless race does not exist."[32]

McCulloch's attitudes were altogether typical of many Texans of the day. But no such notions of manifest destiny, racial superiority, and territorial conquest were foremost in the minds of most Rangers deployed in South Texas. Young Andrew Erskine, who served under Major Ford, was a case in point. During the course of this winter campaign Erskine's letters home to his wife, Ann, revealed not an adventurer or soldier of fortune but a devoted husband and father of two sons. His correspondence expressed nothing of patriotism or principle, only his boredom with the drudgery of daily camp life and the dangers of scouting in the field. "I am getting very homesick and want to see you and the boys very much," he penned on December 1, "but I must denigh [*sic*] myself the pleasure . . . for awhile yet." Although he wrote that the Rangers' quarters at Ringgold Barracks were comfortable, he complained about the long hours in the saddle and simply sitting in the barracks playing cards with comrades and about the lack of mail. "Some of the men have become anxious to go on," he informed Ann on December 7. "I am getting very restless. I for one want to go on and do what we came for and then return home to you and the children." Four days later, from a camp near Edinburg, he again affirmed, "I am growing more impatient . . . to get home every day."[33]

The Rout of Black Cortina

As Christmas approached, Heintzelman and Ford continued to send reconnaissance parties into the field with monotonous regularity. Their troops swept the prairies and thickets of Cameron, Hidalgo, and Starr counties, despite the stinging north winds that blew into the valley on the morning of December 20. All the while they sought to confirm or deny more daily rumors of Cortina's whereabouts.[34]

The calm of those dreary days turned out to be as deceptive as Cortina's tracks through the chaparral thickets. On December 21, Heintzelman assembled his entire combined force, including some 150 regulars and 198 mounted Rangers, and headed northward toward the Baston Ranch, William Neale's brick house and corrals located near Rosario, across the river from La Bolsa, some thirty-five miles upriver from Brownsville. "I had information that was deemed reliable that Cortinas [*sic*] had fortified himself" there, Heintzelman later reported. But the two-day march to this ranch site turned up nothing. On the night of December 23, Major Ford and his scouts found only an abandoned house, sacked by vandals, a fallen fence, and a few burned-out barns and jacales. Of the spacious home left looted but otherwise undamaged by the bandits, Heintzelman wrote, "[I]t was one of the finest houses I have seen on a ranch in Texas." Not a single head of livestock could be located anywhere on the premises. Once again, Cortina had stolen away, apparently with a herd of cattle and all the tools and provisions his men could carry. As on previous occasions, he seemed to have just disappeared into the night, much to the dismay of both Heintzelman and Ford.[35]

"The next place I was told that we should certainly meet him was in a bend of the river a mile beyond . . . Edinburg," Heintzelman recorded. But upon reaching Edinburg on Christmas morning, he found only a ghost town. He only rounded up a handful of Mexicans who had crossed the river from the village of Reynosa, perhaps intending to loot. "Not one could tell us anything about him [Cortina]," the major recalled, "except that he had left after plundering the custom house, post office . . . which we could see ourselves." Saddling up again and riding several miles northward to the canebrake along the river, Heintzelman and company came upon fresh horse tracks and droppings. Cortina once again had stayed a step ahead of his pursuers.[36]

The following day, Heintzelman learned from Colonel Lockridge that Cortina and as many as five hundred armed men were camped on the plaza at Rio Grande City, some twenty miles upriver. The major recorded in his journal that evening that the Cortinistas had occupied the river town and were purportedly "drinking & looting." He and his officers, after holding a war council with Ford and his subordinates, decided upon a forced night march to surprise the enemy at dawn the next day. Waiting until midnight, Heintzelman commanded his columns to mount up and move out, with Ford and eighty-five Rangers leading the way. Although their route ran alongside the Rio Grande, and their movement would be in full view of any spies on the Mexican side of the river, Heintzelman remained confident that his entire command could arrive at Rio Grande City undetected just before sunrise. Despite the fact that he and his men advanced in silence and with extreme caution, their silhouettes were plainly visible in the moonlight. Without a doubt it was the boldest and most dangerous plan Heintzelman had yet initiated.[37]

Thanks to Ford and his scouts, the strategy worked. Aided by a dense fog that settled over the river bottoms, the Rangers advanced in a deliberate order. Sometime after 1:00 A.M., Major Ford and his men approached the houses of several Mexican farmers. Ford's Tejano scouts spoke to a handful of peons, and as Old Rip later recalled, "we were taken to be a reinforcement for Cortina—a mistake we encouraged." Continuing along the road to Rio Grande City, the Rangers arrived at the home of a Mexican "friend" and informant who lived less than two miles south of town. Rancher and former journalist Henry Clay Davis, who rode with the Rangers that night, assured Major Ford that the Tejano who lived just ahead would share with the Texans "reliable information" about the disposition of Cortina's forces.[38]

No one knew better where and how to obtain such intelligence than the Kentucky native known as Clay Davis. Just three days earlier, Cortina's marauders had burned his home and the fences around his residence at Rio Grande City. At the same time, the bandits had stolen fourteen of his horses as well as tools, implements, and stores. In her memoir, Teresa Viele described the forty-six year-old gentleman farmer, trader, and ranchero as "a true specimen of the Texan, tall and athletic." But she observed, too, that Davis's "delicately cut features, carefully trimmed moustache, and *air distingue*, bespoke rather the modern carpet knight than the hero and pioneer of the wilderness." She then noted, "[A]n association with the Mexicans had given him a peculiar manner, a mixture of Western frankness and the stateliness of a Spaniard; a low-toned voice, and a deference mixed with assurance." In sum, Davis—a survivor of the doomed Mier expedition seventeen years earlier—knew the land and the people living along the river, and he had been perfectly positioned by location and by personal association to know more about Cortina's disposition than any other Anglo residing in Starr County.[39]

Less than two miles south of Rio Grande City, Ford's scouting party rode up to the ranch of Davis's spy. Without hesitating, the ranchero revealed that when he had left the border town the previous afternoon, Cortina and his followers were encamped on the main street of the village. He explained that Cortina's right flank rested atop a hill overlooking both the river and the town, providing a commanding field of fire to the south. He also told the Texans that Cortina's left flank was just as heavily fortified by picket lines that extended across a flat prairie east of Ringgold Barracks. "This intelligence made it impossible to . . . attempt to make the flanking movement without arousing Cortina," Ford recalled. Determined to seize the element of surprise and to attack the enemy's weakness, Old Rip remembered, "[W]e were firmly resolved to force him to fight."[40]

That is precisely what Ford did. But first he established sentries along a nearby road, then ordered his men to dismount and wait quietly for Heintzelman's arrival. Each man lay on the ground, holding his reins, trying to get no more than an hour's sleep. "Just before daylight," Ford recollected, "the rumble of the artillery carriages announced the approach of Major Heintzelman." Every man awakened to the gnawing anticipation of battle, each knowing that the long-awaited moment was at hand.[41]

With a calmness that belied the situation, the stoic Major Ford stepped into the road and hurriedly reported to Heintzelman that Cortina's defensive position was not impregnable, that his Rangers could flank the enemy pickets, move north of the village, and cut Cortina's men off, thus preventing their escape upriver. Although Ford later claimed that Heintzelman did not fully understand the Ranger's report, the major nevertheless ordered him to lead his Rangers in the advance of the regular cavalry and artillery and to initiate the attack. So Ford and some eighty Texans eased into their saddles and rode slowly ahead, disappearing into a bank of fog.

At dawn's first light, Ford engaged Cortina's pickets, about a half mile below town. The resulting exchange of gunfire alerted Cortina's camp, but the Rangers easily drove through the line of enemy sentries. Now hastening through the thick haze, Ford's men emerged from the mist within a hundred meters of Ringgold Barracks, where they encountered the perimeter of Cortina's defenses. The reports of revolvers and rifles, accompanied by the shrill, guttural cries of the Texans, pierced the morning stillness. Like howling gray ghosts galloping from the fog, the Rangers charged with such ferocity that, after the first volley, the enemy broke and ran, melting into the morning mists. Surely the sights and sounds that opened the battle at Rio Grande City were as eerie as they were terrifying.[42]

"We moved to the right," Ford recorded, "under an effective fire from Mexicans on tops of houses, and gained the crest of the hill." But he soon discovered that Cortina had already retreated from the river town. Fortunately for Ford, a local Anglo resident named John Phelps informed him that the Mexican force had withdrawn to some ebony trees a mile above the village. Immediately ordering Captain Tobin to wheel to Cortina's left flank, which was positioned on a small cemetery, Ford swept swiftly toward the enemy's right flank, which rested between the river and the nearby Roma road that ran north of town. The center of the Texans' lines was left for Heintzelman's artillery, which was fast bringing up the rear.[43]

For whatever reason, Tobin failed to initiate the attack on the cemetery, although Ford's company swiftly pushed to within 150 yards of the enemy's artillery emplacements. "They opened fire with little effect upon the head of our column," Ford recollected. As Cortina's cannon fired grape and canister, interspersed with buckshot, directly at the Mounted Rangers, Ford ordered his men to spur their ponies through the hail of shrapnel, which consisted of small shreds of scrap iron and lead balls. He observed that being pelted by the stinging shot felt like being "struck by handsful [*sic*] of gravel." Ranger lieutenant James Fry and his detachment on foot, armed with "Minnie rifles," moved into position "to pay . . . respects to the artillerymen," while Ford's company rode bravely ahead at a "brisk gallop," halting and dismounting less than forty yards from the enemy battery and taking cover in a line of chaparral. At that point, both sides engaged in a brief but bloody pitched battle at close range. All the while, as the smoke of gunpowder mixed with fog, Ford noted, conditions made it "difficult to distinguish a Mexican from an American at the distance of twenty yards."[44]

After several moments, a Mexican bugle sounded, and approximately fifty of Cortina's men charged Ford's position. The Ranger commander and his men were ready for them. Kneeling in front of their mounts, the Texans unleashed a deadly fusillade into the Mexican line, leaving the bodies of at least a dozen horsemen littering the field. "Many a charger galloped off," Ford wrote, "carrying an empty saddle. . . [while] Cortina's bold riders were left on the ground."[45]

Meanwhile, to Ford's right, Fry and his volunteers marched forward to seize the artillery. Ford never forgot the bravery of those Rangers who walked into the face of enemy fire. He also vividly recalled the cool manner with which twenty-eight-year-old Colonel Samuel Lockridge led the way, emptying his revolver as he walked to within ten yards of the enemy pickets. A Mexican directly in front of the angular Mississippian took "deliberate aim" at him and fired a single-shot pistol, then reloaded and fired again, failing to find his tall target on both attempts. As the Mexican began loading a third time, Lockridge stared down the barrel of his enemy. At that moment, he turned to Ranger George Morris who had moved forward and stood alongside him. "Good morning, Mr. Morris, would you please kill that Mexican." Then "quick as thought," Ford recollected, "Morris' Sharpe [*sic*] carbine exploded . . . [and] the Mexican fell dead." Showing his appreciation, Lockridge politely bowed, smiled, and nonchalantly walked away, offering: "Very much obliged to you Mr. Morris."[46]

While the battle raged, Heintzelman's troopers moved into position and joined the fight, bringing even more fire upon the enemy. In the face of such force, as many as 400 Cortinistas broke ranks and scattered into the brush. Ranger Rufus Byler of Nueces County recalled that dozens of the enemy ran for the river, waded into the waters, and began swimming for their lives. "Only one of that party lived to tell the tale," Byler wrote home to his fiancée two days later. "Rufe" also claimed that 38 of the enemy were shot dead, either in the river or as they scrambled upon the muddy banks on the Mexican side. Ford confirmed, "[M]any Mexicans were killed in the river. None of them proposed to surrender," he stated, without apology.[47]

The sun had already burned away the morning fog by the time Cortina fled northward along the Roma road, escaping with his two artillery pieces and the main body of his force. Ford and the Texans led Heintzelman's columns in pursuit. Some five miles up the trail, Cortina and his personal bodyguard crossed a shallow washout, halted in a tree line, and dismounted, preparing an ambush. When Ford's Rangers rushed toward the ravine, they discovered the enemy waiting. But instead of firing, Cortina's men first attempted to taunt the Texans into fighting them on foot.

That tactic failed. A ripple of rifle fire greeted the determined Rangers, who charged across the gully with six-guns blazing. "The matter of nationality was decided then and there," Ford remembered. Cortina's lines collapsed, and his men scurried into the thickets, "panic stricken" in their retreat. So fast did the Mexicans flee that they abandoned one of their two cannon, leaving the piece still loaded. In a gesture of both defiance and celebration, the old filibustero Captain William R. "Big" Henry rode to the six-pounder and turned it on the retreating bandits. Not to be outdone by Major Ford, the irrepressible Henry mounted the carriage and fired the piece in victory. Another mile up the road, the Rangers found the second cannon in the brushes. But the Red Robber had ridden away once again.

Although defeated and in full retreat, Cortina had escaped, like so many times before, vanishing into the chaparral, then across the river to the sanctuary of Mexican soil. The Rangers' dogged pursuit thus went unrewarded. Later that morning, the Texans entered Roma. If they expected to corner Cortina and his men there, they were greatly disappointed. The village, called by Heintzelman a "substantial little town on a high bluff overlooking the Rio Grande," was crawling with nothing more than a welter of rumors about the bandit chief and his bodyguard. Most locals insisted that Cortina lurked just across the river with at least sixty armed men.[48]

Despite such reports, Ford and his Rangers assured themselves that Roma's residents were safe and the town secure. Mounting up again, Old Rip and company headed back toward Rio Grande City, fifteen miles to the south. Along the way, they stopped at Heintzelman's camp at Rancho Los Barreros, located halfway between the two river towns. Shortly after dusk, Ford met with Heintzelman and urged the major to allow him to cross into Mexico with two companies of Mounted Rangers. He also reported that fourteen Rangers had been wounded in the battle that day (Heintzelman later claimed sixteen, most "very slight cases"). Among the wounded was Ford, who suffered minor contusions and lacerations as a result of being peppered with the "buck and ball" fired from the enemy artillery. In part as testimony to Ford's stealth and experience, no Texans were killed in the decisive engagement with Cortina that morning. Apparently, not one regular trooper suffered so much as a scratch, probably because the Rangers bore the brunt of the danger, something Major Heintzelman stubbornly refused to acknowledge.

As for enemy casualties, Heintzelman reported sixty Mexican dead in the fight along the river, while Ford estimated that the number was "much greater." Neither commander knew for sure. Still one thing seems certain. From that day forward, Cortina would resort to guerrilla tactics: retreat, evasion, and deception. Although Cortina's supporters were not entirely dispirited, their ranks had been decimated, and from then on he would run and hide—mostly hide—from the guns of *los diablos Tejanos*. And who could blame him?[49] Heintzelman reported the affair that evening in his diary. He wrote simply, "[W]e marched yesterday about 20 miles & this morning 20 more & then 9 in pursuit. Near 50 miles and a fight is pretty good business." Then he boasted, "I hope now that the matter is ended." He later informed U.S. secretary of war John B. Floyd that "the defeat was complete. We captured his guns, ammunition and baggage carts, provisions, everything he could throw away to lighten his flight, and entirely dispersed his force."[50]

Heintzelman, however, not only failed to credit Ford's Rangers with contributing to the success at Rio Grande City but also claimed in official reports that they were disorganized and that they delayed in their pursuit of the bandit chieftain. Perhaps he actually believed in the brilliance of his tactical surprise attack and that his bluecoats had won the day, in spite of the disobedience and dissension that prevailed among the Rangers. Or more likely he just wanted officials in the Department of War to accept his version of events, which was largely self-serving and anything but generous to the state partisans. He depicted the volunteers from Texas as undisciplined, disorderly, strung out during the attack, and straggling back in disarray following Cortina's retreat.[51]

From Roma on December 30 Major Heintzelman penned, "I am satisfied that . . . [Cortina] can't even again collect any force together" and that the defeat at Rio Grande City had placed "a complete damper on his operations." What Heintzelman failed to recognize was that despite his recent victory, he was in reality no closer to capturing or killing Cortina than he had been the day he first arrived in Brownsville. Confident that his chief nemesis was on the run and no longer posed a threat to the border, the major looked forward to the new year and the chance to return to his wife and son at Camp Verde.[52]

Major Heintzelman was not alone in his optimistic assessment of the situation nor in his belief that he—and not Ford—had pressed the fight and forced Cortina's retreat. Pennsylvania native Captain Arthur Tracy Lee of the Eight U.S. Infantry, assigned to Heintzelman during the campaign along the Rio Grande, later wrote a light-hearted poem touting Heintzelman's heroic triumph over the dreaded Red Robber. Titled "The Rout of the Black Cortina: A Legend of the Rio Bravo del Norte," the verse suggested that the intrepid bluecoats of the U.S. Army drove back the enemy that December day along the Rio Grande and that the men from the Lone Star State played only a secondary role.

Heintzelman five hundred strong,
Fresh from the land of doodle dandy;
With Texas Rangers five miles long,
Sweeping up the Rio Grande.

And gaily rode the Heintzelman,
Not he of fear or death e'er dreaming;
Rode proudly as the Ritter Ban,
With trumpet blast, and banners streaming.

And combat burned in every eye,
And brows were flushed as red verbena;
Whilst loud and wild arose the cry
Of "Vengeance on the Black Cortina."

The Heintzelman his sabre drew,
Drew Captain Ford his old revolver;
Cried King, "Charge on my boys in blue,
And give the devils a dissolver."

"Call in the guides"; the guides were called,
Bad Samples of the Texas Ranger;
For they through chaparral had crawled,
Back to the rear, and out of danger. . . .

The Heintzelman, he flashed his blade,
The red legs held their brass guns handy;
The rangers yelled out, "Who's afraid,"
As they swept up the Rio Grande.[53]

Maybe Captain Lee's poem speaks more about the regulars' disdain for the Texas volunteers than it does about the Rangers' role in the fight near Rio Grande City. Despite these verses and, specifically, Lee's contention that the Rangers were "back to the rear" and "out of danger" during Heintzelman's bold attack, one stubborn fact remains. Ford and his detachment of Mounted Rangers demonstrated extraordinary bravery during this pivotal battle, and they carried the wounds to prove it. That is more than could be said for Heintzelman's regulars.

John Coffee “Jack” Hays, “El Diablo.” Courtesy of the Center for American History, University of Texas, Austin, Prints and Photographs Collections.

Samuel H. Walker, “Thunderbolt of the Texas Rangers.” Courtesy of the Library of Congress Prints and Photographs Division, Washington, D.C.

Cartoon caricature of a Texas Mounted Ranger as depicted during the war with Mexico. Courtesy of the Texas State Library and Archives Commission, Austin, Texas.

Ben McCulloch, "Captain Ben." Courtesy of the Texas State Library and Archives Commission, Austin, Texas.

Juan N. Cortina, the storied "Red Robber" of the Rio Grande, ca. 1862–1865. Courtesy of Jerry Thompson, Laredo, Texas.

Major Samuel Peter Heintzelman of the Union Army as he appeared during the American Civil War. Courtesy of the Library of Congress Prints and Photographs Division, Washington, D.C.

Robert E. Lee, as he appeared before the Civil War, painted in 1862 by Benjamin F. Reinhardt. Courtesy of the R. W. Norton Art Gallery, Shreveport, Louisiana.

Sam Houston, full-length portrait, ca.1858. Courtesy of the Library of Congress Prints and Photographs Division, Washington, D.C.

Colonel John S. "Rip" Ford depicted in Confederate uniform, ca. 1865. Courtesy of Lawrence T. Jones III, Austin, Texas.

General David E. Twiggs, "Old Davy." Courtesy of Library of Congress Prints and Photographs Division, Washington, D.C.

Thought to be Ben McCulloch's Rangers atop the Veramendi house, San Antonio, Texas, February 16, 1861. Courtesy of Texas State Library and Archives Commission, Austin, Texas.

John S. “Rip” Ford, Senior Captain, Texas Mounted Rangers. Courtesy of a private collection.

“Old Rip” Ford, a genuine Texas legend. Courtesy of the Center for American History, University of Texas, Austin, Prints and Photographs Collections.

7
The Rio Bravo

On New Year's Eve, 1859, while encamped at the dusty village of Roma, Major Heintzelman scribbled in his journal that a "disgraceful state of affairs" existed at Ringgold Barracks some twenty miles downriver. "The Rangers are shooting all dogs & killing all the chickens, not only in town but in the neighboring ranches," he wrote. He further recorded that the ranks of state volunteers were divided in their loyalties, with Captain Tobin forcing an election to the position of major and threatening to resign if he was not chosen leader over his rival, Rip Ford. Of the Texans and their purportedly despicable conduct, Heintzelman wrote, "[T]hey are doing no service & only bringing disgrace upon the country." He expressed disgust that Tobin was unable to "keep better order" and that his Rangers had allegedly hanged another prisoner rather than turn the accused man over to civil authorities, as Heintzelman had directed.[1]

Heintzelman was not alone in his critical assessment of the petulant and insolent Rangers. While F. M. Campbell of Cameron County, who had been held captive by Cortina for ten days, later reported to U.S. military officials that Mexican marauders had stolen an estimated $200 worth of horses, livestock, firearms and other provisions from him, he claimed that Tobin's Rangers had relieved him of property valued at more than $1,000. "They burnt up my pens and fences for firewood," he charged, "and one horse by accident." These "notorious" state partisans also helped themselves to several of his prized hogs and fifty barrels of sweet potatoes—all without permission or recompense to the owner.[2]

Two days after the battle at Rio Grande City, from his quarters at Ringgold Barracks, Ranger Rufe Byler complained to his fiancée that he could not rest or even concentrate enough to write a lucid and legible letter. "There are many men in the house and some of them are drunk," he complained, "and they keep up so much fuss I can hardly hear myself speak." Amid the celebration and revelry in the aftermath of Cortina's defeat, Byler also concluded that most of his comrades, inebriated or otherwise, failed to understand one important reality: "The war is not ended."[3]

Ranger against Ranger

Indeed, it was not. But the battlefront seemed to have shifted, at least for the moment, from the pursuit of Cortina to the election of a major to command all volunteers in the South Texas theater. In sum, instead of fighting the Red Robber, the Rangers were squabbling among themselves. As was the custom in those days, volunteers had every right to elect their own officers. Former governor Runnels's original orders to Ford the previous November even instructed that such a democratic vote would be in order. As a result, on December 31, Ford finally complied with Captain Tobin's demand and called an election, the outcome of which should have been predictable. After currying favor with enlisted men and officers alike, offering them assurance that they would not be punished for their transgressions, the ambitious Captain Tobin was rewarded as the Rangers chose him over the stern and stoic Major Ford, who refused to campaign. Apparently, the canvas was held at a time when liquid spirits flowed freely through the Ranger camp at Ringgold Barracks, alcohol conceivably being used to influence the outcome of the vote. Even so, Tobin won by a mere six votes. However, the result must be viewed as a vote not for Tobin over Ford as much as for disobedience and debauchery over military discipline and decorum. Perhaps it was altogether fitting that as the year 1859 drew to a close, Ford assembled several companies of Rangers in an open hay lot at Ringgold Barracks and read his report to Governor Houston commending state volunteers for gallantry in action at Rio Grande City. He also announced Tobin's election as major. True to his Spartan-like pride and Athenian sense of honor, Ford offered no criticism of anyone, only gratitude for the opportunity to lead men in battle and to serve the state he loved. Had Old Rip given that speech a day earlier, the outcome of the election might have been different.[4]

Soon after New Year's Day, Ford rode with an escort to Brownsville, apparently having no expectation of returning to the field. Some of his most loyal supporters, however, refused to let the matter go without a challenge. On January 1, 1860, Colonel Lockridge lamented the turn of events and expressed his disdain for Tobin. In a report to Major Heintzelman, he noted that Ford was defeated only because of his "establishing some kind of order and discipline." He also claimed that Ford suffered defeat because he was determined "to prevent this indiscriminate robbing and plundering of the Ranches of the Frontier which is a disgrace to the Ranger Service." Heintzelman agreed but was in no position to intervene, even though he wrote from his headquarters at Roma on January 2 that "the scene of confusion and disorder is shocking at Rio Grande City." His only option now was to divide the Ranger companies and scatter them along the river in small parties, at least until Governor Houston could disband Tobin's tattered rabble and order them to return to their homes.[5]

Lockridge was a different matter altogether. He might have been a brazen filibusterer and an unabashed soldier of fortune, but he was also a southern gentleman who did not prefer the company of common thieves and border ruffians. His earlier experiences in Nicaragua had taught him that a disorderly mob of mercenaries was more a threat to itself than to any organized and armed enemy. Unlike Tobin, he could be depended on to maintain discipline.

Houston, too, understood full well the improvidence of maintaining a riotous and ragged horde of hellions to patrol the Rio Bravo. He received the news of Tobin's election with great alarm. He knew if he was to succeed in "staying the hand of violence" along the border, he had to concern himself not only with Cortina but also with his own partisan Rangers, whose penchant for pillage and plunder was already well established. On January 2, therefore, he appointed two commissioners to "proceed with the greatest dispatch" to Brownsville, "there to enquire into the cause, origin, and progress of the disturbances existing in that region." Instructing his emissaries to gather testimony from "correct sources," the governor directed them to confer with Major Heintzelman and other federal officers stationed in the region.[6]

To undertake the mission of serving as his eyes and ears on the border, Houston summoned two men who had earned his confidence and trust. Ángel Navarro of San Antonio, the third son of José Antonio Navarro, an old Houston confidant and supporter, undoubtedly understood the concerns of Tejanos along the Rio Grande and thus the reasons underlying the border conflict. More important, his very presence would inspire Hispanics to have faith in the governor's goodwill. A descendent of one of the oldest families in San Antonio de Bejar and an 1850 graduate of Harvard Law School, the younger Navarro realized the importance of tradition, cultural inheritance, and land as a legal and social basis for wealth and status. He was, after all, a member of the Texas State House of Representatives.[7]

Thirty-five-year-old state senator Robert H. Taylor might have seemed at first to be an odd choice to serve as commissioner to the Rio Grande, but few could dispute his appointment. After all, he was no stranger to public service. A native South Carolinian, he had settled in Fannin County by 1846 and lived for some fifteen years on Texas's "other border"—that of the Red River. A veteran of the war with Mexico, he practiced law in Bonham and served several terms in the Texas House, then the Texas Senate. Fluent in Spanish and knowledgeable in military and diplomatic affairs, he seemed to have formed few prejudices about the peoples south of the Rio Grande. Known for his unflinching honesty and integrity, he remained through the years a Houston loyalist. So the governor understandably had little hesitation in asking Taylor to undertake such an important task.[8]

Navarro and Taylor traveled to Brownsville, arriving on January 10. It took just two days for the commissioners to dispatch a terse communication to Tobin, ordering him and his men to report to Brownsville for discharge from duty. Four days later, Taylor issued a report to Houston, explaining why Tobin was being summarily dismissed (as if an explanation were needed). "There is nothing like *command* amongst the Rangers," Taylor wrote. Condemning Tobin as "utterly incompetent to command in the field," Taylor described the three companies of volunteers as being in a "state of inaction." He vowed to reorganize these forces by disbanding the existing corps, then reforming two new companies; by doing so, he could "obtain good men and get rid of the bad ones and I am sorry to say [there are] a good many of the latter." He further admitted that "in fact some of them . . . have been burning ranches and hanging and shooting Mexicans without authority . . . [of] law and are more dreaded than Cortinas [*sic*]." Taylor went on to inform the governor that "the whole country down here is in desolation to Rio Grande City" and that no crops would likely be harvested in the coming year because the fields and farms throughout the region were virtually abandoned. Moreover, entire herds of cattle and countless numbers of horses had been driven across the river into Mexico, where neither U.S. troops nor state partisans could recover them, at least not under Heintzelman's standing orders.[9]

On January 17, 1860, the commissioners dispatched a letter to Governor Houston, informing him that Cortina still posed a real threat to residents of the border counties and that his armed force was reportedly "well prepared to give a fight." So, they added, "we will probably be detained longer than we anticipated." Why they were delayed soon became obvious. Apparently, Tobin remained in Rio Grande City for more than ten days after receiving orders to present himself and his men to be mustered out of service. Evidently resisting his discharge as long as possible, even after Ford resumed command of one company with the commission of senior captain (John Littleton led the other), Tobin refused to travel to Brownsville. He later claimed that he had never received the dispatch, which seems unlikely. All the while, some of Tobin's volunteers engaged in horse theft, cattle rustling, the wanton plunder of abandoned ranches and farms, and even the lynching of prisoners suspected of complicity with Cortina. To complicate the situation further, Taylor fell ill sometime in mid-January, and the majority of the responsibility for interviewing witnesses, hearing complaints, and gathering testimony fell upon Navarro.[10]

Most of the evidence collected by the commissioners could be best described as a catalog of crimes purportedly committed by the Cortinistas. No doubt the litany of claims documented the loss of property suffered by residents of the border counties. How exaggerated these claims were—for both financial and political reasons—remains open to conjecture. Yet no one could deny that roaming brigands, no matter their loyalties, had laid waste to the entire lower Rio Grande. Throughout the valley, they had burned ranches and farms, torched crops in the field, driven livestock across the river, and left the cattle to roam the prairies as rancheros fled in fear. On every road running across the landscape of South Texas, they had intercepted mail deliveries, opened delivery bags, then dumped and ransacked their contents. They had stolen horses, mules, and oxen. They had appropriated wagons, carriages, carts, tools, weapons, and stores of assorted supplies. And in the course of their thievery, they had terrorized border residents of both races. Soon the growing number of claims against Mexico, owing to what William Neale termed the "Rio Grande War," would exceed $330,000 in damages. Anglos filed most, but not all, of those claims.[11]

Navarro summarized the commissioners' preliminary findings in a letter to the governor on January 26. He concluded that the disturbances in South Texas "originally arose from private and personal feuds" among warring parties and factions in Cameron County. Yet he also determined that the violence had since "grown to such an extent that I am afraid that it will . . . result in a war of races." He further confirmed that "there is a great deal of animosity and hard feeling existing among the Mexicans on the opposite side of the River" and that, consequently, most people south of the border were sympathetic with Cortina's cause. Of the residents of border towns such as Matamoros, Reynosa, and Mier, he wrote, "I believe that they encourage him and . . . privately give him aid and assistance and wish him God speed in his enterprise." Finally, he warned, unless someone took more decisive action soon to suppress the border upheaval, the conflict could easily escalate into another general war between the United States and Mexico.[12]

Although Taylor and Navarro did not yet specifically recommend that state and federal troops be authorized to cross the border into Mexico, the implications of their preliminary report were clear, at least to Houston. Captain Ford was already known to favor such action, as was Major Heintzelman. The major had notified Navarro and Taylor that he needed no more Ranger companies in the field but admitted that his one company of cavalry was "inadequate" to protect the frontier because he was "not authorized to cross the river into Mexico, where those marauders recruit and organize, and to where they flew to safety when pursued." He then concluded that incursions along the border would continue unabated until he was ordered to cross in strength, occupy the opposite side of the river, and thus deny the raiders sanctuary.[13]

Before long, such an opportunity would present itself. Meanwhile, Ford's frustrations had been mounting. On January 20, he had mustered the newly formed Company A of Rangers into service. Most of his volunteers were raw recruits from the counties bordering the Nueces who signed on to serve twelve months, "unless sooner discharged by order of the Governor." At the same time, Company B had been organized under the command of Captain John Littleton, who in the recent election had thrown his support to Tobin. Just as troublesome, Ford had found it difficult to procure provisions from local merchants and stockmen. "There was no money on hand," he recalled, "and some felt unwilling, and others unable, to await legislative action to provide an appropriation to pay the claims." Even when he could purchase mules, horses, wagons, and stores of supplies, he discovered profiteers to be extremely greedy, charging his quartermaster, Lieutenant William Howard, as much as $100 for a good mule. Ford also had instructions from Taylor and Navarro to "obey all orders" from his commander, Major Heintzelman, who despite a respect for Ford, harbored a most jaundiced view of the irregulars from Texas.[14]

Another Clash with Cortina

By the first of February 1860, events were hastening toward another clash between Cortina and the combined American expeditionary force. Word spread rapidly that the steamer *Ranchero* of the King and Kenedy line was descending the river from Rio Grande City, reportedly carrying more than $200,000 in coin, cash, and valuable commodities. Rumor also said that the Red Robber had recruited at least three hundred more armed vaqueros and rurales to intercept and rob the steamboat and that he lay in wait on the Mexican side near La Bolsa, a sweeping bend in the Rio Bravo some thirty-five miles upriver from Matamoros. In anticipation of an attack upon the vessel, Captain Ford took to the field with his two companies of mounted Rangers. Captain George Stoneman also rode out of Brownsville with two companies of the Second U.S. Cavalry and advanced up the Rio Grande. They skirted the Texas side of the river, with Stoneman marching up the road and Ford scouring the riverbanks between Brownsville and La Bolsa, searching for any sign of banditti. It was also reported that Cortina had crossed the river at Las Rusias and captured a U.S. mail carrier, taking him prisoner and rifling through the contents of his mailbags. Although Cortina purportedly threatened to execute his captive, who was working for the Americans, he instead took the carrier back to La Bolsa. According to Heintzelman, Cortina "only spared him because . . . [he] was a Mexican."[15]

After camping near the river on the night of February 1, no more than six miles upstream from Fort Brown, Ford rose the next morning to lead a scouting party northward to Rancho del Carmen. Alongside him rode Don Sabas Cavazos, the educated half brother of Juan Cortina who apparently held little sympathy for Cheno's cause. What happened that morning was a truly remarkable meeting, one Ford would remember for the rest of his days. Cavazos led the captain and several officers to Dona Estéfana's modest ranch house and invited them in to meet his mother. When the frail elderly woman walked into the room, she looked into Ford's eyes and extended her hand in friendship. Her sincerity and the kindness in her voice and eyes impressed and touched the battle-hardened Texan. "She was a small woman, not weighing more than one hundred pounds," Ford recalled. "She was very good looking, had a pretty face, bright, black eyes, and very white skin. She was a lady of culture, and indicated as much in her actions." Ford also noted that "she had all the politeness of a well-bred Mexican" and "was held in high esteem by both her Mexican and American acquaintances." Her eyes welled with tears, which then streamed in rivulets down her cheeks as she pleaded with Ford to show her son the same mercy he might expect "from his Creator."[16]

According to Ford, at one point the chilling sounds of a woman wailing in agony interrupted their conversation. One of Dona Estéfana's daughters had apparently walked into a small chapel on the premises, there to pray for her brother's soul. Unaware of the Rangers' intent, she probably feared for her own life and that of her aging mother. Ford rushed from the house to the nearby stone sanctuary, where he came upon the hysterical woman lying curled on the floor, sobbing uncontrollably and suffering spasms. Fortunately, an army surgeon, Dr. John Eldridge, was nearby to attend to the woman, whose fear and grief had apparently overwhelmed her. It was an unforgettable scene of pathos.[17] This meeting at Rancho del Carmen was not an isolated case. All along the river tensions heightened, and fear mounted. People on both sides of the border armed themselves and forted up in anticipation of attack. While Anglos huddled and readied themselves for Cortina's avengers, Tejanos and Mexicans prepared themselves for the onslaught of los Rinches. As Heintzelman recorded in his journal, Mexican "authorities have armed the people on the river & are cooperating with Cortinas [*sic*] to have his aid, whether from danger from this side or from the interior. They fear the Rangers and filibusters."[18]

On the evening of February 3, gunfire erupted at the upper ferry in Brownsville, causing "quite an alarm," according to Heintzelman. By all indications, several Rangers unleashed a hail of lead toward the Matamoros side, apparently in response to some Mexican citizens who had earlier hurled stones across the river at the ferry house. Although no injuries were reported, the incident further stirred the emotions of residents in both border towns.[19]

This skirmish turned out to be only a prelude to what followed the next day thirty-five miles upriver. The events of February 4 at Bolsa Bend near Bastone proved that all residents of the lower Rio Grande, regardless of race or nationality, had good reason to fear. Shortly after 1:00 P.M., Captain Ford ordered his scouts, under Corporal Milton A. Duty, to halt their wagons and pack trains at a *ranchito* called Zacatel. Riding ahead from there, making their way to the river, the Ranger advance guard came upon some thirty of Cortina's horsemen, who were crossing the river into Mexico with the plunder of their most recent foray into Texas. An estimated fifty horses and an undetermined number of raiders had already reached the safety of the south banks. Opening fire upon the party, the Ranger scouts engaged in a furious gun battle. Suddenly, the roar of rifle fire and the whir of bullets transformed the river ford into a veritable hornet's nest. After the initial exchange, a brief lull in the shooting occurred. But as soon as a detachment of Tobin's men arrived and took up position on the Texas side of Bolsa Bend, Cortinistas opened up with a volley from the opposite banks, mortally wounding a young Ranger named Fountain B. Woodruff. According to Captain Ford, although Woodruff lay dying, he remained "perfectly cool" as he handed his revolver to a fellow Ranger, acknowledging that he would no longer need it.[20]

As the battle at La Bolsa raged, the steamer *Ranchero* turned the bend a half mile upstream, churning its way slowly toward the position of the two rivals. On board waited Lieutenant Loomis L. Langdon with a squad of U.S. regulars. Langdon had mounted atop the starboard deck the two small cannon taken back from Cortina at Rio Grande City five weeks earlier. When the *Ranchero* reached the narrow neck in the river, which provided the only passage downstream, Cortina's gunmen fired upon the vessel. A hail of bullets pelted the craft, one ripping through the American flag that flew from the masthead. Steamboat captain John Martin continued to steer through the ambush, bravely holding his course. To suppress the hostile fire, Langdon's troopers opened up with artillery on the cluster of clapboard houses, fences, and surrounding undergrowth that curled along the water's edge and provided cover for the enemy. The shooting then became sporadic. Most of the enemy retired after the *Ranchero* had run the gauntlet and pulled alongside the banks on the Texas side with the boat's cache of coins secure and, more important, its occupants, including Mrs. Langdon and several other ladies, frightened but otherwise unharmed.[21]

With the steamer and its cargo safe, Langdon dispatched a courier to notify Captain Ford of the attack. The messenger also carried Captain Martin's scribbled plea for Ford to provide him "all the protection in your power." Around 3:00 P.M., Ford arrived on the scene with a company of volunteers. Upon meeting with Langdon and Martin, the Texan quickly assessed the situation and decided it was time to take the fight to Cortina—wherever he was. Not waiting for Stoneman's company of cavalry, which was scouting inland and presumably several miles away, he prepared to cross the river with more than forty men, including about a dozen of Tobin's volunteers. Of the latter, he wrote that "a large number of . . . [them] pointedly declined to pass the Rio Grande . . . [since] they were on their way to Brownsville to be mustered out of service." As for Tobin, Ford recalled that he "claimed no command, but offered to help us personally."[22]

As a consequence, Ford asked Tobin and Captain Peter Tumlinson to lead a scouting party across the Rio Grande to conduct a reconnaissance of the south bank. He then ordered that ammunition be passed out, and he briefed thirty-five men of his and Captain Littleton's companies that they would go afoot to assume a position on the Mexican side. Around 4:00 P.M., Ford crossed the Rio Bravo, then waited for word from his spies. Within the hour, Tobin and "Uncle Pete" Tumlinson reported that they had seen no one in the immediate area. Ford recalled that Tobin explained simply, "[T]hey have gone." Old Rip was not so sure.[23]

Before crossing, Ford hastily penned a letter to Heintzelman, justifying his decision. He informed the major that he intended to patrol the south bank and "beat the bush in the neighborhood" to determine Cortina's disposition, strength, and movements. He specifically intended to parallel the river on the Mexican side to protect the *Ranchero* in its descent of the river, "keeping as near as possible even pace with the boat." He also suggested that Heintzelman assign a force of regulars to do likewise on the Texas side of the Rio Grande. "By this co-operation only can the life and property on her be secured," he concluded.[24]

Ford wasted little time in locating and engaging the enemy. Not long after disembarking from a crude launch and setting foot on Mexican soil, he espied, through the nearby thickets, a number of the enemy behind houses and fences. Quietly motioning his Rangers to advance in line toward the upper end of the bend, he tried to flank Cortina's force but to no avail. The Rangers' movement caused Cortina to send about sixty mounted men forward. The Mexican horsemen approached to within thirty yards of the Texans but then halted and refused to charge or even fire their weapons. Ford thus had time to order his command back to the river, where they dispersed and formed a skirmish line beneath the bank, which furnished "excellent shelter." Kneeling and peering over the edge of the natural parapet, the Rangers readied their rifles and revolvers and waited for a few tense moments.[25]

Then the firing commenced. The first Mexican volley whistled harmlessly over the Texans' heads into the waters of the Rio Bravo. Ford commanded his men to return fire. With Captain John Littleton on the Texans' extreme right,

Captain Tobin in the center, and Captain Tumlinson nearby (Ford referred to him as a "brave, old frontiersman" who was "not much concerned about questions of military import"), Ford's skirmish line did not lack leadership.[26]

Nor did Ford or his Rangers lack courage. The captain directed twelve men on his right to "keep up a brisk and well-directed fire" on Cortina's mounted gunmen. Despite the "heavy fire" from the enemy, the Rangers discharged their weapons with precision and accuracy, even while exposing themselves to the enemy. Outgunned and outmanned, but determined to hold their precarious position on the water's edge, the Texans stood their ground. Passing up and down the line, Ford urged his men not to waste a single round of ammunition nor to hesitate to draw down on an enemy in range. They "shot to kill," he recalled of his volunteers, "it was victory or death with them."

His inspiring words failed to convince two demoralized young Rangers, one of whom broke and ran at "race horse speed" into the river, where he began to swim frantically for the steamboat still docked on the Texas side. As his frightened friend made a move to follow, Ford let loose with a string of oaths and announced that he would shoot the Ranger if he tried to follow. No matter that the captain was standing along the riverbanks, exposed to the enemy, and not even carrying a sidearm. All the while most of Tobin's men remained safely on the north banks, merely watching the fight unfold as if they were spectators to a sporting contest. Simply put, not all of the state partisans lived up to Ford's lofty standards of valor, much less his own personal example of bravery.[27]

For more than an hour, the fight at Bolsa Bend continued unabated. The firing even intensified as the sun dropped below the western horizon, hindering the vision of Ford's men. At dusk, Cortina's mounted guerrillas, some who may have been rurales from the state of Tamaulipas, retired from the field. Ford's Rangers had emptied several saddles. And now Captain Martin of the *Ranchero* was steaming out into the river and positioning the boat so that Lieutenant Langdon could bring his two field pieces to bear upon the enemy. By then, however, the remainder of Cortina's columns had broken ranks and withdrawn into the thickets. Ford then issued the order to charge, and the Rangers—revolvers loaded—rushed the retreating force, keeping up what Ford termed a "galling fire." All the while, the Texans let out a chorus of blood-curdling cries that would have terrified even the bravest of men. Ford later learned from Mexican sources that twenty-nine of the

Cortinistas lay dead on the field and an undetermined number had been wounded. As for the triumphant Texans, only private Woodruff was lost, while four others were "slightly" wounded. All things considered, the captain could hardly have been more pleased. Cortina was routed; victory was complete.[28]

Ford would record for posterity one last haunting image of the fight at La Bolsa. The figure of Cortina was "the last to leave the field," he observed. "He faced his pursuers, emptied his revolver, and tried to halt his panic-stricken men." As the red-bearded rider reigned up, turned his horse, and galloped away, Lieutenants Dix and Howard, along with Private George Morris, trained their revolvers on him, firing several rounds. "One shot struck the cantle of his saddle," Ford reported, "one cut out a lock of hair from his head, a third cut his bridle, a fourth passed through his horse's ear." Remarkably, the ever elusive Cortina escaped and disappeared into the haze of the river bottoms. "But for the obscurity," Ford insisted, "it almost being dark, the frontier pirate would have been killed."[29]

After sundown on February 4, 1860, Stoneman received word of the fight at La Bolsa. From his bivouac at "Old Camp" near Bastone, he dashed off a note to Heintzelman that he was breaking camp and leaving immediately to render aid to the crew of the *Ranchero.* "I shall not cross the river without instructions," he assured the major, "except to repel an attack upon the boat." Yet it was not the conduct of the cavalry that worried Heintzelman, who from his headquarters at Fort Brown was nervous and concerned about the fast-developing situation upriver. "It is of the utmost importance that you preserve the most rigid discipline amongst your troops," he warned Ford in a dispatch that evening, so that "no injury . . . is done to the inhabitants [on the Mexican side] and their property. Do not allow yourself to be drawn from the river," he further cautioned, "but confine your operations strictly to the protection of the boat."[30]

Ford, although refusing to be lured from the river and into the uncertainties that waited in the high chaparral beyond the south banks, indeed failed to maintain a "rigid discipline" among his ranks. Based on what happened next, therefore, Heintzelman's concerns in this regard proved justified. As soon as Cortina had retreated from La Bolsa, some of the Texan volunteers—acting without orders—set fire to the cluster of jacales, barns, fences, and corrals that had provided cover for their enemies. As the roaring flames rose in the evening sky and illumined the bottomlands of the Rio Bravo, and the cacophony of Ranger yells and hurrahs died down, a few Texans demanded that their captain grant them leave to pursue the Mexican raiders into the interior and even to plunder at will. He refused.[31]

After returning without incident to the Texas side of the river that evening, Ford collected additional cartridges and provisions, then crossed back to the Mexican bank with mounts the following morning aboard the *Ranchero.* As ordered, the Rangers rode in double column, acting as an escort as they wound their way down the water's edge, remaining alongside the vessel as it steamed a safe course toward Brownsville. Hugging the Texas bank, Captain Arthur Tracy Lee and two companies of the Eighth U.S. Infantry likewise paralleled the river for the next two days. At every bend of the river, Ford and his Rangers scanned the horizon for any sign of the banditti. But none were seen between La Bolsa and Fort Brown. Even so, the seasoned Ranger captain knew that they were out there somewhere beyond the forbidding brush and thorny chaparral.[32]

On the afternoon of February 7, the people of Brownsville had cause to celebrate. The steamboat, albeit riddled with bullet holes, pulled into dock, its tattered standard flying proudly from the masthead. Captain Martin sounded a horn that heralded a successful passage through the perilous, sandbar-choked channels of the lower Rio Grande. That same day, Major Heintzelman hoisted the Stars and Stripes over Fort Brown for the first time since his return from the field two weeks earlier. Just the reappearance of the U.S. flag whipping in the winter wind and the beleaguered steamboat glistening in the sun buoyed the spirits of city residents.[33]

Official Assessment of the Cortina Situation

On February 4, 1860, the same day that Cortina ambushed the *Ranchero*, Commissioners Navarro and Taylor submitted an eighteen-page report to Governor Houston. Writing from their quarters in Brownsville, they outlined the causes and consequences of the current border conflict as well as the corrective actions necessary to quell the disturbances. Judging by the tone and text of the report, their conclusions must have been what Houston had anticipated and just what he wanted to hear. They began by reassuring the governor that they had interviewed only trustworthy witnesses to the events of recent months, both Anglo and Tejano. Based on the evidence uncovered by their investigation, they ascertained that, while personal feuds and local disputes underlay the present troubles, the war on the Rio Grande had rapidly escalated into a more general conflict that threatened the stability of the entire international border. In sum, marauding banditti and brigands had devastated the valley. "The *ranchos* and farms are destroyed," they confirmed. "The cattle and horses as far out as the Arroyo Colorado have been driven off, and in fact the whole country from this place to Rio Grande City—a distance of one hundred and thirty miles—is in utter desolation." Anglo rancheros had been threatened and driven from their land, they reported. Mexican peons had fled their fields in fear of their lives; entire families had either left the region altogether or were roaming it in search of shelter and protection, living off the land with little in their possession but the hope of someday returning home. And at the center of it all, the commissioners alleged, stood Juan Cortina, who was in their words "a thief, a pirate and a murderer" who had "collected around him all the *pelados* and desperadoes he could" from the Mexican border states.[34]

Navarro and Taylor, although advising Houston that Ranger companies should continue to play an important role in supporting federal troops and protecting the borderlands of South Texas, expressed no confidence in Captain Tobin and his motley crew of mercenaries and malcontents. They informed Houston that Tobin had disobeyed their direct order to stand down and disband his company, which they described as being "without organization, muster rolls, or any thing like discipline." They vowed to discharge Tobin and his minions as soon as they arrived in Brownsville. Reiterating the sentiments expressed in earlier communications, they wrote, "[I]t is better to have a hundred good men than one thousand indifferent and bad ones."[35]

The commissioners also issued clear words of advice. "The only way to stop these disturbances," they insisted, "is to occupy the right [south] bank of the Rio Bravo." Unaware that Captain Ford was at that very moment in the process of doing just that, they echoed the frustrations of Major Heintzelman and his bluecoats, submitting that "this boundary line is worse than an imaginary one." The distant Juárez government was either unable or unwilling to exert the necessary pressures to control Cortina's insurrection, they accused. U.S. garrisons stationed along the border, too, could do nothing to stop Cortina under the present circumstances. They were understaffed, unprepared for guerrilla warfare, and unnecessarily constrained by political considerations. Their standing orders to remain on the Texas side of the river rendered them ineffective. Moreover, the commissioners charged that U.S. State Department officials seemed able to do little more than complain to disinterested or corrupt Mexican magistrates. The commissioners, therefore, concluded: "We can no longer live as neighbors in peace."[36]

For that matter, the entire frontier of the lower Rio Grande remained a welter of intrigue and machination. The volatile situation spawned by the Rio Grande war provided a breeding ground for the worst of ambitions and conspiracies. Although the commissioners failed to mention any specific names or plots, other than the fact that filibusters were gathering on both sides of the river, the presence of men such as Lockridge, Henry, Tobin, General Carvajal, and even Ford convinced Taylor and Navarro that Texas nationalists and Mexican secessionists were poised to take advantage of the border troubles. On February 7, 1860, Major Heintzelman wrote in his journal that he had been given what he termed a "Spanish pamphlet on the Carvajal correspondence with Ford and the fillibusters [*sic*]." The next day, he noted that Ford had warned him that many of Tobin's men were speaking openly of crossing into Mexico and "going towards Reynosa & Camargo to sack these places & return into Texas." The major also reported that Texas adventurers were planning to cross the river above Brownsville and "make a dash at Matamoros to try to plunder it." It was rumored as well that Ford and Littleton intended to join Carvajal to seize the state capital of Victoria, then "take & hold Tampico." Meanwhile, from Austin to Brownsville town leaders were calling meetings to discuss a filibustering expedition into Mexico. Once again, throughout South Texas, the calls for an independent buffer Republic of the Sierra Madre and the cry to "extend the area of freedom" echoed from one settlement to another. State representative John L. Haynes of Starr County, a Houston loyalist and opponent of private filibustering, claimed that Major Ford attended at least two such meetings, presumably in Brownsville, proclaiming that a "state of war" with Mexico already existed. Haynes also alleged that investors and supporters from as far away as New Orleans were willing to lend a hand, or at least money, to the cause.[37]

Evidence has suggested that President James Buchanan and Secretary of State Lewis Cass were not only aware of such schemes but also carefully monitoring the war along the border. During the previous November, Cass had dispatched a personal emissary to the Rio Grande to determine the nature and extent of the "aggressions upon our territory and the outrages upon our citizens" along the border. To undertake this mission, which was known only to a few, Cass handpicked an enigmatic sixty-eight-year-old master of cloak-and-dagger diplomacy, General Duff Green, to act as "Confidential Agent" to investigate the troubles in South Texas. Longtime publisher of the St. Louis *Enquirer* and avid Jacksonian Democrat, Green had once served as President John Tyler's special agent to Great Britain. In 1848, following the negotiations that concluded the U.S.-Mexican War, he accepted the sensitive assignment as Zachary Taylor's personal plenipotentiary in Mexico City. In sum, Green was no stranger to the shadowy world of diplomatic deception and duplicity.[38]

Arriving by steamboat at Galveston early in December 1859, Green posed as a railroad company executive as he interviewed several individuals who had recently traveled by steamer from Brownsville. He then made his way to Austin, where on December 9 he met with Governor Runnels concerning the state of affairs along the Rio Bravo. He apparently concluded that the disturbances on the border had been greatly exaggerated by Texans who demanded greater federal protection and even planned to extend U.S. dominion south of the Rio Grande. On December 21, he attended Governor Houston's inauguration and no doubt probed the new chief executive about his intentions as to the conflict on the Rio Grande. Whether or not Houston or Runnels knew the nature or reason for Green's mission to Texas remains unclear. But Houston must have at least doubted the sincerity of Green's claims of being just another opportunistic businessman seeking a sound investment.[39]

On several occasions, Green communicated to Cass and at least indirectly to U.S. minister to Mexico Robert M. McLane about his concerns regarding the sanguinary border war, specifically his fears that Texas leaders might attempt to provoke a war with Mexico. Writing from Austin on Christmas Eve, Green informed Cass that, although Cortina threatened to become a "great annoyance" to federal officials, his partisans were fragmented, disorganized, and lacking in cohesion or common cause. The greater danger to peace along the Rio Grande, he warned, was posed by what he termed the "party on the frontier" who sought the annexation of Mexico, and claimed to be "in the Confidence and to have the Sanction of the President . . . to be acting in concert with persons of influence in Northern Mexico." One week later, on New Year's Eve, he reported that Houston "was kind enough" to share with him Ford's official report of Cortina's defeat near Rio Grande City, an event he believed confirmed the imminent demise of the insurrection. On January 8, 1860, Green confirmed that despite Houston's confidence that the rebellion was nearing an end, the governor was privately discussing the possibility of raising a volunteer regiment for "frontier defense." Green wrote that "there is a desire on the part of many in this state to involve the U.S. in a war with Mexico" and that many Texan leaders "openly avowed" a military invasion of the border states below the Bravo. Although Houston "professes to wish for peace," Green believed that the governor's private actions and public posturing revealed a more aggressive plan of action. Two days later, Green repeated, "[T]here are many who hope that the matter of Cortinas [*sic*] will end in war or an invasion of Mexico."[40]

A Conspiracy to Conquer

In the coming days, Houston did little to calm Green's fear that influential Texans—perhaps including the governor himself—were engaged in a conspiracy to conquer at least the borderlands of northern Mexico, if not all of the troubled republic. Houston only hinted at such a grandiose plan in his address to the Texas State Legislature on January 13, 1860. Declaring the lower Rio Grande to be "in a state of tumult and war," Houston warned of the "consequences of further rebellion" along the border. "Lawless chieftains plunder . . . with impunity, and light the torch of civil war at pleasure," he contended. "Riot, murder, and revolution reign above law and order. Separated from Mexico by a narrow river alone, and a continual intercourse going on between its people and ours, it is but natural that the unhappy influences of her condition should extend to our border," he explained. But with a determination that Texans had come to know well, he vowed to marshal all resources at his disposal and exercise the full constitutional authority invested in the chief executive to protect the lives and property of the people of Texas. After detailing the Americans' recent clashes with Cortina's followers, he informed the legislators of Taylor and Navarro's mission. More important, he announced the formation of three more minute companies of Rangers to defend the frontier, one organized by Captain W. C. Dalrymple to be stationed below the Red River on the Big Wichita, a second led by Captain John H. Connor to be posted on the San Saba northwest of Austin, and the third commanded by Edward Burleson, Jr., to patrol the Nueces River region and employ "six Mexican guides," according to the governor's instructions.

Houston further informed the legislature that to defend Texas against all enemies, he was going to sign a pending bill titled "An Act for the Protection of the Frontier," which authorized the governor to organize still more state volunteer ranging companies, even though it neglected to appropriate a single dollar to pay for them. Obviously frustrated by such parsimony, he challenged the legislature to find a way to fund these partisan Rangers. "Common justice demands that the State should recompense them," he declared.[41]

Houston soon issued a series of "Orders to Ranging Companies." He forbade all officers of state volunteer units to allow horse racing, gambling, and drinking in their ranks. Not only were alcoholic beverages prohibited from being sold or consumed within five miles of any Ranger camp, but any volunteer in the service of Texas found "guilty of intoxication or insubordination" would be dismissed without honorable discharge or pay. Considering that state lawmakers had thus far refused to pass an appropriation bill, and given that the word "honorable" was not a part of some Texans' vocabulary, the governor's threat of discharge seemed to carry less weight than a cartridge and one ounce of lead.[42]

Regardless of any questions that might be raised regarding Houston's sincerity in signing such orders of restraint, he diligently prepared the way for a U.S. protectorate over Mexico, perhaps with himself at the head of it. Only this time he had no intention of asking the Congress or anyone else for approval. On January 23, in a letter to Secretary of State Cass, Houston recommended that his old friend, Henry Lawrence Kinney, be named U.S. minister to Mexico. Such a man could surely play an important role in the grand scheme. Fluent in Spanish, familiar with the border as a one-time resident of the frontier that was to become Cameron County, the flamboyant Kinney later helped found Corpus Christi and was by most accounts personally responsible for the construction of many of the wharves, warehouses, and livestock tanks and pens in the fledgling coastal town. The Pennsylvania native was also recognized as one of the finest equestrians in all of South Texas and a seasoned Indian fighter feared by even the Comanche. Such skills stood him tall in the eyes of both the Mexican vaqueros and Texans along the border.

Savvy and even shrewd in matters of politics, Kinney engaged in cattle ranching and land speculation below the Nueces years before Richard King and Mifflin Kenedy dreamed of doing so. In 1846, he served on Governor James P. Henderson's staff in the opening military campaigns in northern Mexico. Following the conflict, Kinney invested in several schemes, from the freighting of commerce along the Nueces and the Rio Bravo, to promoting the idea of a camel corps to transport goods across country from the Gulf Coast to San Francisco, to seeking support for an American colony along the Mosquito Coast of Central America. Evidently, Kinney also supported William Walker's Nicaragua enterprise not only with money and moral backing but also with his presence. He traveled to Nicaragua in 1854 to help establish a "new government" in the steaming tropics of Central America. Like hundreds of other Texans, however, he soon returned with little to show for his efforts except lost investments and a lingering fever. He had even purportedly been involved in fomenting revolts in northern Mexico. And he knew Juan Cortina and other Tejano leaders personally.

Kinney, a profiteer and a promoter of mostly failed ventures during the past decade, fit the description of a dreamer and a designer of empires. Called by one contemporary a "Texan Daniel Boone," he was "an extraordinary man . . . [who probably knew] more of the Mexican character than any one" north of the Rio Grande. By some accounts, he came to own more than five hundred thousand acres of land below the Nueces. He was also a man of extraordinary energy, vision, and imagination—just the type to believe in Houston's idea of a protectorate. Perhaps for the latter reason alone Cass never seriously considered Kinney for an appointment to Mexico City.[43]

Houston was growing ever more impatient with the entire situation, increasingly frustrated and even agitated by the Buchanan administration's glacial-like pace on the great issue of Mexico. Houston's hopes had been raised, albeit briefly, by the news of a negotiated agreement between the United States and Mexico known as the McLane-Ocampo Treaty. Signed in Veracruz on December 14, 1859, by Minister Robert McLane and Minister Melchor Ocampo, representing the fledgling liberal government of Benito Juárez, the pending agreement was more than generous to the United States. First it proposed that for just $4 million, the United States could obtain commercial access to northern Mexico for ninety-nine years. Of that sum, $2 million would be set aside to compensate citizens of the United States—many being Texans—who held damage claims against Mexico. Moreover, by this arrangement U.S. goods could be shipped duty free to and from Mexico. In addition to exclusive rights to "develop" the border states with the construction of railroads, the building of textile factories, the establishment of agricultural "enterprises," and other presumed future investments by willing American entrepreneurs, the treaty also allowed the United States to dispatch troops across the border to maintain order and "protect" U.S. "interests" south of the Rio Grande. Obviously, pursuant to the Monroe Doctrine, the agreement was designed to promote and protect American investments by discouraging, if not prohibiting, any further French and British economic expansion within Mexico. President Buchanan submitted this treaty of "transit and commerce" to a divided U.S. Senate on January 4, 1860. Owing to opposition from the northern states, however, the arrangement was doomed even before the formal debate had begun.[44]

Knowing the views of his old colleagues in the Senate, the same men who had soundly rejected the protectorate just two years earlier and now were consumed in the firestorm over slavery and states' rights, Houston now held out little faith that the treaty would ever be ratified. As it turned out, he was right. While the Senate Committee on Foreign Relations delayed and debated, President Buchanan and his secretary of state patiently waited on word of the doomed treaty's fate.

Undeterred, Houston laid the groundwork for his increasingly elaborate plan. By all indications, the governor had no intention of turning back now. On February 13, he dashed off a short note to his confidant Ben McCulloch, the famed Ranger captain and commander of Texas spy companies during the Mexican War. Whether by coincidence or by design, the Texas border fighter was back east "on business." "There will be stirring times on the Rio Grande ere long," Houston predicted. "What are you doing? See the President and Secretary of War," he urged McCulloch.[45]

That same day, nearly two years to the day since he had first formally proposed the protectorate to the U.S. Senate, Houston issued an ominous warning to Secretary of War Floyd in two dispatches, hand delivered by General Forbes Britton of Corpus Christi, the newly appointed assistant adjutant general of the state of Texas. The second came in the form of an urgent telegram; in it Houston reminded Secretary Floyd of the prevailing responsibility of the federal government to protect the border with Mexico. Houston noted, "if matters new and startling arise, he [the governor of Texas] may feel that it is his duty . . . to meet the emergency in carrying his action so far as not only to repel the aggressions from Mexico, but to adopt such measures as will prevent the recurrence of similar inroads upon our frontier." Then he stated bluntly, "Texas can and will if appealed to, in thirty days be able to muster in the field ten thousand men who are anxious . . . to make reclamations upon Mexico for all her wrongs. Can we hope for aid from the Federal Government?" In closing his brief summary of the outrages and depredations along the border, Houston further cautioned, "[U]nless prompt measures are adopted by the Federal Government circumstances will impel a course on the part of Texas, which she desires to avoid. Texas cannot be invaded with impunity," he defiantly warned. Thus in a few well-placed phrases, Houston unmistakably threatened an invasion of Mexico, with or without the support of the Buchanan administration.[46]

In turn, General Green alerted Secretary of State Cass that he was convinced Houston was not bluffing. "The Governor wants the means to organize one Regiment," he wrote. "I am induced to believe that if authorized . . . he will soon be at the head of four or five [regiments] and that once on the Rio Grande with such a force, with Mexico and the 'Protectorate' before him he will not wait for 'instructions' to cross the River."[47]

Green believed that Houston had even greater ambitions in mind. "All that prevents Governor Houston from moving on Mexico with a large force is money, and a justifiable pretext," he asserted. "He sees a Protectorate in Mexico *in presenti*," Green claimed, "and the presidency of the U.S. *in futuro*." Finally, as evidence, Green reported that Texas secretary of state Eber W. Cave had personally boasted to him that "if Houston did move on Mexico he not only would carry Texas & the South" in the upcoming presidential election but also would make the protectorate "the controlling issue" in the national campaign.[48]

Although the 1860 presidential race never seemed far from his mind, Houston was concerning himself with a campaign of a different sort, one that involved the procurement of firearms and bullets rather than ballots and electoral votes. Never timid in his approach to military matters, Houston wrote a reluctant President Buchanan and Secretary of War Floyd on March 8, offering five thousand Texas volunteers for a campaign in Mexico. "Texas is ready for the emergency," he boasted, "and will act at a moment's warning." But to repel the "invasion" from Mexico, he insisted that state volunteers first needed modern arms and lots of them. Specifically, he requested two thousand percussion rifles, one thousand Sharps rifles, three thousand Colt revolvers, and "cavalry accouterments" for a thousand Mounted Rangers. Calling Texas "deficient in arms," Houston pleaded that "danger is upon her now, and she needs them at once."[49]

Four days later, in what appeared to be an act of near desperation, Houston directed Texas secretary of state Cave to solicit an arms deal with manufacturer

Eli Whitney, Jr., of New Haven, Connecticut, son of the famed inventor. Having no funds in the state treasury for the purchase of weapons, Cave proposed on Houston's behalf the swap of five hundred outdated Pennsylvania flintlock muskets, said to be in "good order" but collecting dust in the state armory in Austin, for an in-kind shipment of newly manufactured rifles and revolvers. Incredibly, in order to make the offer attractive, Cave suggested that once Texans used these firearms in war the guns would "come in general use" and thus Whitney's reputation and, more importantly, his business orders would grow accordingly.[50]

Not surprisingly, Whitney refused the offer. Houston then sought out yet another source of support in his quest to raise both men and arms. On February 29, 1860, he lamented in a confidential letter to wealthy East Texas cotton planter Elkanah Greer that "the State is Bankrupt, so I have neither money, arms, or munitions." Angry that the state legislature departed Austin "without leaving me a dollar," Houston hinted that patriotic men of means could come to the aid of their beleaguered state. This plea, he acknowledged, came despite the fact that "the want of grain as well as grass, on the route to the Rio Grande, would render the advance of a force at this time, impracticable."[51]

One elusive fact makes this fragment of evidence all the more remarkable, especially in light of Houston's known, pro-Union stance. Elkanah Greer held the position of grand commander of a secret, mystical, fraternal order known as the Knights of the Golden Circle (also called KGCs). Dedicated not only to the preservation of the "Peculiar Institution" of slavery but also to the extension of the "great golden circle" of cotton and slaves from the Caribbean islands to the Yucatán and beyond, the Knights boasted of local chapters, or "castles," in every sizeable town in Texas. Like their counterparts in other southern states, the members of this mysterious organization advocated white supremacist doctrines as well as southern nationalism. By February 1860, the most fanatical of them already openly favored secession from the Union. In their zeal to advance the cause of an independent Confederacy, they even vowed to seek the annexation of Mexico by the United States, by diplomacy if possible, military conquest if necessary.[52]

Ben McCulloch, known to be supportive of this clandestine movement and its aims, probably summarized best the enthusiasm that the rank-and-file members of the Knights of the Golden Circle held for the Mexico venture. Writing to his mother on February 26, 1860, he admitted that he was hurrying home to Texas from the nation's capital "as there is trouble brewing on her frontiers & I wish to participate in any war." He confessed that "General Houston" had predicted a "stirring time" on the border, and thus the opportunity for national glory and personal gain awaited him. "This looks like war," McCulloch concluded with excitement.[53]

While McCulloch made no mention of the coveted spoils of war as a motive for the planned invasion, at least one contemporary did. Youthful James Pike, who had served in the Comanche campaign the previous year, recalled that in the early spring of 1860 a certain Captain Davis sought him out at Fort Belknap near the waters of the upper Brazos. "He informed us that he was a member of the Knights of the Golden Circle," Pike remembered, "and that he was fully authorized to receive and initiate men into the order . . . and that when fully initiated, the mysteries and objects of the institution would be explained; that some of the objects must be kept secret." There was an exception, Pike said, that "he could reveal; it was the intention to raise a force of twelve thousand men to invade Mexico, under command of General Sam Houston." The mysterious captain claimed that the movement was financially backed by "English capitalists," and he offered Pike $18 a month to enlist as a private, with the promise of rapid promotion. According to Pike, the brash captain promised that the "great estates" of Mexico, "immense tracts" of land, and many silver mines in Sonora would also be their reward. "Houston was not publicly taking part in the matter, for State reasons," the self-styled captain continued, "but that, in a short time, he would throw off all concealment, and declare his purpose to the world." The man named Davis, a "ready talker" in Pike's words, went on to report that the governor would be paid a "fabulous sum for accomplishing the work," but that there would be plenty of riches for all to share. In sum, the KGC enticed many a young volunteer Ranger with adventure, fame, and as Pike stated "the wealth of an Astor or a Vanderbilt."[54]

Pike admitted that he might have joined in the crusade but for one thing. He was convinced that the organization and its goals were the handiwork of a handful of wealthy and influential planters and merchants. Moreover, he believed that these leaders bought their way into the highest degrees of the society's organization, where decisions were made and plans were hatched. "This was the feature to which I objected," he later confessed. Besides, "I could never take an oath to do an act the nature of which I knew nothing;

nor could I swear to obey irresponsible men, who proposed to do anything unlawful. If the object was legitimate, it occurred to me, why this secrecy?"[55]

No known evidence exists to confirm that the enigmatic captain who approached Pike that spring was Henry Clay Davis of Rio Grande City. But one obscure letter suggests that it might have been the same colorful border ranchero from Starr County who had been traveling through Texas on a recruiting trip. On July 12, 1860, Governor Houston instructed Texas secretary of state Cave to offer Clay Davis a military appointment at the rank of brigadier general in a state militia force soon to be organized. The governor also expressed regret that Davis had not visited him during his recent stay in Austin. Houston asked him to stop by the Governor's Mansion the next time he passed through, then concluded, "I hope [you] will assume, and perform the duties of the station" as commander of state volunteers.[56]

Not all young Texas farm boys and frontiersmen of that generation were as skeptical and suspicious of seductive strangers as James Pike was. That was exactly what General Green and Secretary Cass feared most—thousands of impressionable young Texans led by a few manipulative men of malevolent ambitions and mercenary designs. Fortune-seeking men, they dreaded, poised to unleash an entire legion of well-armed and angry conquerors upon the nation they loved to hate, all in the name of manifest destiny, mission, and patriotism.

At the head of such an army of adventurers, Green believed, would surely ride the Hero of San Jacinto, the favorite protégé of Old Hickory who later laid claim to being the heir to Jackson's legacy and now longed for the presidency and an even higher place in history. During his return trip to Washington on February 20, 1860, Green summarized his concerns that British creditors, already impatient of Mexico's inability to meet its debts, might finance a Texan filibustering expedition and that Houston stood ready to oblige them. "You are well acquainted with General Houston," he wrote Cass. "You know that altho [*sic*] as mysterious as a Delphic Oracle, he is nevertheless vain, excessively vain, and may be led to talk on the subject that has become the *leading idea*. His Ambition is now divided between the Presidency of the United States and the 'Mexican Protectorate.'" Green strongly suspected that the aging colossus of Texas saw this moment as his last opportunity to etch his name in the U.S. pantheon of heroes, alongside those of Washington and Jackson.[57]

For weeks, Green had implied in his communications that the United States needed a more able military commander along the border with Mexico and that perhaps only an officer of great stature and experience could calm the present crisis and capture the "bandit" named Cortina. As fate and Secretary of War Floyd would have it, within days of Green's departure such a soldier of distinction would arrive on the scene to relieve General Twiggs and assume command of the sprawling Eighth Military Department of Texas. Secretary Floyd assured Houston on February 28, 1860, that the new commander was "an officer of great discretion and ability." His name was Robert E. Lee.

8
The Colonel

On the morning of February 10, 1860, Colonel Robert E. Lee pulled on his best field boots, straightened his blue uniform coat, and hastily checked his baggage in preparation for a two thousand–mile journey. Then he bid an emotional goodbye to his dearest Mary and to the warmth and comforts of Arlington House. As his carriage bumped across the bridge extending over the broad Potomac for the short ride to the nation's capital, perhaps he glanced back one last time at the columned mansion resting majestically atop the Virginia hills. Maybe he wondered how many more rivers he would have to cross before he could return to the peaceful slopes of Arlington, with its shaded gardens and spreading oaks. For there, overlooking the bustling city of Washington, he could always find a measure of personal peace. Leaving his wife, his home, his beloved state of Virginia, indeed leaving behind all that he loved most in this world must have been especially painful. But duty, and perhaps destiny, called.[1]

Being, above all else, a soldier devoted to the service of his country, and thus to the Union, Lee understood that summons. He fully understood that soldiers make sacrifices, sometimes sacrifices that seem more than anyone should have to bear. In his long distinguished career as an officer in the U.S. Army, he had served faithfully in many assignments, in war and in peace. From his days as a cadet at West Point to his early years as a junior officer in the U.S. Army Corps of Engineers; to the killing fields of Mexico; and back to the honored halls of the U.S. Military Academy, where he served as superintendent (1852 to 1855); on to the remote borderlands of West Texas, where he had been stationed with the Second U.S. Cavalry for two years, he had already seen more than most men might in several lifetimes. But on this dreary February day, as he looked back at the imposing Greek revival mansion perched on the hill, he may have been struck by an ominous sense of foreboding. Dark clouds appeared to be gathering over Washington City, over northern Virginia, indeed over the entire nation as Lee prepared to board a steamboat that would carry him first to New Orleans, then on to Texas.[2]

Less than four months had passed since Lee had left home to suppress the insurrection that had awakened first the slumbering Virginia village of

Harpers Ferry, then all of the American nation. Lee and two companies of U.S. Marines had surrounded the locomotive roundhouse where radical abolitionist John Brown had struck like a lightning bolt. Brown failed in his attempt to spark an armed slave uprising intended to spread and consume the entire southern countryside. Lee captured Brown, who he characterized as a "fanatic" and a "madman," and delivered him to authorities. Sixty-eight days had passed since Brown had announced that he was prepared to die for "God's eternal truth," just before he was led to the gallows and hanged at nearby Charlestown, Virginia, for treason and murder.

Following the Brown capture, Lee had been on leave from duty, a leave now being interrupted, once again, by insurrection, this time along the distant Rio Grande. By dispatching Colonel Lee to this remote border where he was to assume command of the Military Department of Texas, the president and secretary of war had good reason to be confident that the most accomplished officer in all the army could put down one more rebellion and bring to justice the man named Juan Cortina. After all, the distinguished-looking dark-haired and mustached Colonel Lee, the quintessential soldier and southern gentleman, had never failed in any mission. Surely, if he could not apprehend or kill the Red Robber, no one could.[3]

For the next fourteen months, as Colonel Lee completed his third tour in Texas, he could only read about the gathering storm back East and pray that the nation, and the state he loved, would be spared more bloodshed, the likes of which he had seen firsthand at Harpers Ferry. He could only leave to Providence his own destiny and that of his divided country. He could write to Mary of his enduring affection for her as well as for their three daughters and three sons. He could contemplate the unthinkable—that soon he might be faced with a terrible choice, that of taking up the sword either against his blessed country or his beloved Virginia. He could ponder the solitude of Arlington House and so many summer evenings on the veranda, where he had enjoyed the gentle breezes that blew in from the Chesapeake. He could visualize those serene, winter nights by the hearth and the crackling warmth of the fire, and the joy of walking through sun-splashed meadows and furrowed fields of corn. He could imagine returning again to the joy of morning horseback rides with his children and those precious hours in the company of Mary, his dearest companion. And he could dream of hanging up his uniform, someday, retiring to Arlington, and spending the rest of his days farming.

Lee Arrives in Texas

On February 17, 1860, Lee's steamer arrived at the port of Indianola on Matagorda Bay, where the colonel met a sixty-five-year-old former Tennessee congressman turned railroad investor named Pryor L. Lea. By all appearances, Lea, a longtime Houston ally sympathetic to the Knights of the Golden Circle, sought out the colonel to determine whether he might endorse, even openly support, the governor's scheme to annex Mexico. No record has survived of his conversations with the Virginian, but Lea accompanied the colonel as far as the village of Victoria, where he introduced his younger brother, fifty-one-year-old Albert Miller Lea, to Lee. Reportedly a leading spokesman of the KGCs in Texas, A. M. Lea had served briefly as U.S. secretary of war under President Millard Fillmore. An entrepreneur with an interest in building railroads, not only across the prairies of South Texas but also through the border states of Mexico, he surely sized up Lee as a possible military leader for the Mexico enterprise.[4]

The brothers could not have been more favorably taken with Colonel Lee. As A. M. Lea reported to Governor Houston the following week, "[M]y brother was greatly impressed with his whole bearing." He assured Houston that "you will find that I have not painted an imaginary character. If you invite him to a conference about the defense of the frontier, you will find true all I have said of his manners and ability." Calling Colonel Lee a "*Preaux* [*sic*] *chevalier, sans peur et sans reproche*," Lea cautioned that "he is very careful to do nothing that may cast a slur upon his name. He would not touch any thing that he would consider vulgar filibustering; but he is not without ambition, and *under the sanction of Govt.* he might be more than willing to aid you to pacificate [*sic*] Mexico." Then Lea predicted, "[I]f the people of the U. States should recall you [Houston] from the 'Halls of Montezuma' to the 'White House' at Washington, you will find him well fitted to carry out your great idea of a Protectorate. He is well informed in matters of state, honest, modest, brave and skillful."[5]

Indeed, Robert E. Lee was all those things and more. But he was not a schemer, not a man given to machinations, not Houston's or anyone else's. After being properly circumspect in his discussions with Lea, Colonel Lee headed overland by carriage to San Antonio, arriving on February 19. The next day he arranged for modest quarters on the Military Plaza, then took command of the Military Department of Texas. Soon after assuming his new post, he received three letters from A. M. Lea, although he was too busy to respond until March 1. When he did find time to reply, he was courteous and even complimentary but nevertheless evasive and noncommittal. "I feel that I owe to your kindness rather than to my merit your recommendations to Governor Houston," he began. "I am aware of his ability, and first became acquainted with him upon my entrance into the Military Academy. He was president of the Board of Visitors that year and the impression he made has never been effaced. I have followed with interest his career since," Lee continued, "and have admired his manly qualities and conservative principles. His last position in favor of the Constitution and Union elicits my cordial approbation." But the colonel concluded, "[S]hould military force be required to quiet our Mexican frontier, I have no doubt that arrangements will be made to maintain the rights and peace of Texas, and I hope in conformity with the Constitution and laws of the country. It will give me great pleasure to do all in my power to support both."[6]

Colonel Lee refused to lend his good name to any plot to conquer the Republic of Mexico. Lea, in a subsequent letter to the governor, made it clear that he understood that fact. "This letter from Colonel Lee arrived only last night. Although it is plain from his allusion to the 'Constitution and the Laws' that he wd. [*sic*] not participate in any movement upon Mexico not properly sanctioned by the Government, yet his expressions toward yourself are so justly complimentary that I thot [*sic*] you wd. be glad to see them, coming as they do from a man of high intelligence and sincerity."[7]

Most of Lee's energies in the coming days would be justly devoted not to Houston's obsession with Mexico but to the defense of the far-flung frontier from marauding bands of Indians. For Lee seemed to believe that the fierce Comanche were a greater threat to Texas than "that myth Cortinas [*sic*]," as he first called his adversary on the border. By all indications, after meeting with General Twiggs and others, he drew the preliminary conclusion that the accounts of Cortina's banditry along the border, while disturbing, were most likely exaggerated and thus of lesser importance than the "Indian problem." Still, Lee appeared unwilling to dismiss the troubles on the Rio Grande. In writing his son Custis on March 13, he assumed that Cortina remained on the run and in hiding, yet "there are so many contradictory reports that I think it better to see for myself, that I may if possible give quiet there and rest to the authorities in Washington."[8]

Two days later, before leaving for the border, Lee wrote the adjutant general, Colonel Samuel Cooper, that he had already determined it would be unwise to dedicate more troops to the outposts on the Rio Grande. What he termed the "bold and constant depredations" of the Comanche and the Kiowa along the line of settlement in North Texas would not allow him to retrieve those garrisons on the upper Brazos and Trinity for reassignment along the Mexican border. Just as important, only the acquisition of fresh mounts would allow for the redeployment of forces to South Texas, and he did not have the appropriation or the time to accomplish that. Simply put, the horses and mules available at the "northern" posts were poor, worn down, and underfed after a winter of privation. And the animals would not have good forage on the prairies of South Texas for several more weeks, perhaps not even then. More complicated still, reinforcements from frontier posts in Colorado and Kansas would take several months to arrive. Besides, the need to protect the Colorado miners' frontier from the marauding Cheyenne and the recent conflict over slavery on the Central Plains prevented any serious consideration of withdrawing units from those lines of defense.[9]

Despite such realities, Lee departed San Antonio on March 16 and, accompanied by a single company of the Second U.S. Cavalry under Captain Albert Gallatin Brackett, he struck off for Fort Duncan. From there on March 20, he reported to Colonel Cooper that there seemed to be "no truth" to the rumor that Cortina posed an ongoing threat, at least to the immediate area. He stated that "everything in this section of the country is quiet, and the usual intercourse and commerce between Mexico and the United States is uninterrupted." Then he informed Cooper, "I shall therefore proceed down the Rio Grande to Laredo, and if affairs in that quarter are quiet, will continue to Ringgold Barracks." After making the 120-mile march from Eagle Pass to Laredo in just four days, he noted on March 24 that along the route he "found all alarms about Cortinas [*sic*] . . . false." Reporting only a minor skirmish with marauding Indians along the way, Lee admitted that he was beginning to suspect that the stories of bandit brigades and murdering Mexicans were "all flam and clap trap."[10]

A few days earlier, while en route from San Antonio to the border, Lee received news that would do little to cause him to reconsider his initial assumption that the "Cortina affair" had been exaggerated, if not completely fabricated by Texan filibusters who demanded more federal troops and stood determined to provoke another war with Mexico.

Ford and Stoneman in Mexico

From a report sent by Heintzelman, Lee learned that after patrolling the Texas side of river and reconnoitering the region between Rio Grande City and Brownsville for several weeks without incident, Stoneman and Ford had crossed the river again, but this time with specific orders to do so from Major Heintzelman. In recent days, spies had convinced Stoneman and Ford that Cortina and a personal bodyguard of at least forty men were hiding at a rancho just a few miles south of the border. So had a communication from General Guadalupe Garcia, a Mexican separatist long aligned with General Carvajal who commanded the rural police known as the "line of the Bravo." But Ford, distrusting both Garcia and Carvajal, questioned their motives and their information. More specifically, he suspected that their plea for Heintzelman to order U.S. forces across the river was nothing more than "bait thrown out to get us into trouble." His better instincts told him that something was not right.[11]

Although he had misgivings about dubious reports of Cortina's whereabouts, of General Garcia's promise of support, and of Stoneman's reassurance that Heintzelman had authorized their crossing, Ford reluctantly agreed to accompany federal troopers on a daring night raid south of the river. He had another reason to dread this particular operation. He was still recuperating from an accident nearly a month earlier, when his horse had fallen and rolled over on him during skirmish drills, breaking some of Ford's ribs. Four weeks after the fall, he was still in pain and coughing up blood, a fact that could not have gone unnoticed as he prepared his men to swim their horses across the Rio Bravo.[12]

As events transpired that foggy night of March 17, Ford's suspicions and fears turned out to be well founded. After supervising in the dark the "excavation" of a narrow trench on the north bank of the river, Stoneman directed first Ford's scouts, then his own regular cavalry to follow single file and descend into the waters of the Rio Grande. By 3:00 A.M., the Rangers and both companies of regulars had crossed safely to Mexican soil. Once established on the south bank, the captains agreed to send a skirmishing party of Rangers to the front. Ford handpicked the "self-possessed and fearless" Dan Givens and several other "old and tried" warriors to lead the way to La Mesa, no more than three miles south of the river. Givens not only spoke Spanish fluently but also had good instincts, and he was one of the most seasoned scouts in the Ranger service. Thus Ford and Stoneman took all necessary precautions to ensure that they would not ride unsuspectingly into an ambush.[13]

Their caution soon paid off. Not long after advancing toward the rancho La Mesa, Givens and company reported back to Ford that they had detected a Mexican force on the main rode leading to the suspected enemy stronghold. Even in the dim glow of the moonlight it was obvious that an ambush waited. Ford urged Stoneman to sweep southward through the chaparral and downriver more than a mile to avoid a trap; by doing so, they could also envelop the enemy position and maintain the element of surprise. Stoneman agreed. So in columns of twos, the Rangers kept to the regulars' right and, in so doing, stayed between Stoneman and the enemy. "When within a half mile of La Mesa," Ford remembered, "we saw a light off to our right." Not long thereafter, Ford ordered Lieutenant Mathew Nolan and his scouts forward to determine the disposition of the Mexicans. Soon he learned that those lights were the campfires of enemy sentries who had already fled into the thickets, no doubt to warn their comrades at La Mesa. "It was concluded to follow the picket," Ford recalled, "thus giving the enemy as little chance to get ready as possible." Wasting no time, he divided his company into two platoons and galloped forward at a "brisk" pace, again keeping to Stoneman's right flank. Before Ford had advanced to within sight of the rancho, however, he and his men heard a distant drum roll calling the Mexican garrison to arms. "All of us [now] expected a fight," Ford recalled.[14]

A scene of much confusion followed. While Ford led one Ranger platoon ahead to press the fight, the other moved in the wrong direction and got lost in the darkness. At the same time, Stoneman advanced to the left to initiate the attack, and according to Ford, "the firing began about the same time on both sides." As the Mounted Rangers and Stoneman's cavalry approached the ranch compound, Mexican guards returned fire for several minutes before dropping their weapons and scattering into nearby houses. The Americans dismounted, rushed the cluster of clapboard buildings, and broke into several dwellings. At once, they began dragging men from the cabins. Stoneman ordered his troops to collect the prisoners in one large well-lit house. But before the entire compound could be secured, a captured

Mexican officer suddenly pulled a concealed service revolver and fired at Stoneman from a distance of several yards. Missing his target, he scrambled into a dark doorway.[15]

Then the situation quickly turned tragic. A young Mexican woman emerged from the darkness and slammed the door behind the fleeing officer, presumably to protect him. Just then several of Ford's men leveled their guns and blasted away, shooting through the door and mortally wounding the woman. When her bleeding body was pulled from the house, according to Ford, "a rather exciting commotion arose." A captive, who claimed to be a colonel of the Mexican National Guard, was escorted to the area where dozens of prisoners were being detained. Yelling his protests, the officer demanded to speak to Ford. Obviously agitated that his garrison had been attacked without provocation and that he had been robbed of his sword and other valuables, he issued a string of profane threats in Spanish. If he and his men were not immediately released, he warned, the Americans would suffer death at the hands of the Mexican army.

Ford was neither amused nor impressed. Nor was one of his men. Before Ford could finish the interview one young Ranger interrupted the prisoner's hysterical tirade and blurted out: "we saw his feet sticking out from under a bed, and dragged him out." Ford calmly explained to the captured colonel that his own commander, General Garcia, had informed U.S. officials that Cortina was holed up at this rancho. When the Ranger captain then asked his prisoner what he was doing there and what he knew of the man named Cortina, he received only a defiant response.[16]

Soon after the firing stopped that morning Stoneman and Ford determined that, remarkably, they had suffered no casualties, although four of their horses had been fatally wounded. As for the enemy, they reported one Mexican soldier slightly wounded and one mule killed; Lieutenant Nolan confessed that in the confusion he had shot the animal, mistaking it for a man. The one human fatality resulting from the fight was the woman who had been mistakenly shot and died later that morning.

In acknowledgement of the regrettable shooting of an unarmed woman, Stoneman and Ford ordered their prisoners released and their arms and valuables restored. The Americans then retired a few hundred yards toward the river, where they rested and ate breakfast. In his memoir, Ford confessed that many of his own men, whom he termed "plundering rascals," looted the rancho of food and provisions. Moreover, he admitted that some of his

Rangers shoved, scrambled, and fought over several small loaves of bread. But apparently none of them argued over who was to blame for killing the woman. All things considered, the entire incident at La Mesa would be seen by Mexican officials as an outrage, and by U.S. authorities as an embarrassment. Once again, Texas volunteer Rangers had proved as reckless as they were brutal.[17]

Clear morning skies promised a beautiful warm day ahead as Ford and Stoneman established temporary camp near several wells not far from the river. While the Rangers were still relaxing and allowing their horses to forage, with the regulars resting nearby, Ford noticed Stoneman's cavalry suddenly leaping to their feet and hastily mounting up. The captain looked past the troopers into the brush and saw at least two hundred uniformed Mexicans fast approaching on horseback. "The Rangers were in the saddle quickly," Ford remembered.[18]

A solitary rider spurred his horse ahead and was allowed to advance alone to the American lines. The young Mexican officer reigned up and announced to Stoneman's bluecoats that he served as adjutant to a Colonel Vargas and that his commander demanded an audience with Ford. Already at the front of his men, Ford moved forward and informed the messenger that Captain Stoneman was the ranking officer of the expedition. "No, sir," the adjutant replied in precise English. "The colonel holds you responsible for all that has happened." After receiving a promise that both Ford and Stoneman would parley, the Mexican officer wheeled his mount and galloped back to the columns of Mexican cavalry. Tensions mounted, then moments later the rider returned with his commanding officer. A quiet fell over the field as men on both sides listened to the voices of their leaders.[19]

The young adjutant carefully translated the words of an indignant Colonel Vargas, who angrily demanded to know why U.S. forces had violated Mexican sovereignty and attacked the garrison at La Mesa. Then Vargas fired off what Ford termed a "long string of questions," among them queries regarding who authorized the Americans to cross the border and whether U.S. authorities were prepared to pay damages in recompense for their "outrageous" acts.

Ford responded with an indignation equal to that of his adversary. Through his interpreter, Lieutenant Dix, Old Rip explained that General Garcia had approved of their crossing. Then he unleashed his own litany of tough questions that allowed Vargas little room for obfuscation or evasion. Was Cortina at La Mesa, as had been reported on good authority?

Vargas allegedly admitted that Cortina was, or had been, although the colonel denied knowing Cortina's present whereabouts. Why had the Mexican officer not moved to arrest Cortina? Why had Mexican guardsmen laid an ambush for the Americans, rather than offer cooperation in apprehending the "bandit leader"? Why did their commander fail to hail the Americans, instead sounding the drum call to arms, apparently with hostile intent? And why did Vargas bring so many men with him for merely an interview, Ford growled?

Vargas then intimated that few of Ford's men would have been left alive if his force had been at La Mesa at the time of the attack. Visibly angered at the suggestion, Ford offered a deliberate stare and defiantly challenged, "I will make this proposition: I have two companies of Texas Rangers under my immediate command; you have several hundred men; I am ready and willing to fight it out here, at once. I will even request Captain Stoneman not to take part in the engagement." Vargas declined the challenge, and the captain snapped back, "Then, sir, you will please change your tone as to the probable results of a collision, or prepare to decide matters on the instant." Vargas had apparently met his match.[20]

As the meeting abruptly ended without further incident, Ford and Stoneman walked away convinced that the guerrilla force lying in the thickets near La Mesa was "composed of Cortina and his ruffians." They felt equally certain that Vargas and other Mexican military officials were not only cooperating with Cortina but also harboring and even aiding him. They believed, too, that Vargas had planned to ambush the Americans but "found our united force too strong . . . to venture an attack upon us."[21]

Although Vargas requested that the Americans remain encamped at La Mesa until he could confer with officials in Matamoros, the two U.S. officers refused to do so. As they reported the day after the incident, "[W]e shall remain on the Mexican side of the Rio Grande until the passage down of the steamer [*Ranchero*], or until our presence here is no longer required, unless we receive orders to the contrary."[22]

Stoneman and Ford not only agreed to remain on Mexican soil for the next four days but also led their expeditionary force more than forty miles into the interior, as far as Rancho Cayetano. Although it was rumored that Cortina had escaped again, and that he had made his way safely into the Burgos Mountains of Mexico, no one knew for sure. And if any people of the border knew, they were not talking, at least not to Ford or Stoneman. But that did not deter Captain Ford. Nor did it dissuade Captain Stoneman, the intelligent and resourceful New York native who had graduated from West Point in the famous class of 1846 and later served ably during the U.S.-Mexican War as the quartermaster of General Stephen Kearney's famed Mormon Battalion. Ford and Stoneman marched together from one rancho to another, with Ranger scouts and their hired Mexican spies apparently first "visiting" the inhabitants and "interviewing" them about any knowledge they might have of Cortina's disposition. According to Mexican officials, while doing so Ford's men helped themselves to fresh mounts and what food they could gather up. In several instances, they apparently took prisoners, interrogating them by methods of torture that Rangers had employed in the past. They even executed several captives, one an old bandit, referred to by Ford as "the Indian Faustino," who was captured and shot near the rancho La Bolsa. Another, a purported Cortina associate and alleged horse thief, Elijio Tagle, was gunned down in the chaparral while fleeing the Rancho Maygues.

It was there, upriver from Matamoros, that Ford claimed to have come upon Cortina's wife and his "favorite" daughter, who was apparently moved to tears at the imposing sight of the Mounted Rangers. The captain instructed his officers to ensure that none of the men molested or harmed them in any way. While he had no compunction or restraint about allowing his men to commit acts of vengeance against Cortina's followers, he also had no stomach for harming women. Old Rip was a soldier, not a murderer.[23]

On March 21, in accordance with orders received from Heintzelman, Ford and Stoneman crossed back into Texas and headed southward to Fort Brown, arriving there two days later on a blustery afternoon. Upon his return, Ford visited Heintzelman at his headquarters and issued a verbal report of the past week's events. In a separate meeting, Stoneman briefed the major on recent developments and promised to issue a full written account of the expedition. Based on the note that Heintzelman confided to his journal several days earlier, he probably expressed to Stoneman his private concerns about the Rangers' persistent tendency to act outside the law and the accepted conventions and articles of war. "I wish I could get instructions, so as to dispense with the Rangers," he scribbled in his diary. "Everything is going on well & I fear that they will spoil it." Heintzelman had already concluded that the Texas volunteers had overstayed their welcome.[24]

For several days, the last breath of winter blew over the valley of the lower Rio Grande. Night temperatures plummeted to near freezing as a late norther swept over the South Texas prairies on March 25. The skies grew darker, and rain fell intermittently for the next three days, swelling the muddy Bravo beyond its banks and turning it into a swift, churning brown current. Fallen tree limbs and scattered debris choked the arteries of the great river. Roads leading in all directions became clogged with mud, and surrounding fields were transformed into miles of boggy marshes. Little wonder that Heintzelman suspended military operations for the next three days, until the sun reappeared, the weather warmed, and the drenched earth began to dry.[25]

On the afternoon of March 28, 1860, Heintzelman commanded columns of bluecoats in an advance back upriver, this time with Captain Stoneman's troopers leading the way and Ford's Rangers bringing up the rear. The major noted that the first signs of spring had appeared across the landscape, as the grasses now grew lush and green, and wild flowers decorated the countryside. He admired the stunning beauty of purple verbenas in bloom as he looked out over the prairies. Marching up the river past rancho Rito Ebonal, Heintzelman could not help but notice that the glow of the sun, radiating through a cloudless sky, announced the changing of the seasons. It was a good omen. The long winter had passed.[26]

The next day, with dry roads before them, Heintzelman's command marched another eighteen miles and camped near San Rosario. They covered twenty-four miles the following day, pitching camp at a lagoon six miles outside the village of Edinburg. That evening, Heintzelman's worse suspicions about the Rangers were confirmed. Captain Stoneman visited the major in his tent and confided to him that during their most recent foray across the river, many of Ford's men, and even the captain himself, had wanted to march on Matamoros. As a nervous Major Heintzelman noted that night in his journal, "I had good reason to be uneasy when they were there." This time, Heintzelman was more convinced than ever, his regulars would lead the way and the Texans would follow safely behind them. Not the other way around.[27]

Rangers in Reynosa

On Sunday, April 1, Heintzelman moved out with a small escort and pushed on another eighteen miles past a point on the river opposite the Rancho Las Cuevas. The following morning, after an easy ride of three and a half hours, he arrived at Ringgold Barracks, where Colonel Lee awaited. Sitting on the steps of Lee's quarters, the major and his new commanding officer exchanged information. The colonel informed his subordinate that he had been ordered by higher authorities to end the matter soon, by whatever means at his disposal, and that if Mexican authorities did not "break up" Cortina's bands for him he was to "cross and do it." Lee also explained that he fully intended to communicate his determination to Mexican officials along the border. Either they would accept responsibility for the raiders enjoying refuge south of the Bravo, or they would suffer the consequences of a U.S. military incursion. Clearly, during the last ten days while riding along the border, the stoic colonel had stiffened in his resolve to bring in the "bandit chief," dead or alive. Intelligence gathered along the river had convinced Lee that—despite his initial skepticism—Cortina was indeed a menace who posed a continuing threat to the residents of the lower Rio Grande.[28]

Later that day, April 2, Lee sat in his spacious billet and drafted a stern letter to the governor of Tamaulipas, Andres Trevino, explaining that Lee held the governor and other Mexican officials personally accountable for the outrages committed by Cortina and his followers. "I have been instructed by the Secretary of War of the United States to notify the authorities of Mexico on the Rio Grande frontier that they must break up and disperse the bands of *banditti* which have . . . sought protection within Mexican territory." Lee warned Trevino and his subordinates to be "faithful" in the performance of their duties, to subdue and suppress the border bandits raiding with impunity into Texas and enjoying safe harbor south of the Bravo.[29]

The following morning, Lieutenant Charles William Thomas, Heintzelman's adjutant, galloped off to Camargo to deliver Colonel Lee's letter to Governor Trevino. Later that day, the courier returned to Ringgold Barracks with the distressing news that the local *alcalde* (mayor) had informed him that the governor was traveling and likely at Tampico, or perhaps Tula, and that the delivery of the dispatch by way of the Mexican mail might take at least six weeks.[30]

An impatient Colonel Lee had no intention of waiting for a response. Soon after breakfast on April 4, he greeted two additional companies of the Second U.S. Cavalry, one commanded by Captain Brackett, the other by Lieutenant Robert Nelson Eagle. Later that morning, Lee met with his officers and promised them that they would capture Cortina soon and return the border to normality. Apparently, the colonel, referred to by Heintzelman as "punctilious in Military matters," also addressed his concern about the unacceptable conduct of the Texan partisans. "The Rangers will be dispensed with," Heintzelman penned in his journal that evening.[31]

That very night, Captain Ford and his mounted irregulars would give both Lee and Heintzelman one more reason to disband the Texas companies. After learning from Hidalgo County sheriff Sixto Dominguez that at least seventeen of Cortina's armed bravos were hiding at the Mexican settlement of Reynosa Viejo (Old Reynosa), Ford led eighty-five Rangers to the Tobasco Ranch at a ford some thirty miles below Rio Grande City. Once there on the north bank, Old Rip counseled briefly with Stoneman, then spoke with the proprietor of the rancho, an amiable Francisco Garza, who confirmed that Reynosa Viejo was not only a known haven for Cortinistas but also a place of *mucho mala fama* (much infamy). At eight o'clock that evening, Captain Ford led his men across the river. While most of them crossed aboard a skiff with saddles, firearms, and light provisions, to save time the remainder swam their horses through the river currents to the south bank. Within two hours, Ford and company had remounted and were moving toward the lights of the neighboring settlement of Reynosa Viejo. While Stoneman's regular cavalry remained on the Texas side of the river, Ford's Rangers rode southward toward the village that had reportedly provided so many of Cortina's fighters.[32]

Ford's Rangers spent no more than five hours at Old Reynosa that night. Not surprisingly, two strikingly different accounts tell what happened there and at the town of San Antonio de Reynosa, also known as "New Reynosa," later that morning. In his memoir, Ford contended that his men treated the inhabitants of the little pueblo with "civility," suggesting that they even joined in a fandango that continued until dawn. He claimed that he "purchased" provisions that night from merchants willing to conduct business with the Texans. A Mexican government report issued thirteen years later, however, accused the Rangers of stealing goods, then locking some residents in sheds and barns, and preventing them from warning the people of San Antonio de Reynosa, five miles below, of the Rangers' presence.[33]

If the Rangers actually seized prisoners that night and detained them to prevent any warning to the people living downriver, their efforts obviously failed. When Ford's company moved down the trail after sunrise, word of their coming had already reached New Reynosa—and Ford knew it. So the captain had arranged for Stoneman and young Lieutenant Manning Kimmel of the Second U.S. Cavalry to be positioned on the Texas side, with Stoneman concealed in cane thickets at a bend in the river and Kimmel waiting nearby along a lagoon behind the town of Edinburg. Not far away, a company of Rangers also waited, listening for the sounds of gunfire across the river. Understandably, Ford felt confident that, in the event of trouble, reinforcements were not far away.[34]

Ford led his company toward Reynosa, of which he later wrote: "the place is not remarkable for many things, except rocky streets, stone houses, and a rather strong anti-American feeling." If Ford's men expected the people of Reynosa to be prepared for a fight, they were not disappointed. An estimated four hundred armed men, led by the local commandant, Juan Trevino, were positioned around the main plaza, many of them lining the tile rooftops of every building overlooking the square. Trevino's brother, Don Manuel, placed the only artillery piece in his arsenal—a one-pounder mounted atop a water cart—in the square facing the approaching Rangers. Sometime after 10:00 A.M., the column of sullen and surly looking Texans rode defiantly into the plaza, only to find that every door, window, and building top seemed to be bristling with the barrels of rifles and muskets—each trained down upon them.[35]

The Mounted Rangers entered the town along three different streets. A strange, tomblike silence hung over the scene; the only noises to pierce the tension were the clop of horse hoofs and the creaking of leather saddles. Once inside the town square, several Texans tossed Sharps rifles on the ground in hopes that one might discharge and thus initiate a battle. According to Ford, a few of his men even taunted the Mexicans by shouting, "[F]ire on us if you dare!"[36]

Fortunately, no one on either side was foolish enough to open fire and cause a bloodbath. According to Ford, however, Lieutenant Mathew Nolan came dangerously close to turning Reynosa into a battlefield. When ordered by Don Manuel Trevino to halt, or else the one-pounder would be discharged, Nolan supposedly told his adversary that, if he did fire the weapon, the Rangers would take it from him. One of Nolan's men, a land pirate identified only as "English Tom," asked for permission to kill Trevino, pointing out "he has two six-shooters and a gold watch." Before Nolan could order him to stand down, another Ranger reportedly bellowed, "[N]o, no, don't kill him. We can make him prisoner, carry him back to Texas, and sell him for $1,500." An incensed Don Manuel, who spoke

English, responded with a well-placed curse upon the Texans. But the moment passed without further incident.[37]

Still, the crisis was far from over. Even before the Rangers halted in front of the town *juzgado* (courthouse), several unarmed men emerged and requested that Captain Ford meet with members of the local *ayuntamiento* (town council) to discuss the situation. Accompanied by Captain John Littleton, Lieutenant John Dix, and the company surgeon, John T. Eldridge, Ford dismounted and walked into the local house of justice. As the four men entered the building, armed guards stopped Dr. Eldridge and demanded his Sharps rifle. According to Ford, the feisty physician snapped, "I won't give you my gun, but I will give you its contents."[38]

The negotiations that followed were marked by just as much rancor as the introductions had been. During the private discussions, with Dix acting as interpreter, Ford informed the chief magistrate of the council that he had come for Cortina and his men so that they could be taken back to Texas for trial. He also accused the leaders of the town of challenging the Texans, claiming that they would pay $30,000 to the Rangers if they could capture them and "run things as we did at Las Palmas and La Mesa."

Following the parley between Ford and officials of Reynosa, Don Juan Trevino escorted the column of Rangers to the river, where a ferry carried them back to the Texas side. As might be expected, different versions of this event were told. Ford characterized his exchange with Trevino as "friendly" and their parting amiable. By his account, before leaving Mexican soil he managed to gain the concession from members of the ayuntamiento that all "outlaws and refugees" in their jurisdiction would be "delivered to justice" to Texas authorities. But these officials apparently qualified that pledge, stating that any demands for extradition must first be approved by General Guadalupe Garcia, the regional commander headquartered in Matamoros. They did accept Ford's list of wanted criminals accused of committing outrages against citizens of Texas (Juan Cortina must have been at the top of that list). They also promised to make every effort to apprehend those named under indictment and even announced that two of the accused bandits had already been arrested and taken to Matamoros to stand trial.[39]

According to the official Mexican version, however, only rancor marked the meeting between Captain Ford and the town officials. Rather than leaving Reynosa on good terms, the Texans were "compelled to abandon the town and depart by the public ford, because they would not allow him [Ford] to cross elsewhere." Regardless of the exact circumstances surrounding the Rangers' abrupt departure from Reynosa on April 5, Ford and his men remained encamped near Edinburg for the next two days, with the companies of Stoneman and Kimmel in bivouac nearby. On the morning of April 7, shots were exchanged across the river, apparently with no injuries being reported by either side. Ford and Mexican authorities never agreed as to who fired first.[40]

But it mattered little. Only one casualty (a "slightly wounded" Mexican) was reported as a result of the standoff in Reynosa and the subsequent face-off across the river near Edinburg. In any case, Ford agreed with Stoneman and Kimmel to suspend the operations. Couriers had informed them that Colonel Lee was coming to take command, and thus regulars and Rangers alike stood down, at least for the present.[41]

Lee Takes Command

On the afternoon of April 7, Lee and Heintzelman arrived on the scene. Riding by carriage first to Stoneman's and Kimmel's camp several miles below Edinburg, they continued on to a site located beside the canebrakes about three miles above town. They were accompanied by an escort commanded by Captain Albert G. Brackett who, in Ford's words, "had seen service in Texas and had a good knowledge of Mexican character and . . . the Spanish language." By all indications, Lee, whom Heintzelman termed "an officer of prudence and discretion," wanted a complete assessment of the border situation before determining a proper course of action. He had already conferred with Major Heintzelman and other officers and now wanted to speak with the legendary Ranger captain. In sum, despite the fact that Heintzelman had flattered himself into believing that Lee relied heavily upon his experience and judgment, the truth was that Lee was not one to form judgments before the fact or to trust the counsel of any one man. He had heard enough advice and now wanted to see for himself.[42]

Learning of Lee's arrival, Captain Ford saddled up and rode more than a mile to the colonel's camp near the river. As the Ranger dismounted, Lee emerged from his campaign tent, walked over to the Texan, extended his hand in friendship, and invited him to supper. The two men had much to talk about. That evening, Lee requested a full briefing, which he no doubt received. The Texan not only detailed for his new commander the developments of recent weeks but also apprised him of his belief that Mexican authorities were in league with Cortina and his banditti. None of these so-called authorities across the river were to be trusted, Ford advised. At some point, Lee expressed concern about the well-being of Mexican civilians, and particularly as it related to the reports that Rangers were firing across the river, preventing the people of Reynosa from coming to its banks for water. Ford recalled that the colonel calmly admonished him about the manner in which he rode into Reynosa two days earlier. "You should have sent a courier to inform them who you were."[43]

The two men could hardly have been more different. Although both were southerners by breeding and belief, they seemed to have come from different worlds. The very thought of sending a dispatch ahead, forewarning his proclaimed enemies of his coming, would never have occurred to the rough-hewn, sometimes profane Texan. Military courtesies and diplomatic decorum mattered little to him. A seasoned plainsman and Indian fighter, he much preferred unconventional means and methods of accomplishing his objectives, military or otherwise. For him, expediency guided decisions in the field far more than did the customs and conventions of war. As for the West Point–trained Colonel Lee, he respected martial traditions and the refinements of the military arts. A student of history, he valued the lessons to be learned from examining past wars. Cultured, well educated, a consummate professional and a man of genteel upbringing, he was a scion of the Virginia aristocracy who valued proper etiquette and protocol.

The two men, however, shared the same code of conduct. And each seemed to hold a most genuine respect for the other. Ford recalled that "Lee's appearance was dignified without hauteur, grand without pride, and in keeping with the noble simplicity characterizing a true republican . . . [who] evinced an imperturbable self-possession, and a complete control of his passions. To approach him was to feel your self in the presence of a man of superior intellect," Ford reflected. The Texan also recognized in the Virginian "the capacity to accomplish great ends and the gift of controlling and leading men." In turn, Lee admired Ford's reputation for courage and candor. He recognized his personal charisma and his folksy demeanor. And the Virginian shared the Texan's penchant for discipline and, more important, his almost chivalrous sense of honor.[44]

After his meeting with Captain Ford on the evening of April 7, Colonel Lee dashed off a dispatch to the authorities of Reynosa. The letter was vintage

Lee—terse and to the point. To the town council he said, "I hereby notify you that you must break up and disperse the bands of *banditti* within your jurisdiction engaged in committing depredations upon the persons and property of American citizens." Lee stated, "I shall hold you responsible for the faithful performance of this plain duty on your part." Then in reference to the hostilities along the border, he warned, "[T]his state of things cannot longer exist, and must be put an end to."[45]

The following day, Lee received a response from Francisco Zepeda, president of the ayuntamiento of Reynosa. Zepeda's answer afforded the colonel only some measure of satisfaction, while at the same time raising concerns about the conduct of the partisans from Texas. Zepeda regretted the depredations of bandits from the south banks, who he termed "mere skulking vagabonds." He assured Lee that the people of the border town wished to enjoy "the most pleasant relations with a friendly people" across the river and pledged his full cooperation in apprehending any criminals infesting the town and vicinity. State authorities, he told Lee, had ordered local officials to "pursue, arrest, and punish any and every band of men" that the "fractious" Juan Cortina collected south of the Rio Bravo. At the same time, however, Zepeda complained bitterly about the "injurious prejudices" of the Texas volunteers. He accused Ford of an unwarranted "sudden invasion" of sovereign Mexican soil, "which he had no right to make." And he dismissed those accusations that his town was a nest of thieves as a "fabrication." He also alleged that during the past four days the Rangers had repeatedly fired across the river at unarmed Mexican civilians, using the customs house for target practice, wounding one guard there, and even slightly injuring a young man in the fields nearby. He concluded that his people lived in "continued fear" of the Rangers and that women and children, believing their lives to be in danger, could not even draw water from the river.[46]

Less than twenty-four hours after receiving Zepeda's letter, Lee ordered Ford to investigate the reports of Ranger misconduct. By all indications the Texan looked into the matter. Although no record exists of any volunteers being singled out or reprimanded for their behavior, Ford admitted that some of his men had been guilty of firing upon the south bank "contrary to his orders." At the same time, Lee cautioned Zepeda that he would not be patient but expected the town council to be "prompt and efficient" in their pursuit of Cortinistas said to be infesting their town.[47]

Lee did disapprove of the Rangers' reported insubordination and disorderly conduct, a fact that became apparent two days later. When Lee and his escort rode into Brownsville on the morning of April 11, he found a message and a messenger from the governor of Texas waiting for him. Representative George McKnight, a member of the Texas State Legislature from Rusk County and consummate politician known for his penchant for fine suits and stovepipe hats, had arrived days earlier and taken up temporary residence in the Miller Hotel. Like Houston, a native Tennessean, practicing attorney, and lifelong Democrat of the old Jacksonian mold, the portly McKnight carried a letter from the governor instructing him to confer with Colonel Lee about the border situation. Specifically, the governor's special agent was to inquire of Lee whether he wished to keep Ranger units in the field alongside regulars to patrol the Rio Grande border. If so, McKnight was to request that the U.S. government pay for their expenses, from payroll costs to the procurement of provisions. If not, McKnight was authorized to disband the volunteer units. According to Ford, word and even suspicion soon spread that Governor Houston had dispatched his friend and ally to South Texas not to solicit federal funds but "to keep the [Ranger] command from stealing," then to muster them out of service.[48]

Just hours after receiving McKnight's letter, Lee sat down in his quarters at Fort Brown and crafted a tactful response. Claiming that he had "no authority . . . to receive into the service of the United States any portion of volunteers," he informed McKnight that he could not retain the Rangers "on the conditions you propose." Then he wrote that Major Heintzelman and he agreed that the "present conditions of affairs" on the lower Rio Grande did not warrant the continuing presence of state partisans and that the federal troops already deployed along the border were "sufficient to preserve order." He concluded, "[T]he services then of the rangers may at this time be more important on the Indian . . . [frontier] than on this."[49]

Lee only hinted at his dissatisfaction with the performance of the Texas mounted volunteers in his report of April 11, 1860, to Adjutant General Cooper. From Fort Brown he reported, "I have . . . arrived here today, having descended the left bank of the Rio Grande from Eagle Pass. I found the frontier on the river quiet." Describing the Anglo and Mexican populace as "much embittered against each other," he intimated that the prospects for future violence remained high. "Most of the ranches on the river in Texas, between Rio Grande City and this place, have been abandoned or destroyed," he informed Cooper. "Those spared by Cortinas [*sic*] have been burned by the Texans."[50]

Lee gladly allowed McKnight to muster out the Ranger companies and remove them to Goliad on the lower San Antonio River, or anywhere else that Houston wanted to send them, as long as it was far from the Mexican border. Lee had apparently seen enough to convince him that the Texas Rangers were an impediment to improving conditions on the Rio Grande.

Governor Houston likewise seemed resigned to withdrawing the state volunteers from the Rio Grande and stationing them along the line of the Indian frontier. Yet, as always, even in the face of criticism he remained the Rangers' most faithful advocate and their greatest defender. In a letter to Secretary of War John B. Floyd on April 14, Houston explained first that, while regular troops were ineffective, even "useless" in defending western settlements from the marauding Comanche, the Mounted Rangers were "superior" in arms, tactics, and methods of warfare. Whereas U.S. infantry units provoked the ridicule of the native tribesmen, and the cavalry were little more than a "source of amusement" to the Plains Indian warriors, Houston claimed, the Rangers remained the only fighting force that had proven time and again to be up to the task. In a phrase, they were "the only class of troops fitted for such service."[51]

"They are excellent horsemen, accustomed to hardship," Houston wrote of *his* Rangers, "and the horses of Texas, having been raised on grass, can perform service without requiring grain to subsist them, except to recruit their strength for a few days when returned from a hard scout." Furthermore, "the Texans are acquainted with Indian habits, and also their mode of warfare. They are woodsmen and marksmen. They know where to find the haunts of the savage, and how to trail and make successful pursuit after them," he continued. "They, too, have their families, their kindred, and their neighbors to protect. They have the recollection of a thousand outrages, committed upon those dear to them . . . to impel them onward; and if, in the pursuit of the foe, they get out of rations, they can subsist on game, being dexterous hunters. What are privations, suffering, and danger to them?" he asked. "They are accustomed to the heat of the prairies, and the severe northers to which we are subject. They need no tents to shield their hardy frames from the night winds, but are content with the earth for a bed, and a blanket for a covering," he concluded. "Such a force as this, continually on the alert, will be a terror to the savage."[52]

No one ever offered a better summary of the reasons for the Rangers' success in border warfare, no one a more concise synopsis of the enduring Ranger mystique. And no one of the day provided a more vigorous defense of the rationale behind the deployment of state volunteers along the frontier. As in the past, Houston still preferred to rely upon the Rangers as opposed to federal regulars, who in his view resented their assignment defending the Texas frontier and did not possess the will, the wherewithal, nor the training to accomplish the task.

Lee remained unconvinced about the value of the Rangers in the field. From his headquarters at Fort Brown, he ventured into town each day to confer with various civil officials and his own staff about the conditions along the river. For him, the time in Brownsville proved less than satisfying. He confined himself mostly to exchanging letters with Mexican authorities in Matamoros and Reynosa, in each case reinforcing his determination to hold these leaders strictly accountable for the actions of Cortina's marauding bands. With every dispatch, he restated his demands that officials south of the border apprehend Cortina and his followers. Apparently, that was all that he could do.[53]

On April 16, in a private letter to his son Custis, Lee revealed his reason for not crossing the river and going after the elusive Red Robber, who had reportedly fled into the Burgos Mountains more than a hundred miles beyond the Bravo. "I do not like to enter a blind pursuit after a man so far in the interior with broken down horses," he explained. "If it was prairie or grass country in which horses could live, I would try him."[54]

Lee knew that the best mounts on the border belonged to the very Texas Rangers he wished to be rid of. As Heintzelman recorded in his journal on April 22, when he observed Ford's volunteers assembled alongside his regulars for inspection in the compound at Fort Brown, the Rangers sat atop "the finest horses ever seen in Texas." And these well-groomed, well-proportioned animals, as Houston had pointed out, could range far over desolate country, living only on what nature offered. The quartermaster had provided Lee's troops with inferior stock. The colonel had neither the appropriation nor the time to procure better mounts. The windswept plains of Tamaulipas, largely unknown to Lee, were fraught with uncertainty. He thus had good reason for his reluctance to venture into such a semi-arid region, knowing neither the location of Cortina nor the water and forage available for his horses, which were fatigued and in poor condition, especially after a hard winter.[55]

Thus frustrated by the constraints placed upon him by the elements and the Department of War, Lee waited at Fort Brown and prepared for a return trip to San Antonio. But the colonel stayed long enough to see the Rangers off. Late in April, when it became apparent that state troops were being withdrawn from the river, the citizens of Brownsville held a banquet and ball in honor of the departing Rangers. At this festive occasion, Colonel Lee, ever the proper gentleman and consummate diplomat, raised his glass and offered an appropriate toast in a subtle play on words. "To the men who could always find a 'ford' across the Rio Grande," he announced to the pleasure of the assembled crowd. When called upon to respond, Old Rip thanked the colonel for his support and offered his own toast to the preservation of the Union. It was a fitting sendoff for the Rangers, many of whom were ready to go home after a difficult winter campaign. No doubt, Lee was happy to accommodate them.[56]

Several days later, on May 1, 1860, as ordered by George McKnight, Captain Littleton's company left Brownsville for Goliad, there to be mustered out of service. Three days later, Captain Ford's company departed the border along the same trail northward beyond the Arroyo Hondo and across the windy, dusty plain known as the Wild Horse Desert. As for Ford, he did not ride out of Brownsville until May 7, when he, too, headed northward, accompanied by an old companion, Ranger John Ingram, and Dr. Charles Combe of Brownsville. That same day, Colonel Lee left Fort Brown with his personal escort riding alongside his ambulance. Ironically, on May 10 both Ford and Lee joined up with Major Heintzelman at Rancho Cavazos in northern Kenedy County, the sprawling estate of the fifty-one year-old landowner Sabas Cavazos, half brother of Juan Cortina. The next day, the entire party continued on, past Captain King's Rancho Santa Gertrudis to the tiny hamlet of Banquete, located nine miles south of San Patricio. After parting company with Captain Ford on the morning of May 13, Heintzelman and Lee pushed on to the banks of the Nueces, which the major described as only "knee deep to horses."[57]

While Lee and Heintzelman rode west along the road to San Antonio, arriving there in the early morning of May 17, Ford waited at Banquete for his company so that he could join them for the trip to Goliad. According to Ford, a humorous incident occurred en route to the historic village near the Presidio La Bahia. Apparently somewhere along the line of march, George McKnight's favorite stovepipe hat had disappeared or, more accurately, was stolen. That evening when the column halted to pitch camp, Lieutenant Howard produced the hat, which had been crushed almost beyond recognition. Howard apologized to the nattily attired politician and explained that someone must have sat on it. As Ford remembered, an irritated McKnight insisted on wearing the hat for the remainder of the trip, even though its accordion-like appearance evoked snickers from the Rangers. By the time the party reached Goliad, the article of ridicule had become, in Ford's words, "one of the most uncouth-looking objects a white man ever placed on his head." McKnight was probably the only member of the column who failed to see the levity of the situation.[58]

What happened when they arrived in Goliad, however, was no laughing matter. The portly McKnight, upon assembling the Rio Grande squadron for one final formation, refused the assistance of the Ranger officers. As he called the names on the company rolls, he requested that each man step forward one at a time and hand his firearms to an enlistee standing in front of a covered wagon. Then, without emotion, McKnight discharged the entire command without further ceremony. As Ford stated, scores of young Rangers then "bade each other good-bye—in many cases for the last time on this earth—and dispersed to many points of the compass."[59]

An Era Ends

It was not only the end of a campaign but also the end of an era. With the removal of the Rangers from the border, Lee's return to San Antonio, and Heintzelman's departure from Fort Brown, the Rio Grande war of 1859–1860—Cortina War, as it has been called—came to a close. Still the consequences of the conflict would endure long after the events of these tumultuous years. Juan Cortina, although hiding for several months in the shadows of the Burgos Mountains, returned to the lower Rio Grande before the year was out. Moving from one border town to another, he inspired the indigenous people of the border to believe they could liberate themselves from the land-hungry gringos who had dispossessed them. In every village on both sides of the river, crowds of poor and landless peons soon gathered again—in even greater numbers—to hear their champion vow to break their bonds of misery and oppression. For those who heard Cortina's cries for social justice, the voice of hope would echo in the valley for the next sixteen years and more. "*Viva Cheno Cortina*," they would shout. "*Mueran los gringos*!"[60]

By Heintzelman's account, some eighty-five individuals died in the violence of this border war and an estimated $330,000 in property had been destroyed or stolen. Moreover, these figures only took stock of the losses on the Texas side of the river. Worse still, the war was not really over. Anglo residents along the border understood that the smoldering conflict could erupt again at any time. Most Texans continued to seethe about what they considered to be Governor Houston's betrayal and abandonment of the region. Embittered in their belief that they were now left to the mercy of gun-wielding bandits and cattle rustlers, they remained uneasy about the removal of state Rangers from the river frontier.[61]

And they deeply resented the reduction, once again, of federal forces along the Rio Bravo. As Francis Hardman wrote in 1860, they "saw themselves, with no very patient feeling, under the rule of a people both morally and physically inferior to themselves. They looked with contempt . . . on the bigoted, idle, and ignorant Mexicans, while the difference of religion, and the interference of priests, served to increase the dislike between the Spanish and Anglo-American races."[62]

Of the Anglo principals who commanded troops in the border campaign, only Rip Ford remained a factor in the future development of the region known as "the Valley." Within two months. he would return to Brownsville, take up residence there, and enjoy the fruits of this land of sunshine, at least until the war clouds gathered again. Although his tenure as a commander of Mounted Rangers had ended after fourteen years of service to the state, his career as a soldier was far from over.

Major Heintzelman would not look upon the Rio Grande again for nine years. After resuming his command at the tiny outpost of Camp Verde, he ended his tour of duty in Texas before the year was out. As for the unflappable Colonel Lee, he would never returned to the Rio de las Palmas, although he had many more rivers to cross before he could hang up his sword and retire to private life. Failing to bring in "that myth" Cortina, he would only be able to write to his son Rooney about the one that got away. "I could not catch Cortinas [*sic*], which I very much regret, but drove him to the mountains and dispersed his party. I also gave the Mexican authorities to understand that if they permitted him to molest our frontier again, I should cross the river in force and they must take the consequences."[63]

Perhaps Lee never really understood the nature of the conflict along the lower Rio Grande. Surely, he underestimated both Juan Cortina and his cause. To the Mexican people on both sides of the serpentine river, Cortina had already become, rightly or wrongly, justifiably or not, a symbol of the larger cultural conflict that transcended the geographic and political border that separated the two nations. In the words of famed Texan folklorist J. Frank Dobie, the Red Robber was "the most striking, the most powerful, the most insolent, and the most daring as well as the most elusive bandit, not even excepting Pancho Villa, that ever wet his horse in the muddy waters of the Rio Bravo." Maybe Dobie also failed to understand that the downtrodden peasants of the Rio Grande Valley looked upon this mythic figure on horseback, no matter his faults and failings, not as a bandit but as a liberator, indeed a modern-day Robin Hood who defied the Texas devils and lived to tell about it.[64]

Cortina, the man and the legend, thus assumed a special place in the memory and imagination of the Mexican people of the border. His exploits and his legacy would live long after he was gone. So would his bold message to the conquerors from the North. The Texans could occupy the country of the Rio Bravo. They could fly their flag over it. They could even burn their brands into the cattle that ranged over it. But they could never conquer the irrepressible spirit of the proud people who worked the Rio Grande Valley. Like the winds that whispered across the prairies of South Texas, and like the river that ran through it, Juan Cortina's people belonged there. And they would always belong there.

9
The Rebels

The so-called Cortina War ended all too soon to suit the rawboned Ranger turned fortune seeker known as "Captain Ben." While visiting Washington, D.C., in February 1860, the restless adventurer with the familiar receding hairline, renowned for his daring exploits in the U.S.-Mexican War, received a personal audience with Secretary of War John B. Floyd. Although skeptical of the administration's position on frontier defense, Ben McCulloch accepted Floyd's assurances that President Buchanan had promised to dispatch more federal troops to the Rio Grande to protect the border from Mexican banditti and marauding Indians. On February 21, the legendary Ranger informed his old friend Governor Houston that he would "soon hear from the government." Then he affirmed, "I am at all times ready to serve Texas." Confident that the legislature in Austin would soon authorize a new regiment of state volunteers and that he would ride at the head of it, he wrote his mother, Frances McCulloch, five days later that he would soon be returning to Texas. "There is trouble brewing on her frontiers," he penned with excitement, "and I wish to participate in any war in which she may engage." Understating the growing discord over slavery and southern rights that foreshadowed a great national crisis, he observed, "[T]here seems to be a storm cloud on the horizon." He reminded his mother that she had taught her boys "never to refuse to serve your country when it becomes a duty." He assured her further that "no son of yours will ever disgrace himself on the battlefield." Even if he were to die in the defense of Texas, or in an invasion of Mexico, he "could not fall in a better cause." So he pleaded with her to understand that the time was fast approaching when he must "take his chance for glory or the grave."[1]

Not since his days as a commander of Texas scouts serving under General Zachary Taylor had the restive McCulloch been so determined to force a fight. At the same time, however, his recent letters home revealed not only a man consumed with the prospect of personal failure but also one faced with the specter of his own mortality. Hopelessly broke and in debt, he had reported to his mother the previous December, "I am making nothing and spending rapidly what I have. The time may soon come when I must commence to replenish my purse." In a haunting prophecy of national doom, he predicted, "[T]he union is gone and *civil war will follow*. May God prevent such a calamity from falling on my country. But if it does come," he continued, "I was born on the southern side and owe my allegiance to the South, and I will fight her battles no matter who may be her enemies." Four weeks later, on New Year's Day, 1860, he again lamented to his mother, "[W]e are . . . getting old. It seems but the other day when I was a mere youth, now almost fifty years old, I can hardly believe it other than in a dream. In fact life is but a dream after all when compared with eternity. Tis a grave thing to reflect on," he wrote in an almost morbid tone. "But none can live long . . . so we ought to live in this life so as to take the best chances in the future. . . . God is good. God is great," he pronounced as his mother had taught him to pray all those many years ago. "He far surpasses His creature man in all his attributes."[2]

Thus fatalistic and impatient, McCulloch was obviously a man in a hurry to make his mark upon the world—and to do so while he still had a little time, if not much money. Certain that fate would soon force him to take up arms in another great cause, he still hoped that his next call to service would be in a glorious crusade on the borders of Mexico, not in a war of southern independence against his own brethren in the North. He truly believed that, if a military enterprise along the Rio Grande came to fruition, he and other patriots could turn their guns on Mexico again instead of turning them on one another. Thus hoping to incite Houston to action, on March 4, 1860, McCulloch confided again to his mentor that the standing orders for U.S. regulars on the Rio Bravo were so restrictive, so constraining that "no officer (unless a very bad man) will cross the River in pursuit of the enemy." Pointedly, he reminded Houston that, while the U.S. Congress was debating another New Regiments Bill, which, if passed, would authorize several new units for frontier defense, including at least one in Texas, the Congress seemed unlikely to appropriate any funds to support these regiments. Such proposed units would thus exist on paper only. McCulloch believed that it would be left to Houston—or maybe to a commander of Houston's choosing—to lead a Texan army into Mexico and complete the task that had been left unfinished by the Treaty of Guadalupe Hidalgo.[3]

Like other leaders from the Lone Star State, McCulloch refused to acknowledge that Texans wanted to start *another* war with Mexico. Instead, he privately hoped and even publicly hinted that they simply wanted the opportunity to finish the last one. On February 29, the Dallas *Herald* quoted the Galveston *News* in announcing Houston's summons of the much-celebrated Ranger leader. "We understand that Major McCulloch has been telegraphed to return to the State. When we see the governor calling around him the military men of the State, and organizing the militia, it looks to us as if something of moment is threatening."[4]

A Spirit of Vigilantism

Indeed, what threatened was a general spirit of vigilantism, one sweeping over the entire state, including the border counties of South Texas. While rumors abounded that more federal troops were on their way to the Rio Grande, a military buildup of a different sort was under way. Already, hundreds of members of the Knights of the Golden Circle had assembled in Gonzales, the village on the Guadalupe long known as the "Lexington of Texas" (the first shots of the Texas Revolution were exchanged there). Elsewhere that March, in towns across South Texas, swelling numbers of armed citizens gathered to discuss the present state of affairs along the border. In San Antonio, a so-called citizens' committee made up of self-appointed avengers, most no doubt members of the KGC, held town meetings near the Main Plaza. As San Antonio resident Morgan Wolfe Merrick wrote of the Knights, they stood as a "military organization" that had been in existence in the city "for some time," a force that was "powerful and whose principle object was the acquisition of territory outside the United States." In Castroville and Corpus Christi, even in the hamlet of Banquete and elsewhere, men came from miles around to join local castles. Farther south, the streets and boarding houses of Brownsville also overflowed with brooding men who claimed affiliation with the KGC and whose avowed objective was the conquest of Mexico. In his last days on the border, Major Heintzelman expressed grave concern that several hundred of these border ruffians were "behaving badly," and he confided in his diary that nightly they were spilling into the cantinas of Matamoros. Worse still, he noted, these armed malcontents openly boasted that two thousand of their fellow Knights would soon join them on the Rio Grande. "They will give us trouble," Heintzelman grimly predicted.[5]

All across the Lone Star State that spring, the Knights held initiation ceremonies as elaborate as they were secretive. In the first degree, or military degree, they proclaimed their belief in the Bible, particularly the laws of Moses. They pronounced their unflinching faith in the "Anglo-Saxon race" and declared their allegiance to the South. They also swore to defend the institution of slavery and to promote the "objects and aims" of the society. Then they received the secret signs, passwords, handshake, and history of the organization. In the second degree of the rites, they recited the Lord's Prayer, then pledged their financial support for an incursion south of the Rio Bravo; in return, they received a promise of 960 acres of Mexican soil if they participated in a successful invasion or 320 acres for merely contributing money to the glorious cause. Only in the third degree, or political degree, were they entrusted with the highly sensitive information about the membership and makeup of the society's hierarchy. While learning more about the leadership of their movement, they also accepted a card with a crude code for deciphering messages of instructions from their commanders. Such words as "Mexico," "Rio Grande," "Matamoros," "Monterrey," and "Gulf of Mexico" left little doubt as to the intentions of this mystical fraternal order.[6]

The KGC's published initiation rites expressed clearly the purposes and goals of the organization. With virtually anyone able to obtain a printed copy of the ritual, the planned invasion of Mexico could have been said to be the worst kept secret in Texas. "Christian men ought to go to war," the text proclaimed. "Every step of our race has been marked by the bloody footprints of revolution." According to the scriptures of the Old Testament, the KGC pronounced, "[T]he most warlike nation of antiquity were God's chosen people—the Jews—and the Great Jehovah ordered the destruction of whole peoples, so that the enlightened Jew might go forth and possess their lands. The Anglo Saxon race has never found its equal in all walks of intelligence and virtue," the rites announced. Furthermore, "[I]t has never displaced a race equal to itself. . . . It gives peace and protection to every one, and plants a religion of which every *true* Christian may approve." The initiation proceedings also announced that the Knights sought "the development of this white race, and this people's empire. We would go forth with our country's institutions and civilization and subdue the mongrel races on our southern border." So in the name of Protestantism, patriotism, and personal profit (not necessarily in that order), Texans should carry the blessings of "liberty" and spread their "superior" Anglo-American ideals to the impoverished and oppressed peoples of Mexico.

The Knights proclaimed, therefore, that it was their manifest destiny to establish a "defensive colony" south of the Rio Bravo, then "spread out until the whole [of Mexico and Latin America] is Americanized and Southernized." After all, the ceremonial booklet proclaimed, "no greater calamity could befall the South than the planting of free soil colonies in Northern Mexico." According to the society's literature, a vast dominion of some 854,000 square miles awaited the American conquerors. Better yet, most of these sprawling lands were "admirably adapted to tillage or grazing." Then the official document declared, "[T]hese lands are within our reach, and the KGC should be at the vanguard of their acquisition." Finally, the pamphlet revealed the full extent of this ambitious enterprise, declaring that it was the Knights' "intention to cross the Rio Grande with four divisions of 4,000 men each." As for an instrument to further their ambitions, the Knights needed to look no further than the state volunteers known as Mounted Rangers.[7]

The membership of the Knights, and the moral as well as monetary support for their cause, extended all the way to the corridors of power in Washington, D.C. In the capital, Ben McCulloch was not alone in promoting Houston's grand design during the last weeks of the Cortina War. State senator Forbes Britton of Corpus Christi, recently commissioned by the Texas State Legislature a brigadier general and chief of staff to the governor, traveled to Washington City to hand deliver Houston's message of February 13 to Secretary Floyd. Upon his arrival on February 29, Britton met first with Floyd at the Department of War, then later that evening with President Buchanan at the White House. When asked by the president whether Houston intended an invasion of Mexico, Britton answered that federal authorities could render such a military action unnecessary by simply dispatching more federal regulars to defend the border. The Texan was disappointed to hear the commander in chief hedge on the subject, remarking that the Congress must take the lead by appropriating funds for an additional regiment for Texas defense. During the next three days, Britton intensified his lobbying efforts, canvasing members of the Congress and the president's cabinet. On March 3, he reported to Houston that, in one private meeting at the Department of War, he had pressed Floyd to explain whether he would order U.S. regulars to restrain Texas volunteers if they crossed the Rio Grande without expressed orders from Washington. An amused Floyd replied, "No, Sir, but I would stand upon this side and clap my hands & holler hurrah."[8]

Lemuel D. Evans, one of Houston's longtime allies from Harrison County in East Texas, was also visiting Washington City during this period. Not surprisingly, he joined the chorus favoring a U.S. protectorate over Mexico. Writing Houston on March 19, Evans speculated that Buchanan privately hoped that the governor of Texas would seize the initiative along the border and thus decide with brute force what diplomacy could not. In reference to Houston's well-chronicled popularity among female socialites in the nation's capital, Evans commented that the governor's "lady friends" in Washington longed to see the Hero of San Jacinto "make a grand *coup de main* . . . upon the Rio Grande immediately."[9]

Back in Texas, hardly a day passed that Houston did not receive at least one unsolicited letter advising him to launch an invasion of Mexico. On March 1, T. T. Gammage of Cherokee County, Texas, urged the governor to "bestow that vengeance upon the Border Mexicans . . . that they so richly deserve." To assist in this war of reprisal, Gammage even offered a minute company of men "with as brave hearts and strong arms as any in the state." One week later, twenty-six-year-old George F. Walker of Galveston likewise informed the governor that he could easily organize a force "for the purpose of chastizing [*sic*] Mexico." While stating that he had no personal ambition to rule the fertile regions of Mexico, he admitted that his motives emanated from "a long and deep seated hatred as well as a desire to avenge the murder of a friend and relative." William Robertson Henry, former Ranger and notorious filibuster of Nicaragua fame, wrote from San Antonio on March 15 that he would proudly join in an expedition across the Rio Bravo. A man given to histrionics, he went so far as to compare Houston, himself, and other Texan patriots to the legendary King Leonidas and his Spartan warriors, who had fought valiantly to the death at the pass of Thermopylae some 2,300 years earlier.[10]

As could have been expected, southerners were the most eager to lead the charge in the Mexico venture. On March 6, F. G. Nicholson of Mississippi summarized the sentiments of many when he informed Houston, "I glory in your cause, and you will find many others who deeply sympathize with Texas. If you raise an army to march into Mexico," he wrote, "I would like to have the honor to belong to your command." Of Mexico, he opined, "[S]he should belong to the United States, and he who is the chief instrument of our attaining her will confer a great blessing upon *both* Mexico and the Southern states." Four days later, writing from Lynchburg, Virginia,

Thomas Sears and Charles Browning concurred: "[W]e are ready to enlist under your patriotic banner which has never known defeat nor been tarnished by dishonor." In offering their services to Houston in a letter dated March 14, John Stubbs, John Patton, and several other aspiring filibusters from Macon, Georgia, also typified the passion that southerners held for "carrying the war into the heart of Mexico." Ten days later, Mississippian Wiley Morgan, Jr., wrote less eloquently, "I offer you my company to fight those dam [*sic*] Mexicans if you except [*sic*] my services. . . . Please write to me so my expenses are paid. That's all I care for." From throughout the Cotton Belt, similar offers of men, muskets, and moral as well as monetary backing flowed into the office of the governor. Most of these letters were laced with a curious mixture of manifest destiny and southern nationalism.[11]

Houston could not have expected a greater outpouring of support from his native South. But not all such enthusiastic expressions of encouragement emanated from Dixie. From as far away as the Ohio Valley and the Atlantic seaboard the correspondence poured in. Writing on March 3 from the nation's capital, S. N. Solomon implored the governor of Texas: "I think the time has arrived when you should act as the deliverer of Mexico. Do for her what you performed for Texas. Grant liberty to Mexico, drive out her *banditti*, establish our form of government, and in return receive the thanks and prayers of the whole civilized world." Echoing that sentiment on March 10, Jacob Davis and C. M. Bacon, both twenty-five-year-old adventurers from Philadelphia with mercenary motives, wrote to Houston, begging him to accept them into the Texas volunteer Rangers. "We are not rich," they confessed. So they hoped that the governor could "make arrangements that will be satisfactory to us." Young David Cahill, a law student from rural Ohio, likewise offered his enthusiastic support to Houston. "You will not be without one volunteer from the Buckeye state," he began. "Humble in life and poor in property, I yet have a good frame and a patriotic heart. If the drama of San Jacinto is to be played over again, and by you," he vowed, "I desire to be an actor in the play."[12]

Despite his determination to bring Mexico under the aegis of the United States, Governor Houston justly feared the possibility, even the likelihood, that the pandemic of violence that plagued northern Mexico might soon spill into South Texas. Understandably, he also remained apprehensive that the agents of anarchy might not be Mexican insurrectos but Texas patriots, the very ones poised to carry out *his* conquest south of the border. Concerned, therefore, about the issue of a military incursion into Mexico, the governor penned an executive order on March 21, 1860, titled "Proclamation Declaring an Expedition to Mexico Unauthorized." Unconvincingly, Houston claimed that only in the "last two days" had it come to his attention that some citizens of Texas were contemplating an invasion of Mexico. He decried such extralegal military ventures, then reminded fellow Texans that Secretary of War Floyd had not yet replied to Houston's offer to call into service five thousands Texas volunteers.[13]

To issue, or even to allow, a call to arms without federal consent would be "rash," surely precipitous, a certain prescription for disaster, Houston warned. "Unauthorized expeditions can eventuate in nothing favorable to humanity," he prophesied, "but in general evil to those who engage in them; and will tend to strengthen those who oppose American influence in Mexico. Neither freedom can be extended, or glory achieved," he contended. Recalling the failed campaign to Mier nearly two decades earlier, he cautioned, "[T]he most calamitous disasters that have befallen Texas have grown out of expeditions not Sanctioned by Law." Then he concluded that Texas would be better served if those who responded to the call of duty would turn their attention—and their weapons—on the Plains Indians who plundered with impunity the settlements scattered along the borders of the upper Brazos, San Saba, Colorado, Blanco, and Guadalupe rivers. "Our Bleeding and Suffering fellow Citizens of the frontier call for aid," he declared.[14]

On April 6, 1860, McCulloch issued an impassioned plea of his own. That day, he scribbled a letter asking the governor to reconsider his recent rejection of a planned military invasion of Mexico. He admitted that the inexperienced rabble assembled at Gonzales had neither the means nor the moral leadership to launch such a great enterprise, which he confessed was "fortunate for them and the Mexicans." With a sense of urgency, he implored Houston to settle the issue by placing himself at the head of the movement. "No one could succeed so easily as yourself," he stated. McCulloch even predicted that half the people of Mexico would rise up in arms to join Houston in liberating their nation from native tyrants and Old World imperialists. Surely, he insisted, the poverty-ridden populace of Mexico would see the Hero of San Jacinto as "their savior from their own leaders, who are no better than . . . robbers." Only Houston could "redeem" Mexico, he suggested. Only Houston could rescue the war-torn country from the clutches of European opportunists and from its own people.

Only Houston could lift the divided nation from the darkness of despotism and chaos. If the governor failed to mount this mighty movement, McCulloch warned, lesser men would surely try. "There is no telling the effusion of blood" that might result in such a case, he proffered.[15]

"Reflect gravely," McCulloch pleaded of Houston. "Reflect well." Remember, too, he urged his friend, "you need not fear for wanting men or money. Thousands of men and millions of . . . [dollars] will be placed at your disposal. To do this will be the crowning act of your life and will make your name greater than if you had been President of the United States."[16] McCulloch understood Houston well. He knew that, notwithstanding his friend's noble qualities, he was still a man of vaulting ambition and enormous ego.

In truth, however, McCulloch held out little hope that Houston would listen to his advice. Even if the governor did listen, McCulloch did not believe he would receive a commission from Houston to lead the advance into Mexico. "The Governor has no use for me," he complained to his mother five days after Houston issued his proclamation declaring any invasion of Mexico "unauthorized." Frustrated and disappointed that Houston had "abandoned the idea of crossing the Rio Grande for the present," McCulloch determined to focus on the upcoming national political campaign and, more specifically, on the lofty stakes for the Lone Star State. By the summer of 1860, he was, therefore, more concerned than ever that his military career might be over and with it the opportunity to "free" Mexico from the restraints of grinding poverty and brutal despotism. Perhaps of greater importance to the ambitious Ranger captain, gone too was the chance to extend the empire of slavery and cotton across the vast dominions of Mexico. And vanished with it the glory, the land, and his own lofty place in history.[17]

A Pax Americana

In the coming weeks, Houston said little and wrote even less about the Mexico venture. Given the stunning events in Texas during that turbulent summer of 1860—the summer of the "Great Fear"—no wonder Houston shifted his attention away from the Rio Grande. Smoldering discontent over the Mexican boundary and the recent rash of violence along the Rio Grande soon became engulfed by a raging firestorm that swept North Texas and then the nation, a firestorm over slavery, states' rights, and secession. Rabid proslavery firebrands rioted on the wharves of Galveston, mobbing Yankee merchant seamen and brutally beating them, simply because of their criticisms of slave owners. Across the state, newspapers reported angry southern fanatics ransacking and torching shops and stores owned by northerners and known Unionists. Then in the intense heat of July, the fires of suspicious origin erupted across North Texas, in Gainesville, Pilot Point, Denton, McKinney, Waxahachie, Fort Worth, and Dallas, where on a searing Sunday afternoon flames swept swiftly through the town's commercial district, reducing twenty-five businesses to cinder and ashes. In the subsequent hysteria, three black men, two of them slaves—all suspected of arson—were arrested, jailed, then lynched. Less than two months later, in neighboring Fort Worth, one hundred vigilantes dragged a northern Methodist minister into the town streets, tossed him into a wagon, escorted him to a site west of town, and without benefit of a trial hanged him, all because of his purported incendiary statements intended to incite a slave insurrection. Throughout Texas, committees of "public safety" formed. The KGC mobilized its members, and wherever these vigilantes suspected the threat of "John Brownism," they took the law into their own hands and carried out terrible acts of reprisal: barn burnings in the night, "necktie parties" organized under the cover of darkness, savage floggings of allegedly insolent slaves. It was a wicked time when, as one contemporary put it, a "monster of the human heart" was unleashed upon the land. And South Texas was no exception.[18]

Yet amid the spreading flames of discord, Houston never gave up on the notion of the protectorate. In August, he apparently received two letters from Colonel Mann, most likely the same Charles L. Mann of Dallas who had led a company of "free Rangers" to Central America three years earlier to aid William Walker in his war to "liberate" Nicaragua. Houston's cryptic reply of August 27 alluded to ongoing clandestine plans to raise money in support of a filibustering expedition to Mexico. The governor must have been well acquainted with Mann, for he not only referred to the recent birth of his son, Temple, a "fine child in midwife parlance," but he also admitted that since the delivery of the child on August 12, his wife, Margaret Lea, had been "so unwell that for ten nights I was not undressed, so you may think that I have had a protectorate at home to claim my attention." On a more serious subject, the governor alluded to the sale of bonds to willing investors from as far away as New York and even London and to the need for funds to purchase firearms for Texas volunteers. The thinly veiled reference to the "plan of operation" and the "glorious result" left little doubt that Houston, despite his public pronouncements, not only knew about but also privately endorsed the scheme to launch an invasion of Mexico.[19]

And Houston had in mind the man who could lead the march across the Rio Bravo. "I will write today to General Ben McCulloch," he informed Mann. "You can let him see my letter. Ben will do for a very 'big Captain' as my Red brothers say."[20]

The following day, Houston dispatched correspondence to McCulloch, referring to him as "My Dear General." In this letter, the governor again revealed his support for raising a Texas army to carry a Pax Americana into Mexico. But he also informed his old friend from Gonzales that, as chief executive of the state, he could not initiate such an action. "I am for some work if it is undertaken," he confided. Referring to the scheme to establish a protectorate south of the Rio Grande, he admitted, "[W]e look on it as a mission of mercy and humanity . . . [but] it must not sink into the character of spoil and robbery." Instead, he insisted, "it must be to elevate and exalt Mexico to a position among the nations of the world."[21]

Meanwhile, Houston understandably wished to guard carefully the secrecy of the enterprise. He privately asked McCulloch to solicit inventor and arms manufacturer Colonel George W. Morse of Washington, D.C., regarding the cost of his state-of-the-art carbines and the possibility of delivering between seven and ten thousand of the weapons "If this question should . . . get out," Houston cautioned, "it would do no good, and might create a thousand foolish or silly rumors. So it is best to keep it *Sub Rosa*."[22]

Few Texans of the day knew more about firearms than McCulloch. From his boyhood in Tennessee to his military service on the borders of Texas and Mexico, he had handled just about every weapon in the American arsenal. Then during his brief tenure as a member of President Buchanan's peace commission dispatched to Utah Territory during the so-called Mormon War of 1857, he had familiarized himself with the latest in shoulder weapons—from the Sharps rifle, to the Springfield carbine, to Morse's newest rifle. Of the reliability of the latter, McCulloch had written that he had "met with no gun or carbine that equaled it in accuracy or length of range." Moreover, he had contended that the improved metallic cartridge was "for all practical use, the best that has been invented." Houston apparently agreed with him that, if a Texas volunteer brigade were to be raised for a campaign in Mexico, it should be armed with nothing less than the best, provided of course that the money could be raised and the shipment delivered.[23]

No one who knew Ben McCulloch should have been surprised that the famed former Ranger would not wait on his governor—or anyone else—to instruct him to take up arms again in the service of Texas. Aspiring firearms merchant, advanced agent of manifest destiny, McCulloch remained, above all else, an adventurer and a soldier who longed to return to the field of glory. Being also the only one of Frances McCulloch's four sons who was a bachelor, he had no marital ties, no children, nothing to prevent him from risking his life in what he considered a great and glorious cause. In a word, he was the only McCulloch who could be "spared." As revealed in his most private correspondence, he seemed tormented by the specter of growing old and penniless and dying without a legacy or, worse yet, living out his years in anonymity and poverty, becoming a burden to his family. At the age of forty-eight, therefore, the legendary Ranger scout remained a man of almost excessive pride and desperate ambitions, one overly consumed with his reputation and his deteriorating financial condition. Surely he was not the type to be denied or underestimated. In other words, he had everything to gain and nothing to lose by leading an expeditionary force into Mexico—nothing but his life. And that seemed to matter less and less to him with each passing year.[24]

As events hurled the nation toward civil war, McCulloch continued to believe that a military invasion of Mexico might be just what the country needed. A potential diversion from the sectional strife that was fast dividing the nation, such an expedition could possibly distract southern firebrands and northern radicals alike and maybe unite them in a common cause. Together, he hoped, enemies from all sections of the fractious republic could rediscover their sense of national purpose. Besides, once the conquest of Mexico was under way, not even the most fanatical abolitionists in the North could oppose the acquisition of new territories south of the Rio Grande for fear of political ruination. Privately, he expressed confidence that another campaign in Mexico would allow Texans and southerners everywhere an outlet for both their ambitions and their nationalistic pride. Finally, he was just as certain that such a war—if fought on the same scale as the last one had been—would surely serve as a catalyst for agricultural production in the South as well as for the manufacturing economy of the North. At least the annexation of Mexico would allow the cotton kingdom of the Gulf Plains to expand all the way to the tropics of Central America. Of that he remained certain.[25]

But Governor Houston was not so sure—not yet anyway. There seemed little doubt that the hero of San Jacinto still hoped to carry out his plans to create a protectorate south of the Rio Grande. Most certainly, too, he saw the enterprise not only as a moral obligation but also as an opportunity for further territorial expansion. He even considered the conquest of at least a portion of Mexico to be his destiny as well as the destiny of the United States. Unlike those who suggested that a military incursion might be a desperate measure to preserve the Union, he feared that such an action might have the opposite effect, dividing further the North and the South on the issue of slavery and its extension into new territories. Moreover, the ever cautious and restrained Houston understood that the venture would be doomed to fail unless the might and majesty of a united American nation were fully behind it.

The Crisis Builds

As late as the autumn of 1860, the scheme to invade Mexico was still afoot. Even if Houston had his doubts, the leadership of the Knights of the Golden Circle did not. On October 10, "General" George Bickley, the eccentric founding father and spiritual head of the KGC, arrived on the Gulf Coast admitting to the Galveston *News* that events beyond his control had forced him to delay but not to abandon plans for crossing the "Mexican Rubicon." The recent failures of filibustering expeditions in Honduras, the logistical problems with transporting thousands of troops and supporting materials across country or by sea to Texas, and the looming presidential election had all demonstrated "how necessary to success is the element of timing." Furthermore, "arms that ought to have been at our rendezvous have not arrived, and agents have to be sent in search of them." Nor had corn, wheat, and other necessary staples promised by supporters in the Ohio Valley arrived. "All this is the work of time," he confessed. "To throw ourselves and a body of 400 or 500 men only across the river would insure disaster," he admitted. "This will not do—if I cross, it must be with every element of success in my hands . . . men, arms, and material." He concluded by promising, "[W]e shall cross at the earliest possible moment."[26]

Bickley's movements and his message during a recruiting tour of Texas that fall and winter revealed clearly what the Knights were planning. On October 30, Bickley was visiting the town of Houston, soliciting money and men for the Mexico enterprise and helping to organize new castles across Texas. The following week he passed through East Texas, first to Huntsville, then Marshall, Jefferson, and Henderson. By November 13, he had arrived in San Antonio, the cradle of the KGC movement in Texas. For the next several weeks, he remained in the Alamo City, raising still more support for secession, southern independence, and of course, the planned military occupation of northern Mexico. During these weeks, he also worked diligently to organize new castles in towns throughout the state. All the while, he maintained a line of communication with his growing ranks by publishing a series of letters addressed to editor Edward H. Cushing of the Houston *Telegraph* but surely intended for the people of Texas.[27]

Bickley's letters reflected the crescendo of dissonance sounding across the Lone Star State. Most notably, in his letter from Marshall, dated November 15, 1860, he reacted harshly to recent criticism launched by an unnamed "Black republican correspondent" writing from Brownsville. In response to the charges that a mob sponsored by the KGC had gathered along the lower Rio Grande with the expressed intention of invading Mexico, he confessed that "it is true that a few misguided men assembled upon the Rio Grande, in violation of my special orders." But he also admitted that "we made provision for these men that they might not be compelled to return home until we knew what the south would do in reference to Mr. Lincoln's election." He then warned the voices of abolitionism and Unionism that "we hope yet to have the pleasure of hanging each and every lying correspondent living in our midst."[28]

News of the November presidential election confirmed the worst fears of southern fire-eaters such as Bickley. The northern Republican Party and its standard-bearer, Abraham Lincoln, won on a free-soil platform calling for the restriction of slavery to states where it already existed. With Lincoln's victory, therefore, both Bickley's plotted invasion and Houston's parallel plans for a protectorate were delayed, if not ultimately doomed. No matter that Lincoln would soon plead with his countrymen to listen to the "better angels" of their nature. The time had come, as Houston had prophesied, when Texas and the nation would be hurled into the madness of total war. What Houston termed the "demons of anarchy" would now be unleashed.

Or as Texan Noah Smithwick aptly wrote: "the dogs of war were . . . turned loose, and the devil concealed in men unchained."[29]

While the ensuing secession crisis summoned forth the best in some men, it brought out the worst in others. Fueled by fears encouraged by firebrand secessionists and flaming abolitionists alike, radicalism swept over Texas that winter. In towns across the state, vigilantism supplanted both the U.S. Constitution and the state constitution as so-called committees of public safety, made up mostly of members of the KGC, formed outside the framework of the law.

What happened in San Antonio, the statewide headquarters of the KGCs, was no exception. On November 24 the local leadership of the Knights, composed of respectable merchants and public officials, including longtime Houston loyalist Asa Mitchell, joined an undisciplined rabble of border ruffians to hold a prosecession rally in the shadow of the Alamo. With Bickley also in attendance, a frenzied mob of well-armed fanatics, numbering more than one thousand, crowded into the open plaza to hear the celebrated Reverend Jesse Boring of the Methodist Episcopal Church deliver a stirring address that belied his unusual name. For more than an hour, Reverend Boring, a well-known divine of secessionism, railed out against the dangers of abolitionism and northern "oppression." In the words of one observer, Boring "set the hearts of the Southern men on fire by his strong appeals to . . . patriotism, and the excitement rose to a fever heat."[30]

After a number of overzealous men, perhaps inspired by liquid spirits, fired their revolvers in celebration of their "sacred rights," a native Kentuckian and known Unionist, Charles Anderson, rose to deliver a rebuttal. As soon as he stepped up to the speaker's stand in front of the Menger Hotel and began his message, however, the heckling mob jeered him in an attempt to disrupt his speech. A riot then erupted as armed bullies of the KGC pulled pistols and again began shooting wildly into the air, sending the crowd scurrying for cover. Several of "Colonel" Anderson's admirers, and even a few officers of the KGCs, saved him from the clutches of the mob as they pushed him through the throng and into the lobby of the Menger.[31]

This incident in San Antonio seemed a metaphor for the spiraling anarchy that swirled across the Lone Star State. Meanwhile, as fire-eating secessionists tugged their fellow Texans toward rebellion, self-styled "Higher law" men from the North likewise expressed their willingness to resort to extralegal means to rid the country of slavery, even if it meant purging the land with blood. To extremists on both sides of the sectional conflict, therefore, the covenant of the U.S. Constitution dissolved, a climate of civil disorder prevailed, and a general attitude of disrespect for established authority descended over a divided people. Not surprisingly, amid this growing crisis, community leaders called town meetings in dozens of counties across Texas. From these tumultuous assemblages, the call sounded forth for a secession convention to gather in Austin the following month. In hopes of heading them off, Governor Houston called a special session of the Texas State Legislature for January 21, 1861.

Despite Governor Houston's public appeals and private maneuvering to preserve the Union and his state's place in it, secessionist leaders went ahead with their plans to hold a special convention in the Texas capital. Unable to work with the governor, the secessionists went around him by calling for an election on January 8, 1861, to choose delegates for the special convention. Meanwhile, Houston acted upon disturbing reports that the radical pro-slavery faction was preparing to settle the matter, preferably with ballots but with bullets if necessary. On January 20, he dispatched a "confidential agent," Ranger captain and Indian fighter John M. Smith, with a secret message to General David E. Twiggs, commanding the Military Department of Texas at San Antonio. Houston's letter warned Twiggs that an "unauthorized mob" was privately plotting to seize the federal arsenal in San Antonio as well as other Union forts around the state. He offered Twiggs his assistance in protecting the armory in San Antonio, which held the largest store of weapons and munitions west of the Mississippi. He even suggested that Twiggs consider turning over possession of such properties to the state government rather than surrendering them to an armed mob. In so doing, he implied that, as the state's chief executive, he would defend these posts and their ordnance from those seeking to sever Texas's ties with the Union.[32]

Twiggs was everything that Houston was not—timid, lacking in confidence, weak and indecisive, in sum anything but a leader. Worse yet, he was unfit for duty, much less command. As Charles Anderson remembered, "[I]t was certainly amusing to hear the poor old invalid tattling over his complaints, organs, functions, remedies, and the like . . . charming topics of conversation. One of his concepts was that his gall bladder had burst an opening into either his stomach or his heart, I forget which." Given the fact that, as a native of Georgia, Twiggs was also sympathetic to the causes of secession, southern independence, and slavery, he could hardly have been expected to put up much of a fight. Indeed, he would not.[33]

Surrender in San Antonio

The tempo of events accelerated and passions mounted. On January 21, Houston implored the state legislature to help him stay the hand of secession, but most representatives were in no mood for compromise, either on their unyielding defense of slavery or on the issue of states' rights. Emotions rose to a fever pitch as Houston and the legislature, many of its members being the very same delegates elected earlier in the month to the upcoming special convention on secession, reached an impasse. So when Texas Supreme Court justice Oran M. Roberts, a slave owner and a leader of secessionist leanings, called the convention to order on January 28, the outcome of the proceedings seemed a foregone conclusion. In the words of Unionist delegate James Throckmorton, a "wild spirit of revolution" reigned in the convention as elsewhere throughout the state. Accordingly, delegates voted to form a Committee of Public Safety and to encourage other "vigilance" committees in every county and township in Texas. One member appointed to this committee was the revered Rip Ford, a delegate from Cameron County. Predictably, on February 1, when Justice Roberts, the pipe-smoking jurist, slammed the gavel and demanded order in the meeting hall, fanaticism prevailed as jeering radicals shouted down the few voices of reason in attendance. It was as if every man had become a law unto himself, and a howling mob had replaced the democratic processes of government.[34]

The grave moment of decision was at hand. The great issue on the floor was a proposed ordinance of secession. As the raucous assembly descended into a din of discord, Roberts called the roll of delegates. Through the back of the convention hall walked the tall, brooding figure of Sam Houston. Gray and grim faced, the ailing governor took his seat just as the clerk began to read the historic document proclaiming Texas's separation from the Union. Houston spoke not a word; he did not have to. As Throckmorton wrote admiringly, "[T]o those who tell of his charge at San Jacinto, I say it took a thousand times more courage when he stalked [into the hall] alone, and . . . awed them by his mere presence."[35]

Only 7 of more than 160 delegates cast dissenting votes. But Houston was not done–not yet. The convention called for the people to vote on the secession question on February 23, and Houston arose from his sick bed one last time to tour the state and appeal to his fellow Texans. It was his finest hour. Even in the face of certain defeat, and despite failing health, the aging titan of Texas braved death threats to take his case to the people he had served so faithfully for a quarter of a century. As one who heard him speak that February recalled, he stood "magnificent in form" and mesmerized hostile crowds with his "voice of deep base tone, which shook and commanded the soul of the hearer."[36]

Speaking to a camp of fervent young volunteers near his namesake town of Houston, Old Sam delivered one of many impassioned speeches, which in the words of contemporary Ralph Smith were "calculated to dampen the ardor of men . . . intoxicated . . . with the pomp and glory of war." He warned them that the "resources of the North were almost exhaustless. That time and money would wear us out and conquor [*sic*] us at last." But Smith remembered that Houston "might as well . . . [have] been giving advice to the inmates of a lunatic asylum. For we knew no such word as fail."[37]

Houston concluded his speaking tour before a belligerent crowd in Galveston. With a spellbinding eloquence and an almost haunting sense of doom reminiscent of the prophet Jeremiah, he issued his admonition from the balcony of the Tremont House. "Some of you laugh to scorn the idea of bloodshed as a result of secession. . . . But let me tell you what is coming . . . your fathers and husbands, your sons and brothers, will be herded together like sheep and cattle at the point of the bayonet. You may, after the sacrifice of countless millions of treasure, and of hundreds of thousands of precious lives . . . win Southern independence, if God be not against you, but I doubt it . . . [for] the North is determined to preserve the Union."[38]

Houston's warnings that the North would fight went unheeded. Meantime, the secession convention appointed three commissioners to negotiate with General Twiggs the terms of a timely surrender of all federal properties in Texas. The three Texan leaders appointed by the Committee of Public Safety were surely well prepared to demand that Twiggs turn over the federal arsenal in San Antonio and then all military stores and properties within the state. They were Philip N. Luckett, the thirty-six-year-old physician from Corpus Christi who had once ridden with Rip Ford's Rangers in pursuit of Comanches; Thomas Jefferson Devine, forty-year-old district judge and practicing attorney from San Antonio; and the venerable fifty-seven-year-old Samuel Maverick, land baron, livestock raiser, lawyer, legislator, and civic leader in San Antonio. It was for the latter, legend has it, that the very label *maverick* was first applied, owing to Sam's wandering herds of unbranded cattle that were left to drift over the prairies of the Gulf coastal plain.[39]

On the afternoon of February 9, the commissioners met briefly in San Antonio with members of Twiggs's staff, including the quartermaster for the Department of Texas, Major David H. Vinton. Over the next several days, they exchanged notes with Twiggs and Vinton in an effort to arrange a peaceful transfer of Union posts and properties to the state government and to effect the removal of some 2,600 federal troops stationed in Texas. But those delicate negotiations broke down when Twiggs stubbornly refused to allow his troops to surrender their shoulder weapons, side arms, and light artillery before vacating their posts and evacuating the state.[40]

While the commissioners and General Twiggs talked, the irrepressible Ben McCulloch prepared for war. Commissioned a colonel of state volunteers by the Committee on Public Safety on February 8, the "gallant old Ranger," as the San Antonio *Herald* called him, was encamped on his brother Henry's ranch near Seguin, where he gathered around him volunteers, friends, supporters, spies, and weapons. Confidently, he awaited word from Austin. Writing of the Rangers' storied tradition as being the western equivalent to the tradition of the minuteman of colonial times, he boasted, "[T]o Texans a moment's notice is sufficient when their state demands their service." Amazingly, in a few precious days, McCulloch mustered into service hundreds of eager volunteers, the "real bone and sinew" of southern and central Texas, as he called them. In reality, although many of these mounted border fighters were experienced in the "ranging service," they resembled an assorted rabble more than a regiment. Many, if not most, of these men were determined to do more than simply defend Texas.[41]

As Major John T. Sprague of the Eighth U.S. Infantry, a native New Yorker, observed, this surly looking lot of state partisans was a poor imitation of the "roving and daring class of men known as Texas Rangers." He further noted of the martial traditions of the Lone Star State, "[A]s it is generally supposed an American is born a soldier, so in this . . . [state] every man is by inheritance a Texas Ranger. With his horse, rifle, and powder horn, and ten days subsistence in his saddle bags, he takes to the field, confident of success." Sprague also correctly assessed that many, if not most, of McCulloch's motley assemblage were not merely citizen soldiers but also mercenaries and "true believers," secretly sworn to promote the goals and aims of the Knights of the Golden Circle. He failed to understand, however, that only a thin line separated the mythic Rangers of the imagination from McCulloch's mob of mounted riflemen.[42]

While McCulloch prepared for an assault upon San Antonio, the commissioners waited to meet with Twiggs again, at 11:00 A.M. on Saturday, February 16. What they did not know, however, was that the old general had received orders the previous day relieving him of his duties and appointing in his place Colonel Carlos Adolphus Waite, a native of New York and a known Unionist stationed at Camp Verde in the hill country, more than sixty miles away. The changeover of command mattered little. By the time Waite learned of his appointment, however, events had already hastened toward an appeal to arms. In the predawn hours of February 16, a bitter chill hung in the air. Shortly after midnight, an armed force of more than six hundred determined Texan "Rangers," who styled themselves "McCulloch's Army of the Knights of the Golden Circle," gathered along the banks of Salado Creek some five miles above San Antonio. While encamped there, McCulloch's men fed their horses, cleaned and fired off their weapons, and anxiously awaited orders from their commander. Around 2:30 A.M., McCulloch directed his men to mount up, and they "started with a rush," according to young James K. Polk Blackburn, on a night march made with "much caution and secrecy." As the volunteers proceeded southward, they hardly spoke a word, for in the assessment of participant Robert H. Williams, "the rank and file expected a sharp tussle." By 4:00 A.M., the columns of horsemen had slipped quietly into San Antonio. At that point, McCulloch ordered ninety of his riflemen to continue on foot and fan out to strategic points in the city. Of this rowdy regiment of armed men, Williams recollected, "[I]t was a formidable force . . . for though it couldn't boast much discipline, all the men were well mounted, most of them expert rifle and revolver shots. With just a little training, what a brigade of irregular cavalry it would have made."[43]

Some on horseback, others astride mules, still others on foot, advancing slowly and in silence through the streets of San Antonio as city residents—and General Twiggs—slept, they entered the military plaza with their Lone Star flag waving before them. Not a single Union picket awaited the Texans as they took up positions in the darkness around the armory, with its coveted stores of ordnance. Many of McCulloch's sharpshooters scaled roofs and scrambled for a clear view of the streets below. McCulloch himself climbed to the top of the Veramendi house on Soledad Street, a popular tavern and watering hole adjacent to the armory, where several young sentries of the KGC's local "Alamo Guards" were already waiting. All the while, only a few citizens had been awakened by the sounds of barking dogs and the cries of frightened slaves living near the arsenal. As Carolyn Darrow, wife of one of Twiggs's clerks, observed in the faint glow of moonlight, "[T]he revolutionaries appeared, two by two . . . mounted and on foot—a motley though quite orderly crowd."[44]

By dawn, when the sun first glinted off the adobe walls of the old Spanish town, scores of Texas rebels rested atop roofs, scanning the horizons, with their rifles drawn and ready. As one young recruit recalled, "[W]e stood with loaded rifles for four mortal hours, and still no shot was fired, though every moment we expected the balls would open" up. Everywhere, it seemed, the rebels had swarmed into public buildings and even into the compound around the arsenal.[45]

Around six o'clock in the morning, McCulloch and the commissioners summoned General Twiggs from his quarters on the outskirts of town. Less than an hour later, the Stars and Stripes were hauled down from the Military Plaza, and as one observer recollected, the Lone Star flag "floated in its place amidst the wild cheers and hurrahs of all our 'Boys.'" Twiggs wept openly at the formal surrender ceremony held in the Main Plaza that morning. His subsequent report of the surrender was typically terse and without embellishment. "I immediately . . . proceeded to my office and found the troops and public property surrounded by the Texans. After a conversation with the commissioners, and in the presence of my staff and the officers of the post, it was agreed that the United States troops should march out of the city, taking with them . . . all the necessities for a march out of Texas."[46]

By noon it was over. Twiggs had agreed to order his troops, numbering no more than 160, to stand down. And so, as the twenty-fifth anniversary of the storied siege and fall of the Alamo approached, "Old Davey" Twiggs—unlike the immortal Crockett and company—surrendered San Antonio without fanfare and without firing a shot. The Texas devils thus gained, in one bold act, what their leaders had failed to acquire with diplomacy or to purchase with a depleted public treasury—more than two thousand Springfield rifles, several batteries of light artillery, and substantial stores of munitions and stocks of provisions. The only question left unanswered now was whether they would use these implements of war against Union troops and in the defense of Texas or turn them toward the Mexican border for deployment in another war of conquest.

At midday armed sentries patrolled every street, most of the riflemen distinguished by their red flannel armbands, the unofficial uniform of the Knights of the Golden Circle. Otherwise they bore no evidence of rank or military affiliation. Throngs of pistol-toting citizens also crowded into the major plazas. "All the stores were closed; men, women, and children armed themselves, and the excitement was intense," Carolyn Darrow remembered. Were it not for all the firearms being brandished in the streets, the scene might have resembled a carnival.[47]

Around two o'clock that afternoon, a U.S. Army transport with escort arrived in Alamo Plaza. Down from the horse-drawn ambulance stepped a distinguished-looking officer dressed in his traditional blue field jacket and trousers. He carried himself with the pride and bearing of a patrician. Relieved of his duties as commander of the Military Department of Texas and replaced by the feeble old General Twiggs just weeks earlier, the colonel was tired after traveling three days from his last post on the Texas frontier, Fort Mason situated in the rugged, cedar-covered crags of the hill country. Visibly shaken by the scene of armed vigilantes roaming the square in front of the shrine of Texas independence, he looked up and noted that the Stars and Stripes had been hauled down from the pole in front of the ruins of the old chapel, now used as a storehouse by the army quartermaster. Only the Lone Star flag of Texas waved in the breeze of that gray winter day.

Through the swirling dust and bustling confusion in the plaza, Carolyn Darrow emerged from the Menger Hotel and rushed into the street to meet the gentleman she immediately recognized as Colonel Robert E. Lee. As she greeted the handsome officer, an unidentified young Texan galloped by on horseback and nearly brushed against him, whether by accident or as a defiant gesture to demonstrate his disdain for "Yankee blue bellies." Amid the tumult, the colonel stiffened, momentarily stunned and speechless. He looked over the mob that had gathered in front of the Alamo chapel. After collecting his emotions, he finally asked, "Who are these men?" Mrs. Darrow responded, "They are McCulloch's Rangers. General Twiggs surrendered everything to the state this morning and we are all prisoners of war." Then she recalled, "I shall never forget his look of astonishment. With his lips trembling and his eyes full of tears, he exclaimed, 'Has it come as soon as this?'" His head bowed, the colonel then walked undisturbed through a barricade of men and horses into the lobby of the Menger and disappeared into a private room to change out of his dust-covered uniform. Sitting alone, he may have wondered if the rebels' action in seizing a federal arsenal was tantamount to treason, a traitorous deed no better than that committed by John Brown.[48]

Shortly after 4:00 P.M., federal troops assembled to prepare for their formal evacuation from the city. Captain John King formed three companies of the Eighth U.S. Infantry Regiment, column on line, for the inglorious march to a camp on San Pedro Creek outside San Antonio, where they would bivouac and await further word of their orderly removal to Indianola on the shores of Matagorda Bay. According to the Unionist newspaper the *Alamo Express*, it was an emotional scene never to be forgotten. The bluecoats marched grimly "with colors flying and band playing the national airs, and the old bullet-riddled and war-stained [regimental] banner . . . floating in the breeze." The journalist who witnessed the event further described "a most profound sensation among the people–strong men wept and hung their heads in shame. We never have seen so much feeling evidenced on any occasion," the reporter continued. "The people cheered the troops all along the streets, and many followed them to the head of the San Pedro." A "sullen gloom" settled over the city as many loyal Unionists felt "humiliated to see the glory of their country departing."[49]

Before nightfall, Colonel Lee met with General Twiggs and his command staff to be briefed on the crisis. That evening, according to Darrow, Lee "returned and shut himself in his room, which was over mine, and I heard his footsteps through the night . . . and the murmur of his voice, as if he were praying." Meanwhile, outside in the streets the sounds of gunfire continued until dawn. In the words of Mrs. Darrow, gunmen were "drinking and shouting in the streets, recklessly shooting at anyone who happened to displease." No wonder Lee believed his life to be in danger.[50]

More important, Lee realized, the life of the republic was in peril. The following day, February 17, 1861—exactly one year to the day after his arrival at Indianola to take command of the Military Department of Texas—the colonel continued to agonize over the terrible decision that now confronted him and all Americans. Like other officers on the scene, Lee was first saddened, then indignant to learn from rebel commanders that, if he resigned his commission and joined the newly formed Confederate armed forces, he would be provided free transportation and safe passage to his home in Virginia. Otherwise, he would not be allowed to carry his personal baggage and effects with him to the Gulf Coast for the trip north. He might even be arrested.[51]

Charles Anderson, a stockman and landowner who had recently befriended Lee, recalled his meetings with the colonel during that weekend. He never forgot Lee's composure and self-control amid the growing tempest. He remembered Lee's "grave, cold dignity of bearing and the prudential reserve of his manners." He further observed that the colonel was "diligent, faithful, and universally trusted . . . in all his duties."In Anderson's opinion, "[O]f all the officers and men I ever knew, he came . . . the nearest in likeness to the classical ideal" of the honorable man who was ever beyond reproach. In fact, Anderson saw in the Virginian the same qualities that he admired in his brother, Major Robert Anderson, who was then awaiting his own appointment with destiny at Fort Sumter, South Carolina, where he commanded the quiet island citadel that guarded the entrance to Charleston Harbor.[52]

The War Begins

As Saturday's tumult gave way to a somber Sunday morning, church and cathedral bells tolled across San Antonio, calling the faithful to worship. According to Robert Williams, a solemn Colonel Lee attended services of the Episcopal Church held in the Masonic Hall. Williams described his future Confederate commander as "tall, and somewhat spare in figure, with a soldierly bearing that revealed his profession at a glance." Lee "looked every inch a gentleman. Courteous and dignified in manner, but without the slightest assumption"; his "dark hair was untinged with gray, and his blue eyes were bright and undimmed beneath his black eyebrows."[53]

No one could blame Lee for preparing to leave San Antonio as soon as possible. "When I get home to Virginia, I think the world will have one soldier less," he confided to a fellow officer. "I shall resign [my commission] and go to planting corn." To another friend he explained that, while he would never draw his sword against the United States, he would, without hesitation, lift it in defense of Virginia. So while he packed his bags for the long trip home, hoping to avoid the gathering conflict, he contemplated the weighty responsibilities of the professional soldier. And he knew that, like the boys in blue who had served with him on the Texas frontier, and like those volunteer Rangers who rode with Ben McCulloch, he could not escape what Lincoln would term the "fiery trial" of the coming Civil War.

As expected, the following week, on February 23, Texans voted three to one in favor of secession. Then on March 2, 1861, on the twenty-fifth anniversary of Texas independence from Mexico, state officers officially severed their ties with the Union. Two weeks later, state officials gathered to take the oath of allegiance to the newly formed Confederate States of America—all leaders that is all except one—Sam Houston. Unyielding in his stand for the Union, unbending in his refusal to support secession and any standard of rebellion against the United States, Houston was forced to relinquish the office of governor and was replaced by his lieutenant governor and longtime protégé, Edward Clark. Saddened, embittered, heart broken in defeat, the aging colossus of Texas soon rode off to his home at Cedar Point near Galveston Bay and into the mists of history and legend.

For Houston, not only had his brief but courageous tenure as governor ended all too soon, but so too had his spectacular public career. Gone, too, was the historic moment to establish a U.S. protectorate and, more specifically, Texan hegemony over Mexico. As he retired to private life, and to the comforting love of his adoring Margaret Lea, he therefore knew that for him and, in a larger sense, for the people the United States, it was an opportunity lost forever.

As for Robert E. Lee, he traveled to Indianola, arriving there on February 22. He continued on the three-day journey by steamer to New Orleans. By March 1, he was back in Virginia, back to the peaceful hills of Arlington and to the protective embrace of his dearest Mary. Back to the land, the fallow cornfields, the spreading oaks and shaded gardens overlooking the Potomac. Back to the warmth of the hearth and the home filled with so many fond memories. In the coming days, as Colonel Lee rested on the veranda of Arlington House and contemplated the fate of his troubled country, he also pondered the awful decision that weighed so heavily upon him. Pensive and melancholy in mood, he reflected on the gathering storm and what it all meant. For in his thirteen-month absence, he understood that, while his surroundings remained as familiar as ever, so much had changed. The country had changed. So had he. And nothing would ever be the same again.[54]

Indeed, within six weeks the word came, the word that Lee had been anticipating with dread. In the early morning darkness of April 12, 1861, with the firing on Fort Sumter, the day and the hour had at last arrived. The war that almost started on a chilly February morning in San Antonio had instead begun with the surrender of another federal installation, this one at Charleston Harbor, South Carolina. To paraphrase Lee biographer, Douglas Southall Freeman, it was the war that "Bobby" Lee, Ben McCulloch, and so many others of their generation were born to fight.

10
Requiem

On February 21, 1861, the squall of war again swept over the Rio Grande Valley. That morning, the steamer *General Rusk*, commissioned from the Southern Steamship Company, and the schooner *Shark* appeared over the horizon, just off shore from Brazos Island. Both vessels flew only the banner bearing the Lone Star of Texas. On the bridge stood the imposing figure of Colonel John S. Ford, Old Rip himself. Now grizzled haired, Ford looked older, with a stubby growth of whiskers that covered his prominent jaw and chin. Still his familiar voice could be heard resonating above all others, encouraging his men and subordinate officers, who included second in command forty-six-year-old Colonel Hugh McLeod of Galveston, best remembered as Mirabeau Lamar's handpicked leader of the ill-fated Santa Fe expedition twenty years earlier. Ford commanded them to prepare to board skiffs and go ashore. Draw weapons, he ordered; and be ready to use them if Union troops offered armed resistance.[1]

Ford had surely come far in the past three weeks. In many ways, his journey paralleled that of his adopted state of Texas. First named to the Texas Committee of Public Safety on February 1, then commissioned two days later by that body as commander of all state forces in the Rio Grande District, he received orders to enlist six hundred armed volunteers. Before leaving Austin, he hastily scribbled orders to three Ranger captains, two of whom had served ably under him in the past: young Mat Nolan of Corpus Christi and John Littleton of Karnes County, both veterans of the Comanche campaigns and the Cortina War, and John Donelson, who had yet to prove himself in the ranging service. Ford authorized each to raise a company of Mounted Rangers and ride southward to join him on the border. After traveling by stagecoach from Austin to the tiny town of Hempstead, then on to Houston by train during the second week of February, Old Rip hastened to Galveston, where he assembled his regiment for the defense of the Rio Grande. Then on the night of February 19, he sailed with more than five hundred volunteers, including more than fifty Irish immigrants eager for a fight.[2]

The regiment that Ford raised for the Rio Grande campaign resembled the companies of Rangers already renowned for their service along the border.

Ford wrote of them: "they knew little of each other; many of them were not secessionists by belief; yet they were true Texians . . . and could be depended on." Many were experienced Indian fighters, frontiersmen familiar with the ways of plains warfare. Some were soldiers of fortune eager for adventure and territorial conquest, but most were mere farm boys, young and untested in battle. Few owned slaves or held any exalted notions of southern nationhood or states' rights. Fewer still could boast of much formal education. To a man, their abiding allegiance—if they had any—was not so much to any league or confederacy of southern states but to Texas and to Texas alone.[3]

Ford Seizes Federal Properties

When Ford and his officers disembarked from the *General Rusk*, rowed ashore, and stepped on the beaches of Brazos Island around noon that February 21, they found less resistance than expected. Only twelve young Union artillerymen awaited them, their single shore battery of siege guns and mortars already disabled, the powder holes spiked, trunnions broken, and barrels removed from carriages. Fortunately for both sides, the surrender came quickly. With General Ebenezar B. Nichols, commissioner of the state of Texas, at his side, Ford approached the federal stockade overlooking the pass at the northern tip of the island. From the cluster of modest buildings stepped an inexperienced first lieutenant, James Thompson.

While one company of Texans formed on the beach in battle order, Ford and Nichols walked slowly ahead to parley with Thompson. They explained that, under the authority of the state of Texas, they had come to seize all federal properties on the island as well at the outposts upriver from Fort Brown and northward along the entire length of the lower Bravo. "After some hesitation," Ford reported, Thompson agreed to turn over possession of his post without an armed confrontation. "No unpleasant remark dropped from either party during the affair, and a high-toned courtesy seemed to prevail throughout," Ford wrote. As ordered, the Texas volunteers fired a thirty-three-gun salute while the soldiers slowly lowered the Stars and Stripes "in respectful silence." Tears formed in Ford's eyes, for it was the first time he had ever seen his national banner folded in defeat. As he summarized the emotional scene, "It was a trial of no ordinary character."[4]

After a few moments, a Texas color guard hoisted the Lone Star flag, and as the standard unfurled, a cheer went up from the ranks of Ford's recruits.

The next day, Ford continued upriver some thirty-five miles to Brownsville. By the time he arrived at Fort Brown, word of his march had preceded him. As directed by the statewide Committee of Public Safety, his official purpose was threefold. First, he should secure all federal properties and posts along the border and, if possible, do so without provoking hostilities. Second, they had instructed him to occupy these forts and to protect the same line of the Bravo from any invasion of Mexican banditti and marauding Indians. Third, the commissioners had implored Ford to conduct himself in such a way as to ensure "friendly intercourse" and "feelings of amity" with local Mexican authorities.[5]

When Ford arrived at Brownsville about noon on February 22, he found only four companies of federal troops occupying Fort Brown. Confidently, he assessed the situation, informing John C. Robertson, chairman of the Texas Committee of Public Safety, that his forces would have "no great trouble" in gaining possession of the fort and the surrounding city of some five thousand inhabitants. But Ford quickly learned that the task would not be as easy as he had first hoped. On the morning of February 23, he met with a determined Captain Bennett H. Hill of the First U.S. Artillery, commander of Fort Brown, who not only refused to capitulate and surrender his post but even threatened to order Ford's arrest for treason. An angry Colonel Ford responded that such an action would inevitably lead to bloodshed on both sides. And he implied that Hill's blood might be the first to be spilled. Following the heated exchange between the two officers, Old Rip returned to his headquarters in town and prepared to besiege the sprawling cantonment and its recalcitrant commander. The standoff dragged on for another week.[6]

As the crisis heightened during the final days of February, Ford ordered Colonel McLeod to return to Brazos Santiago and fortify the island for a possible Union attack, whether by land or by sea. All the while, he kept up his surveillance of Hill's position in Fort Brown and readied his volunteers for the grim prospect of an assault on the well-defended stockade with its heavy artillery emplacements and four companies of regulars entrenched behind well-built earthworks.

When two companies of the Eighth U.S. Infantry arrived from Ringgold Barracks on February 28, Hill could claim that his position was further fortified. But within two days so could a confident Colonel Ford. On March 2, 1861, the same day that officials in Austin formally severed their ties to the Union and forged a state government under the newly formed Confederate States of America, Captains Nolan, Littleton, and Donelson rode into Brownsville with reinforcements numbering nearly 200. That day as well Nichols arrived with another 325 Rangers under the command of Colonel Benjamin Franklin Terry, their welcomed appearance bringing the Texan force to more than a thousand.[7]

Although outnumbered by more than two to one, Captain Hill stood defiant. Fortunately, diplomacy prevailed. Now refusing to discuss terms of surrender with the obstinate and prideful commander at the scene, Ford sent for his old friend Captain George Stoneman of the Second U.S. Cavalry, still on patrol duty upriver from Fort Brown. In at least one private meeting, Ford pleaded with Stoneman to advise Hill to adopt a more conciliatory posture. Ford admired the stoic Captain Stoneman and correctly surmised that his old comrade from the Cortina campaign would intercede, not to help him seize federal property, but to avoid needless bloodshed. He knew that Stoneman would listen to him, that he would negotiate, and that he would persuade his fellow officers and troopers to accept the inevitable. Stoneman proved him correct on all accounts.

As events unfolded during the next forty-eight hours, Ford received still more support from an unexpected source. On the morning of March 3, the New York–based steamer *Daniel Webster* arrived off Brazos Island, carrying Major Fitz-John Porter, assistant adjutant general of the U.S. Army, who had received orders to oversee the peaceful evacuation of all federal troops from the border. After boarding the vessel and meeting briefly with Porter, Ford and Nichols were satisfied as to his intentions, and the three officers started out later that afternoon for Fort Brown. By the time Major Porter entered the beleaguered post the following day, Captain Hill was already contemplating surrender. With provisions dwindling daily, with Stoneman's quiet counsel, and now with the reassurance of a superior officer that a transport awaited at Point Isabel to carry his troops to safety, the lanky bearded artillery commander finally agreed to evacuate his post. But not before ordering a twenty-one-gun salute in honor of the inauguration—that very day—of the new president of the United States, Abraham Lincoln.[8]

The irony of such a celebration was not lost on Ford and his fellow Texans. Despite the largely symbolic thunder of federal twenty-four-pound artillery on the afternoon of March 4, Hill quietly began preparations for an orderly and peaceful withdrawal.[9] That Rip Ford played a vitally important role in negotiating an amicable resolution of the crisis appears certain. In fact, if not for Colonel Ford's patience and diplomacy, the American Civil War—the conflict that was almost ignited days earlier in San Antonio—might well have begun on the lower Rio Grande. Justice Oran Roberts later praised Old Rip: "I do believe that, but for his prudence and masterly management of the troops, and his address with the United States officers, the war would have opened there, before we had finally seceded, and very probably to our disadvantage greatly."[10]

During the dreary days of March 1861, other federal forts upriver fell in rapid succession. From Ringgold Barracks to Fort McIntosh, Fort Duncan, and Fort Clark, northward to Fort Bliss at El Paso, and into the interior along a line running from Fort Inge on the upper Nueces to Fort Mason in the hill country, a steady stream of Union stragglers—more than one thousand of them—marched to the Gulf Coast for evacuation. Mostly resigned to a peaceful removal from Texas soil, they abandoned their posts with little ceremony or resistance to the occupying state volunteers. The last federal troops to pass down river en route to Brazos Island did not depart until March 13.

For Colonel Ford, it was a sad farewell to arms. As he watched the bluecoats board a steamer at Brownsville that day for the short passage to the coast, he recognized many of them as men he had served and shared danger with. An abiding mutual respect prevailed as Ford waved goodbye to the regulars while their steam transport pushed off, then puffed down river. "The future was full of uncertainty, dark and lowering," Ford recalled thinking at that moment. "Each one of us felt a dread of what might befall us. A terrible foreboding of civil war warned us that we might meet again as foes and, under a sense of duty, might take the life of a valued friend." Understandably, he recollected, "it was a dreadful feeling."[11]

Indeed, the terrible, fratricidal war that Ford feared was at hand. But that is another story.

The Legacy

It has been said that every story has two sides. Certainly, this statement is true of the American Civil War, and as it is of the early history of the Texas

Mounted Rangers. Nowhere is this sharp disagreement in interpreting Ranger traditions more magnified than along the border with Mexico, especially on the lower Rio Grande.

As a general rule, almost every story also produces its share of extraordinary heroes and ordinary villains. Such is certainly the case with the American Civil War. In the remote corner of the Confederacy, along the waters of the lower Rio Grande, both the most valiant of soldiers and the vilest of ruffians rode across the pages of border history. Union and Confederate, Anglo and Mexican, some famous, others anonymous—they shall ever remain in the collective conscience of the people of the Rio Grande Valley.

The legacy of the mounted volunteers of Texas who, even in the service of the Confederacy, still proudly styled themselves Rangers would outlive this great conflict, as it had the last one. For better—and for worse—these Texan partisans would continue the traditions of those who a generation earlier had carried the Lone Star flag all the way to Mexico City. Like the federal regulars they fought alongside, and the Texans of Mexican heritage who continued to claim the brush country of South Texas as *their* birthright, they imparted a rich, though barbaric, heritage of border conflict, one that would divide people as much as any great river that delineates the boundary separating nations.

Many of the principals of this story died violent deaths, seemingly before their times. Only a few lived to be old men. Most were lost to history or forgotten by future generations. For those who went on to future fame, or further infamy, the stories of their lives were largely ones of men guided by vaulting ambitions—some fulfilled, most never realized.

The legendary John Coffee "Jack" Hays—El Diablo to the people south of the border—left Texas soon after the war with Mexico. Making his way west, like so many soldiers of fortune, he was destined to leave even larger footprints across the history of California than he had in Texas. In 1850, he won election to the post of sheriff of San Francisco County; soon thereafter, California officials appointed him state surveyor general. Two years later, he moved his wife and children across the San Francisco Bay and became one of the founders of the city of Oakland. He launched a lucrative career as a venture capitalist, building an impressive fortune from wealth accrued in real estate and ranching. He never talked much about his service in the U.S.-Mexican War, and he wrote even less about his exploits as a Ranger captain.

On April 4, 1883, he died quietly in bed at the age of sixty-five. He left behind a wife, Susan, and six children—three sons and three daughters.[12]

Captain Ben McCulloch devoted the rest of his life to the cause of southern independence. He rose to the rank of brigadier general in the Confederate Army, first fighting bravely at the Battle of Wilson's Creek southwest of Springfield, Missouri, in August 1861, then at Pea Ridge, or Elkhorn Tavern, in northwestern Arkansas, where he fell—while leading a cavalry charge—on March 7, 1862. A single bullet to the right breast apparently killed him instantly. Buried first on the battlefield, then near Bentonville, Arkansas, and later disinterred, placed in a pine coffin, and transported back to Texas by his friend John Henry Brown. Countless hundreds of fellow Texans turned out to pay their respects as his remains were carried through the streets of Sherman, McKinney, Dallas, Waco, and a half dozen other towns along the way. Six weeks after his death, hundreds looked on as the beloved Ben McCulloch was laid to rest in the State Cemetery in Austin. The star-crossed adventurer was only fifty years old.[13]

John Glanton, the infamous scalp hunter, returned to San Antonio following the war with Mexico. Like many others of the day, he became infected with the gold fever in 1849. He left his wife, Joaquina Menchaca, and their daughter and joined a party of gold seekers bound for the promised land of California. He never made it. After contracting first with the state of Chihuahua, then with officials of Sonora, to hunt down and kill menacing Indians, the knife-wielding Glanton finally crossed paths with the wrong band of Indians. In the summer of 1850, somewhere on the northern border of Sonora, a party of Yuma killed Glanton and his comrades. Fittingly, Glanton was scalped.[14]

After his Corpus Christi Rangers were mustered out of active service at Camargo in July 1847, Mabry B. "Mustang" Gray returned to the Nueces Strip. He died the following year at Rio Grande City, probably of cholera, although some believe of yellow fever. Ten years later, a varnished version of his life, titled *Mustang Gray: A Romance,* by Jeremiah Clemens, perpetuated his legend as a gallant warrior. A poem that eulogized the late Ranger appeared in 1884 in Andrew Jackson Sowell's *Rangers and Pioneers of Texas.* No less than the fabled folklorist J. Frank Dobie wrote of Gray's exploits in his 1932 study *Mustang Gray: Fact, Tradition, and Song.* Time filtered many of the reports of Gray's misdeeds, and Dobie believed that a modern revision of his story was in order. The people of the border, at least those of Mexican heritage, had long held that Gray was nothing more than a murderous devil, a dreaded villain whose name remains synonymous with atrocities and injustice.[15]

Following his service in the U.S.-Mexico War, Samuel Chamberlain, soldier and artist, returned home to New England. A resident of Boston, he began working on his watercolor paintings depicting American troops in the field. The more than 140 paintings, which remain arguably the best renderings of scenes from that conflict, are housed at the San Jacinto Battlefield Museum near Houston.

Chamberlain married Mary Keith on July 4, 1855, in Boston. During the Civil War, Brevet Brigadier General Chamberlain returned to East Texas as a member of the Fifth Massachusetts Cavalry, an African American unit. He lived out the last four decades of his life in Boston, where he died on November 10, 1908. His colorful memoir, titled *Confessions of a Rogue,* was not published until 1956. A classic in the historical literature of the U.S.-Mexican War, the book remains in print to this day.[16]

President Antonio Lopéz de Santa Anna went into exile after General Winfield Scott's occupation of Mexico City in 1847. Before leaving the country, however, the old hero of Tampico (where Mexicans defeated the Spanish invasion in 1829) appeared at a formal surrender ceremony during which he reviewed the U.S. occupational force. Eyewitnesses remembered that, as he rode along the columns of General Scott's troops, he quickened his pace when he looked up and saw the Lone Star flag flapping in the wind above one unit. Staring into the grimy faces of surly looking Texan Rangers, he reportedly trembled and turned pale with fear.

Santa Anna's short-lived return to power in Mexico City in 1853 was his last. Scheming as always to regain a place in the corridors of influence, he offered his services—and his political soul—to the French-installed emperor Maximilian but to no avail. From 1867 to 1874, Santa Anna lived in seclusion in Cuba, then for a time in Puerto Rico and finally in Nassau. Hoping for history's redemption, he spent several years writing his memoirs. He returned to Mexico in 1874 with plans to resurrect his reputation, if not his political career. He died on June 22, 1876, at the age of eighty-two. To the end he insisted that he had conducted himself honorably in 1836 during his victorious siege of the Alamo, after his subsequent capture at

San Jacinto, and even a decade later during the U.S.-Mexican War. Few Texans ever believed him.[17]

After being ousted as governor in March 1861, Sam Houston, the colossus of Texas, left Austin and returned to his modest summer home at Cedar Point, overlooking Galveston Bay. Retiring from public life, he never completely abandoned dreams of conquest. As late as March 1863, while on a final journey to his home in Huntsville, Texas, he expressed privately to longtime protégé Eber Cave his hope that Texans would leave the Confederacy and again proclaim an independent Lone Star Republic. Visions of grandeur and of a great Texan empire sweeping well beyond the Rio Grande still stirred within him. But it was not to be. On July 26, 1863, he died at the age of seventy. His wife, Margaret Lea, reported that his last words were of Texas.[18]

After his return from the Rio Grande in the autumn of 1855, Captain James Hughes Callahan failed to gain support in Austin for a second expedition to the Mexican border. Unsuccessful in his efforts to persuade Governor Pease and the state legislature to outfit yet another company to punish the Lipan Apache and round up runaway slaves in Mexico, he returned home to Blanco, where the following April he was shot to death during an argument with rival Woodson Blassingame. The next year, the legislature named Callahan County for him. He was later reburied in the State Cemetery in Austin.[19]

Like many others who attempted to escape Reconstruction, Dr. Philip N. Luckett fled to Mexico in the spring of 1865. The following November, he returned to Texas, only to be arrested as a war criminal and imprisoned in a federal prison in the cypress swamps near Fort Jackson, Louisiana. Although released later that year, he never fully recovered his health. He died in Cincinnati, Ohio, on May 21, 1869.[20]

At the outbreak of the Civil War, Edward Burleson, Jr., joined the First Texas Mounted Rifles and held the rank of major in Ben McCulloch's command. He saw action in Tennessee and Arkansas. After the war, he returned home to his farm in Hays County, where he and his wife, the former Emma Kyle, raised ten children. Burleson died in Austin on May 12, 1877. He had just celebrated his fiftieth birthday.[21]

Andrew Jackson "Andy" Walker, Ranger and adventurer, once a Mustang Gray protégé, remained a filibuster and supporter of General José María de Jesús Carvajal to the end. After the aborted attempts to achieve a Republic of the Sierra Madre, Walker retired from Ranger service, owing to failing health. In 1855, he died of tuberculosis on his farm in Nueces County.[22]

Ranger John Littleton, after serving briefly during the Cortina War under Captain William G. Tobin, enlisted in the battalion commanded by Major John S. Ford and soon rose to the rank of captain. During the Civil War, Littleton rejoined Old Rip, accepting a commission as captain of the Second Texas Mounted Rifles. He participated in Ford's Rio Grande expedition of 1864 and fought at the Battle at Palmito Ranch on May 13, 1865. Following the conflict, he returned home to Karnes County, where as a bounty hunter he soon found himself embroiled in the violent Sutton-Taylor feud. In the spring of 1868, the forty-two-year-old Captain Littleton and a companion were ambushed by outlaws on the Old Gonzales Road, and both were gunned down in a murderous crossfire. No one was ever arrested for the crime, but most locals knew that Creed Taylor's sons had boasted of the cowardly deed. They had vowed to get Littleton before he could kill or capture them. Apparently, they succeeded.[23]

General Carvajal eventually gave up all designs on founding an independent republic of the Sierra Madre. After commanding Liberal troops in Tamaulipas for four bloody years and serving as a Juárez loyalist in the struggle against French imperialism, he was appointed governor of Tamaulipas and San Luis Potosi in 1865. To escape the political storms of his homeland, he later lived for several years in Hidalgo County, Texas, then again crossed the border into Mexico. In 1874, he died in relative obscurity at Soto La Marina, Tamaulipas.[24]

Early in 1857, just over a year after fighting Callahan's Rangers at San Fernando, Coacoochee, better known to Texans as Wild Cat, disappeared into the Sierra Madre Mountains. Soon thereafter, he reportedly contracted smallpox and died somewhere in the remote deserts of Coahuila. His name is still honored among the Seminole descendents living on both sides of the border.[25]

Samuel Lockridge, the vaunted veteran of William Walker's ill-fated exploits in Nicaragua, never realized his dreams of empire. Like other filibusteros and defenders of slavery who looked with a lustful eye toward Mexico, Central America, and the Caribbean Basin, he supported the southern cause without qualification. Soon after the beginning of the Civil War, he joined the Confederate Army and accompanied Brigadier General Henry H. Sibley on his campaign in northern New Mexico. While commanding an artillery battery in the southern Sangre de Cristo Range, he was mortally wounded during savage hand-to-hand fighting at the Battle of Valverde on February 21, 1862.[26]

After commanding a company of Rangers ordered to the border in response to Juan Cortina's raid on Brownsville in 1859, William G. Tobin served briefly in the Confederate Army. Following the war, he drifted into a series of unsuccessful business ventures. After enjoying limited success as the proprietor of the Vance Hotel in San Antonio, Tobin persuaded U.S. Department of War officials to tender him a contract to produce canned chili con carne for both the army and navy. Just days after his promising enterprise began, the fifty-year-old native of South Carolina suffered severe cramps and died suddenly at his home in San Antonio on July 28, 1884.[27]

Following his career as a filibuster and his brief service in Captain Tobin's company during the Cortina War, William Robertson "Big" Henry returned to his family in San Antonio. In 1861, the people of Bexar County elected him sheriff for the second time. In that capacity, he exerted influence not only over law enforcement but also over the local home guard. On March 15, 1862, following a bitter dispute over military command in San Antonio, Henry was shot to death on the north side of the Main Plaza by a local ruffian named William Adams. Henry's killer was later judged to have acted in self-defense and was acquitted by a jury of his Bexar County peers.[28]

Henry Clay Davis remained a prominent cattleman in Starr County. Although he gave up on any future filibustering activities along the border, he stood as a staunch proponent of Anglo supremacy in South Texas. Ironically, the settlement that he founded, Rio Grande City, is inhabited today mostly by people of Mexican descent. His brick home on Britton Street, once a symbol of Anglo conquest, no longer stands. Few locals even remember the man and his Texas-size dreams.[29]

Henry Lawrence Kinney was financially ruined by his support for William Walker's Nicaragua venture. He served briefly in the Texas State Legislature but resigned office in 1861, owing to his bitter opposition to secession. Bankrupt and fearful of reprisal, "Colonel" Kinney moved to Matamoros to escape the wrath of his enemies. But he found no escape from the secessionists who stalked him. On March 3, 1862, during an exchange of gunfire between rebel and Unionist factions in the streets of Matamoros, he sustained a fatal wound. He was only forty-seven.[30]

Major Samuel Peter Heintzelman went on to enjoy a distinguished career in the U.S. Army. Although suffering serious wounds at the First Battle of

Manassas, he recovered and soon received promotion to brigadier general and commanded a brigade of Union troops at the Second Battle of Manassas. In 1863, he earned a field command. But Major General Heintzelman spent most of the last months of the conflict on court martial duty in Washington, D.C. He retired from the army in February 1869 and remained in the nation's capital until his death at the age of seventy-four on May 1, 1880. He is buried in Buffalo, New York.[31]

After surrendering the federal arsenal at San Antonio to McCulloch's Rangers in 1861, General David E. Twiggs left Texas for New Orleans. Following a brief stint in the District of Louisiana, he suffered infirmities that forced him to retire. In Augusta, Georgia, on July 15, 1862, "Old Davey" died at the age of seventy-two. He never admitted to any act of dishonor and claimed to his last days that only his age and poor health had prevented him from fighting the mob of secessionists in San Antonio. Many Texans celebrated the news of his passing.[32]

Following General Twiggs's surrender at San Antonio, Captain George Stoneman enjoyed a remarkable military and political career. He served with distinction in a series of campaigns in Virginia, achieving the rank of major general while being decorated for gallantry at the Battle of Petersburg. Surviving the Battle of the Crater and the fight at the Bloody Angle in 1865, he recuperated from serious wounds. After serving for two years in the Twenty-first U.S. Infantry on the Arizona frontier, Stoneman retired from the army in 1871 and moved to Los Angeles. He accepted an appointment as California state railroad commissioner in 1879. Four years later, he gained the Democratic Party gubernatorial nomination over George Hearst, father of the famed newspaper mogul, then was elected governor. First as commissioner, then during his four years as the state's chief executive, he earned the reputation as an honest public servant and a courageous leader who resisted the unbridled influence of powerful railroad corporations. In 1891, he retired from public life and returned to his San Gabriel Valley ranch. After suffering a debilitating stroke, he moved to Buffalo, New York, to be close to family. On September 4, 1894, he died and was buried in the city's Lakewood Cemetery.[33]

In the autumn of 1864, Lieutenant Colonel Mat Nolan, the "Boy Bugler of the Battle of Cerro Gordo," returned to his home in Corpus Christi, where he won election as sheriff of Nueces County. Following a dispute involving Nolan's purported plans to arrest anyone cooperating with Yankee troops stationed on Mustang Island, he became the target of assassins. On the night of December 22, 1864, Nolan and a well-known horse trader named McDonald were called into the street by two local hellions—known as the "Gravis boys"—who murdered both men with shotgun blasts to the face and pistol shots to the head. Nolan's killers were never brought to justice.[34]

As every American schoolchild should know, Robert E. Lee achieved immortality as the commander of the Army of Northern Virginia. His brilliant defense of the South—against overwhelming odds—established his reputation as a modern-day Hannibal, indeed a military genius who arguably stands as one of the greatest field strategists in history. After his surrender to General Ulysses S. Grant at Appomattox, Virginia, on April 9, 1865, Lee rode back to civilian life for the first time in forty years.

But he could never return home. By the end of the war he had lost something more cherished than his freedom: the scenic Arlington House, or Custis-Lee estate, overlooking the Potomac, which had been seized in 1864 by act of the U.S. Congress for the creation of what became Arlington National Cemetery. In the autumn of 1865, therefore, dispossessed and even denied access to his own home, Robert E. Lee and his wife, Mary, moved to Lexington, Virginia, where the general assumed the post of president of Washington College (now Washington and Lee University). He died there on October 12, 1870, of heart disease. Ineligible for burial on the grounds of his beloved Arlington, the much-venerated General Lee was laid in a simple wooden casket beneath the Washington College campus chapel.[35]

For the rest of his days, Captain Richard King continued to cast a long shadow over South Texas. In the spring of 1865, he escaped Reconstruction by fleeing to Mexico. He soon returned to the Nueces River region after receiving a pardon from President Andrew Johnson. In 1868, he dissolved his partnership with fellow livestock baron Mifflin Kenedy, retaining his sprawling Santa Gertrudis Ranch and the storied "Running W" brand. During the post–Civil War era, his cowhands drove a quarter million of his cattle up the Chisholm Trail then later the Western Trail. By the time of his death, King had amassed more than 614,000 acres, which would become the nucleus of the storied King Ranch.

In the twilight of his life, Richard King moved to San Antonio. The crippled old hacendado, the son of Irish immigrants who had helped to introduce scientific breeding to the ranges of South Texas, died in the Menger Hotel adjacent to the Alamo on April 14, 1885, at the age of sixty-one. Few did more to revolutionize the range cattle industry, and few did more to incite political revolution along the Rio Grande.[36]

Mifflin Kenedy, who in earlier times had also repeatedly offered to finance filibustering expeditions into Mexico, recalled late in life, "[F]or almost fifty years Captain King and I attempted to Americanize the border, without much success." But Kenedy enjoyed tremendous success as a pioneering rancher and later as a railroad financier. After his partnership with Captain King ended in 1868, he enclosed almost all of his Rancho Laureles on the lower Nueces, no small accomplishment for the owner of more than 242,000 acres of rugged ranch country. Among the first to fence his grazing lands with barbed wire, he sold his entire estate in 1882, then purchased an even larger empire, more than 400,000 acres in northern Cameron County (later appropriately renamed Kenedy County). He called the spread La Parra for the wild grapevines that covered the rangelands. Earlier, in 1876, he had helped finance the Corpus Christi, San Diego, and Rio Grande Railway from the lower Nueces to Laredo. He also extended terms of credit for the construction of a line from San Antonio to Aransas Pass. He lived out his last years in Corpus Christi, dying at home on March 14, 1895, at the age of seventy-six—nearly ten years after the passing of his more famous collaborator, Captain King.[37]

Juan Nepomuceno Cortina continued to elude officials of Texas and the United States. In 1862, he left the border for central Mexico, where he joined the fight against French imperialism. He was even at Querétaro to observe the execution of the emperor Maximilian. The following year, he rose above the turmoil within his troubled homeland, accepting an appointment by President Benito Juárez as general of the Mexican Army of the North. That same year, he effectively proclaimed himself governor of Tamaulipas, a post he again held briefly in 1866.

For the next decade, Cortina helped fund and encourage the largest cattle theft operation ever seen in South Texas. Instigating an accompanying reign of lawlessness, he left the border in a constant state of turmoil. Not even the likes of Rip Ford or the young and fearless Ranger Captain Leander H. McNelly could find, much less punish, him. Owing in part to continuing diplomatic pressure from the Grant administration, newly ascended president of Mexico Porfirio Díaz ordered Cortina's arrest and removal from the border in July 1875. For the last twenty years of his life, Cortina lived under the watchful eye of the Porfiriato. Although he receded from the public arena, Cortina basked in the leisure and comfort that belied his past as the most famous of "bandit chieftains." Some said that near the end of his life the ailing Cortina longed to see Colonel Ford one last time. He died in bed at Atzcapozalco on October 30, 1894, at the age of seventy. Along the Rio Grande border, they still sing corridos (ballads) about the storied Red Robber.[38]

Ford's Final Years

As for John S. "Rip" Ford, in March 1861 he organized and commanded the state volunteer unit designated as the Second Texas Mounted Rifles. Less than three months later, however, he was relieved of his command, probably for political reasons. Reluctantly, he accepted an appointment as superintendent of the newly created Texas Bureau of Conscription. Leaving his pregnant wife, Addie, in Brownsville at the home of her father, Major Eliju Smith, Ford traveled first to Houston, then on to Austin to organize the office charged with the onerous task of administering the first draft law in American history.[39]

It was perhaps the supreme irony for Ford. Long a champion of the citizen-soldier and arguably the greatest Ranger commander in the post–Mexican War era, Ford now faced the dreaded responsibility of carrying out a law that he did not believe in and had even opposed. As he recollected years later, the Confederate conscription measure of April 1862 was "an unfortunate enactment" that "did great harm" on the home front as it exempted prominent officeholders and wealthy slave owners.[40]

For Ford, the next two years spent in Austin and San Antonio could hardly have been less satisfying. Overseeing the machinery of the state conscription board, employing enrolling officers and sending them throughout the state with armed escorts to confront frightened and angry conscripts, shuffling endless stacks of papers and writing tedious reports, dealing with officious politicians more concerned with their own reelection than with the success of the war effort, Old Rip was simply out of place.[41]

In his most private moments of despair, Ford longed to mount up again and ride to the border to battle the enemies of Texas. At last, with news of a Union invasion of the Rio Grande Valley in November 1863, Ford began expressing his disdain for the desk job and his renewed desire to return to the field. Just days before Christmas, 1863, he got his wish. General John

Bankhead Magruder called on the legendary Ranger captain to drive the federals from Brownsville, just as he had done three years earlier.

Not surprisingly, given the obvious obstacles confronting him during the last phase of the war, Ford fell back on his experience as a Ranger and relied mostly on men he knew—and trusted—from past campaigns. Deception, disruption, evasion, interdiction, secrecy, and surprise would be the elements of his strategy along the lower Rio Grande. To carry out his tactical plans for an unconventional campaign designed to harass and frustrate Union forces, Ford relied on the very guerrilla tactics he had learned from Jack Hays in Mexico, then refined in the Indian campaigns and the subsequent Cortina War of 1859–1860. Understandably, he again chose to depend on such men as Mat Nolan, John Littleton, Philip Luckett, and Santos Benavides—men who had learned field tactics and leadership skills from him.[42]

State volunteer Robert H. Williams had more than a measure of respect for Rip Ford—and for good reason. Like other Ranger leaders of the time, Ford was quiet, even solitary, not given to conversation. He was reticent to reveal his plans to anyone. When he did speak, his men listened and listened attentively. No one could mistake his commanding presence, his bellowing voice, or his infectious confidence. At times, however, these Spartan qualities only isolated the brooding Colonel Ford from even his most trusted officers and enlisted men.

Still, virtually all who served with Ford held a genuine admiration for his strength of character and rare qualities of leadership. At the same time, that admiration was tempered by the understanding that he was a soldier, not a saint. Captain Williams remembered the fabled Texan as the "most inveterate gambler and the hardest swearer I ever met, even out West; indeed his power of 'language,' especially when the luck went against him, was almost grotesque in its resourcefulness." Williams recalled that Ford, whether raising a glass of whiskey in a formal toast or just imbibing whiskey in a saloon while playing poker, was not only the proverbial "hail fellow well met" but also an earthy character, always "free with his money, and equally free with his six-shooter," not to mention his strongly held opinions.[43]

Perhaps it was altogether fitting that Rip Ford rode at the head of a ragtag group of young Texans, remnants of the legendary Second Texas Mounted Rifles, when they routed elements of the Sixty-second Colored U.S. Infantry and the Thirty-fourth Indiana Infantry some eight miles below Brownsville at the Palmito Plain on May 13, 1865. On this field, at a bend of the Rio

Grande no more than twenty miles southeast of the Palo Alto Prairie where the U.S.-Mexican War had begun almost two decades earlier, Ford and his young volunteers drove Colonel Theodore Barrett's federal force downriver and toward the sea in one final act of Texan and southern defiance. No matter that the Battle at Palmito Ranch came nearly five weeks after General Robert E. Lee's surrender to General Ulysses S. Grant at Appomattox, Virginia; the motley collection of mounted Texans still cheered their commander that afternoon as the guns fell silent and the sun dropped below the western horizon. "Rip!" "Rip!" "Rip!" the rebels reportedly chanted in unison as Barrett's disorganized troops ran from the field. All was strangely quiet by the time dusk turned to twilight and the gray smoke of gunpowder finally lifted over the South Texas plain.

One day after he and his fellow Texans heard the echoes of the last shots of the American Civil War, Old Rip returned to Brownsville. Like so many of his compatriots, however, he soon slipped across the river to Matamoros and remained there for several months. He reestablished himself in Texas, living on the border during the next decade, ever the stalwart citizen. In 1868, he resumed a career in the newspaper business, taking the post of editor of the Brownsville *Sentinel*. In 1873, amid the so-called Skinning Wars along the lower Rio Grande, he served as cattle and hide inspector for Cameron County. Although no longer a Ranger, he nevertheless devoted his energies to thwarting the largest ring of cattle rustlers in the history of South Texas, the operation directed by none other than his longtime antagonist Juan N. Cortina. The following year, Ford served as mayor of Brownsville. To no one's surprise, in 1875 Ford was elected to represent Cameron County in the state constitutional convention held in Austin. During the critical months that concluded Reconstruction rule, he helped to draft the Texas constitution of 1876, still the framework of government in the Lone Star State. For the next three years he held a seat in the state senate and soon thereafter became superintendent of the Texas School for the Deaf, still located today in Austin.

By 1885, an aging John Ford and his wife, Addie, had moved to San Antonio to be near their daughter, Mary Louise, and her husband, Joe Maddox, a prominent real estate broker in the Alamo City. Ford assumed the post of deputy internal revenue collector for Bexar County, spending most days working at his office at 285 West Commerce and many of his evenings and weekends supporting civic causes and renewing his association with the Masonic Lodge. For the next decade, the Fords lived comfortably in their modest residence at 213 Avenue C, where Old Rip enjoyed his celebrity among the residents of San Antonio.[44]

When the famed frontier artist Frederick Remington visited San Antonio in 1891 to interview old Texan "originals," he found Ford to be the most original of them all. Impressed with Ford's flair as a storyteller and his gift for recalling details, Remington listened intently as the legendary Ranger regaled him with colorful accounts of border wars against Mexican bandits and marauding Indians. Remington described the flinty Captain Ford as "a very old man, with a wealth of snow white beard—bent but not withered . . . with stiffened limbs." Their meeting was one that the aspiring writer, painter, and sculptor would never forget. Remington surely understood that, in the person of Ford, he was witnessing the passing of an era.[45]

During his last years, Ford penned his memoirs and collected manuscripts and documents relating to his life and times, all the while devoting himself to the preservation of Texas history. Toward that end, in March 1897, during a gathering of prominent Texans in the state capitol, the assemblage including former governors Oran M. Roberts and Francis Lubbock, Ford helped to establish the Texas State Historical Association. This statewide organization continues to promote the rich cultural heritage of the Lone Star State.

Later that spring, the stooped but dignified Texan was often seen walking the streets of San Antonio with a gold-beaded cane in hand, sometimes sitting on a park bench in Alamo Plaza, where he liked to chat of the long ago. Local residents could not help but notice the tall figure of Old Rip strolling through the lobby of the historic Menger Hotel, where he frequently met with old friends and newer acquaintances. After suffering a series of strokes, which left him partially paralyzed, Ford convalesced in the Maddox home at 322 King William Street, a short carriage ride from the Alamo.

On July 8, 1897, Ford answered correspondence from an admirer, apologizing that the "ills of advancing age" had prevented him from doing more than dictating his thoughts to one Will Lambert, identified only as "secretary, etc." While his body was fast giving way, his mind remained clear and purposeful. He managed to sign his name to a letter that might well have served as his own eulogy. Declaring that he had always been an "unceasing advocate" of deploying Rangers in time of crisis, he added that his fellow state partisans had been "tireless defenders of the people of

Texas in the dark hours of danger and trouble." He expressed his lifelong admiration for the citizen-soldiers of Texas who had repeatedly responded to the call "not from any order of an official, but from a sense of duty to their neighbors and themselves." Finally, he concluded, "The Rangers did all brave men could do. In God's name let them organize, and give to the world an idea of their services and their sacrifices."[46]

By the autumn of 1897, Ford had been left an invalid, bedridden, dependent, for the first time, on others. He could only look out his bedroom window as the leaves of giant oaks fell. For several weeks, his condition worsened. As he labored even to breathe, his physician informed family members that there was nothing left to do but keep him comfortable. Surrounded in the end by Addie, Mary Louise, and a loving family, John Salmon Ford died in his sleep shortly after seven o'clock on the evening of November 3, 1897. Two days later, mourners gathered for a memorial service at the Westminster Presbyterian Church in San Antonio, after which Old Rip was buried in the city's Confederate Veterans Cemetery, where his remains rest in peace to this day.[47]

As for Rip Ford's enduring legend, and that of his Texas Mounted Rangers, it lives still—on *both* sides of the border.

A Mixed Legacy

To the Anglo populace of Texas, the Rangers stand alone in the lore and legends of the Lone Star State as righteous agents of justice and vengeance, who hastened the triumph of "civilization" over "savagery" and "democracy" over "despotism." For the Spanish-speaking peoples of the border, however, these very same Rangers left only a bitter legacy—one that yet lives in the dark legends of what is still a troubled border. That fact alone should relegate the early Rangers of the lower Rio Grande to a tragic chapter of the past that might well be titled "Burdens of Texas History." For people of Mexican heritage, the Texas Rangers appeared on the historical landscape like the Devil's horsemen, terrifying figures galloping straight out of the cryptic prophecies in the Book of Revelation. Like apparitions from hell, these Texan devils rode through border history as harbingers of death and destruction. They were soldiers of fortune, not of freedom; mercenaries and not missionaries of civilization; privateers rather than patriots. Even now, almost a century and a half later, Tejanos and Mexicanos recall in the lyrics of their border ballads a just fear of the hated mounted militia of the Lone Star State known simply as los Rinches.

Memories of past sorrows echo still on a border where such long-standing mistrust continues to separate people along lines of race, religion, language, and nationality. And just like the river that courses its way through the region, dividing one nation from another, the tradition of los diablos Tejanos stands between two peoples and two cultures that must share a common border and a common future.

Along the lower Rio Grande, the legend of the Texas devils remains as real as the historical record of the long and brutal war of ethnic conquest that forever shaped the character of the region. Throughout the ages, conquerors have always written their own history. And their accounts have inevitably filled the annals of what they, the victors, accept and promote as truth. In sum, as one sage historian liked to lament, "[H]istory too often belongs to the winners." Such has been the case with the Lone Star State and with the iconic Rangers of Texas tradition and American popular imagination.

But as with all legends that last through time and truly live, somewhere, in the mists between myth and documented fact, there exists the compelling necessity of reconciliation. In other words, historical controversy shall always exist, but the bitterest of legacies can only be put to rest when longtime adversaries are willing to make peace with the legend. Such a reconciliation must begin with an acknowledgment of past wrongs and the acceptance that conquest has a moral cost. And that cost to losers and victors alike *cannot* be measured in monetary or material terms.

As long as people on both sides of the lower Rio Grande read and remember, the Rangers' deeds—and misdeeds—shall not be forgotten. Nor should they be. The past should always be reappraised by each generation in light of its own experiences. Professor Walter Prescott Webb, too, would have understood that.

So the question remains: Were they heroic Rangers or riders from hell? A large body of evidence—much of it previously neglected if not ignored—points to a few of the former, but an even greater number of the latter.

Notes

Introduction

1. Walter Prescott Webb, *The Texas Rangers: A Century of Frontier Defense* (Austin: University of Texas Press, 1973), ix, 11–15; for the most thorough modern survey of the subject, albeit one that offers little to revise the Webb thesis, see Robert M. Utley, *Lone Star Justice: The First Century of the Texas Rangers* (New York: Oxford University Press, 2002).

2. Walter Prescott Webb, *The Texas Rangers in the Mexican War* (Austin: Jenkins Garrett Press, 1975), 8. For other useful treatments of the Rangers in the U.S.-Mexican War, see Henry W. Barton, *Texas Volunteers in the Mexican War* (Wichita Falls, Tex.: privately printed, 1970); Frederick Wilkins, *The Highly Irregular Irregulars: Texas Rangers in the Mexican War* (Austin: Eaken Press, 1990). For a traditional interpretation, consult also the Ranger trilogy of Frederick Wilkins, particularly the second volume, *Defending the Borders: The Texas Rangers, 1848–1861* (Austin: State House Press, 2001). A sweeping revisionist interpretation of the role and effectiveness of Texas volunteer Rangers in the nineteenth century that challenges Webb's thesis, particularly in relation to campaigns against the American Indians in Texas, may be found in Gary Clayton Anderson, *The Conquest of Texas: Ethnic Cleansing in the Promised Land, 1820–1875* (Norman: University of Oklahoma Press, 2005).

3. Charles M. Robinson III, *The Men Who Wear the Star: The Story of the Texas Rangers* (New York: Random House, 2000), xxi; Chuck Parsons and Marianne E. Hall Little, *Captain L. H. McNelly: Texas Ranger* (Austin: State House Press, 2001), xi.

Chapter 1

1. Luther Giddings, *Sketches of the Campaign in Northern Mexico by an Officer of the First Ohio Volunteers* (New York: G. P. Putnam & Co., 1853), 97.

2. Ibid., 10–32; Samuel C. Reid, *The Scouting Expeditions of McCulloch's Texas Rangers* (Philadelphia: G. B. Lieber, 1848), 26; Allan Peskin, ed., *Volunteers: The Mexican War Journals of Private Richard Coulter and Sergeant Thomas Barclay, Company E, Second Pennsylvania Infantry* (Kent, Ohio: Kent State Press, 1991), 218; Maurice Garland Fulton, ed., *Diary and Letters of Josiah Gregg* (Norman: University of Oklahoma Press, 1941), 218–19; Jonathan Duff Brown, "Reminiscences of Jon.

Duff Brown," *Quarterly of the Texas State Historical Association* 12 (April 1909): 296–311; Rhoda Doubleday, ed., *Journals of the Late Brevet Major Philip Norbourne Barbour, a Captain in the Third Regiment, United States Infantry, and His Wife Martha Isabella Hopkins Barbour, Written during the War with Mexico, 1846* (New York: G. P. Putnam's Sons, 1936), 50–53 (hereafter cited as Doubleday, *Barbour Journals*); Grady McWhiney and Sue McWhiney, eds., *To Mexico with Taylor and Scott, 1845–1847* (Waltham, Mass.: Blaisdell Publishing Co., 1969), 36.

3. Samuel Chamberlain, *My Confession: Recollections of a Rogue*, ed. William Goetzmann (Austin: Texas State Historical Association, 1996), 61, 92; Robert H. Ferrell, ed., *Monterrey Is Ours: The Mexican War Letters of Lieutenant Dana, 1845–1847* (Lexington: University Press of Kentucky, 1990), 14.

4. George Wilkins Kendall, *Dispatches from the Mexican War* (Norman: University of Oklahoma Press, 1999), 48; George Winston Smith and Charles Judah, eds., *Chronicles of the Gringos: The U.S. Army in the Mexican War, 1846–1848, Accounts of Eyewitnesses and Combatants* (Albuquerque: University of New Mexico Press, 1968), 42–43; Brown, "Reminiscences of Jon. Duff Brown," 304–11.

5. Albert G. Brackett, *General Lane's Brigade in Central Mexico* (Cincinnati: H. W. Derby & Co., 1954), 173–74.

6. Ibid.; Rankin Dilworth, *The March to Monterrey: The Diary of Lieutenant Rankin Dilworth*, ed. Lawrence R. Clayton and Joseph E. Chance (El Paso: Texas Western Press, 1996), 37, 63, 67.

7. Nelson Lee, *Three Years among the Comanches: The Narrative of Nelson Lee, the Texas Ranger* (Norman: University of Oklahoma Press, 1957), 14.

8. Webb, *Texas Rangers: A Century of Frontier Defense*, 11–15; Ben Procter, "The Texas Rangers: An Overview," in *The Texas Heritage*, ed. Ben Procter and Archie McDonald, 3rd ed. (Wheeling, Ill.: Harlan Davidson, 1998), 209; Joseph E. Chance, ed., *Mexico under Fire: Being the Diary of Samuel Ryan Curtis, 3rd Ohio Volunteer Regiment during the American Military Occupation of Northern Mexico, 1846–1847* (Fort Worth: Texas Christian University Press, 1994), 200–202.

9. Dilworth, *March to Monterrey*, 24; J. Jacob Oswandel, *Notes of the Mexican War, 1846–47–48* (Philadelphia: n.p., 1885), 363.

10. John Salmon Ford, *Rip Ford's Texas*, ed. Stephen B. Oates (Austin: University of Texas Press, 1963), 61, 72–73.

11. Chamberlain, *My Confession*, 98; Joseph Chance, ed., *The Mexican War Journal of Captain Franklin Smith* (Jackson: University of Mississippi Press, 1991), 166. See also E. M. Daggett "Advances with Guerrillas," in *Heroes and Incidents of the Mexican War*, ed. Isaac George (Greensburg, Pa.: Review Publishing, 1903), 209–13; for a firsthand account of the Mexican side of the war, and for reference to the guerrilla war among the civilian populace, see Ramón Alcaraz, *Apuntes para la*

historia de la guerra entre México y los Estados Unidos (Mexico City: Siglo Veintiuno Editores, 1974), 385–90 (hereafter cited as Alcaraz, *Historia de la guerra*).

12. Reid, *Scouting Expeditions of McCulloch's Texas Rangers*, 53.

13. Alexander Lander, *A Trip to the Wars: Comprising the History of the Galveston Riflemen, Formed April 28, 1846, at Galveston, Texas; Together with the History of Monterrey, also Descriptions of Mexico and Its People* (Monmouth, Ill.: Atlas Office of the Publisher, 1847), 24; Chance, *Mexican War Journal of Captain Franklin Smith*, 100; Doubleday, *Barbour Journals*, 107.

14. Chamberlain, *My Confession*, 61–63, 267–70; Ford, *Rip Ford's Texas*, 64; Walter P. Lane, *The Adventures and Recollections of General Walter P. Lane* (Marshall, Tex.: News Messengers Publishing Co., 1928), 57–59. Lane mistakenly refers to Glanton as "Glandon." See also Thomas Wilhelm, ed., *History of the Eighth U.S. Infantry, from Its Organization in 1838* (New York: Regimental Headquarters, Eighth Infantry, 1873), 2:348; Horace Bell, *Reminiscences of a Ranger: Early Times in Southern California* (Norman: University of Oklahoma Press, 1999), 273–80.

15. Chamberlain, *My Confession*, 201–202.

16. Ibid.

17. Ibid.

18. Chance, *Mexico under Fire*, 173, 261; Charles D. Spurlin, *Texas Volunteers in the Mexican War* (Austin: Eakin Press, 1998), 64–65, 118; Mexican War Correspondence, 30th Cong., 1st sess., 1848, H. Exec. Doc. 60, serial 520, 1138.

19. James Kuykendall, "Sketches of Early Texians," Center for American History, University of Texas, Austin, 8; Brackett, *General Lane's Brigade in Central Mexico*, 77; Charles Wilson James, *Address on the Occasion of Removing the Remains of Captains Walker and Gillespie on the 21st of April, A.D., 1856*, Center for American History, University of Texas, Austin, 14; Chamberlain, *My Confession*, 86.

20. Chamberlain, *My Confession*, 92; William S. Henry, *Campaign Sketches of the War with Mexico* (New York: Harper Brothers, 1847), 88–90, 113–15; *General Taylor and His Staff: Comprising Memoirs of /Generals Taylor, Worth, Wool, and Butler* (Philadelphia: Grigg, Elliot & Co., 1848), 179.

21. Oswandel, *Notes of the Mexican War*, 348–54; J. Frost, *The Mexican War and Its Warriors: Comprising a Complete History of All the Operations of the American Armies of Mexico* (New Haven, Conn.: H. Mansfield, 1848), 301.

22. Marilyn McAdams Sibley, ed., *Samuel H. Walker's Account of the Mier Expedition* (Austin: Texas State Historical Association, 1978), 59; see also Samuel H. Walker Papers, Texas State Library and Archives, Austin (hereafter cited as SWP).

23. Samuel Walker to "Dear Sister," August 26, 1845, SWP; Oswandel, *Notes of the Mexican War*, 147–53.

24. Samuel Walker to Jonathan Walker, June 6, 1847, SWP.

25. Smith and Judah, *Chronicles of the Gringos*, 269–71.

26. Ibid., 349; for a slightly different account of Walker's death, see *General Taylor and His Staff*, 185–94.

27. Jerry Thompson, ed., *Fifty Miles and a Fight: Major Samuel Peter Heintzelman's Journal of Texas and the Cortina War* (Austin: Texas State Historical Association, 1998), 8. Heintzelman's actual journal may be found in the Henitzelman Papers, located in the Manuscript Division of the Library of Congress, Washington, D.C.; Oswandel, *Notes of the Mexican War*, 350–51.

28. Smith and Judah, *Chronicles of the Gringos*, 269–71.

29. Alcaraz, *Historia de la guerra*, 350; Webb, *Texas Rangers: A Century of Frontier Defense*, 81–86; Walter Prescott Webb, *The Great Plains* (New York: Grosset & Dunlap, 1931), 171–73, 177; Oswandel, *Notes of the Mexican War*, 147–53.

30. Bell, *Reminiscences of a Ranger*, 151–52.

31. Reid, *Scouting Expeditions of McCulloch's Texas Rangers*, 23.

32. For an early biographical treatment of McCulloch, see Victor M. Rose, *The Life and Services of General Ben McCulloch* (Philadelphia: Pictorial Bureau of the Press, 1888); Thomas W. Cutrer, *Ben McCulloch and the Frontier Military Tradition* (Chapel Hill: University of North Carolina Press, 1993); Webb, *Texas Rangers: A Century of Frontier Defense*, 58–62, 74, 84.

33. Webb, *Texas Rangers: A Century of Frontier Defense*, 94–113; *General Taylor and His Staff*, 200–203; Kendall, *Dispatches from the Mexican War*, 50–57, 91–95, 100–109, 118–41; George Wilkins Kendall, *Letters from a Texas Sheep Ranch: Written in the Years 1860 and 1861 by George Kendall to Henry Stephens Randall*, ed. James Brown (Urbana: University of Illinois Press, 1959), 101–107.

34. Giddings, *Sketches*, 287; Webb, *Texas Rangers: A Century of Frontier Defense*, 113; Isaac Stevens, *Campaigns of the Rio Grande and of Mexico* (New York: D. Appleton & Co., 1851), 43.

35. Mexican War Correspondence, 30th Cong., 1st sess., 1848, 1178. H. Exec. Doc. 60, serial 520; Lane, *Adventures and Recollections of General Walter P. Lane*, 56; Abner Doubleday, *My Life in the Old Army: The Reminiscences of Abner Doubleday*, ed. Joseph E. Chance (Fort Worth: TCU Press, 1998), 101–16; Abriel Abbot Livermore, *War with Mexico: Reviewed* (Boston: American Peace Society, 1850), 148, 234; Charles Porter, *Review of the Mexican War* (Auburn, N.Y.: Alden & Parsons, 1849), 79; Webb, *Texas Rangers: A Century of Frontier Defense*, 112–15; Henry, *Campaign Sketches of the War with Mexico*, 222–25; Fulton, *Diary and Letters of Josiah Gregg*, 218–19.

36. Webb, *Texas Rangers in the Mexican War*, 60, 70–74.

37. John C. Caperton, "Sketch of Colonel John C. Hays, Texas Ranger," typescript, Center for American History, University of Texas, Austin; Charles Adams Gulick et al., eds., *The Papers of Mirabeau Buonaparte Lamar*, 6 vols. (Austin: Von

Boeckmann-Jones, 1920–27), 5:409; John H. Jenkins III, ed., *Recollections of Early Texas: The Memoirs of John Holland Jenkins* (Austin: University of Texas Press, 1987), 144–46; Eugene C. Hollon, ed., *William Bollaert's Texas* (Norman: University of Oklahoma Press, 1956), 225, 241.

38. James K. Greer, *Colonel Jack Hays: Texas Frontier Leader and California Builder* (College Station: Texas A&M Press, 1987), 52–53, 118; Frederick Wilkins, *The Legend Begins: The Texas Rangers, 1823–1845* (Austin: State House Press, 1996), 202–205; Robinson, *Men Who Wear the Star*, 65–66; Reid, *Scouting Expeditions of McCulloch's Texas Rangers*, 111–12.

39. Reid, *Scouting Expeditions of McCulloch's Texas Rangers*, 107–15; Frost, *The Mexican War and Its Warriors*, 305–306; Ferrell, *Monterrey Is Ours*, 14; John Q. Anderson, ed., *Tales of Frontier Texas, 1830–1860* (Dallas: Southern Methodist University Press, 1966), 171–73.

40. Brackett, *General Lane's Brigade in Central Mexico*, 173–74; Ford, *Rip Ford's Texas*, 68–69; *General Taylor and His Staff*, 211; see also John S. Ford, "The Services of Col. John C. Hays," Texas Confederate Museum Collection, The Haley Memorial Library and History Center, Midland, Texas (hereafter cited as TCMC).

41. Ford, *Rip Ford's Texas*, 107; Robert Hall, *Life of Robert Hall: Indian Fighter and Veteran of Three Great Wars* (Austin: State House Press, 1992), 104–105; Brackett, *General Lane's Brigade in Central Mexico*, 194–95; Reid, *Scouting Expeditions of McCulloch's Texas Rangers*, 107–12.

42. Ferrell, ed., *Monterrey Is Ours*, 132–33; *General Taylor and His Staff*, 203; Doubleday, *Barbour Journals*, 107; Thomas B. Thorpe, *Our Army at Monterrey: Being a Correct Account of the Proceedings and Events Which Occurred to the Army of Occupation under the Command of Major General Taylor* (Philadelphia: Carey & Hart, 1847), 63–64.

43. James K. Holland, "Diary of a Texan Volunteer in the Mexican War," *Southwestern Historical Quarterly* 30 (July 1926): 22.

44. Greer, *Colonel Jack Hays*, 137–53; Doubleday, *My Life in the Old Army*, 73–99; Chance, *Mexican War Journal of Captain Franklin Smith*, 150–51; Henry, *Campaign Sketches of the War with Mexico*, 192–205; Spurlin, *Texas Volunteers in the Mexican War*, 90; *General Taylor and His Staff*, 203.

45. Reid, *Scouting Expeditions of McCulloch's Rangers*, 192; Kendall, *Dispatches from the Mexican War*, 94–116.

46. Lee, *Three Years among the Comanches*, 73; McWhiney and McWhiney, *To Mexico with Taylor and Scott*, 52–61; Thorpe, *Our Army at Monterrey*, 120; Alcaraz, *Historia de la guerra*, 65. For an early translation of Alcaraz, which was published in the United States, consult Albert C. Ramsey, trans. and ed., *The Other Side: Or Notes from the History of the War between Mexico and the United States* (New York: Wiley, 1850).

47. *General Taylor and His Staff*, 110–11.

48. Mexican War Correspondence, 30th Cong., 1st. sess., 1848, H. Exec. Doc. 60, serial 520, 430; Giddings, *Sketches*, 221–22; see also an anonymous pamphlet published under the title *General Taylor's Rough and Ready Almanac* (Philadelphia: Turner & Fisher, 1848), 4.

49. Brackett, *General Lane's Brigade in Central Mexico*, 173–74; Dumont's quote in the *Indiana Register* appeared in the Lone Star State in the *Democratic Telegraph and Texas Register*, February 24, 1848.

50. 30th Cong., 2nd sess., 1848, H. Exec. Doc. 1, 86–88.

51. Ford, *Rip Ford's Texas*, 81–82; *Democratic Telegraph and Texas Register*, February 24, 1848.

52. Lee, *Three Years among the Comanches*, 74–75.

53. New Orleans *Picayune*, December 29, 1847, as quoted in Greer, *Colonel Jack Hays*, 181.

54. Ethan Allen Hitchcock, *Fifty Years in Camp and Field: Diary of Major General Ethan Allen Hitchcock U.S.A.*, ed. W. A. Croffut (New York: G. P. Putnam's Sons, 1909), 310.

55. Ford, *Rip Ford's Texas*, 81–82; Lee, *Three Years among the Comanches*, 74–76; Mark Nackman, "The Making of the Texan Citizen Soldier," *Southwestern Historical Quarterly* 78 (January 1975): 243.

56. Ford, *Rip Ford's Texas*, 81–85.

57. Ibid.

58. Ibid.

59. Ibid.; Lee, *Three Years among the Comanches*, 76; see also John C. Hays to Joseph Lane, March 1, 1848, TCMC.

Chapter 2

1. Numerous mid-nineteenth-century descriptions of the Nueces Strip are available. See Albert J. Myer, "I Am Already Quite a Texan: Albert J. Myer's Letters from Texas, 1854–1856," ed. David A. Clary, *Southwestern Historical Quarterly* 82 (July 1978): 35–36; John Russell Bartlett, *Personal Narrative of Exploration and Incidents in Texas, New Mexico, California, Sonora, and Chihuahua* (New York: D. Appleton & Co., 1854), 2:522–30; Frederick Law Olmsted, *A Journey through Texas: Or, A Saddle Trip on the Southwestern Frontier* (Austin: University of Texas Press, 1978), 270–76, 441–45; William H. Emory, *Report on the United States and Mexican Boundary Survey: Made under the Direction of the Secretary of the Interior* (Austin: Texas State Historical Association, 1987), 1:56; Lydia Spencer Lane, *I Married a Soldier* (Albuquerque: New Mexico Press, 1964), 28–30.

2. For the standard study of the Rio Grande and its significance in the history of the American Southwest, see the classic Paul Horgan, *Great River: The Rio Grande in North American History*, 2 vols. (New York: Rinehart & Co., 1954).

3. Richard Griswold del Castillo, *The Treaty of Guadalupe Hidalgo: A Legacy of Conflict* (Norman: University of Oklahoma Press, 1990), 3, 10–11, 172–76, 187.

4. J. Frank Dobie, *The Longhorns* (New York: Grosset & Dunlap, 1941), 10–11, 17–18, 20–25, 28–30, 33–38, 42; Joseph G. McCoy, *Historic Sketches of the Cattle Trade of the West and Southwest* (Lincoln: University of Nebraska Press, 1985), 77–84.

5. Emory, *Report on the United States and Mexican Boundary Survey*, 1:56; Bartlett, *Personal Narrative*, 2:529–30; Caleb Coker, ed., *The News from Brownsville: Helen Chapman's Letters from the Texas Military Frontier, 1848–1852* (Austin: Texas State Historical Association, 1993), 386 (hereafter cited as Coker, *Helen Chapman's Letters*); John C. Rayburn and Virginia Rayburn, eds., *Century of Conflict: 1821–1913, Incidents in the Lives of William Neale and William A. Neale, Early Settlers in South Texas* (Waco: Texian Press, 1966), 58.

6. Olmsted, *Journey through Texas*, 443.

7. *Reports of the Committee of Investigation Sent in 1873 by the Mexican Government to the Frontier of Texas* (New York: Baker, Godwin Printers, 1875), 11–17.

8. Frederick Wilkins, *Defending the Borders*, 10–13; Ford, *Rip Ford's Texas*, 141, 147–48; J. W. Wilbarger, *Indian Depredations in Texas: Reliable Accounts of Battles, Wars, Adventures, Forays, Murders, Massacres, etc., Together with Biographical Sketches of Many of the Most Noted Indian Fighters and Frontiersmen of Texas* (Austin: Hutchings Printing House, 1889), 309–13.

9. W. J. Hughes, *Rebellious Ranger: Rip Ford and the Old Southwest* (Norman: University of Oklahoma Press, 1964), 5–7, 15–16.

10. Ibid.

11. Ford, *Rip Ford's Texas*, 141–48; John S. Ford, "Memoirs of John S. Ford and Reminiscences of Texas History, 1836–1888," typed mss. See also the typed and bound copies of Ford's original memoir, later edited by Stephen Oates, in the John S. Ford Papers, Center for American History, University of Texas, Austin. The author obtained copies from the Pan American University Library in Edinburg, Texas (hereafter cited as Ford, "Memoirs").

12. Ford, *Rip Ford's Texas*, 141–48; Ford, "Memoirs," 533–37; see also *Annual Report of the Commissioner of Indian Affairs, 1850* (Washington, D.C.: Office of the Commissioner of Indian Affairs, 1850), 10–13.

13. Ford, *Rip Ford's Texas*, 141–48: Ford, "Memoirs," 533–37, 549–57.

14. Ford, *Rip Ford's Texas*, 141–48.

15. Ibid; Ford, "Memoirs," 539–45.

16. Ford, *Rip Ford's Texas*, 156–57.

17. Ibid.; Ford to Major George Deas, May 21, 1850, Correspondence and Reports Relating to Special Subjects, 1830–1851, Record Group 393, Department of the Army, National Archives, Washington, D.C; A. J. Sowell, *Early Settlers and Indian Fighters of Southwest Texas* (Austin: State House Press, 1986), 819–21.

18. Sowell, *Early Settlers and Indian Fighters*, 819–20; Ford, *Rip Ford's Texas*, 158–60; Ford, "Memoirs," 549–57.

19. Ford, *Rip Ford's Texas*, 160–61.

20. Ibid.

21. Ibid.; Ford, "Memoirs," 558.

22. Dorman H. Winfrey, ed., *Texas Indian Papers, 1846–1859*, vol. 3 (Austin: Texas State Library, 1960), 119–20.

23. Ibid., 138–39; Utley, *Lone Star Justice*, 90–94; For a recent treatment of the contrast of views and contradicting interests that led to the clash between state and federal officials on the Indian "menace" along the borders of the Lone Star State, consult Anderson, *Conquest of Texas*, 240–45.

24. Ford, *Rip Ford's Texas*, 161–63.

25. Ibid., 164–65; Ford, "Memoirs," 575–76.

26. Ford, *Rip Ford's Texas*, 170–72; Hughes, *Rebellious Ranger*, 92–93.

27. Wilbarger, *Indian Depredations in Texas*, 614–16.

28. Ibid.; Ford, *Rip Ford's Texas*, 171–72.

29. Ibid.; Wilbarger, *Indian Depredations in Texas*, 614–16.

30. Ford, "Memoirs," 571–74; Ford, *Rip Ford's Texas*, 171–72.

31. Ford, *Rip Ford's Texas*, 171–73. For a representative statement reflecting the views of Texas leaders on Indian depredations in South Texas, especially spokesmen for South Texas such as state senator and Committee on Indian Affairs cochair Henry L. Kinney of Corpus Christi; see also the *Report of the Committee on Indian Affairs, Journals of the Senate of the State of Texas, Extra Session, Third Legislature* (Austin: Gazette Office, 1850), 75–78.

32. Ford, *Rip Ford's Texas*, 173–74; Sowell, *Early Settlers and Indian Fighters*, 821–22.

33. Sowell, *Early Settlers and Indian Fighters*, 821–22; for background on Walker's activities as an adventurer guiding and assisting travelers through Mexico to California following the war, see John W. Audubon, *Audubon's Western Journal: 1849–1850, Being the Ms. Record of a Trip from New York to Texas, and an Overland Journey through Mexico and Arizona to the Goldfields of California.* (Glorietta, N.M.: Rio Grande Press, 1969), 75–77; Ford, *Rip Ford's Texas*, 174–76.

34. Ford, *Rip Ford's Texas*, 174–76; Sowell, *Early Settlers and Indian Fighters*, 821–22.

35. Wilbarger, *Indian Depredations in Texas*, 616–19; Ford, *Rip Ford's Texas*, 177–79.

36. Ford, *Rip Ford's Texas*, 177–79; Wilbarger, *Indian Depredations in Texas*, 616–19.

37. Ford, *Rip Ford's Texas*, 184–87; *Annual Report of the Commissioner of Indian Affairs, 1851* (Washington, D.C.: Gideon & Co., Printers, 1851), 43, 254.

38. Teresa Viele, *Following the Drum: A Glimpse of Frontier Life* (Lincoln: University of Nebraska Press, 1984), 149–50; Emory, *Report on the United States and the Mexican Boundary Survey*, 1:56–62; Olmsted, *Journey through Texas*, 323–26; Coker, *Helen Chapman's Letters*, 160–61, 373–77.

39. Bartlett, *Personal Narrative*, 1:36; Emory, *Report on the United States and Mexican Boundary Survey*, 1:61; Melinda Rankin, *Twenty Years among the Mexicans: A Narrative of Missionary Labor* (Cincinnati: Central Book Concern, 1881), 39; Olmsted, *Journey through Texas*, 443; P. F. Parisot, *The Reminiscences of a Texas Missionary* (San Antonio: St. Mary's Church, 1899), 84–85; Viele, *Following the Drum*, 151–52.

40. William R. Manning, ed., *Diplomatic Correspondence of the United States, Inter-American Affairs, 1831–1860*, vol. 9, *Mexico* (Washington, D.C.: Carnegie Endowment for International Peace, 1937), 47; Smith and Judah, *Chronicles of the Gringos*, 445–47.

41. Doubleday, *My Life in the Old Army*, 48–49, 122–24,175.

42. Fitzhugh Lee, *General Lee: A Biography of Robert E. Lee* (New York: Da Capo Press, 1994), 58–69; Carl Coke Rister, *Robert E. Lee in Texas* (Norman: University of Oklahoma Press, 1946), 83–94.

43. Coker, *Helen Chapman's Letters*, 373–77, 390; R. H. Williams, *With the Border Ruffians: Memories of the Far West, 1852–1868*, edited by E. W. Williams (Lincoln: University of Nebraska Press, 1982), 152–56; Richard Maxwell Brown, *Strain of Violence: Historical Studies of American Violence and Vigilantism* (New York: Oxford University Press, 1975), 237–39; Joe B. Frantz, "The Frontier Tradition: An Invitation to Violence," in *A History of Violence in America: A Report to the National Commission on the Causes and Prevention of Violence*, ed. Hugh Davis Graham and Ted Robert Gurr (New York: Bantam Books, 1969), 130–40, 150–52.

44. Cora Montgomery, *Eagle Pass: Or, Life on the Border* (New York: George Putnam & Co., 1852), 153–55.

45. *Texas State Gazette* (Austin), December 29, 1849; Galen Greaser and Jesus F. de la Teja, "Quieting Title to Spanish and Mexican Land Grants in the Trans-Nueces: The Bourland and Miller Commission, 1850–1852," *Southwestern Historical Quarterly* 95 (April 1992): 446–50. For surveys of Anglo-Mexican relations in South Texas, see David Montejano, *Anglos and Mexicans in the Making of Texas, 1836–1986* (Austin: University of Texas Press, 1987); and Armando C. Alonzo, *Tejano Legacy: Rancheros and Settlers in South Texas, 1734–1900* (Albuquerque: University of New Mexico Press, 1998).

46. *Texas State Gazette* (Austin), February 23, 1850.

47. "To the Citizens of the Valley of the Rio Grande," undated news clipping in *The Intelligencer* (Austin), John L. Haynes Papers, Center for American History, University of Texas, Austin (hereafter cited as JLHP).

48. *Texas State Gazette* (Austin). February 23, 1850; Frank H. Dugan, "The 1850 Affair of the Brownsville Separatists," *Southwestern Historical Quarterly* 61 (October 1957): 270–72; various undated news clippings may also be found in JLHP.

49. *Texas State Gazette* (Austin), February 23, 1850; Dugan, "The 1850 Affair of the Brownsville Separatists," 270–87.

50. *Texas State Gazette* (Austin), March 9, 1850.

51. Greaser and De la Teja, "Quieting Title to Spanish and Mexican Land Grants," 450–54.

52. For biographical information of Bourland and Miller, see John L. Haynes, "The Rio Grande Commissioners," in *The Intelligencer* (Austin), JLHP. See also William S. Speer and John Henry Brown, eds., *The Encyclopedia of the New West* (Marshall, Tex.: United States Biographical Publishing Co., 1881), 139, 573; Texas Legislature, House of Representatives, *Biographical Directory of the Texan Conventions and Congresses, 1832–1845* (Huntsville, 1942), 54; *Message of the Governor Transmitting the Report of the Commissioners to Investigate Land Titles West of the Nueces* (Austin: Cashney & Hampton, 1851), 3–7. See also William Bourland to Governor Peter H. Bell, August 24, 1850; Bourland to Bell, October 6, 1850; and James B. Miller to Bell, November 28, 1850, Peter H. Bell Papers, Texas State Library and Archives, Austin (hereafter cited as PHBP).

53. Peter H. Bell, *Message of the Governor, Transmitting the Report of the Commission to Investigate Land Titles West of the Nueces* (Austin: *State Gazette* Office, 1851), 5–6.

54. Miller to Bell, November 28, 1850, PHBP.

55. Greaser and De la Teja, "Quieting Title to Spanish and Mexican Land Grants," 459–64.

56. Arnoldo De Leon, *They Called Them Greasers: Anglo Attitudes toward Mexicans in Texas, 1821–1900* (Austin: University of Texas Press, 1983), 16–20, 28–34, 65–83; Arnoldo De Leon, *Mexican Americans in Texas: A Brief History* (Arlington Heights, Ill.: Harlan Davidson, 1993), 40–42; Bruce Cheeseman, ed., *Maria Von Blucher's Corpus Christi: Letters from the South Texas Frontier, 1849–1879* (College Station: Texas A&M Press, 2002), 84–85.

57. Montgomery, *Eagle Pass*, 154, 159–60; Olmsted, *Journey through Texas*, 265–66, 455.

58. Ford, *Rip Ford's Texas*, 205; Olmsted, *Journey through Texas*, 456; John J. Linn, *Reminiscences of Fifty Years in Texas* (Austin: State House Press, 1986), 310.

59. Emory, *Report on the United States and Mexican Boundary Survey*, 1:59–67.

60. Montgomery, *Eagle Pass*, 111–12; Viele, *Following the Drum*, 149; Parisot, *Reminiscences of a Texas Missionary*, 100–101; Emory, *Report on the United States and Mexican Boundary Survey*, 1:56–62; Olmsted, *Journey through Texas*, 452–453.

61. Montgomery, *Eagle Pass*, 147–51; Ford, *Rip Ford's Texas* 195–205; Bartlett, *Personal Narrative*, 2:511–12; Rankin, *Twenty Years among the Mexicans*, 40; Ernest C. Shearer, "The Carvajal Disturbances," *Southwestern Historical Quarterly* 55 (October 1951): 201–30; Charles Brown, *Agents of Manifest Destiny: The Lives and Times of Filibusters* (Chapel Hill: University of North Carolina Press, 1980), 151–53; John Wright and William Wright, *Recollections of Western Texas: Descriptive and Narrative, Including an Indian Campaign, 1852–55*, ed. Robert Wooster (Lubbock: Texas Tech University Press, 2001), 78; Ford "Memoirs," 880; Coker, *Chapman's Letters*, 264–65. For a recent study that sheds new light on the career of Carvajal, including the so-called Merchant's War, see Joseph E. Chance, *Jose Maria De Jesus Carvajal: The Life and Times of a Mexican Revolutionary* (San Antonio: Trinity University Press, 2006).

62. Ford, *Rip Ford's Texas*, 201; Emanuel Domenech, *Missionary Adventures in Texas and Mexico: A Personal Narrative of Six Years' Sojourn in Those Regions* (London: Longman, Brown, Green, Longmans, & Roberts, 1858), 334.

63. Ford, *Rip Ford's Texas*, 201.

64. Domenech, *Missionary Adventures in Texas and Mexico*, 340–45.

65. Ibid.; Ford, *Rip Ford's Texas*, 196; *Reports of the Committee of Investigation*, 188–90; "The Rio Grande Commissioners," JLHP.

66. *Reports of the Committee of Investigation*, 202–203.

67. Ibid.

68. Manning, *Diplomatic Correspondence of the United States*, 9:48–56.

Chapter 3

1. Ford, *Rip Ford's Texas*, 187–88.

2. The editorial from the *Ledger* was reprinted in the *Texas State Gazette* (Austin), October 11, 1851.

3. Winfrey, *Texas Indian Papers, 1846–1859*, 3:173.

4. Ibid., 3:174–75; see also Anna Maria Kelsey, *Through the Years: Reminiscences of Pioneer Days on the Texas Border* (San Antonio: Naylor Co., 1952), 19–25.

5. E. J. McLane to Governor Bell, June 30, 1852, PHBP; Winfrey, *Texas Indian Papers, 1846–1859*, 3:176.

6. Bell to Millard Fillmore, August 20, 1852, PHBP; Winfrey, *Texas Indian Papers, 1846–1859*, 3:179–80.

7. Wilkins, *Defending the Borders*, 39–41.

8. Charles Conrad to Bell, September 30, 1852, PHBP.

9. Ibid.

10. Owen Shaw to Bell, September 22, 1852; and Henry Clay Davis to Bell, December 12, 1852, PHBP.

11. Elisha M. Pease to James H. Callahan, July 5, 1855, Elisha M. Pease Papers, Texas State Library and Archives, Austin (hereafter cited as EPP); *Annual Report of the Commissioner of Indian Affairs, 1851*, 41–43, 254–56, 259.

12. Linn, *Reminiscences of Fifty Years in Texas*, 185; James T. DeShields, *Border Wars of Texas* (Austin: State House Press, 1993), 324; Wilbarger, *Indian Depredations in Texas*, 376; Homer Thrall, *A Pictorial History of Texas: From the Earliest Visits of European Adventurers, to A.D. 1879* (St. Louis: N. D. Thompson & Co., 1879), 520–21; John H. Jenkins III, ed., *The Papers of the Texas Revolution, 1835–1836* (Austin: Presidial Press, 1973), 7:86; John Henry Brown, *Indian Wars and Pioneers of Texas* (Austin: State House Press, 1988), 84, 601–602.

13. Pease to Callahan, July 5, 1855; Pease to Callahan, July 25, 1855; and Callahan to Pease, August 10, 1855, EPP. See also extracted from the governor's papers in the Texas State Library and Archives, Pease to Citizens of Bexar County, July 25, 1855, and W. E. Jones to Pease, September 22, 1855, in Winfrey, *Texas Indian Papers, 1846–1859*, 3:228–29, 243–46.

14. Pease to Callahan, July 5, 1855; and Pease to Callahan, July 25, 1855, EPP; Anderson, *Conquest of Texas*, 268–69.

15. Callahan to Edward Burleson, Jr., August 15, 1855; Callahan to Pease, August 18, 1855; and Callahan to Burleson, August 31, 1855, Edward Burleson, Jr., Papers, Center for American History, University of Texas, Austin (hereafter cited as EBP).

16. Callahan's muster roll may be found in Ranger Muster Rolls, Texas State Library and Archives, Austin; Amelia Barr, *All the Days of My Life: An Autobiography* (New York: D. Appleton, 1913), 217–18.

17. Manning, *Diplomatic Correspondence of the United States*, 9:192–93. A poignant inquiry into the fugitive slave question may be found in Ronnie C. Tyler, "The Callahan Expedition of 1855: Indians or Negroes?" *Southwestern Historical Quarterly* 70 (April 1967): 574–85; J. D. B. Stillman, *Wanderings in the Southwest in 1855*, ed. Ron Tyler (Spokane, Wash.: Arthur H. Clark Co., 1990), 119–20.

18. Callahan to Burleson, August 15, 1855; and Callahan to Burleson, August 18, 1855, EBP.

19. Marcus Duval to Bell, October 20, 1850, PHBP.

20. Doubleday, *My Life in the Old Army*, 349–50; see also Olmstead, *Journey through Texas*, 314–55; Montgomery, *Eagle Pass*, 137–41.

21. Duval to Bell, October 20, 1850; and John H. Rollins to Bell, October 30, 1850, PHBP; *Annual Report of the Commissioner of Indian Affairs, 1851*, 42–44, 253–59.

22. Webb, *Texas Rangers: A Century of Frontier Defense*, 127–36.

23. Doubleday, *My Life in the Old Army*, 179, 349–50; see also Jesse Sumpter, *Paso del Aguila: A Chronicle of Frontier Days on the Texas Border as Recorded in the Memoirs of Jesse Sumpter*, comp. by Harry Warren (Austin: Encino Press, 1969), 4, 61–70 (hereafter cited as Sumpter, *Memoirs*); *Reports of the Committee of Investigation*, 409–11.

24. William Banta and J. W. Caldwell, Jr., *Twenty-Seven Years on the Texas Frontier* (Council Hill, Okla.: L. G. Park, 1933), 54–58, 77–86; Montgomery, *Eagle Pass*, 73–77.

25. William R. Henry to Pease, September 2, 1855, EPP; Elton Cude, *The Wild and Free Dukedom of Bexar* (San Antonio: Munguia Printers, 1978), 43–44; Ernest C. Shearer, "The Callahan Expedition, 1855," *Southwestern Historical Quarterly* 54 (April 1951): 432–34; Manning, *Diplomatic Correspondence of the United States*, 9:782–89; Stillman, *Wanderings in the Southwest in 1855*, 119–20. The *Texas State Gazette* (Austin), August 11, 1855, and the *San Antonio Herald*, August 14, 1855, carried reports of Henry's boasts of his incursions into Mexico that spring and summer.

26. Sowell, *Early Settlers and Indian Fighters*, 248, 527, 530–32; Winfrey, *Texas Indian Papers, 1846–1859*, 3:243–47; Shearer, "Callahan Expedition, 1855," 435–37.

27. Sowell, *Early Settlers and Indian Fighters*, 530–32; Shearer, "Callahan Expedition," 437–39.

28. Sowell, *Early Settlers and Indian Fighters*, 531–33.

29. Ibid.; William Kyle to Burleson, October 7, 1855, EBP; John Henry Brown, *History of Texas from 1685 to 1892*, 2 vols. (St. Louis: L. E. Daniell, 1893), 2:369–71.

30. Sowell, *Early Settlers and Indian Fighters*, 527, 533–35; Brown, *History of Texas*, 2:369–71.

31. Kyle to Burleson, October 7, 1855, EBP; Brown, *History of Texas*, 2:369–71; Sowell, *Early Settlers and Indian Fighters*, 248, 532–34; Callahan's handwritten notes regarding those killed and wounded at Escondido Creek may be found on his company's muster roll in Ranger Muster Rolls, Texas State Library and Archives, Austin.

32. McDowell's eyewitness account of the burning of Piedras Negras may be found in the New Orleans *Picayune*, January 8, 1893; Shearer, "Callahan Expedition," 438–42; Winfrey, *Texas Indian Papers, 1846–1859*, 3:253–57.

33. Kyle to Burleson, October 7, 1855, EBP; see also Winfrey, *Texas Indian Papers, 1846–1859*, 3:253–54.

34. Sowell, *Early Settlers and Indian Fighters*, 533–34.

35. New Orleans *Picayune*, January 8, 1893.

36. Sidney Burbank to Samuel Cooper, October 4, 1855; and Burbank to Cooper, October 8, 1855, Ranger Correspondence, Texas State Library and Archives, Austin (hereafter cited as RC).

37. Burbank to Cooper, October 8, 1855, RC; Sumpter, *Memoirs*, 63–68.

38. New Orleans *Picayune*, January 8, 1893; Sumpter, *Memoirs*, 68.

39. Manning, *Diplomatic Correspondence of the United States*, 9:193; Shearer, "Callahan Expedition," 442–43; Langberg's letter was published in the *Texas State Times* (Austin), November 17, 1855; *Reports of the Committee of Investigation*, 192–93; Burbank to Cooper, October 8, 1855, RC.

40. Winfrey, *Texas Indian Papers, 1846–1859*, 3:253–57; Governor Elisha M. Pease, "Address to the Texas State Legislature," November 5, 1855, EPP; *Texas State Gazette* (Austin), October 20, 1855; *San Antonio Herald*, October 16, 1855; W. R. Henry to Santiago Vidaurri, August 12, 1856, Santiago Vidaurri Papers, Center for American History, University of Texas, Austin (hereafter cited as SVP).

41. Manning, *Diplomatic Correspondence of the United States*, 9:197–200.

42. Ibid., 9:788–789, 800–802.

43. Ibid., 9:816–17.

44. *Reports of the Committee of Investigation*, 192–93; see also, *Preliminary Report of J. Hubley Ashton, Agent of the United States, before the United States and Mexican Claims Commission, to the Secretary of State, November 23, 1876*, in 44th Cong., 2nd sess., 1876, S. Exec. Doc. 31, serial 1720, 18–67.

Chapter 4

1. Myer, "I Am Already Quite a Texan," 43.

2. *Annual Report of the Commissioner of Indian Affairs, 1851*, 257–58. For an overview of Texan filibustering activities during the period, see Earl W. Fornell, "Texans and Filibusters in the 1850s," *Southwestern Historical Quarterly* 59 (April 1956): 411–28.

3. Michael Baldridge, *A Reminiscence of the Parker H. French Expedition through Texas and Mexico to California in the Spring of 1850* (Los Angeles: privately printed, 1959), 10–11.

4. Randolph Barnes Marcy, *Thirty Years of Army Life on the Border* (New York: Harper & Brothers, 1866), 351.

5. Domenech, *Missionary Adventures in Texas and Mexico*, 175–76, 226–30; Rayburn and Rayburn, *Century of Conflict*, 64.

6. Domenech, *Missionary Adventures in Texas and Mexico*, 230–41; Parisot, *Reminiscences of a Texas Missionary*, 84–90, 94–98.

7. Hughes, *Rebellious Ranger*, 121–22; Viele, *Following the Drum*, 149.

8. Ford to Burleson, February 15, 1855, EBP.

9. William Walker, *The War in Nicaragua* (Tucson: University of Arizona Press, 1985), 2–6, 147–48, 264–65.

10. Houston *Telegraph*, August 25, 1856; New Orleans *Picayune*, November 26, 1856; Fornell, "Texans and Filibusters," 411–17.

11. Galveston *News*, January 22, 1857; Houston *Telegraph*, February 16 and 25, 1857.

12. Fornell, "Texans and Filibusters," 419.

13. Galveston *News*, May 16, 1857.

14. William Walker, *War in Nicaragua*, 334–35; Fornell, "Texans and Filibusters," 423–24.

15. Galveston *News*, September 5, 1857.

16. Fornell, "Texans and Filibusters," 421–23; Galveston *Civilian*, October 27, 1857.

17. Galveston *News*, November 26, 1857.

18. Gulick, *Papers of Mirabeau Buonaparte Lamar*, 3:284–86; 4:38–39, 45–48, 68–73, 78–79.

19. Ibid., 4:109–13.

20. For an excellent survey of filibustering in Mexico, see Joseph A. Stout, *The Liberators: Filibustering Expeditions in Mexico, 1848–1862, and the Last Thrust of Manifest Destiny* (Los Angeles: Westernlore Press, 1973). A more recent treatment is Robert E. May, *Manifest Destiny's Underworld: Filibustering in Antebellum America* (Chapel Hill: University of North Carolina Press, 2002).

21. Lockridge to Vidaurri, March 29, 1858; Lockridge to Vidaurri, April 7, 1858; and Lockridge to Vidaurri, April 8, 1858, SVP; Albert Z. Carr, *The World and William Walker* (New York: Harper & Row, 1963), 206–13.

22. Linn, *Reminiscences of Fifty Years in Texas*, 352–54.

23. De Leon, *They Called Them Greasers*, 82–83.

24. *Nueces Valley Weekly* (Corpus Christi), December 19, 1857, as quoted in De Leon, *They Called Them Greasers*, 82–83.

25. Emory, *Report on the United States and Mexican Boundary Survey*, 1:61–73; M. L. Crimmins, ed., "Colonel J. K. F. Mansfield's Report of the Inspection of the Department of Texas in 1856," *Southwestern Historical Quarterly* 41 (October 1938): 128–29.

26. Montgomery, *Eagle Pass*, 119–20, 153.

27. John Hoyt Williams, *Sam Houston: A Biography of the Father of Texas* (New York: Simon & Schuster, 1993), 305–307; *Congressional Globe*, 35th Cong., 1st. sess., 1858, 115, pt. 2:716.

28. *Texas Star Gazette*, January 12, 1850, and December 28, 1850; Wright and Wright, *Recollections of Western Texas*, 55–57.

29. *Congressional Globe*, 35th Cong., 1st. sess., 1858, 115, pt. 2:716.

30. Wright and Wright, *Recollections of Western Texas*, 17; Williams, *Sam Houston*, 306–307.

31. *Congressional Globe*, 35th Cong., 1st. sess., 1858, 115, pt. 2:716.

32. Ibid.; Amelia Williams and Eugene C. Barker, eds., *The Writings of Sam Houston, 1813–1863*, 8 vols. (Austin: University of Texas Press, 1938–43), 7:85–86.

33. Williams and Barker, *Writings of Sam Houston*, 7:85–86.

34. Ibid.

35. Ibid., 7:89–95.

36. Ibid.

37. Ibid., 7:96–99.

38. *Texas State Gazette* (Austin), September 4, 1858; Williams and Barker, *Writings of Sam Houston*, 7:100, 181–82; Donald Day and Harry Herbert Ullom, eds., *The Autobiography of Sam Houston* (Norman: University of Oklahoma Press, 1954), 254; Williams, *Sam Houston*, 308.

Chapter 5

1. Charles Anderson, *Texas before and on the Eve of the Rebellion* (Cincinnati: Peter G. Thompson, 1884), 21; John T. Sprague, *The Treachery in Texas: The Secession of Texas, and the Arrest of United States Officers and Soldiers Serving in Texas* (New York: New York Historical Society, 1862), 111; Thompson, *Fifty Miles and a Fight*, 20; Ford, *Rip Ford's Texas*, 308–309.

2. "Difficulties on the Southwestern Frontier," 36th Cong., 1st. sess., 1859, H. Exec. Doc. 52, 65.

3. Rayburn and Rayburn, *Century of Conflict*, 64–65.

4. Ibid.

5. Ibid.

6. *Texas Border Troubles*, 44th Cong., 1st. sess., 1876, H. Misc. Doc. 343, 118.

7. For an exhaustive study of the land politics that consumed Cortina's family, see Charles W. Goldfinch, "Juan N. Cortina, 1824–1892: A Re-Appraisal," in *Juan N. Cortina: Two Interpretations* (New York: Arno Press, 1974), 33–41. Goldfinch's 1950 master's thesis at the University of Chicago, later published and reprinted in the study cited above, was a ground-breaking work on Cortina and his life and career along the border.

8. Nannie M. Tilley, ed., *Federals on the Frontier: The Diary of Benjamin F. McIntyre, 1862–1864* (Austin: University of Texas Press, 1963), 293; Ford, *Rip Ford's Texas*, 261; Parisot, *Reminiscences of a Texas Missionary*, 99–100; Ford, "Memoirs," 783–89.

9. For a recent reinterpretation of Cortina's career, see Carlos Larralde and Jose Rodolfo Jacobo, *Juan N. Cortina and the Struggle for Justice in Texas* (Dubuque, Iowa: Kendall Hunt, 2000), 3–10: see also De Leon, *They Called Them Greasers*, 53–55, 83–85.

10. Goldfinch, "Juan N. Cortina," 42–43.

11. W. H. Chatfield, *The Twin Cities of the Border and the Country of the Rio Grande* (New Orleans: E. P. Brandao, 1893), 23.

12. "Difficulties on the Southwestern Frontier," 28–30; Rayburn and Rayburn, *Century of Conflict*, 66–67.

13. Rayburn and Rayburn, *Century of Conflict*, 66–67.

14. Ibid.; "Difficulties on the Southwestern Frontier," 28–30; Edmund J. Davis to Hardin R. Runnels, October 7, 1859, Hardin R. Runnels Papers, Texas State Library and Archives, Austin (hereafter cited as HRRP).

15. Chatfield, *Twin Cities of the Border*, 23.

16. *Texas Border Troubles*, 4; Rayburn and Rayburn, *Century of Conflict*, 68; Parisot, *Reminiscences of a Texas Missionary*, 97–98; Rankin, *Twenty Years among the Mexicans*, 81–82.

17. *Texas Border Troubles*, 4; Thompson, *Fifty Miles and a Fight*, 24.

18. "Difficulties on the Southwestern Frontier," 31–32.

19. Ford, *Rip Ford's Texas*, 3

20. Jerry Thompson, ed., *Juan Cortina and the Texas-Mexican Frontier* (El Paso: Texas Western Press, 1994), 14–18; "Difficulties on the Southwestern Frontier," 69–73.

21. "Difficulties on the Southwestern Frontier," 31.

22. Ibid.; Stephen Powers to Runnels, October 23, 1859, HRRP.

23. "Difficulties on the Southwestern Border," 31–35.

24. Ibid.; Rankin, *Twenty Years among the Mexicans*, 82–83.

25. Powers to Runnels, October 23, 1859, HRRP; Thompson, *Fifty Miles and a Fight*, 26.

26. Thompson, *Fifty Miles and a Fight*, 26; "Difficulties on the Southwestern Border," 34.

27. Runnels to William G. Tobin, October 13, 1859, HRRP.

28. Thompson, *Fifty Miles and a Fight*, 26–27; Rankin, *Twenty Years among the Mexicans*, 82–83; Parisot, *Reminiscences of a Texas Missionary*, 97–98.

29. "Difficulties on the Southwestern Frontier," 44–49, 68–69.

30. Ibid.; Neale's recollection of Thompson's expedition was later printed in *The Evening Ranchero*, July 5, 1876, and also appears in Chatfield, *Twin Cities of the Border*, 15.

31. Chatfield, *Twin Cities of the Border*, 15.

32. Ibid.; see also Thompson, *Fifty Miles and a Fight*, 27; Rayburn and Rayburn, *Century of Conflict*, pp. 69–70; Parisot, *Reminiscences of a Texas* Missionary, 98–99.

33. Tobin to Runnels, October 26, 1859; and Latham to Tobin, October 26, 1859, HRRP; "Difficulties on the Southwestern Frontier," 34; Thompson, *Fifty Miles and a Fight*, 27–28.

34. Major Samuel Peter Heintzelman kept letters, notes, and articles from the *American Flag* (Brownsville). See his notes in the October 15 and October 25 editions, Samuel Peter Heintzelman Papers, Manuscripts Division, Library of Congress, Washington, D.C. (hereafter cited as SPHP).

35. "Difficulties on the Southwestern Frontier," 53.

36. Ibid.; Corpus Christi *Ranchero*, November 12, 1859; Galveston *Daily Civilian*, November 11, 1859; San Antonio *Herald*, n.d., as quoted in Thompson, *Fifty Miles and a Fight*, 28. See also Wilhelm, *History of the Eight U.S. Infantry*, 2:375–76; Cheeseman, *Maria Von Blucher's Corpus Christi*, 117–18.

37. For the clipping from an extra edition of the San Antonio *Herald*, n.d., see Adjutant General's Office, Letters Received, Record Group 94, U.S. Department of War, Washington, D.C.; Thompson, *Fifty Miles and a Fight*, 30.

38. Brown, *Strain of Violence*, 8; Michael L. Collins, "Statehood, 1845–1860," in *The Texas Heritage*, 3rd ed., ed. Ben Procter and Archie P. McDonald (Wheeling, Ill.: Harlan Davidson, 1998), 64.

39. Ford, "Memoirs," 790; Ford, *Rip Ford's Texas*, 265.

40. Runnels to Ford, November 17, 1859, HRRP.

41. Thompson, *Fifty Miles and a Fight*, 31; Corpus Christi *Ranchero*, November 26, 1859.

42. Corpus Christi *Ranchero*, November 26, 1859.

43. Webb, *Texas Rangers: A Century of Frontier Defense*, 181–82; Rister, *Robert E. Lee in Texas*, 111; and see Tobin to Runnels, November 16, 1859, HRRP. Tobin identifies the injured man simply as Lieutenant Jackson; see also Washington D. Miller Papers, Texas State Library and Archives, Austin.

44. Corpus Christi *Ranchero*, November 26, 1859; Thompson, *Fifty Miles and a Fight*, 32; *Troubles on the Texas Frontier*, 36th Cong., 1st. sess., 1860, H. Exec. Doc. no. 81, 5.

45. David E. Twiggs to John B. Floyd, November 17, 1859, Letters Received, Adjutant General's Office, Record Group 94, U.S. Department of the Army, National Archives, Washington, D.C. (hereafter cited as LR, AGO); Twiggs to Floyd, November 21, 1859, LR, AGO, as quoted in Thompson, *Fifty Miles and a Fight*, 31.

Chapter 6

1. "Difficulties on the Southwestern Frontier," 176–84; Thompson, *Fifty Miles and a Fight*, 1–7, 33–35, 88–99.

2. Thompson, *Fifty Miles and a Fight*, 1–7, 33–35, 88–89.

3. Ibid., 124–26.

4. Tobin to Runnels, November 27, 1859, Sam Houston Papers, Texas State Library and Archives, Austin (hereafter cited as SHP).

5. Ibid; *Troubles on the Texas Frontier*, 5–7; Andrew Erskine to Ann Erskine, December 1, 1859, Andrew Erskine Papers, Center for American History, University of Texas, Austin (hereafter cited as AEP).

6. Andrew Erskine to Ann Erskine, December 1, 1859, AEP.

7. Ibid.; Tobin to Runnels, November 27, 1859, SHP.

8. Thompson, *Juan Cortina and the Texas-Mexico Frontier*, 23–28.

9. Ibid.

10. Hughes, *Rebellious Ranger*, 147–59; Ford, *Rip Ford's Texas*, 223–40; Webb, *Texas Rangers: A Century of Frontier Defense*, 151–61.

11. Tom Lea, *The King Ranch* (Boston: Little, Brown & Co., 1957), 1163–64; Ford, *Rip Ford's Texas*, 260–66.

12. Ford to Runnels, November 17, 1859, HRRP.

13. Ibid.; Ford to Runnels, November 22, 1859; and Edmund J. Davis et al., to Runnels, November 30, 1859, HRRP.

14. Thompson, *Fifty Miles and a Fight*, 126; Ford, *Rip Ford's Texas*, 267–74.

15. Thompson, *Fifty Miles and a Fight*, 126–31. Regarding W. R. Henry, Rip Ford described the adventurer as "indignant" because he had not been appointed captain of state volunteers in November 1859; see Ford, "Memoirs," 793–94.

16. Thompson, *Fifty Miles and a Fight*, 132.

17. Ibid.

18. *Troubles on the Texas Frontier*, 7–8.

19. Thompson, *Fifty Miles and a Fight*, 137–44; *Troubles on the Texas Frontier*, 8–13.

20. *Troubles on the Texas Frontier*, 8–13; see also Ford, "Memoirs," 791–96.

21. Thompson, *Fifty Miles and a Fight*, 136; *Troubles on the Texas Frontier*, 75. Judging by Heintzelman's journal entry, Featherstone must have been killed on December 10 or 11, not December 15, as erroneously listed in Heintzelman's later report of casualties.

22. "Proclamation of the Governor," December 12, 1859, HRRP.

23. Thompson, *Fifty Miles and a Fight*, 136–39; *Troubles on the Texas Frontier*, 7–8; "Difficulties on the Southwestern Frontier," 89–90.

24. Thompson, *Fifty Miles and a Fight*, 139–42; *Troubles on the Texas Frontier*, 7–8; Webb, *Texas Rangers: A Century of Frontier Defense*, 184.

25. Webb, *Texas Rangers: A Century of Frontier Defense*, 184; Ford to Houston, December 16, 1859, SHP; Thompson, *Fifty Miles and a Fight*, 139–42; Ford, *Rip Ford's Texas*, 267.

26. Ford, *Rip Ford's Texas*, 267; Ford to Houston, December 16, 1859, SHP.

27. Thompson, *Fifty Miles and a Fight*, 143; Andrew Erskine to Ann Erskine, December 18, 1859, AEP.

28. Ford, *Rip Ford's Texas*, 267; F. F. Fenn to Houston, December 16, 1859, SHP; Thompson, *Fifty Miles and a Fight*, 143.

29. Thompson, *Fifty Miles and a Fight*, 146–48.

30. Williams and Barker, *Writings of Sam Houston*, 7:379–85.

31. Ibid.; Williams, *Sam Houston*, 317–18.

32. Williams, *Sam Houston*, 317–18; Ben McCulloch to his mother, July 28, 1859, McCulloch Family Papers, Center for American History, University of Texas, Austin (hereafter cited as MFP).

33. Andrew Erskine to Ann Erskine, December 1, 7, and 11, 1859, AEP.

34. Thompson, *Fifty Miles and a Fight*, 146–51.

35. *Troubles on the Texas Frontier*, 8, 48–50; Thompson, *Fifty Miles and a Fight*, 148–51; Ford, *Rip Ford's Texas*, 269–70.

36. Ford, *Rip Ford's Texas*, 269–70; *Troubles on the Texas Frontier*, 8–9; Thompson, *Fifty Miles and a Fight*, 153–54.

37. Thompson, *Fifty Miles and a Fight*, 155; Ford, *Rip Ford's Texas*, 270–71; *Troubles on the Texas Frontier*, 9.

38. Ford, *Rip Ford's Texas*, pp. 270–71; Ford, "Memoirs," 798–99.

39. Ford, "Memoirs," 798–99; Viele, *Following the Drum*, 145–46; Thompson, *Fifty Miles and a Fight*, 145.

40. *Troubles on the Texas Frontier*, 9; Ford, *Rip Ford's Texas*, 270–71.

41. Ford, *Rip Ford's Texas*, 270–71.

42. Ibid., 271–72.

43. Ibid.; Ford, "Memoirs," 799–801.

44. Ford, "Memoirs," 798–99; Ford, *Rip Ford's Texas*, 270–71; *Troubles on the Texas Frontier*, 9. In "Difficulties on the Southwestern Frontier," 97–99, Heintzelman was more charitable to Ford and his men than he was in his more terse comments issued in *Troubles on the Texas Frontier*; see also Thompson, *Fifty Miles and a Fight*, 153.

45. Ford, *Rip Ford's Texas*, 273.

46. Ibid.; Ford, "Memoirs," 805–806; Rufus Byler to Martha Fusselman, December 29, 1859, Dobie Byler Family Papers, Center for American History, University of Texas, Austin (hereafter cited as DBFP).

47. Byler to Fusselman, December 29, 1859, DBFP; Ford, *Rip Ford's Texas*, 273–74.

48. Ford, *Rip Ford's Texas*, 274; Thompson, *Fifty Miles and a Fight*, 155–58; Noah Cox to Heintzelman, December 27, 1859, SPHP; Tobin to Houston, December 28, 1859, RC; Ford to Houston, December 29, 1859, SHP.

49. Ford, *Rip Ford's Texas*, 274–75; Thompson, *Fifty Miles and a Fight*, 155–58.

50. Thompson, *Fifty Miles and a Fight*, 155–56; *Troubles on the Texas Frontier*, 9–10.

51. "Difficulties on the Southwestern Frontier," 97–99; *Troubles on the Texas Frontier*, 9–10; Thompson, *Fifty Miles and a Fight*, 159–60.

52. Thompson, *Fifty Miles and a Fight*, 159–60.

53. Wilhelm, *History of the Eighth U.S. Infantry*, 2:403–405. The term "red legs" refers to field artillerymen. The verbena is a flowering plant native to the region of South Texas.

Chapter 7

1. Thompson, *Fifty Miles and a Fight*, 161–62.

2. *Troubles on the Texas Frontier*, 19.

3. Byler to Fusselman, December 29, 1859, DBFP.

4. Ford, *Rip Ford's Texas*, 276–77; Ford, "Memoirs," 810–11; Thompson, *Fifty Miles and a Fight*, 161–62; *Troubles on the Texas Frontier*, 10; Webb, *Texas Rangers: A Century of Frontier Defense*, 186–87.

5. Samuel Lockridge to Heintzelman, January 1, 1860, SPHP; Thompson, *Fifty Miles and a Fight*, 164–65.

6. Williams and Barker, *Writings of Sam Houston*, 7:395–96, 409–410.

7. Ibid.

8. Ibid.

9. Robert Taylor to Houston, January 16, 1860, SHP; Thompson, *Fifty Miles and a Fight*, 177–80; Ford, *Rip Ford's Texas*, 278–79.

10. Taylor and Ángel Navarro to Houston, January 17, 1860; Navarro to Houston, January 26, 1860; and Charles Stillman to Taylor and Navarro, January 18, 1860, SHP; *Troubles on the Texas Frontier*, 10; Thompson, *Fifty Miles and a Fight*, 180.

11. Stillman to Taylor and Navarro, January 18, 1860; Adolphus Glaevecke to William D. Thomas, January 16, 1860; William Neale to Navarro and Taylor, January 16, 1860; and Francisco Itrurria to Navarro and Taylor, January 19, 1860, SHP.

12. Navarro to Houston, January 26, 1860, SHP.

13. Heintzelman to Navarro and Taylor, February 2, 1860, SHP; the letter is also printed in *Troubles on the Texas Frontier*, 62. See also undated news clippings in JLHP.

14. Ford, *Rip Ford's Texas*, 280; *Troubles on the Texas Frontier*, 62–63.

15. Ford, *Rip Ford's Texas*, 281; *Troubles on the Texas Frontier*, 10–11.

16. Ford, *Rip Ford's Texas*, 282.

17. Ibid.

18. Thompson, *Fifty Miles and a Fight*, 180.

19. Ibid., 187.

20. Ford, *Rip Ford's Texas*, 282–83.

21. Ibid.; *Troubles on the Texas Frontier*, 10, 63–64.

22. *Troubles on the Texas Frontier*, 63–64; Ford, *Rip Ford's Texas*, 283; Tobin to Navarro, February 6, 1860; and Tobin to Houston, February 6, 1860, SHP; John Martin to Ford, February 4, 1860, SPHP.

23. Ford, *Rip Ford's Texas*, 283.

24. *Troubles on the Texas Frontier*, 63–64.

25. Ford, *Rip Ford's Texas*, 284.

26. Ibid.; Ford, "Memoirs," 819–20.

27. Ford, *Rip Ford's Texas*, 284.

28. Ibid.

29. Ibid.; Ford, "Memoirs," 820–821; Tobin to Houston, February 6, 1860; and Ford to Houston, February 9, 1860, SHP.

30. Thompson, *Fifty Miles and a Fight*, 187–90; *Troubles on the Texas Frontier*, 10, 63–65; Webb, *Texas Rangers: A Century of Frontier Defense*, 188–89; Ford, *Rip Ford's Texas*, 285–86.

31. Ford, *Rip Ford's Texas*, 285–87; *Troubles on the Texas Frontier*, 96–98.

32. Heintzelman to Arthur Tracy Lee, April 28, 1860, LR, AGO; *Troubles on the Texas Frontier*, 64–67; Heintzelman's report of the incident at La Bolsa, including Stoneman's and Ford's reports of the fight and the ensuing operation, may be found in "Difficulties on the Southwestern Frontier," 114–15.

33. Thompson, *Fifty Miles and a Fight*, 194.

34. Navarro and Taylor to Houston, February 4, 1860, SHP.

35. Ibid. See also Tobin to Houston, February 6, 1860, SHP.

36. Navarro and Taylor to Houston, February 4, 1860, SHP.

37. Ibid. See also Navarro to Tobin, February 6, 1860; and Taylor to Houston, February 5, 1860, SHP; Thompson, *Fifty Miles and a Fight*, 194–95; John L. Haynes scrapbook, JLHP, 14–18.

38. Manning, *Diplomatic Correspondence of the United States*, 9:278–80; Thompson, *Fifty Miles and a Fight*, 183–84.

39. Thompson, *Fifty Miles and a Fight*, 183–84; Manning, *Diplomatic Correspondence of the United States*, 9:1135–36, 1153–55.

40. Ibid., 9:1153–56; Williams, *Sam Houston*, 318–19.

41. Williams and Barker, *Writings of Sam Houston*, 7:407–421.

42. Ibid., 7:421–29, 508–509.

43. Ibid., 7:441–44; Wilbarger, *Indian Depredations in Texas*, 65–71. See also Peter F. Stout, *Nicaragua* (Philadelphia: Potter Co., 1859), for a contemporary description of the Central American venture; Robert Anderson, *An Artillery Officer*

in the Mexican War, 1846–7: Letters of Robert Anderson (Freeport, N.Y.: Libraries Press, 1911), 19.

44. J. Fred Rippy, *The United States and Mexico* (New York: Alfred A. Knopf, 1926), 223–27; Manning, *Diplomatic Correspondence of the United States*, 9:1119; John Bassett Moore, ed., *The Works of James Buchanan: Comprising His Speeches, State Papers, and Private Correspondence*, 12 vols. (New York: Antiquarian Press, 1960), 10:353–60 and 373–75, 12:248–61.

45. Williams and Barker, *Writings of Sam Houston*, 7:473.

46. Ibid., 7:474.

47. Manning, *Diplomatic Correspondence of the United States*, 9:1161–62.

48. Ibid. See also Webb, *Texas Rangers: A Century of Frontier Defense*, 197–215; Williams, *Sam Houston*, 317–25.

49. Williams and Barker, *Writings of Sam Houston*, 7:502–507.

50. Ibid., 7:502–509, 518.

51. Ibid., 7:495–96.

52. Ibid.

53. McCulloch to Frances McCulloch, February 26, 1860, MFP; Williams, *Sam Houston*, 320.

54. James Pike, *Scout and Ranger: Being the Personal Adventures of James Pike of the Texas Rangers in 1859–60* (Princeton: Princeton University Press, 1932), 124–25.

55. Ibid.

56. Madge Thornall Roberts, ed., *The Personal Correspondence of Sam Houston*, vol. 4, *1852–1863* (Denton: University of North Texas Press, 2001), 376.

57. Manning, *Diplomatic Correspondence of the United States*, 9:1163–164.

Chapter 8

1. Douglas Southall Freeman, *R. E. Lee: A Biography* (New York: Charles Scribner's Sons, 1934), 1:404.

2. Ibid. For contemporary impressions of Lee's character, see J. William Jones, *Personal Reminiscences of General Robert E. Lee* (New York: Tom Doherty Associates, 2003), 63–65, 134, 151–52, 215, 447.

3. Robert E. Lee, *Recollections and Letters of General Robert E. Lee* (New York: Doubleday, Page & Co., 1904), 3–23.

4. A. M. Lea to Houston, February 24, 1860, SHP; the letter is quoted in Webb, *Texas Rangers: A Century of Frontier Defense*, 206.

5. Ibid.

6. Robert E. Lee to A. M. Lea, March 1, 1860, SHP.

7. A. M. Lea to Houston, April 3, 1860, SHP; Webb, *Texas Rangers: A Century of Frontier Defense*, 207; Rister, *Robert E. Lee in Texas*, 102–106.

8. Freeman, *R. E. Lee*, 1:404; Rister, *Robert E. Lee in Texas*, 113.

9. John H. Jenkins III, ed., *Robert E. Lee on the Rio Grande: The Correspondence of Robert E. Lee on the Texas Border, 1860* (Austin: Jenkins Publishing Co., 1988), 8–10; *Troubles on the Texas Frontier*, 78.

10. Jenkins, *Robert E. Lee on the Rio Grande*, 10–12.

11. Ford, *Rip Ford's Texas*, 290–91; *Troubles on the Texas Frontier*, 71, 79–81; Thompson, *Fifty Miles and a Fight*, 213–16.

12. Ford, *Rip Ford's Texas*, 291.

13. Ibid.

14. Ibid.; *Troubles on the Texas Frontier*, 80–81.

15. Ford, *Rip Ford's Texas*, 292–93.

16. Ibid; Thompson, *Fifty Miles and a Fight*, 214; *Troubles on the Texas Frontier*, 80–81.

17. Ford, *Rip Ford's Texas*, 292–94. The official Mexican version of this controversial raid is told in *Reports of the Committee of Investigation*, 195–97.

18. Ford, *Rip Ford's Texas*, 293–94; Thompson, *Fifty Miles and a Fight*, 214.

19. Ford, *Rip Ford's Texas*, 294.

20. Ibid., 294–95.

21. Ibid.; *Troubles on the Texas Frontier*, 80–81.

22. *Troubles on the Texas Frontier*, 80–81.

23. Ibid., 80–83; *Reports of the Committee of Investigation*, 196–97; Ford, *Rip Ford's Texas*, 297–98; Thompson, *Fifty Miles and a Fight*, 214–19.

24. Thompson, *Fifty Miles and a Fight*, 214–19; Stoneman to Heintzelman, March 23, 1860; and Ford to Heintzelman, March 24, 1860, SPHP.

25. Thompson, *Fifty Miles and a Fight*, 219–21.

26. Ibid.

27. Ibid., 221–22; Ford, "Memoirs," 852–68.

28. Thompson, *Fifty Miles and a Fight*, 223–24; Elizabeth Brown Pryor, *Reading the Man: Robert E. Lee through His Private Letters* (New York: Viking, 2007).

29. Jenkins, *Robert E. Lee on the Rio Grande*, 12–13; *Troubles on the Texas Frontier*, 84–85.

30. Thompson, *Fifty Miles and a Fight*, 223–24.

31. Ibid., 224–25.

32. Ford, *Rip Ford's Texas*, 299–300.

33. Ibid.; *Reports of the Committee of Investigation*, 196–97.

34. Ford, *Rip Ford's Texas*, 300; Ford to Heintzelman, April 5, 1860, SPHP.

35. Ford, *Rip Ford's Texas*, 300–301; *Reports of the Committee of Investigation*, 196–97.

36. Ford, *Rip Ford's Texas*, 301.
37. Ibid., 301–302.
38. Ibid.
39. Ford to Heintzelman, April 5, 1860; and Ford to The Authorities, Civil and Military, of Reynosa, n.d., SPHP; Ford, *Rip Ford's Texas*, 302–303.
40. Ford, *Rip Ford's Texas*, 302–303; *Reports of the Committee of Investigation*, 196–97; Thompson, *Fifty Miles and a Fight*, 227.
41. Thompson, *Fifty Miles and a Fight*, 226–27; Ford, *Rip Ford's Texas*, 305.
42. Thompson, *Fifty Miles and a Fight*, 227.
43. Ford, *Rip Ford's Texas*, 301–305; Ford to Heintzelman, April 5, 1860, SPHP; *Troubles on the Texas Frontier*, 87–88.
44. Ford, "Memoirs," 867–868; Ford, *Rip Ford's Texas*, 301–305.
45. *Troubles on the Texas Frontier*, 85; Jenkins, *Robert E. Lee on the Rio Grande*, 14.
46. *Troubles on the Texas Frontier*, 85–87.
47. Jenkins, *Robert E. Lee on the Rio Grande*, 15–16; *Troubles on the Texas Frontier*, 87–88.
48. Williams and Barker, *Writings of Sam Houston*, 7:541–43; *Troubles on the Texas Frontier*, 88–89; Thompson, *Fifty Miles and a Fight*, 229–30.
49. *Troubles on the Texas Frontier*, 89.
50. Jenkins, *Robert E. Lee on the Rio Grande*, 17–18.
51. Williams and Barker, *Writings of Sam Houston*, 8:13–21; *Troubles on the Texas Frontier*, 90–95.
52. Williams and Barker, *Writings of Sam Houston*, 8:13–21; *Troubles on the Texas Frontier*, 90–95.
53. Ibid., 100–104; Jenkins, *Robert E. Lee on the Rio Grande*, 18–23.
54. Jenkins, *Robert E. Lee on the Rio Grande*, 23–24.
55. Ibid., 23–24.
56. Ford, *Rip Ford's Texas*, 307.
57. Thompson, *Fifty Miles and a Fight*, 242–48.
58. Ford, *Rip Ford's Texas*, 307–308.; Thompson, *Fifty Miles and a Fight*, 242–43.
59. Ford, *Rip Ford's Texas*, 308.
60. Ibid., 309.
61. *Texas Border Troubles*, 2–6.
62. Francis Hardman, *Frontier Life: Or Tales of the Southwestern Border* (New York: C. Saxton, Barker & Co., 1860), 171; "Difficulties on the Southwestern Frontier," 79–83.
63. Emory Thomas, *Robert E. Lee: A Biography* (New York: W. W. Norton, 1995), 184.

64. J. Frank Dobie, *A Vacquero of the Brush Country: The Life and Times of John D. Young* (Austin: University of Texas Press, 1998), 49.

Chapter 9

1. Ben McCulloch to Frances McCulloch, February 26, 1860, MFP; Cutrer, *Ben McCulloch and the Frontier Military Tradition*, 170.

2. Ben McCulloch to Frances McCulloch, December 4, 1859; and Ben McCulloch to Frances McCulloch, January 1, 1860, MFP.

3. Ben McCulloch to Houston, March 4, 1860, SHP.

4. Dallas *Herald*, February 29, 1860.

5. Thompson, *Fifty Miles and a Fight*, 230–31; Benson Bobrick, ed., *Testament: A Soldier's Story of the Civil War* (New York: Simon & Schuster, 2003), 37–43, 143–44.

6. Knights of the Golden Circle, *By Laws, Castroville Chapter, K. G. C.* (n.p.: n.p., 1861); Knights of the Golden Circle, *First, Or Military Degree: Castroville Chapter* (n.p.: n.p., 1861); a copy of these rare documents may be found in the Center for American History, University of Texas, Austin. See also Dallas *Herald*, February 29, 1860; Galveston *Weekly News*, February 16, 1860; Pike, *Scout and Ranger*, 124–25.

7. Knights of the Golden Circle, *By Laws, Castroville Chapter, K. G. C.*; Knights of the Golden Circle, *First, Or Military Degree: Castroville Chapter.*

8. Britton to Houston, March 3, 1860, SHP, as quoted in Llerena Friend, *Sam Houston: The Great Designer* (Austin: University of Texas Press, 1954), 305; Williams and Barker, *Writings of Sam Houston*, 7:473–76; Corpus Christi *Ranchero*, February 25, 1860.

9. Lemuel D. Evans to Houston, March 19, 1860, SHP, as quoted in Friend, *Sam Houston*, 305–306.

10. T. T. Gammage to Houston, March 1, 1860; George F. Walker to Houston, March 8, 1860; and W. R. Henry to Houston, March 15, 1860, SHP.

11. F. G. Nicholson to Houston, March 6, 1860; Thomas Sears and Charles Browning to Houston, March 10, 1860; R. W. James to Sam Houston, March 13, 1860; G. W. Williams to Houston, March 13, 1860; John Stubbs et al. to Houston, March 14, 1860; Wiley Morgan, Jr., to Houston, March 24, 1860; and S. B. Day to Houston, March 20, 1860, SHP.

12. S. N. Solomon to Houston, March 3, 1860; Jacob Davis and C. M. Bacon to Houston, March 10, 1860; and David Cahill to Houston, March 21, 1860, SHP.

13. Williams and Barker, *Writings of Sam Houston*, 7:534–35.

14. Ibid.

15. McCulloch to Houston, April 6, 1860, Amelia Williams Collection, Center for American History Center, University of Texas, Austin, as quoted in Cutrer, *Ben McCulloch and the Frontier Military Tradition*, 171–72.

16. Ibid.
17. Ben McCulloch to Frances McCulloch, March 26, 1860, MFP.
18. Thomas North, *Five Years in Texas: Or What You Did Not Hear during the War from January 1861 to January 1865* (Cincinnati: Elm Street Publishing Co., 1870), 161; Noah Smithwick, *The Evolution of a State: Or Recollections of Old Texas Days* (Austin: University of Texas Press, 1983), 244–58.
19. Williams and Barker, *Writings of Sam Houston*, ,8:126–27.
20. Ibid.
21. Ibid., 8:127–28.
22. Ibid.
23. Ben McCulloch's letter to G. W. Morse, August 17, 1858, was later reprinted in a pamphlet for distribution by the arms manufacturer; General Joseph Lane's endorsement of Morse's newest weapon, dated December 19, 1859, may also be found in MFP. See also Cutrer, *Ben McCulloch and the Frontier Military Tradition*, 152–53.
24. Ben McCulloch to Frances McCulloch, February 26, 1860, MFP.
25. Cutrer, *Ben McCulloch and the Frontier Military Tradition*, 166–75.
26. Bickley's letter to the people of Texas, first published in the Galveston *News* was reprinted in New Orleans *Picayune*, October 26, 1860.
27. Jimmie Hicks, ed., "Some Letters Concerning the Knights of the Golden Circle in Texas," *Southwestern Historical Quarterly* 65 (July 1961): 80–86.
28. Ibid., 84–85.
29. Smithwick, *Evolution of a State*, 262.
30. Williams, *With the Border Ruffians*, 159–60.
31. "Speech of Charles Anderson, Esq., in Reply to Rev. Dr. Boring, Delivered November 24, 1860," copy in the Center for American History, University of Texas, Austin; M. L. Crimmins, "Colonel Charles Anderson Opposed Secession in San Antonio," *West Texas Historical Association Yearbook* 29 (October 1953): 113–14.
32. *The War of the Rebellion: A Compilation of the Official Records of the Union and Confederate Armies*, ser. 1, vol. 1 (Washington, D.C.: Government Printing Office, 1894), 583; Williams and Barker, *Writings of Sam Houston*, 8:234.
33. Anderson, *Texas before and on the Eve of the Rebellion*, 23–24.
34. Ernest Winkler, ed., *Journal of the Secession Convention in Texas, 1861* (Austin: Texas State Library and Historical Commission, 1912), 14–15, 18–21, 27–47, 49–61; Francis R. Lubbock, *Six Decades in Texas, or Memoirs of Francis Richard Lubbock, Governor of Texas in Wartime, 1861–1863: A Personal Experience in Business, War, and Politics*, ed. C. W. Rains (Austin: Ben C. Jones & Co., 1900), 304–309; for a recent treatment of Houston's role during the secession crisis in Texas, see James L. Haley, *Sam Houston* (Norman: University of Oklahoma Press, 2002), 382–94.

35. North, *Five Years in Texas,* 88–95; see also Ralph Smith, *Reminiscences of the Civil War and Other Sketches* (Waco: W. M. Morrison, 1962), 2–3; S. G. Davidson to Mary Davidson, January 30, 1861; and S. G. Davidson to Mary Davidson, February 1, 1861, S. G. Davidson Papers, Center for American History, University of Texas, Austin.

36. North, *Five Years in Texas,* 89–95.

37. Smith, *Reminiscences of the Civil War,* 1–2.

38. Ibid.; Anderson, *Texas before and on the Eve of the Rebellion,* 23–24.

39. *War of the Rebellion,* ser. 1, vol. 1, 504–10.

40. Ibid.

41. Cutrer, *Ben McCulloch and the Frontier Military Tradition,* 179; James "Buck" Barry, *A Texas Ranger and Frontiersman* (Lincoln: University of Nebraska Press, 1978), 126–28.

42. Sprague, *Treachery in Texas,* 110.

43. Williams, *With the Border Ruffians,* 162–64; J. K. P. Blackburn, "Reminiscences of the Terry Rangers," in *Terry Texas Ranger Trilogy* (Austin: State House Press, 1996), 91–93; *War of the Rebellion,* ser. 1, vol. 1, 524; J. J. Bowden, *The Exodus of Federal Forces from Texas* (Austin: Eaken Press, 1986), 50–51.

44. Bowden, *Exodus of Federal Forces from Texas,* 50–51; Carolyn Darrow, "Recollections of the Twiggs Surrender," in *Battles and Leaders of the Civil War: Being for the Most Part Contributions by Union and Confederate Officers,* ed. Robert Underwood Johnson and Clarence Clough Buel (New York: T. Yoseloff, 1956), 1:33–36

45. Bowden, *Exodus of Federal Forces from Texas,* 49–54, 503–504; Morgan W. Merrick, *From Desert to Bayou: The Civil War Journal and Sketches of Morgan Wolfe Merrick,* ed. Jerry Thompson (El Paso: Texas Western Press, 1991), 2–6; Sprague, *Treachery in Texas,* 111–14; Williams, *With the Border Ruffians,* 157–64.

46. Bowden, *Exodus of Federal Forces from Texas,* 49–54; Sprague, *Treachery in Texas,* 111–14.

47. Darrow, "Recollections of the Twiggs Surrender," 33–36; Edward S. Hartz to Samuel Hartz, February 25, 1861; and Edward S. Hartz to Samuel Hartz, March 11, 1861, Edward S. Hartz Papers, Manuscripts Division, Library of Congress, Washington, D.C.; Samuel Maverick to William Edgar, February 16, 1861, Daughters of the Republic of Texas Archives, San Antonio; Mary A. Maverick, *Memoirs of Mary A. Maverick,* ed. Rena Maverick Green (Lincoln: University of Nebraska Press, 1989), 113–14.

48. Darrow, "Recollections of the Twiggs Surrender," 33–36.

49. *Alamo Express,* February 19, 1861, as printed in Bowden, *Exodus of Federal Forces from Texas,* 56.

50. Ibid., Darrow, "Recollections of the Twiggs Surrender," 33–36.

51. Anderson, *Texas before and on the Eve of the Rebellion*, 32–37.
52. Ibid., 24.
53. Williams, *With the Border Ruffians*, 161–63; Pryor, *Reading the Man*, 257.
54. Freeman, *R. E. Lee: A Biography*, 1:428–31.

Chapter 10

1. Winkler, *Journal of the Secession Convention in Texas*, 321–25; Ford, *Rip Ford's Texas*, 318–19.
2. Ford, *Rip Ford's Texas*, 318–19; Winkler, *Journal of the Secession Convention in Texas*, 321–25.
3. Ford, *Rip Ford's Texas*, 320–31.
4. *War of the Rebellion*, ser. 1, vol. 1, 537–39; Lubbock, *Six Decades in Texas*, 309; Winkler, *Journal of the Secession Convention in Texas*, 324–25.
5. *War of the Rebellion*, ser. 1, vol. 1, 537–39.
6. Ibid.
7. Ibid., 539–40; Winkler, *Journal of the Secession Convention in Texas*, 343–48.
8. Winkler, *Journal of the Secession Convention in Texas*, 325–29; Ford, *Rip Ford's Texas*, 320–21.
9. Winkler, *Journal of the Secession Convention in Texas*, 325–29.
10. Ford, *Rip Ford's Texas*, 321; Hughes, *Rebellious Ranger*, 197.
11. Ford, *Rip Ford's Texas*, 320–21.
12. Ron Tyler et al., eds., *The New Handbook of Texas* (Austin: Texas State Historical Association, 1996), 3:519.
13. Ibid., 4:384.
14. Ibid., 3:180
15. Ibid., 3:293.
16. Ibid., 2:28.
17. Ibid., 5:881.
18. Ibid., 3:717.
19. Ibid., 1:905.
20. Ibid., 4:329.
21. Ibid., 1:838.
22. Ibid., 6:793.
23. Ibid., 4:238.
24. Ibid., 1:971.
25. Ibid., 2:170.
26. Don Alberts, ed., *Rebels on the Rio Grande: The Civil War Journals of A. B. Peticolas* (Albuquerque: University of New Mexico Press, 1984), 46–48; Martin Harwick Hall, *Sibley's New Mexico Campaign* (Austin: University of Texas Press,

1960), 88–91; Donald S. Frazier, *Blood and Treasure: Confederate Empire in the Southwest* (College Station: Texas A&M Press, 1995), 174–75.

27. See William Tobin Biographical File, Local History Collection, San Antonio Public Library, San Antonio.

28. Tyler et al., *New Handbook of Texas,* 3:564.

29. Historical traces of Henry Clay Davis, the founder of Rio Grande City, appear to have all but vanished. His brick home, once a landmark and fixture on Britton Street, was apparently razed sometime after 1936. There is no entry on Davis included in *The New Handbook of Texas.* The author was unable to ascertain the date of Davis's death.

30. Tyler et al., *New Handbook of Texas,* 3:1117.

31. Ibid., 3:543.

32. Ibid., 6:602.

33. Robert Sobel and John Raimo, eds., *Biographical Directory of the Governors of the United States, 1789–1978* (Westport, Conn.: Meckler Books, 1978), 1:111.

34. Ford, *Rip Ford's Texas,* 384–85.

35. Tyler et al., *New Handbook of Texas,* 4:142.

36. Ibid., 3:1107.

37. Ibid., 3:1064.

38. Ibid., 2:343.

39. Ford, *Rip Ford's Texas,* 331–32.

40. Ibid.; North, *Five Years in Texas,* 117–18, 167.

41. Ford, *Rip Ford's Texas,* 332–37, 341.

42. Ford to James E. Slaughter, May 16, 1864, TCMC.

43. Williams, *With the Border Ruffians,* 365.

44. For fragments of biographical material relating to John S. Ford during his last years, consult the San Antonio City Directory for the years 1878 to 1897; for further references to Ford and his family, see Hughes, *Rebellious Ranger,* 265–71.

45. Frederick Remington, "How the Law Got into the Chaparral," *Harper's New Monthly Magazine* 94 (1896): 160; Hughes, *Rebellious Ranger,* 265.

46. Ford to Foreman, July 8, 1897, John S. Ford File, Texas Rangers Museum and Hall of Fame, Waco.

47. Copies of Ford's published obituaries may be found in the John S. Ford Biographical File, Local History Collection, San Antonio Public Library, San Antonio.

Bibliography

Manuscript Collections

Anderson, Charles. "Speech of Charles Anderson, Esq., in Reply to Rev. Dr. Boring, Delivered November 24, 1860." Center for American History, University of Texas, Austin.

Bell (Peter H.) Papers. Texas State Library and Archives, Austin.

Blake (Robert Bruce) Collection. Daughters of the Republic of Texas Library at the Alamo, San Antonio.

Broadside File. Texas State Library and Archives, Austin.

Burleson (Edward, Jr.) Papers. Center for American History, University of Texas, Austin.

Byler (Dobie) Family Papers. Center for American History, University of Texas, Austin.

Caperton, John C. "Sketch of Colonel John C. Hays, Texas Ranger." Typescript. Center for American History, University of Texas, Austin.

Clark (Edward) Papers. Texas State Library and Archives, Austin.

Davidson (S. G.) Papers. Center for American History, University of Texas, Austin.

Erskine (Andrew) Papers. Center for American History, University of Texas, Austin.

Ford (John S.) Biographical File. Local History Collection. San Antonio Public Library, San Antonio, Texas.

Ford (John S.) File. Texas Rangers Museum and Hall of Fame, Waco.

Ford (John S.) Papers. Center for American History, University of Texas, Austin.

Hartz (Edward S.) Papers. Manuscripts Division, Library of Congress, Washington, D.C.

Haynes (John L.) Papers. Center for American History, University of Texas, Austin.

Heintzelman (Samuel Peter) Papers. Manuscripts Division, Library of Congress, Washington, D.C.

Houston (Sam) Papers. Texas State Library and Archives, Austin.

Hunter, John Warren. "The Fall of Brownsville on the Rio Grande, November, 1863." Center for American History, University of Texas, Austin.

Kuykendall, James. "Journal of James Hampton Kuykendall." Center for American History, University of Texas, Austin.

———. "Sketches of Early Texians." Center for American History, University of Texas, Austin.

Maverick, Samuel, to William Edgar, February 16, 1861. Daughters of the Republic of Texas Archives, San Antonio, Texas.
McCulloch Family Papers. Center for American History, University of Texas, Austin.
Miller (Washington D.) Papers. Texas State Library and Archives, Austin.
Murrah (Pendleton) Papers. Texas State Library and Archives, Austin.
Pease (Elisha M.) Papers. Texas State Library and Archives, Austin.
Ranger Correspondence. Texas State Library and Archives, Austin.
Ranger Muster Rolls. Texas State Library and Archives, Austin.
Robertson (George Lee) Papers. Center for American History, Austin.
Runnels (Hardin R.) Papers. Texas State Library and Archives, Austin.
Texas Confederate Museum Collection. Haley Memorial Library and History Center, Midland, Texas.
Tobin (William) Biographical File. Local History Collection, San Antonio Public Library, San Antonio.
Vidaurri (Santiago) Papers. Center for American History, University of Texas, Austin.
Walker (Samuel H.) Papers. Texas State Library and Archives, Austin.
Williams (Amelia) Collection. Center for American History, University of Texas, Austin.

Government Documents

Annual Report of the Commissioner of Indian Affairs, 1850. Washington, D.C.: Office of the Commissioner of Indian Affairs, 1850.
Annual Report of the Commissioner of Indian Affairs, 1851. Washington, D.C.: Gideon and Co., Printers, 1851.
Annual Report of the Commissioner of Indian Affairs, 1855. Washington, D.C.: Gideon and Co., Printers, 1855.
Consular Dispatches, Matamoros, Mexico, 1826–1906. Record Group 59, Records of the U.S. Department of State, Washington, D.C. Microfilm edition.
Correspondence and Reports Relating to Special Subjects, 1830–1851. Record Group 393, U.S. Department of the Army, National Archives, Washington, D.C.
Letters Received, Adjutant General's Office, 1780s to 1917. Record Group 94, U.S. Department of the Army, National Archives, Washington, D.C.
Message of the Governor Transmitting the Report of the Commissioners to Investigate Land Titles West of the Nueces. Austin: Cashney and Hampton, 1851.
Report of the Committee on Indian Affairs. Journals of the Senate of the State of Texas, Extra Session, Third Legislature. Austin: Gazette Office, 1850.
Reports of the Committee of Investigation Sent in 1873 by the Mexican Government to the Frontier of Texas. New York: Baker, Godwin Printers, 1875.
U.S. Congress. *Congressional Globe.* 35th Cong., 1st. sess., 1857–1858.

U.S. Congress. House. 30th Cong., 2nd sess., 1848, H. Exec. Doc. 1.

U.S. Congress. House. "Difficulties on the Southwestern Frontier." 36th Cong., 1st. sess., 1859, H. Exec. Doc. 52.

U.S. Congress. House. Mexican War Correspondence. 30th Cong., 1st sess., 1848, H. Exec. Doc. 60, serial 520.

U.S. Congress. House. *Texas Border Troubles.* 44th Cong., 1st. sess., 1876, H. Misc. Doc. 343.

U.S. Congress. House. *Troubles on the Texas Frontier.* 36th Cong., 1st. sess., 1860, H. Exec. Doc. 81.

U.S. Congress. Senate. *Preliminary Report of J. Hubley Ashton, Agent of the United States, before the United States and Mexican Claims Commission, to the Secretary of State, November 23, 1876.* 44th Cong., 2nd sess., 1876, S. Exec. Doc. 31, serial 1720.

The War of the Rebellion: A Compilation of the Official Records of the Union and Confederate Armies. 128 vols. Washington, D.C.: U.S. Government Printing Office, 1880–1901.

Books

Alberts, Don, ed. *Rebels on the Rio Grande: The Civil War Journals of A. B. Peticolas.* Albuquerque: University of New Mexico Press, 1984.

Alcaraz, Ramon. Apuntes para la historia de la guerra entre Mexico y los Estados Unidos. Mexico City: Siglo Veintiuno Editores, 1974.

Alonzo, Armando C. *Tejano Legacy: Rancheros and Settlers in South Texas, 1734–1900.* Albuquerque: University of New Mexico Press, 1998.

Anderson, Charles. *Texas before and on the Eve of the Rebellion.* Cincinnati: Peter G. Thompson, 1884.

Anderson, Gary Clayton. *The Conquest of Texas: Ethnic Cleansing in the Promised Land, 1820–1875.* Norman: University of Oklahoma Press, 2005.

Anderson, John Q., ed. *Tales of Frontier Texas, 1830–1860.* Dallas: Southern Methodist University Press, 1966.

Anderson, Robert. *An Artillery Officer in the Mexican War, 1846–7: Letters of Robert Anderson.* Freeport, N.Y.: Libraries Press, 1911.

Audubon, John W. *Audubon's Western Journal: 1849–1850, Being the Ms. Record of a Trip from New York to Texas, and an Overland Journey through Mexico and Arizona to the Goldfields of California.* Glorieta, N.M.: Rio Grande Press, 1969.

Baldridge, Michael. *A Reminiscence of the Parker H. French Expedition through Texas and Mexico to California in the Spring of 1850.* Los Angeles: privately printed, 1959.

Banta, William, and J. W. Caldwell, Jr. *Twenty-Seven Years on the Texas Frontier.* Council Hill, Okla.: L. G. Park, 1933.

Barney, Chester. *Recollections of Field Service with the Twentieth Iowa Infantry Volunteers: Or What I Saw In the Army*. Davenport, Iowa: privately printed, 1865.

Barr, Amelia. *All the Days of My Life: An Autobiography*. New York: D. Appleton and Co., 1913.

Barry, James "Buck." *A Texas Ranger and Frontiersman*. Lincoln: University of Nebraska Press, 1978.

Bartlett, John Russell. *Personal Narrative of Exploration and Incidents in Texas, New Mexico, California, Sonora, and Chihuahua*. New York: D. Appleton and Co., 1854.

Barton, Henry W. *Texas Volunteers in the Mexican War*. Wichita Falls, Tex.: privately printed, 1970.

Bell, Horace. *Reminiscences of a Ranger: Early Times in Southern California*. Norman: University of Oklahoma Press, 1999.

Blackburn, J. K. P. "Reminiscences of the Terry Rangers." In *Terry Texas Ranger Trilogy*. Austin: State House Press, 1996.

Bobrick, Benson, ed. *Testament: A Soldier's Story of the Civil War*. New York: Simon and Schuster, 2003.

Bowden, J. J. *The Exodus of Federal Forces from Texas*. Austin: Eaken Press, 1986.

Brackett, Albert G. *General Lane's Brigade in Central Mexico*. Cincinnati: H. W. Derby and Co., 1954.

Brown, Charles. *Agents of Manifest Destiny: The Lives and Times of Filibusters*. Chapel Hill: University of North Carolina Press, 1980.

Brown, John Henry. *History of Texas from 1685 to 1892*. 2 vols. St. Louis: L. E. Daniell, 1893.

———. *Indian Wars and Pioneers of Texas*. Austin: State House Press, 1988.

Brown, Richard Maxwell. *Strain of Violence: Historical Studies of American Violence and Vigilantism*. New York: Oxford University Press, 1975.

Castillo, Richard Griswold del. *The Treaty of Guadalupe Hidalgo: A Legacy of Conflict*. Norman: University of Oklahoma Press, 1990.

Chamberlain, Samuel. *My Confession: Recollections of a Rogue*. Edited by William Goetzmann. Austin: Texas State Historical Association, 1996.

Chance, Joseph E. *Jose Maria De Jesus Carvajal: The Life and Times of a Mexican Revolutionary*. San Antonio, Tex.: Trinity University Press, 2006.

———, ed. *The Mexican War Journal of Captain Franklin Smith*. Jackson: University of Mississippi Press, 1991.

———, ed. *Mexico under Fire: Being the Diary of Samuel Ryan Curtis, 3rd Ohio Volunteer Regiment during the American Military Occupation of Northern Mexico, 1846–1847*. Fort Worth: Texas Christian University Press, 1994.

Chatfield, W. H. *The Twin Cities of the Border and the Country of the Rio Grande*. New Orleans: E. P. Brandao, 1893.

Cheeseman, Bruce, ed. *Maria Von Blucher's Corpus Christi: Letters from the South Texas Frontier, 1849–1879.* College Station: Texas A&M Press, 2002.

Coker, Caleb, ed. *The News from Brownsville: Helen Chapman's Letters from the Texas Military Frontier, 1848–1852.* Austin: Texas State Historical Association, 1993.

Collins, Michael. "Statehood, 1845–1860." In *The Texas Heritage*, 3rd ed. Edited by Ben Procter and Archie P. McDonald. Wheeling, Ill.: Harlan Davidson, 1998.

Cude, Elton. *The Wild and Free Dukedom of Bexar.* San Antonio: Munguia Printers, 1978.

Cutrer, Thomas W. *Ben McCulloch and the Frontier Military Tradition.* Chapel Hill: University of North Carolina Press, 1993.

Daggett, E. M. "Advances with Guerrillas." In *Heroes and Incidents of the Mexican War.* Edited by Isaac George. Greensburg, Pa.: Review Publishing, 1903.

Darrow, Carolyn. "Recollections of Twiggs Surrender." In *Battles and Leaders of the Civil War: Being for the Most Part Contributions by Union and Confederate Officers.* Edited by Robert Underwood and Clarence Clough Buel. New York: T. Yoseloff, 1956.

Day, Donald, and Harry Herbert Ullom, eds. *The Autobiography of Sam Houston.* Norman: University of Oklahoma Press, 1954.

De Leon, Arnoldo. *Mexican Americans in Texas: A Brief History.* Arlington Heights, Ill.: Harlan Davidson, 1993.

———. *They Called Them Greasers: Anglo Attitudes toward Mexicans in Texas, 1821–1900.* Austin: University of Texas Press, 1983.

DeShields, James T. *Border Wars of Texas.* Austin: State House Press, 1993.

Dilworth, Rankin. *The March to Monterrey: The Diary of Lieutenant Rankin Dilworth.* Edited by Lawrence R. Clayton and Joseph E. Chance. El Paso: Texas Western Press, 1996.

Dobie, J. Frank. *The Longhorns.* New York: Grosset and Dunlap, 1941.

———. *A Vacquero of the Brush Country: The Life and Times of John D. Young.* Austin: University of Texas Press, 1998.

Domenech, Emanuel. *Missionary Adventures in Texas and Mexico: A Personal Narrative of Six Years' Sojourn in Those Regions.* London: Longman, Brown, Green, Longmans, and Roberts, 1858.

Doubleday, Abner. *My Life in the Old Army: The Reminiscences of Abner Doubleday.* Edited by Joseph E. Chance. Fort Worth: TCU Press, 1998.

Doubleday, Rhoda, ed. *Journals of the Late Brevet Major Philip Norbourne Barbour, a Captain in the Third Regiment, United States Infantry, and His Wife Martha Isabella Hopkins Barbour, Written during the War with Mexico, 1846.* New York: G. P. Putnam's Sons, 1936.

Emory, William H. *Report on the United States and Mexican Boundary Survey: Made under the Direction of the Secretary of the Interior.* 2 vols. Austin: Texas State Historical Association, 1987.

Ferrell, Robert H., ed. *Monterrey Is Ours: The Mexican War Letters of Lieutenant Dana, 1845–1847.* Lexington: University Press of Kentucky, 1990.

Ford, John Salmon. *Rip Ford's Texas.* Edited by Stephen Oates. Austin: University of Texas Press, 1963.

Frantz, Joe B. "The Frontier Tradition: An Invitation to Violence." In *A History of Violence in America: A Report to the National Commission on the Causes and Prevention of Violence.* Edited by Hugh Davis Graham and Ted Robert Gurr. New York: Bantam Books, 1969.

Frazier, Donald S. *Blood and Treasure: Confederate Empire in the Southwest.* College Station: Texas A&M Press, 1995.

Freeman, Douglas Southall. *R. E. Lee: A Biography.* 4vols. New York: Charles Scribner's Sons, 1934–1935.

Fremantle, Arthur James. *The Fremantle Diary: Being the Journal of Lieutenant Colonel Arthur James Lyon Fremantle, Coldstream Guards on His Three Months in the Southern States.* Short Hills, N.J.: Burford Books, 1954.

Friend, Llerena. *Sam Houston: The Great Designer.* Austin: University of Texas Press, 1954.

Frost, J. *The Mexican War and Its Warriors: Comprising a Complete History of All the Operations of the American Armies of Mexico.* New Haven, Conn.: H. Mansfield, 1848.

Fulton, Maurice Garland, ed. *Diary and Letters of Josiah Gregg.* Norman: University of Oklahoma Press, 1941.

General Taylor and His Staff: Comprising Memoirs of Generals Taylor, Worth, Wool, and Butler. Philadelphia: Grigg, Elliot and Co., 1848.

General Taylor's Rough and Ready Almanac. Philadelphia: Turner and Fisher, 1848.

Giddings, Luther. *Sketches of the Campaign in Northern Mexico by an Officer of the First Ohio Volunteers.* New York: G. P. Putnam and Co., 1853.

Goldfinch, Charles W. "Juan N. Cortina, 1824–1892: A Re-Appraisal." In *Juan N. Cortina: Two Interpretations.* New York: Arno Press, 1974.

Grant, Ulysses S. *Personal Memoirs of U. S. Grant and Selected Letters, 1839–1865.* Edited by Mary McFeely and William S. McFeely. New York: Library Classics of the United States, 1990.

Greer, James K. *Colonel Jack Hays: Texas Frontier Leader and California Builder.* College Station: Texas A&M Press, 1987.

Guilick, Charles Adams, Katherine Elliott, Winnie Allen, and Harriet Smither. *The Papers of Mirabeau Buonaparte Lamar.* 6 vols. Austin: Von Boeckmann-Jones Co., 1920–1927.

Haley, James L. *Sam Houston.* Norman: University of Oklahoma Press, 2002.

Hall, Martin Harwick. *Sibley's New Mexico Campaign.* Austin: University of Texas Press, 1960.

Hall, Robert. *Life of Robert Hall: Indian Fighter and Veteran of Three Great Wars.* Austin: State House Press, 1992.

Hardman, Francis. *Frontier Life: Or Tales of the Southwestern Border.* New York: C. Saxton, Barker and Co., 1860.

Henry, William S. *Campaign Sketches of the War with Mexico.* New York: Harper Brothers, 1847.

Hitchcock, Ethan Allen. *Fifty Years in Camp and Field: Diary of Major General Ethan Allen Hitchcock, U.S.A.* Edited by W. A. Croffut. New York: G. P. Putnam's Sons, 1909.

Hollon, Eugene C., ed. *William Bollaert's Texas.* Norman: University of Oklahoma Press, 1956.

Horgan, Paul. *Great River: The Rio Grande in North American History.* 2 vols. New York: Rinehart and Co., 1954.

Hughes, W. J. *Rebellious Ranger: Rip Ford and the Old Southwest.* Norman: University of Oklahoma Press, 1964.

Hunt, Jeffrey William. *The Last Battle of the Civil War: Palmetto Ranch.* Austin: University of Texas Press, 2002.

Irby, James A. *Backdoor at Bagdad: The Civil War on the Rio Grande.* El Paso: University of Texas at El Paso, 1977.

James, Charles Wilson. *Address on the Occasion of Removing the Remains of Captains Walker and Gillespie on the 21st of April, A.D., 1856.* Center for American History, University of Texas, Austin.

Jenkins, John H., III, ed. *The Papers of the Texas Revolution, 1835–1836.* 10 vols. Austin: Presidial Press, 1973.

———, ed. *Recollections of Early Texas: The Memoirs of John Holland Jenkins.* Austin: University of Texas Press, 1987.

———, ed. *Robert E. Lee on the Rio Grande: The Correspondence of Robert E. Lee on the Texas Border, 1860.* Austin: Jenkins Publishing Co., 1988.

Jones, J. William. *Personal Reminiscences of General Robert E. Lee.* New York: Tom Doherty Associates, 2003.

Kelsey, Anna Maria. *Through the Years: Reminiscences of Pioneer Days on the Texas Border.* San Antonio: Naylor Co., 1952.

Kendall, George Wilkins. *Dispatches from the Mexican War.* Norman: University of Oklahoma Press, 1999.

———. *Letters from a Texas Sheep Ranch: Written in the Years 1860 and 1861 by George Kendall to Henry Stephens Randall.* Edited by James Brown. Urbana: University of Illinois, 1959.

Knights of the Golden Circle. *By Laws, Castroville Chapter, K. G. C.* N.p.: n.p., 1861.

———. *First, Or Military Degree: Castroville Chapter.* N.p.: n.p., 1861.

Lander, Alexander. *A Trip to the Wars, Comprising the History of the Galveston Riflemen, Formed April 28, 1846, at Galveston, Texas; Together with the History of Monterrey, also Descriptions of Mexico and Its People.* Monmouth, Ill.: Atlas Office of the Publisher, 1847.

Lane, Lydia Spencer. *I Married a Soldier.* Albuquerque: University of New Mexico Press, 1964.

Lane, Walter P. *The Adventures and Recollections of General Walter P. Lane.* Marshall, Tex.: News Messengers Publishing Co., 1928.

Larralde, Carlos, and Jose Rodolfo Jacobo. *Juan N. Cortina and the Struggle for Justice in Texas.* Dubuque, Iowa: Kendall Hunt, 2000.

Lea, Tom. *The King Ranch.* 2 vols. Boston: Little, Brown and Co., 1957.

Lee, Fitzhugh. *General Lee: A Biography of Robert E. Lee.* New York: Da Capo Press, 1994.

Lee, Nelson. *Three Years among the Comanches: The Narrative of Nelson Lee, the Texas Ranger.* Norman: University of Oklahoma Press, 1957.

Lee, Robert E. *Recollections and Letters of General Robert E. Lee.* New York: Doubleday, Page and Co., 1904.

Linn, John J. *Reminiscences of Fifty Years in Texas.* Austin: State House Press, 1986.

Livermore, Abriel Abbot. *War with Mexico: Reviewed.* Boston: American Peace Society, 1850.

Lubbock, Francis R. *Six Decades in Texas, or Memoirs of Francis Richard Lubbock, Governor of Texas in Wartime, 1861–1863: A Personal Experience in Business, War, and Politics.* Edited by C. W. Rains. Austin: Ben C. Jones and Co., 1900.

Malone, Dumas, ed. *Dictionary of American Biography.* 23 vols. New York: Charles Scribner's Sons, 1936.

Manning, William R., ed. *Diplomatic Correspondence of the United States, Inter-American Affairs, 1831–1860.* 9 vols. Washington, D.C.: Carnegie Endowment for International Peace, 1937.

Marcy, Randolph Barnes. *Thirty Years of Army Life on the Border.* New York: Harper and Brothers, 1866.

Maverick, Mary A. *Memoirs of Mary A. Maverick.* Edited by Rena Maverick Green. Lincoln: University of Nebraska Press, 1989.

May, Robert E. *Manifest Destiny's Underworld: Filibustering in Antebellum America.* Chapel Hill: University of North Carolina Press, 2002.

McCoy, Joseph G. *Historic Sketches of the Cattle Trade of the West and Southwest.* Lincoln, University of Nebraska Press, 1985.

McWhiney, Grady, and Sue McWhiney, eds. *To Mexico with Taylor and Scott, 1845–1847.* Waltham, Mass.: Blaisdell Publishing Co., 1969.

Merrick, Morgan W. *From Desert to Bayou: The Civil War Journal and Sketches of Morgan Wolfe Merrick.* Edited by Jerry Thompson. El Paso: Texas Western Press, 1991.

Montejano, David. *Anglos and Mexicans in the Making of Texas, 1836–1986.* Austin: University of Texas Press, 1987.

Montgomery, Cora. *Eagle Pass: Or, Life on the Border.* New York: George Putnam and Co., 1852.

Moore, John Bassett, ed. *The Works of James Buchanan: Comprising His Speeches, State Papers, and Private Correspondence.* 12 vols. New York: Antiquarian Press, 1960.

Newcomb, James P. *Sketch of Secession Times and Journal of Travel through Mexico and California.* San Francisco: privately printed, 1863.

Nichols, James W. *Now You Hear My Horn: The Journal of James W. Nichols, 1820–1888.* Edited by Catherine W. McDowell. Austin: University of Texas Press, 1967.

North, Thomas. *Five Years in Texas: Or What You Did Not Hear during the War from January 1861 to January 1865.* Cincinnati: Elm Street Publishing Co., 1870.

Oates, Stephen. "John S. 'Rip' Ford: Prudent Cavalryman, CSA." In *Lone Star Blue and Gray: Essays on Texas in the Civil War.* Edited by Ralph Wooster. Austin: Texas State Historical Association, 1995.

Olmsted, Frederick Law. *A Journey through Texas: Or, a Saddle Trip on the Southwestern Frontier.* Austin: University of Texas Press, 1978.

Oswandel, Jacob. *Notes on the Mexican War, 1846–1848.* 2 vols. Philadelphia: n.p., 1885.

Parisot, P. F. *The Reminiscences of a Texas Missionary.* San Antonio: St. Mary's Church, 1899.

Parsons, Chuck, and Marianne E. Hall Little. *Captain L. H. McNelly: Texas Ranger.* Austin: State House Press, 2001.

Peskin, Allan, ed. *Volunteers: The Mexican War Journals of Private Richard Coulter and Sergeant Thomas Barclay, Company E, Second Penn. Infantry.* Kent, Ohio: Kent State Press, 1991.

Pierce, Frank Cushman. *Texas' Last Frontier: A Brief History of the Lower Rio Grande Valley.* Menosha, Wis.: George Banta Publishing, 1917.

Pike, James. *Scout and Ranger: Being the Personal Adventures of James Pike of the Texas Rangers in 1859–60.* Princeton: Princeton University Press, 1932.

Pomfrey, J. W. *A True Disclosure and Exposition of the Knights of the Golden Circle, Including Secret Signs, Grips, and Charges of the Three Degrees as Practised by the Order.* Cincinnati: privately printed, 1861.

Porter, Charles. *Review of the Mexican War.* Auburn, N.Y.: Alden and Parsons, 1849.

Procter, Ben. "The Texas Rangers: An Overview." In *The Texas Heritage*, 4th ed. Edited by Ben Procter and Archie McDonald. Wheeling, Ill.: Harlan Davidson, 2003.

Pryor, Elizabeth Brown. *Reading the Man: A Portrait of Robert E. Lee through His Private Letters.* New York: Viking, 2007.

Ramsey, Albert C., trans. and ed. *The Other Side: Or Notes from the History of the War between Mexico and the United States.* New York: Wiley, 1850.

Rankin, Melinda. *Twenty Years among the Mexicans: A Narrative of Missionary Labor.* Cincinnati: Central Book Concern, 1881.

Ransleben, Guido. *A Hundred Years of Comfort in Texas: A Centennial History.* San Antonio: Naylor Co., 1954.

Rayburn, John C., and Virginia Rayburn, eds. *Century of Conflict: 1821–1913, Incidents in the Lives of William Neale and William A. Neale, Early Settlers in South Texas.* Waco: Texian Press, 1966.

Reid, Samuel C. *The Scouting Expeditions of McCulloch's Texas Rangers.* Philadelphia: G. B. Lieber, 1848.

Rippy, J. Fred. *The United States and Mexico.* New York: Alfred A. Knopf, 1926.

Rister, Carl Coke. *Robert E. Lee in Texas.* Norman: University of Oklahoma Press, 1946.

Roberts, Madge Thornall, ed. *The Personal Correspondence of Sam Houston.* 4 vols. Denton: University of North Texas Press, 1995–2001.

Roberts, Oran M. "Texas." In *Confederate Military History: A Library of Confederate States History.* Edited by Clement A. Evans. 12 vols. Atlanta: Confederate, 1899.

Robinson, Charles M., III. *The Men Who Wear the Star: The Story of the Texas Rangers.* New York: Random House, 2000.

Rose, Victor M. *The Life and Services of General Ben McCulloch.* Philadelphia: Pictorial Bureau of the Press, 1888.

Santleben, August. *A Texas Pioneer: Early Staging and Overland Freighting Days on the Frontiers of Texas and Mexico.* New York: Neale Publishing Co., 1910.

Sibley, Marilyn McAdams, ed. *Samuel H. Walker's Account of the Mier Expedition.* Austin: Texas State Historical Association, 1978.

Smith, George Winston, and Charles Judah, eds. *Chronicles of the Gringos: The U.S. Army in the Mexican War, 1846–1848, Accounts of Eyewitnesses and Combatants.* Albuquerque: University of New Mexico Press, 1968.

Smith, Ralph. *Reminiscences of the Civil War and Other Sketches.* Waco: W. M. Morrison, 1962.

Smithwick, Noah. *The Evolution of a State: Or Recollections of Old Texas Days.* Austin: University of Texas Press, 1983.

Sobel, Robert, and John Raimo, eds. *Biographical Dictionary of the Governors of the United States, 1789–1978.* 3 vols. Westport, Conn.: Meckler Books, 1978.

Sowell, A. J. *Early Settlers and Indian Fighters of Southwest Texas.* Austin: State House Press, 1986.

Speer, William S., and John Henry Brown, eds. *The Encyclopedia of the New West.* Marshall, Tex.: U.S. Biographical Publishing Co., 1881.

Sprague, John T. *The Treachery in Texas: The Secession of Texas, and the Arrest of United States Officers and Soldiers Serving in Texas.* New York: New York Historical Society, 1862.

Spurlin, Charles D. *Texas Volunteers in the Mexican War.* Austin: Eakin Press, 1998.

Stevens, Isaac. *Campaigns of the Rio Grande and of Mexico.* New York: D. Appleton and Co., 1851.

Stillman, J. D. B. *Wanderings in the Southwest in 1855.* Edited by Ron Tyler. Spokane, Wash.: Arthur H. Clark Co., 1990.

Stout, Joseph A. *The Liberators: Filibustering Expeditions in Mexico, 1848–1862, and the Last Thrust of Manifest Destiny.* Los Angeles: Westernlore Press, 1973.

Stout, Peter F. *Nicaragua.* Philadelphia: Potter Co., 1859.

Sumpter, Jesse. *Paso del Aguila: A Chronicle of Frontier Days on the Texas Border as Recorded in the Memoirs of Jesse Sumpter.* Compiled by Harry Warren. Austin: Encino Press, 1969.

Thomas, Emory. *Robert E. Lee: A Biography.* New York: W. W. Norton, 1995.

Thompson, Jerry. *Cortina: Defending the Mexican Name in Texas.* College Station, Tex.: Texas A&M Press, 2007.

———, ed. *Fifty Miles and a Fight: Major Samuel Peter Heintzelman's Journal of Texas and the Cortina War.* Austin: Texas State Historical Association, 1998.

———, ed. *Juan Cortina and the Texas-Mexican Frontier.* El Paso: Texas Western Press, 1994.

———. *Mexican Texans in the Union Army.* El Paso: Texas Western Press, 1986.

———. *Sabers on the Rio Grande.* Austin: Presidial Press, 1974.

———. *Vacqueros in Blue and Gray.* Austin: State House Press, 2000.

Thompson, Jerry, and Lawrence T. Jones, III. *Civil War and Revolution on the Rio Grande Frontier: A Narrative and Photographic History.* Austin: Texas State Historical Association, 2004.

Thorpe, Thomas B. *Our Army at Monterrey: Being a Correct Account of the Proceedings and Events Which Occurred to the Army of Occupation under the Command of Major General Taylor.* Philadelphia: Carey and Hart, 1847.

Thrall, Homer. *A Pictorial History of Texas: From the Earliest Visits of European Adventurers, to A.D. 1879.* St. Louis: N. D. Thompson, 1879.

Tilley, Nannie M., ed. *Federals on the Frontier: The Diary of Benjamin F. McIntyre, 1862–1864.* Austin: University of Texas Press, 1963.

Tyler, Ron, Douglas E. Barnett, Roy R. Barkley, Penelope C. Anderson, and Mark F. Odintz, eds. *The New Handbook of Texas.* 6 vols. Austin: Texas State Historical Association, 1996.

Utley, Robert M. *Lone Star Justice: The First Century of the Texas Rangers.* Oxford: Oxford University Press, 2002.

Viele, Teresa. *Following the Drum: A Glimpse of Frontier Life.* Lincoln: University of Nebraska Press, 1984.

Walker, William. *The War in Nicaragua.* Tucson: University of Arizona Press, 1985.

Webb, Walter Prescott. *The Great Plains.* New York: Grosset and Dunlap, 1931.

———. *The Texas Rangers: A Century of Frontier Defense.* Austin: University of Texas Press, 1973.

———. *The Texas Rangers in the Mexican War.* Austin: Jenkins Garrett Press, 1975.

Wilbarger, J. W. *Indian Depredations in Texas: Reliable Accounts of Battles, Wars, Adventures, Forays, Murders, Massacres, etc., Together with Biographical Sketches of Many of the Most Noted Indian Fighters and Frontiersmen of Texas.* Austin: Hutchings Printing House, 1889.

Wilhelm, Thomas, ed. *History of the Eighth U.S. Infantry, from Its Organization in 1838.* 2 vols. David's Island, N.Y.: Regimental Headquarters, Eighth Infantry, 1873.

Wilkins, Frederick. *Defending the Borders: The Texas Rangers, 1848–1861.* Austin: State House Press, 2001.

———. *The Highly Irregular Irregulars: Texas Rangers in the Mexican War.* Austin: Eaken Press, 1990.

———. *The Legend Begins: The Texas Rangers, 1823–1845.* Austin: State House Press, 1996.

Williams, Amelia, and Eugene C. Barker, eds. *The Writings of Sam Houston, 1813–1863.* 8 vols. Austin: University of Texas Press, 1938–1943.

Williams, John Hoyt. *Sam Houston: A Biography of the Father of Texas.* New York: Simon and Schuster, 1993.

Williams, R. H. *With the Border Ruffians: Memories of the Far West, 1852–1868.* Edited by E. W. Williams. Lincoln: University of Nebraska Press, 1982.

Winfrey, Dorman, and James M. Day, eds. *Texas Indian Papers.* 4 vols. Austin: Texas State Library, 1959–1961.

Winkler, Ernest, ed. *Journal of the Secession Convention in Texas, 1861.* Austin: Texas State Library and Historical Commission, 1912.

Wright, John, and William Wright. *Recollections of Western Texas: Descriptive and Narrative, Including an Indian Campaign, 1852–55.* Edited by Robert Wooster. Lubbock: Texas Tech University Press, 2001.

Articles

Bridges, C. A. "The Knights of the Golden Circle: A Filibustering Fantasy." *Southwestern Historical Quarterly* 44 (January 1941): 287–302.

Brown, Jonathan Duff. "Reminiscences of Jon. Duff Brown." *Quarterly of the Texas State Historical Association* 12 (April 1909): 296–311.

Crimmins, M. L. "Colonel Charles Anderson Opposed Secession in San Antonio." *West Texas Historical Association Yearbook* 29 (October 1953): 113–14.

———. "Colonel J. K. F. Mansfield's Report of the Inspection of the Department of Texas in 1856." *Southwestern Historical Quarterly* 41 (October 1938): 128–29.

Dugan, Frank H. "The 1850 Affair of the Brownsville Separatists." *Southwestern Historical Quarterly* 61 (October 1957): 270–87.

Dunn, Roy Sylvan. "The KGC in Texas, 1860–1861." *Southwestern Historical Quarterly* 70 (April 1967): 543–73.

Fornell, Earl W. "Texans and Filibusters in the 1850s." *Southwestern Historical Quarterly* 59 (April 1956): 411–28.

Greaser, Galen D., and Jesus F. de la Teja. "Quieting Title to Spanish and Mexican Land Grants in the Trans-Nueces: The Bourland and Miller Commission, 1850–1852." *Southwestern Historical Quarterly* 95 (April 1992): 446–50.

Hicks, Jimmie, ed. "Some Letters Concerning the Knights of the Golden Circle in Texas." *Southwestern Historical Quarterly* 65 (July 1961): 80–86.

Holland, James K. "Diary of a Texan Volunteer in the Mexican War." *Southwestern Historical Quarterly* 30 (July 1926): 1–33.

Myer, Albert J. "I Am Already Quite a Texan: Albert J. Myer's Letters from Texas, 1854–1856." Edited by David A. Clary. *Southwestern Historical Quarterly* 82 (July 1978): 25–76.

Nackman, Mark. "The Making of the Texan Citizen Soldier." *Southwestern Historical Quarterly* 78 (January 1975): 231–53.

Remington, Frederick. "How the Law Got into the Chaparral." *Harper's New Monthly Magazine* 94 (1896): 60–69.

Shearer, Ernest C. "The Callahan Expedition, 1855." *Southwestern Historical Quarterly* 54 (April 1951): 430–51.

———. "The Carvajal Disturbances." *Southwestern Historical Quarterly* 55 (October 1951): 201–30.

Tyler, Ronnie C. "The Callahan Expedition of 1855: Indians or Negroes?" *Southwestern Historical Quarterly* 70 (April 1967):574–85.

Newspapers

Brownsville *Daily Ranchero*

Corpus Christi *Ranchero*

Daily Picayune (New Orleans).

Dallas *Herald*

Democratic Telegraph and Texas Register (Houston)

Fort Brown Flag (Brownsville)
Galveston *Daily Civilian*
Galveston *News*
Galveston *Weekly News*
Houston Telegraph
New Orleans *Picayune*
Nueces Valley Weekly (Corpus Christi)
San Antonio Herald
Texas Star Gazette (Austin)
Texas State Gazette (Austin)
Texas State Times (Austin)

Index

References to illustrations are in italic type.